# THE LAND
# THAT
# ENGLAND LOST

## Argentina and Britain,
## a Special Relationship

# THE LAND THAT ENGLAND LOST

## Argentina and Britain, a Special Relationship

*Edited by*
Alistair Hennessy and John King
*Department of History and*
*School of Comparative American Studies*
*University of Warwick*

British Academic Press – an imprint of I.B. Tauris

Published in 1992 by

The British Academic Press
110 Gloucester Avenue
London NW1 8JA

An imprint of I.B. Tauris & Co Ltd

In the United States of America
and Canada distributed by
St Martin's Press
175 Fifth Avenue.
New York
NY 10010

A CIP record for this book is available from the British Library.

Library of Congress Catalog card number:

A full CIP record is available from the Library of Congress.

ISBN 1 85043 491 3

# Contents

# List of Maps

To Juan Lopez and John Ward

*They would have been friends ... each
one was Cain and each one was Abel*

# Foreword

*Guido Di Tella*

The resumption of full diplomatic relations between Argentina and the United Kingdom in the early part of 1990, has been accompanied by renewed mutual interest in many fields. We cannot but welcome this trend, particularly in view of the very long and extremely fruitful relations which our two countries had enjoyed for more than a century before the 1982 war, and we hope, will continue to enjoy.

Argentina was a magnet for British investments from the nineteenth century and also for a significant and selective immigration. British influence was so great that at times Argentina was considered part of the British informal empire, with the ambivalence that such status elicits. It is clear that Argentina developed a special relationship with Britain; this stemmed from the complementary character of the two economies, and this relationship defined Argentina's position in the world. This also contributed to Argentina's alienation from the Americas, and enhanced her resistance to the attempts of the United States to establish continental hegemony. Argentina's special relation with Britain was the counterpart of Argentina's conflictive relation with the United States, at least during the first half of the twentieth century.

British trade practices, entrepreneurial behaviour and important aspects of British culture, become significant components in Argentina's contemporary reality. Moreover, the so-called Anglos, estranged in the midst of two cultures they loved, became identifiable characters in the Argentine social scene.

Too much influence – so it was felt by many – guaranteed the strong reactions, positive and negative – noticeable since the 1930s. But it was not surprising that, during the Second World War, Great Britain understood Argentina much better than any other country. While the United Kingdom appreciated Argentina's war efforts – proportionately greater than those of Canada – the United States objected to Argentina's neutral stand, and wanted a declaration of war with the Axis. The United Kingdom did not favour this at all, considering it a hindrance to the stream of essential, and ample, supplies coming from Argentina. The strained Argentine-United

ix

States relations, the advent of Peronism, and the intensification of the conflict, meant a continuation of British influence longer than might have been expected, given the general world trend; another example of the unintended consequences of human actions.

From the 1960s on Argentina and Britain ignored each other to a surprising degree, given the past intimate relations. The 1982 war was in a way the tragic apex of this trend; a monument to human folly that left more than one thousand young men dead. There is a need to remember but not for nostalgia. The world is changing at an impressive pace and it would be pitiful not to make the most of the significant good will prevailing on both sides of the Atlantic and the intensive recent rekindling of good relations.

This book written by some of the top British scholars in their fields is an excellent expression of the renewed mutual interest and is commendable for the level of its contributors, for the range of topics which goes beyond the usual analysis of the commercial aspects of the relation, and also for delving into the historical, cultural and demographic aspects.

A similar work by Argentine scholars will, if fulfilled, be a significant complement of this very important book, one of the first to come out after the fortunate resumption of full diplomatic relations, and one to be welcomed, from every point of view.

# Introduction

## *Alistair Hennessy*

This book originated in a symposium at the University of Warwick convened in the aftermath of the Falklands/Malvinas conflict in an effort to explain why hostilities should have broken out with the country in Latin America with which Britain had had the closest relationship for a hundred and fifty years. So close had this been that Argentina was sometimes described as the 'sixth dominion' or as part of Britain's 'informal empire'.

For Britain to go to war with a Latin American country over a group of islands the population of which was no larger than a small English village and which most Britons apart from philatelists and a few experts, could not point out on a map seems preposterous and surreal. And yet what appears to the outsider to be an aimless and unnecessary quarrel not only involved firmly held and sincere beliefs on both sides but marked a turning point in the domestic politics of both countries. Argentina has its 'Malvinas factor' as Britain has its 'Falklands factor'. As a British defeat in 1807 gave an impetus to Argentine independence so a British victory in 1982 was one cause of the fall of military dictatorship ushering in a period of democratic government. Britain has thus been a catalyst of change at two of the most critical points in Argentina's history. In Britain, the Falklands War was the apotheosis of Thatcherite triumphalism:

> There were those who would not admit it ... that Britain was no longer the nation that had built an Empire and ruled a quarter of the world. Well they were wrong. The lesson of the Falklands is that Britain has not changed and that this nation still has those sterling qualities which shine through our history. [1]

For many it is seen as the turning point in the administration, enabling the Prime Minister to tap atavistic memories, instilling a sense of national self-confidence and releasing new energies.

In 1982 publishers seemed uninterested in discussions concerning Argentina other than those on the war, its immediate causes and repercussions. No one expressed a concern for the 'Forgotten Colony' – the title of a book on the Anglo-Argentine community which appeared the year before hostilities began. Based on secondary sources

and the files of newspapers one of which the author, Andrew Graham-Yool, was sometime editor, that book is a quarry of information
on the British in Argentina and an invaluable starting point for
further research.

Since 1982 the Falklands crisis (and there is *still* a crisis, and not
to recognise that there is, is to fall into the mistakes of the pre-war
period) has generated an enormous literature, most of it concerned,
on the British side, with the mechanics of domestic politics, and
analyses of why the war was 'nothing less than the inevitable result
of a collision of misperceptions' [2] but in most of these books Argentina
is only discussed peripherally.

The purpose in commissioning these essays, aiming at both a
general and academic readership, was to probe more deeply into the
cultural and social aspects of the British-Argentine relationship. As
the gap of incomprehension remains and solutions seem as far away
as ever we felt the need for a book which might make a modest
contribution to understanding. There is no shortage of analyses by
both British and Argentine scholars, many of a collaborative nature,
exploring the economic aspects of the relationship but the cultural
dimension with its wider social implications has gone largely un-
charted. This is scarcely surprising as the relationship was primarily
commercial, based on a complementarity of interests, but even commercial relations have cultural implications and one of the questions
posed by this book is the nature of the links between culture and
commerce. It is an apposite question in the aftermath of empire, in a
period of fierce competition for markets and influence. The importance of the link, which the French have never doubted, has at last
been recognised in official quarters with the recent House of Commons Select Committee Report on Cultural Diplomacy.

Argentina, in common with Latin America generally, provides a
particularly interesting case-study for comparing the influence of
different external cultural influences as since independence at the
beginning of the nineteenth century it has been an area of free
competition, both in terms of trade and ideas, and so British culture
there cannot be taken for granted as to a large extent it can in the
English-speaking Commonwealth with its linguistic, legal and educational affinities, and the shared mysteries of cricket. Argentine
admirers of Britain tended to be drawn from the landowning elite for
whom the moderation of liberalism and the rules of comparative
advantage made state intervention and protection unnecessary.
Wealth, it was comfortingly believed, would always be dispersed
through the anodyne 'trickle-down' effect. With the emergence of

Peronism and its challenge to this assumption both the anglophile elite and their British associates were united in their dislike for the vulgar assertiveness of the emergent mass society. Cultural influences have therefore always been restricted to a narrow elite and only with the popularity of football and pop music did the area of cultural influence widen, although how deeply is a moot point.

The title of this book calls for an explanation. It is, in fact, taken from W.H. Hudson's first novel, written in 1885, *The Purple Land That England Lost* and although that is set in Uruguay it is applicable to Argentina which in 1806 a *Times* headline announced had become part of the British Empire.

That novel was, in Jason Wilson's words, a 'private fantasy revenge' against Charles Darwin. The intellectual conflict between these two writers on Argentina goes to the heart of the cultural relationship between the two countries. Hudson's vision of Britain was very different from the reality of living in fog-engirdled London, with no hope of return, and in his autobiographical fragment *Far Away and Long Ago*, written towards the end of his life he was to idealise the Argentina of his youth. These two books, novel and autobiography, encapsulate the tension between the 'innocence' of barbarism and the 'savagery' of civilisation, with its Darwinian materialism that he so disliked. It was a reversal of the categories of that debate provoked by the 'civilisation' versus 'barbarism' dichotomy which runs througout Argentine and Latin American cultural history.

The title also poses the question of the extent to which mistaken British policies, misunderstandings and lack of empathy with Argentina and its many problems destroyed British influence there and led to the final confrontation of 1982. The shift in the subtitle to British-Argentine relations poses the question as to whether these misunderstandings were a specifically *English* responsibility. At a time when the United Kingdom may be becoming more disunited, analysis needs to focus on those strains and tensions which have always existed between the English, Irish, Scots and Welsh. Although smoothed over during the century of emigration before 1914 once that safety-valve began to close these tensions found a more forceful expression – most violently in the case of Ireland. In studies of the British diaspora insufficient attention has perhaps been paid to the different experiences and responses of Britain's major ethnic groups. In Argentina these can be studied in a linguistically and culturally alien environment. Argentina invites comparison with the United States in the scale and importance of the immigrant experience. Many of the problems of Argentine society both in its political and economic

development are closely related to this experience and to the processes of assimilation, acculturation, and identity. Each immigrant
group had its schools and societies which perpetuated links with the
mother country and this has contributed to the unique ethos of
Argentine nationalism and provides one key to understanding its
complexities. How under conditions of informal empire did British
behaviour and performance compare with those of other Europeans?
How perceptive was Philip Guedalla's observation in 1932? [3]

> Seventeen miles out of Buenos Aires a charming suburb clusters
> round an admirable club. It has its games, its dances and its life
> and its contacts with Buenos Aires are almost confined to the
> successful effort of its male population to catch the morning train
> to town or lunch on Saturdays in Harrods. One begins to wonder
> whether the prim British instinct of keeping oneself to oneself
> dictated this retreat. Was Hurlingham the cause of the surprising
> segregation of the races? Or was it just a consequence?

In analyzing the British in Argentina one often has to explain
attitudes of xenophobia, philistinism and ethnocentrism. In Britain
today there is a striking mismatch between a flourishing academic
community of Latin American specialists and of those who have lived
there capable of empathy, and widespread persistence of ingrained
stereotypes inherited from the past. This book touches on this issue,
especially with regard to Peronism and its legacies which raised a
wall of incomprehension between the two countries.

Argentina was an 'area of new settlement' in common with the
United States, Canada, Australia and New Zealand and shares with
them some similar economic problems as well as those of nation-
building. The differing experiences in these areas have stimulated
comparative work in economic history which seeks to explain the
reasons for the puzzling decline of Argentina from the pinnacle and
promise of the early twentieth century – a decline which is partly
mirrored in the British experience too. [4] There is also a field of cultural
comparison which needs to be explored.

Culture is a slippery term and may be used in a variety of ways
stretching from the anthropological interpretation of a society's total
way of life, reflected in social myths and behaviour patterns at one
end of a spectrum of definition to the narrow view of culture as the
thought and expression of an intellectual minority, with this 'high'
culture differentiated from 'popular' culture. Whatever definitions
are used to interpret a culture or to evaluate the extent of cultural

influences they have to be set within a wide framework. For this reason this book is multi-disciplinary and to read through it may make demands on those brought up in our restricted academic tradition. But to understand the relationship between the developed and developing world (and Argentina has always defied easy classification) requires a multi-disciplinary approach. The demarcation of disciplines in which academics can outdo trade unionists can be a barrier to understanding the complexities of dependence in which culture, economic and political factors are often woven together in a seamless web.

The book is divided into four sections. In the first Hennessy looks at the British in relation to other immigrant groups and poses some of the questions of cultural identity and response: Ferns examines the concept of 'informal empire' placing Argentina in the wider context of other new areas of settlement while Jones's chapter analyses the philosophical underpinning of the economic nexus and the change at the end of the nineteenth century in Argentina from an acceptance of *laissez faire* to a nascent economic nationalism: Mac-Donald covers the inter-war years when Britain had to bear the brunt of a new and strident nationalism, and Gravil examines the official and bewildered response to the puzzling phenomenon of Peronism. In the second section the experience of the constituent groups are examined: Williams looks at the Welsh experience in Chubut, the only colony with settlers from Britain still retaining part of its identity: Keogh discusses the Irish, arguably the most successful in terms of assimilation, and Marshall considers the last British agricultural colony to be established which, in contrast to Chubut, was a complete failure. In accounting for these differing experiences cultural factors are crucial. In the third section specific aspects of the cultural relationship are analysed. King's chapter is an overview of British cultural influences in Argentina: Wilson compares W.H. Hudson and Charles Darwin's responses to the imperial relationship of Victorian Britain to Argentina: Walker's chapter on travel writers emphasises the key role which they (and the Scots in particular) played in the nineteenth century in contributing to the Argentine self-image: Fishburn examines the work of Jorge Luis Borges, the most anglophile of all Latin American writers, who has been admitted into the canon of English Literature: Collier charts the rise and decline of the short-lived tango craze in Britain: Howells analyses attitudes to the Peróns as reflected in the British popular press when for the first time in recent history relations with Argentina intruded into British domestic politics, and Crawley explores the paradox that at the lowest ebb of British-Argentine relations, Argentine influence in London had probably never been greater.

In the final section, assessments are made of future prospects. Beck examines the wider implications of the Antarctic treaties which are due for renewal in 1991 and Little looks specifically at the Falklands/Malvinas issue. Finally, in an epilogue Hennessy assesses the current situation, and poses further questions, and proposes a solution, albeit of a counter-cultural nature.

All the contributors are from the United Kingdom except for Keogh who is from Eire and Crawley, an Argentine long resident in England and Ferns a Canadian also long resident here. Four are from the University of Warwick, reflecting its interest in Argentine affairs. A companion volume could give an Argentine perspective: this volume concentrates on the view from this country.

It is hoped that these essays may open up a neglected field of study – even among professional Latinamericanists – and make some contribution towards increasing mutual understanding – a task to which in the past only the Anglo-Argentine Society and a handful of otherwise dedicated people and, more recently, the South Atlantic Council have shown much concern. It is also hoped that by raising some key questions further enquiry and research may be stimulated.

The editors would like to thank the Research and Innovations Committee of the University of Warwick and its Chairman, Professor Alec Ford, an erstwhile specialist himself on economic aspects of the British-Argentine relationship, Dr. Harold Blakemore lately of the Institute of Latin American Studies, University of London and the Latin American Publications Fund for financial support, and our publisher Dr. Lester Crook for recognising the need for such a volume.

## Notes

1. Margaret Thatcher, Speech at Cheltenham, 3 July 1982.
2. Virginia Gamba, The Falklands/Malvinas War: a model for North-South crisis prevention, Allen and Unwin, London, 1987, p.xi.
3. Philip Guedalla, Argentine Tango, Hodder and Stoughton, London, 1932.
4. Guido di Tella and Christopher Platt, *Argentina, Australia and Canada: studies in Comparative Development, 1870-1965*. Macmillan, London, 1985. Solberg, C.E. *The Prairies and the Pampas: agrarian policy in Canada and Argentina 1880-1930*. Stanford University Press, Stanford, 1987. Fogarty, J., Gallo, E. and Dieguez, H. *Argentina y Australia*. Instituto di Tella, Buenos Aires 1979.

# THE POLITICAL,
# ECONOMIC
# AND
# DIPLOMATIC
# CONNECTION

# 1

# Argentines, Anglo-Argentines and Others

*Alistair Hennessy*

On the eve of the First World War Buenos Aires was one of the great cities of the world, justifiably proud of its pretensions to be the 'Paris of the Southern Hemisphere', capital of a country which was fulsomely described as an El Dorado of the future and which had expanded in terms both of population and of economic prosperity faster than any other country at that time. Buenos Aires itself had grown three-fold in twenty years from 666,000 to 1.5 million whilst the national population had increased from 3.9 to 7.8 million. By 1914 Argentina was overwhelmingly an immigrant country. In each of the ten years before 1914 there had been a net balance of 100,000 immigrants per year. One-third of the nation's population and 50 per cent of that of Buenos Aires was foreign-born, and 80 per cent were descendants of immigrants who had entered since the 1860s. Of this foreign population there were approximately 1 million Italians, 800,000 Spaniards, 94,000 Russians and Poles (many of whom were Jews), 86,000 French, 80,000 'Turcos' (the generic term for anyone from the Middle East), 35,000 Germans and some 40,000 British, making it the largest British community outside of the Empire.[1]

In its cosmopolitan mixture Buenos Aires was a South American New York (and was the third largest Jewish city after New York and Tel Aviv), although *porteños* would still not have welcomed this title, accustomed as they were to comparing themselves with Europe, the centre of the pre-war world. Indeed Europeans would have felt at home in the Second Empire boulevards of Buenos Aires with its Beaux Arts architecture and urban palaces which would not have been out of place in Paris. If urban architectural styles were predominantly French, the floridity of public monuments and ornate villas betrayed their Italian provenance, and in the barrack slums of the *conventillos* Neapolitans would have felt at home. A non-Hispanic European veneer overlaid the new metropolis, transformed from the *'gran aldea'* within a period of only thirty years. Only the older provincial towns remained unmistakably Hispanic in appearance and sentiment.[2]

Much influenced by *fin de siècle* racial theories, Argentines predicted a future unencumbered by an African legacy as in neighbouring Brazil, ridden by self-doubts and imbued with pessimism over their mixed racial stock. It is true that some 25 per cent of Buenos Aires had been blacks at the beginning of the nineteenth century — descendants of those slaves introduced under the *asiento* of 1714, a baleful example of early British influence, but Afro-Argentines had virtually disappeared by the end of the century.[3] Nor were Argentina's prospects to be clouded by an unassimilable Indian population as existed in the Andean countries. Such few pampas Indians as survived the War of the Desert (1879-85), far greater in scale than the Indian Wars of the American mid-west, lived dejectedly in near slavery.

Immigrants from northern Europe were the preferred choice of the Argentine elite but those from Germany, France and Britain were only to be a trickle and employers had to make a virtue out of the necessity of Spaniards and Italians who constituted the bulk of migrants. Useful as a source of cheap labour they were an embarrassment to governments wishing to preserve social order and were regarded as the harbingers of crime, violence, disease and strikes.

At the same time as European immigrants poured in so did European capital. Of this foreign investment 60 per cent was British with an estimated £400 million by 1914; Argentina attracted 10 per cent of Britain's total investment abroad. This combination of immigrants and capital fuelled a spectacular economic growth. In the six years before 1914 Argentina had outstripped by half again the foreign trade of its much larger neighbour Brazil; its foreign trade was larger than Canada's with a faster expansion of the wheat trade in which, in some years, it was the world's second largest exporter. Exports from Rosario at times exceeded those from Chicago. Argentina was the world's largest corn and linseed producer, second largest wool exporter and third largest exporter of cattle.

From the earliest years of independence the British had been the most influential commercially and financially of the foreign community, growing from 124 in Buenos Aires in 1810 to 3,000 in the 1820s, to about 5,000 in the 1830s. By the 1860s this had increased to 32,000 of whom the majority, some 28,000, were Irish. Proportionally this number started to fall after the 1860s as political stability and the opening of the pampas began to attract mass immigration mainly from southern and, to a lesser extent, eastern Europe. But although the British were to increase only to 40,000 by 1914, they were still to remain the dominant commercial and financial presence, exerting an influence over the ruling oligarchy out of all proportion to their numbers.

Such had been the extent of British dominance that it has become customary to describe Argentina as part of Britain's 'informal empire'.[4] Indeed as the 'sixth dominion' Argentina was a vindication of the Gladstonian Liberal view of the expensive irrelevance of territorial empire.

Argentina's railway system was the visible symbol of this British dominance growing from the first line in 1854 with redundant Crimean War broad gauge locomotives to become the tenth largest network in the world.[5] In 1910 the 'Big Four' companies controlled 50 per cent of the nations's track, 61 per cent of its locomotives, carried 84 per cent of the nation's passengers and 62 per cent of its freight, employing 64 per cent of railway employees and earning three-quarters of total railway revenues. Although the design of railway termini may have been French inspired, the fretted canopies of rural stations were a visible reminder of the British presence as was the English spoken by clerks, engineers and drivers. With the British owning three smaller companies as well, the domination of the transport system was almost total. The same was true of urban transport in Buenos Aires where from 1876 until the 1940s the street car system was British managed. British dominance extended to most of the capital's infrastructure — the docks after a long period of in-fighting were to be built by British engineers with British capital. Similarly, gas works, water works, the sewage system and the first underground railway in South America were all British financed.

Although British shopkeepers had been numerous in the 1820s they were to be swamped by Italians, Spaniards and the ubiquitous 'turco' pedlars. Wholesaling replaced retailing except for a number of prestigious names, Maples, Mappin and Webb, Gath and Chaves, and the crowning glory of Harrods.[6] Not much of this dominance though was expressed in British architectural forms. Mansard roofs betrayed French influence but in the aptly named Plaza Británica, situated in front of the Retiro railway terminus, the Torre Inglés, presented by the British community on the occasion of the centenary of independence, was a fit expression of that nostalgia which was to be a feature of Anglo-Argentines.[7] The British community eschewed living in centrally located ornate palaces, preferring the dullness — and coolness — of the suburbs Hurlingham and Temperley, relieved by playing the games they introduced — polo, tennis, golf, soccer and

rugby. Visible architectural influences were confined to such extravaganzas as the pampa gothic of Eton-educated Martínez de Hoz's
castellated *estancia* at Chapadmalal. The severe neo-classic style of
the Episcopalian Church of 1831 — the first of its kind in Argentina
— had few imitators, except in the Welsh chapels of Chubut.

Few Argentines of any standing were to question the dominance
of the British until the great financial crash of 1890, known as the
Baring crisis, the dominant bank since the first loan of 1824, but it
was not until the 1930s that criticisms of British hegemony were to
gather mass support among a public increasingly resentful of inefficient monopolies represented by a run down transport system.[8] The
Great War was to make inroads on British predominance but it was
finally with the Peronist nationalisation of the railways, 'the mainstay, the backbone of our whole position ... if they go, we all go', in the
prophetic words of one British ambassador, that the decline, implicit
even before 1914, could no longer be hidden.[9]

The British in Argentina started inauspiciously with the humiliation of military defeats in 1806 and 1807, first of the expedition of Sir
Home Popham, mounted on his personal initiative after the successful seizure of the Cape of Good Hope from the Dutch and secondly of
General Whitelocke's punitive expedition in the year following. Once
the locally recruited creole militia had conquered one of the leading
military powers of the day the Spanish presence was no longer
necessary. Captured regimental flags hanging in a Buenos Aires
church stood as a memorial to the hapless General Whitelocke (court-
martialed and dismissed from the service) who had so obligingly
made victory for the creoles possible.

The loot from Sir Home Popham's expedition had been ostenta-
tiously paraded at Portsmouth, where such scenes of enthusiasm
were not to be seen again until the departure to and return of the fleet
from the Falklands in 1982. This display whetted the appetites of
British merchants, long excluded — legally at least — from the
putative wealth of the Spanish Empire, and sharpened their expectations of finding an alternative market to replace those in Europe
cut off by Napoleon's Continental System. Spanish America held out
a promise which only British India could rival. Recent enmities were
forgotten as merchants descended in droves on Buenos Aires deposi-
ting in a 'harum-scarum sort of shipment' some £1 million-worth of
goods by 1810, much of it unsaleable, and flooding a market which
proved to be far more restricted than that conjured up by the febrile
imagination of marketless merchants.[10]

Subsequent British influence would be exerted without the benefit of military coercion (except in the unsuccessful blockade of the 1840s) and being a *nouveau riche* society, business would be conducted without the niceties of aristocratic protocol. A 'High Aristocrat', commented Sir Woodbine Parish the first British representative in Buenos Aires,[11] on Lord Ponsonby's appointment as ambassador in 1826, 'is little qualified to treat with the lowest of the low democrats we have to deal with here.' It was as well for Anglo-Argentine relations that Ponsonby only stayed two years in Buenos Aires (time enough though to invest in a *saladero*). Appointed, so gossip had it, to remove him from the attentions of one of George IV's favourites, he arrived with nine servants to comment that 'no eye saw so odious a country as Buenos Aires is ... I do not recollect having ever before disliked a place so much ... this land of mud and putrid carcasses.'

'Informal Empire' would be a middle-class affair with merchants and financiers being left to work the market in the true spirit of laisser-faire capitalism. Argentina, together with Latin America generally, was a fully competitive market where merchants, without the benefit of imperial support would have to face the cold winds of competition alone when they came in the closing decades of the nineteenth century, but in 1810 with their control of the sea the British had a head start and were able to carve out enclaves of opportunity and activity. 'A stranger seeing so many English faces would suppose it an English colony' commented an anonymous writer.[12] British merchants were admired for their honourable principles and enlightened views as it was believed these would be a model to emulate but the British commercial invasion was profoundly disruptive by contributing to the bifurcation of Argentine society into the coastal provinces and those of the interior. The former prospered from their links with Europe. The latter, geographically isolated and already crippled by the decline of the Andean mining economy, for which they provided the mules on which that economy depended, became economically depressed and a source of social and political disturbance. Domestic industries were swamped by cheap British imports on which even the gauchos were dependent, as Parish observed:

Take his whole equipment, examine everything about him — and what is there not of hide that is not British? If his wife has a gown, ten to one it is from Manchester. The camp kettle in which he cooks his food — the common earthenware he eats from — his knife, spoons, bits, and the poncho which covers him — are all imported from England. [13]

The wealth of the Plata region did not lie in mines as Head, Beaumont and other early prospectors soon discovered (as did those like Benjamin Disraeli who speculated in mining shares and lost his money in 1825) but in the rich earth of the pampas stretching inland, hill-less, for 500 miles.[14] Bernardo Rivadavia, the anglophile first president of the new nation between 1826 and 1827, established an Immigration Commission to attract settlers to promote arable farming but early immigration schemes collapsed through civil disturbances, inadequate government support, Indian raids, ignorance of conditions and the higher wages to be earned in the city. The Robertson brothers were nearly bankrupted by their Monte Grande colony, with its 220 Scottish settlers.[15] The pastoral idyll of Scottish milkmaids introducing *porteños* and gauchos to the delights of milk and butter was an expensive dream.

Although by the 1825 Treaty of Recognition the British were granted favours and state protection this counted for little beyond the confines of Buenos Aires. By the 1820s the frontier of settlement had scarcely advanced beyond that of 1580. While Head was in Argentina, riding across the pampas four times, the Indians 'with nothing in their hands but the lance ... were twice within fifty leagues of Buenos Aires'. The threat remained until the genocidal War of the Desert of 1879-1885 finally removed them and opened the frontier to settlement and Head's sympathetic and apocalyptic vision did not materialise:

> as soon as firearms shall get into the hands of these brave naked men ... who can venture to say that the hour may not be decreed, when these men mounted upon the descendants of the very horses which were brought over the Atlantic to oppress their forefathers may rush from the cold region to which they have been driven, and with irresistible fury proclaim to the guilty conscience of our civilized world that the hour of retribution has arrived ...[16]

Indians, beyond the pale and condemned as irredeemable savages were the major deterrent to sedentary agriculture, forcing Buenos Aires to be dependent on imports of wheat from the United States until the cereal boom of the 1880s. The failure of immigration schemes perpetuated the unfavourable man-land ratio, condemning Argentina to remain a country of limitless emptiness. The population at independence was a mere 406,000 and if the population in 1914 had the same density as that of Great Britain it would have numbered 400 millions instead of a bare 8 millions. Even the target of 40 millions hopefully envisaged by politicians early in the twentieth century has still to be reached.

The La Plata region had emerged at the end of the eighteenth century from being a backwater of the Spanish Empire through its wealth in cattle; its hides satisfying the voracious demands for leather of European armies and its carcasses providing the salted beef for the basic food of Brazilian and Cuban slave plantations and ocean-going sailors. Wealth, power and influence stemmed from cattle. From 1829 until his overthrow in 1852 the dictator Juan Manuel de Rosas, 'a man of extraordinary character' in Charles Darwin's judgment on meeting him, condemned Argentina to be a Big Man's frontier.[17] Cattle-ranching was an inevitable response to market demand and the scarcity of labour.

Outsiders found it difficult to break in to this hide-bound cattle culture, breeder of *caudillismo* and the macho ways so despised by Domingo Faustino Sarmiento and attacked in *Facundo Civilization and Barbarism* (1845), his blistering anti-Rosas polemic. Mavericks like Cunninghame Graham could identify with this ethos from which he derived a 'bleakly compassionate view of humanity'[18] but by the time the British were heavily involved in the cattle economy the barbed wire revolution had changed it out of recognition. As early as 1844 Richard Newton an English rancher had started to use wire fencing on his land, foreshadowing the introduction of barbed wire in the 1870s which enabled cattle to be domesticated. Fencing the pampas was as revolutionary in its social consequences as enclosures had been in sixteenth-century England, signalling the end of the open range and transforming the free-ranging gaucho into a hired hand.

Selective breeding was now possible with Tarquin the prize bull, imported from England, becoming a culture hero in a cattle-dominated society. The cattle show became the most important event in the economic calendar. The growing power of this cattle interest was represented by the Sociedad Rural founded in 1866, of which several Britons were members. With the invention of the *frigorífico* in 1876 Argentine beef could now be bred for the English palate, soon to comprise two-thirds of beef imports into Britain and becoming one of the staples of that cheap food policy pursued by British governments of all persuasions until the 1960s.[19] Corned beef — the bully beef which sustained British armies in two world wars — Liebig, Oxo, Bovril, all now became household names.

The majority of British *estancieros* however, were sheep-herders importing Spanish merinos and English breeds such as Lincolns and Southdowns much as cattlemen had imported Durhams, Herefords and other breeds. The shift from cattle to sheep occurred in the 1840s and twenty years later many of the largest sheep-herders were British in origin, a high proportion coming from Ireland in the famine and when entry to the United States declined during the Civil War. Recruited as shepherds by Irish *estancieros* some were able to acquire their own flocks by the *medianero* system which allowed them to keep a proportion of the lambs born or wool shorn. Some wealthy Irish-Argentine families owe their origins to these humble beginnings.

'The Irish', commented McCann 'are particularly acceptable as they are willing to do the heavy manual labour which creoles are reluctant to do, and so get whatever they ask'. Ditching, although strenuous, was profitable.[20] The Irish in Argentina may indeed have fared better than those in the United States where they were opprobiously termed 'white niggers'. Unlike slaves in whom capital had been invested they were expendable and so were preferred as ditchers in the fever-ridden Mississippi delta. Of all the immigrant groups from Britain in Argentina the Irish were the most numerous and from the point of view of assimilation the most successful. Hard workers, thrifty, with modest expectations, used to harsh working conditions they adapted better than their English counterparts, but above all being Catholics they could marry creole women and so avoid the complications of mixed marriages such as in the Lafone affair of 1832-3 where the refusal to permit a prominent Anglican businessman to marry a Catholic unless he changed his religion became a *cause célèbre*.[21]

The British responded to the challenges of a sheep and cattle economy but not to those of arable agriculture, and in this way they were to be accomplices in the development of the Big Man's frontier. With the fall of Rosas in 1852 an attempt was made to reverse his policy by encouraging immigration and agriculture as Rivadavia had tried to do earlier but few British settlers responded to the initiative of Aron Castellanos in Santa Fe and Entre Rios where a rural middle class, comparable to homesteaders in the United States were settled in agricultural colonies. Although Juan Alberdi, the originator of the phrase '*Gobernar es Poblar*' was anxious to attract settlers from Northern Europe, describing the British as the 'most perfect of men', few Britons reciprocated by embracing farming. It was Swiss, Germans, French, Italians who accepted the challenge.[22]

Had the Santa Fe experience been extended to the expanding pampas as Sarmiento envisaged in his Chivilcoy speech of 1868 the history of Argentina might have been very different, but attempts to introduce laws comparable to the Homestead Act of 1862 in the United States all failed due to speculation and the use of land grants as political rewards.[23]

There were, however, some exceptions, but only one of which involved settlers from Britain. In 1862 the Argentine government wishing to attract colonists to settle in bleak and underpopulated Patagonia, to forestall possible Chilean infiltration or the attention of European powers, welcomed a group of Welsh immigrants who settled in the Lower Chubut valley in 1865. Like the Irish, the Welsh were escaping from religious, economic and political discrimination, but their experiences in Argentina were markedly different. The Irish, partly through their Catholicism, were absorbed fairly painlessly into Argentine society whereas the Welsh were marginalised geographically and in terms of language and religion. Behind the Welsh exodus was the yearning to find the solitude where Welshness could be preserved. In the isolation of the desert the dream might be realised. All the factors causing the collapse of earlier British colonies were present in Chubut — distance from markets, natural obstacles, undercapitalisation and lack of official support but nevertheless, the Welsh settlement survived due to its religious and nationalistic faith, to temperance and to a rare ability on the part of the settlers to relate to the local Indians. The settlement went through many crises but it still survives today, a remarkable example of cultural persistence, many of its members speaking Welsh and Spanish but not English.[24]

Secular utopian dreams had less chance of being realised as shown by the case of Nueva Australia in Paraguay founded by William Lane whose oratory had fired the grandparents of Gladys Adamson to leave a freezing Edinburgh to help found a socialist community in Paraguay. When this broke up, the Adamson family moved to Entre Rios, leaving a valuable memoir of immigrant life there.[25]

Nothing could have been further removed from the Welsh experience than Puerto Victoria, the last British colony to be established in Argentina, at the other end of the country in Misiones in 1932.[26] The name recalled the great days of Empire. The settlement was a speculative venture, an imperial hangover where a disparate collection of people, some after a career in the Empire — ex-planters, ex-officers and public schoolboys out for adventure, all in the hope of making a profit from yerba maté and cheap labour, but in the post-Depression years the bottom had fallen out of the market and the settlers had no spiritual reserves or strong beliefs to sustain them in adversity.

At the southernmost end of the country in Santa Cruz and Tierra del Fuego there were Scottish sheep farmers on farms the size of European principalities and often under corporate ownership as in the Falklands, where the Falkland Islands Company was founded in 1851 to linger on until 1982. Hardy men in a harsh climate, they were demanding taskmasters, toasting in their club in Rio Gallegos, Major Varela the 'hyena of Patagonia' who had suppressed an anarchist-inspired rising among their immigrant Chilean farm hands in 1922 in which as many as 2,000 may have been killed. For long this rising was only a distant echo until uncovered by Osvaldo Bayer's book in 1972 and made into a film two years later as *Patagonia Rebelde*.[27]

Here was rough pioneering country captured in Lucas Bridge's classic *Uttermost Part of the Earth* but although there might be possibilities for becoming a manager on some company *estancia* the chances of actually owning land diminished as it rocketed in price through speculative deals. After the 1860s it is rare to find newly established British farmers or independent owners and there is an almost total absence of agricultural workers:

> The English labourer does not, or will not, adapt himself to new conditions or face unaccustomed hardships. He is not content to 'rough it'.[28]

By the beginning of this century the Emigrants' Information Office in London was advising prospective emigrants against going to Argentina in a speculative search for employment unless having at least £1,000 of capital, some knowledge of Spanish and farming skills.

This was justifiable caution at a time when the frontier had closed. Earlier in the 1860s when the Indian threat was a reality only the adventurous could have been expected to take the risk of pioneering on the pampas as R. A. Seymour did, recounting it in a book of that title published in 1869.[29] The threat from Indian raids runs throughout his account of farming between Rosario and Córdoba only five years before the British-financed railway would link the two cities.

Pampas Indians did not capture the imagination as did the Indians of the Great Plains of North America although G. A. Henty made a determined bid to do so. Always on the look out for rollicking yarns to fire the spirit of adventure among Victorian youth, he published in 1871 *Out on the Pampas, or the Young Settlers*, a fictional echo of Seymour. It interestingly reflects one motive for migrating, that which saw no openings in England where the professions were crowded and expensive to enter. A period in Argentina, therefore, with its 'magnificent rivers', (echoing promotional literature), 'its boundless extent of fertile land, its splendid climate, its cheap labour and its probable prospects offered the greatest advantage'. For the children it was a matter of 'having fights with Indians and all that sort of thing. Oh, it would be glorious'. Glorious it was for the survivors who return at the age of thirty to settle down in England in very comfortable circumstances, to amuse their children with tales of how their fathers and mothers fought the Indians on the pampas of South America.

Anyone fired to try their luck by Henty's tale might have had second thoughts the next year when news of the Tandil massacre filtered back to England, and after reading the report of the British Consul in 1872 strongly advising against emigration to Argentina. This time it was not the Indians but the *gaucho malo* who was the villain, killing fourteen settlers including Englishmen in a nativist outburst against the disrupting effect of foreigners settling on the pampas.[30]

Henty's moral though was that life in the Argentine offered plenty of scope for adventure as well as opportunities to accumulate enough capital to enjoy life in England. In this respect at least the British shared the *'hacer la América'* mentality of many Spaniards. It would need detailed research to establish that the English were more prone to do this than the Scots or Irish who adapted more readily than the English to the environment and:

> assumed the habits of the people among whom they had cast their lot ... Apart from investing in railways and other undertakings the English were considered to have played less part in the actual labour of developing Argentina than the energetic Scots or Irish.[31]

The English were the ones who tended to return to Southern England where Hobson located the imperialist rentier class living in 'plush parasitism', drawing tribute from overseas via the City.[32]

In Argentina itself religion became a major bonding force among migrants and a touchstone of class and ethnic differentiation. The 1825 Treaty permitted the building of an Anglican church which came to be attended by respectable merchants the majority of whom were English. When the Scots petitioned for a Presbyterian church for a congregation which was to comprise mechanics, agricultural emigrants and clerks, an unsympathetic Parish prevaricated mindful of

rousing Catholic resentment and it was left to his successor to get the
government's agreement to the building of the Scots church in 1833.
The Catholic Irish did not encounter such difficulties and under the
dynamic Father Fahy 'indispensable to his countrymen' in Mac-
Cann's view, and with the support of the Sisters of Mercy who came
from Ireland in 1856 they constituted what amounted to a sub-culture
of their own.[33]

Who went to Argentina and why did they do so when there was a
British Empire crying out for its own kith and kin? In the early days
it was common to find the British running shops, hotels, boarding-
houses, and even practising medicine and architecture in Buenos
Aires but this changes as Italians and Spaniards take over. As the
riverine provinces and the Pampas opened up for settlement from the
1860s so also the post-bellum American West, Canada, Australia and
New Zealand opened up for the British settler with more attractive
prospects of free and cheap land, similar culture and language,
religious freedom as well as varying degrees of political representation. Argentina had to compete for the migrant flow and this
explains the liberality of its immigration laws. Although all children
born to immigrants were Argentine citizens few first generation
immigrants were naturalized — a mere 1.6 per cent by 1914. Why
close off the option of return unless as a political exile return was
impossible? Unlike the United States where migration was a political
issue as Democrats and Republicans sought recruits to their ranks,
this was not the case in Argentina with its oligarchical political
system and even as late as 1916 only four men of foreign birth were
serving in Congress and only 12 per cent of the Chamber of Deputies
and 4 per cent of the Senate were first generation Argentine.[34] But
lax immigration laws could not divert the flow from the Empire and
the percentage of British to the total population of Buenos Aires
dwindled from 3.5 per cent in 1860 to 0.93 per cent in 1914.[35]

As British immigrants were swamped by southern Europeans so
immigration increasingly becomes a matter of capital and not of
people, with a subsequent narrowing and specialisation of occupational roles. Between 1904 and 1913 as much British capital was
invested in Argentina as in the whole of the nineteenth century. From
the 1870s the majority of Britons went out as clerks to work in
British-owned banks, shipping companies, export-import houses,
wholesale businesses and high class retail emporia — the way to
self-advancement for those of meagre means, or as technicians or
clerks in one of the seven British-owned railway companies or in one
of the many British-owned public utility and land companies. Con-

spicuous by their absence were industrialists. Capital tended to be invested in land (many English came as merchants and stayed as landowners), public utilities, or was repatriated.[36]

'As a people', complained Sir Horace Rumbold, ambassador in 1880, 'we do not take in this country the leading part we occupy elsewhere ... and in many branches of industry we allow ourselves to be outstripped by the French and Germans'.[37] He could well have added Italians.

Younger sons of good family — remittance men from minor public schools might be attracted to the 'camp' — as the *campo* was called — working their way up, or if with skills already, managing an *estancia* with the attendant chances of marrying a rich heiress or a British governess. Rumbold saw horse-breeding as a 'paying and congenial occupation for young Englishmen who might be tempted to try their future in this country' — something at which Cunninghame Graham had tried his hand in the early seventies. The open spaces of the Pampas also offered possibilities of acting out the fantasies of English country gentlemen, hunting ostriches instead of foxes, the drink-sodden types who so disgusted the hero in Hudson's *The Purple Land*.[38] Drunkenness is a running theme in the British experience. Six hundred *pulperías* in Buenos Aires in the early nineteenth century and the cheapness of liquor were a constant temptation, but drunkenness seems to have been as much a consequence of solitude as of conviviality. In the early years of the British Hospital in the 1840s some 70 per cent of recorded deaths were caused by alcoholism.[39]

To the outsiders the British appeared to be a tight supportive clique, Germans especially envied the way in which the British looked after their own but the smaller the group, the smaller the occupational niche — at least in the case of the British. Of all the foreign communities the German was closest in many respects to the British.[40] Greater in size, numbering some 140,000 in the inter-war years, and with a sense of cultural superiority, like the British it exercised an influence out of all proportion to its numbers. Although German economic influences never challenged that of the British — as it was to do in Brazil where the German presence was far stronger, it was nevertheless considerable — third in the size of its investments in 1910 after Britain and France, but on the eve of the First World War the number of German real-estate owners had already overtaken the British, steel and iron exports to Argentina exceeded those from Britain and Germans controlled 60 per cent of grain exports. Whereas the British ran the gas company, the Germans dominated the electricity supply under C.A.T.E. (*Companía Alemana Transatlántica de Electricidad*) the largest unified system in the world.[41] Germans were represented in a much wider range of occupations as *estancieros*, farmers, as skilled craftsmen and unskilled workers, as industrialists, financiers, shippers and most strikingly as academics and professionals. Germans conducted scientific missions and established a science department in the University of Córdoba. Several hundred German academics had as well spent time in Argentine universities. Most important of all, a German military mission modernised the Army. If the British community was divided ethnically, German speakers were even more divided between Swiss, Austrian, *Kleindeutsche* then, after unification in 1871, the *Reichsdeutsche* as well as *Volksdeutsche* from Eastern Europe. But nevertheless they were drawn together under the umbrella of *Deutschtum* — a unity of sentiment through a shared language.

Somewhat surprisingly, in contrast to the usual view, Germans admired the British for their efficiency, newcomers envying the humane way the British treated their immigrants. 'When someone knocks on the door' wrote one 'and says *civis britannicus sum*, the simple fact that he is a British subject suffices to get him a position right away.' [42] Another commented that in the British community 'even the least significant person is somebody'. It was believed that Englishmen seldom came to Argentina on the off-chance as they were sure to find employment in British trading houses in which at every rank they were better paid than their German counterparts, a view substantiated by the fact that between 1872 and 1923, 27 per cent of all German immigrants were placed in their first job by the officials at the Hotel de Inmigrantes which was rarely used by high-status immigrants like the British. German employers, for their part, tended to prefer non-German workers not only because they were considered to be less demanding but also for political reasons. The German community was markedly different from the British in its political divisions — the old pre-war *Reichsdeutsche* regarding the post-war immigrants from the Weimar Republic with contempt. Some Irish may have been critical of those compatriots like the Mulhalls, the editors of the *Handbook of the River Plate*, (the indispensable *vade mecum* of the 1870s), for their pro-English attitude but the closest to the widening gulf between the *Geld-Aristokratie* and German workers who comprised a far higher proportion of the German community (about a third) than the British, was the mutual resentment between old established British families with a standing among the land-holding elite and the commercial influx from the

1880s onwards, as the former strove to retain their social exclusiveness.

The influence of British socialist ideas was minimal in Argentina (in contrast, for example, to Australia with its Chartist and Irish radical traditions) whereas the Argentine socialist party was a creation of Germans — mostly printers and typographers — who left Germany during Bismarck's anti-socialist decrees of the 1880s. In 1882 the socialist association *Vorwärts* was founded, publishing a weekly from 1886-97 in which it urged workers to acquire citizenship and help to democratise Argentine politics — an aim inconceivable to the British.

For many Germans, political exile meant permanent exclusion from the homeland whereas the British were never under the same compulsion to put their roots down and rarely regarded themselves as immigrants. There was always the possibility of return — if not to Britain then to a part of the Empire as in the case of some disillusioned Welsh settlers who went to Canada.[43] One consequence was that the British did not take learning Spanish as seriously as the Germans who ran regular classes for workers. Another was that there was never the same need to make agricultural colonies succeed. The Germans' success in their El Dorado colony in Misiones was a standing affront to the neighbouring failed British colony at Puerto Victoria, where one disgruntled settler attributed German success to providing their own labour force by 'spawning like rabbits'.

To offset the failure of British colonies some might point, in contrast, to the success of the Forestal Land, Timber and Railway Company founded in 1906, the largest of its kind in Argentina — and in its day in Latin America.[44] It was the antithesis of an agricultural colony and was more akin to a plantation with its 8,000 workers, company stores and rigid discipline. Cutting down quebracho forests for tannin and railway sleepers (and for fuel to replace coal during the First World War when supplies dwindled) it set a precedent for the desertification with which we are all too familiar today.

In the same year as *Patagonia Rebelde* (1974) was filmed, *Quebracho* also appeared. Both films reflected the growing resentment at British exploitation of Argentina's human and natural resources and were symptomatic of how by the mid-1970s, the negative counter-image of British influence had taken root. The positive British contributions to Argentina were discounted and were regarded as the imposition of an arbitrary pattern of development as in the case of the 'spider web' railway network which served the interests of British investors and their Argentine clients but did nothing to knit together isolated towns and so foster viable rural communities.

In the inter-war years mutual perceptions changed as new social groups emerge who had little contact with the British. Part of the decline of British influence in the course of the late 1930s lay in the inability to diversify their economic interests and hence their social contacts. With few of these outside Buenos Aires, Rosario, and the closed world of the *estancia*, the English tended to live a club life in their suburbs, holding aloof from those expressions of popular culture, football (now professionalised and far-removed from the amateur pre-war model of the Corinthian Casuals), boxing and the vaudeville, which were portents of the emergence of a mass society and harbingers of the popular mobilisation of the Peronist period in the late 1940s and early 1950s.

We can see the slippage by comparing the two chapters in Sir David Kelly's memoirs where he recounts his Argentine experiences. In the first as a young attaché fresh from the Great War the old verities still stand; the Jockey Club and the inner sanctum of the fencing club were where deals were made on the 'old boy net' as often as not between Britons and Argentines who had been to the same public schools in Britain or to one of the British schools in Buenos Aires.

In the second period, as ambassador in the 1940s, he was on the defensive, contacts now had to be worked for and the old magic no longer counted either in dealing with the military with their German and Italian links or the new politicians round Perón who did not have the *savoir faire* of the old anglophile elite. Also, an uncomprehending U.S. State Department now had to be mollified. Well-fed Americans could not understand the British obsession with meat supplies which always tempered dealings with Perón.[45] Nor could they appreciate Kelly's assessment of Perón as an opportunist rather than a fascist. There were deeper undercurrents to this incomprehension stemming from rivalry over influence and trade. Kelly's views were more balanced and less jaundiced than some of his intemperate colleagues who, when faced with an assertive, articulate and radical nationalist intelligentsia, resorted to popular stereotypes.

In these days when racialism is equated with colour prejudice it is too easily forgotten how prejudiced British views of southern Europeans have been. Spaniards have always suffered from the legacies of the Black Legend and some of this has rubbed off on to Spanish Americans, especially where there has been race-mixing.[46] Sarmiento shared these views as did many other Spanish American intellectuals for whom as with Bolívar, Spain was the *madrastra* (stepmother) and not the *madre* (mother). The assumed creole aversion to work had been attributed by many British writers to Spanish influence, and Spanish immigrants 'did not show the aptitude for all kinds of work which characterises Italians'. Basques were excluded from these strictures and were, 'by universal consent', in the opinion of one writer 'to be considered the best kind of man who comes to Argentina'.[47] They monopolised dairying, finding in the growth of a mass market in Buenos Aires the enduring success which had eluded the Robertsons' butter makers in the 1820s.

The saying that an 'Argentine is an Italian who speaks bad Spanish and aspires to be English' is one of those *chistes* which indicates an attitude. Argentina is unique in being predominantly an Italo-Hispanic society for which there were no precedents elsewhere. The complexities of the assimilation process as reflected in *lunfardo* speech or the figure of *cocoliche* eluded the British community many of whom, not feeling themselves to be immigrants, did not need to come to terms with the inner complexities of Argentine culture.[48] Cunninghame Graham's empathy with gauchos was an individual response whereas the gaucho clubs of Italian immigrants in the early years of this century where they dressed up in *bombachos* and held *asados* in the *campo* at week-ends was a group attempt to identify with the symbol of *argentinidad* and to slough off the pejorative attributes associated with migrants.

British attitudes towards Italians have always been ambivalent — and it must have been difficult to reconcile what had been learnt at school about the Roman Empire (a model for the British Empire), the glories of the Renaissance or to relate Victorian enthusiasm for the Risorgimento and its colourful leader Garibaldi (who had served his military apprenticeship at the 9-year seige of Montevideo — the 'modern Troy' as it was fancifully described) with the flood of poor Italian immigrants — nearly a million of whom poured in to Argentina in the forty years before 1914 — the poorest of them from Sicily and the South tending to stay in Buenos Aires.

There was little opportunity for the British community to form a balanced view of Italians as those with whom they came into contact were labourers, servants, shoeshine boys, waiters or shop-keepers, nor would there be opportunities to meet upwardly mobile Italians socially. Each group had their own clubs, schools and newspapers. Few Britons entered the professions or the universities. In any case, many Italians, especially of the second generation, were aspiring businessmen and industrialists who lobbied for tariff protection and

so tended to be those whom the British saw as a threat to their own
hegemony.

Although the British shared the creole's disdain for poor Italians
who were held responsible for crime, disease, immorality and political
extremism, they acknowledged their capacity for hard work attributing their success to being prepared to accept conditions which British
workers would reject. Italian labour in Koebel's opinion was 'accepted
with alacrity: that of the British — such little as has been offered —
with misgiving ... in Argentina the common opinion has almost
passed into a proverb that the British, whether mechanic or agricul-
turalist, is of little account in the first rung of the ladder. Unless a
foreman, he may be ranked one of the useless class'.[49]

It was impossible to ignore the Italian presence. Buenos Aires was
largely built by Italian architects using Italian construction firms,
employing Italian labourers although the influence of the *Ecole des
Beaux Arts* began to popularise French styles from the 1880s. Opera,
the art form par excellence of the *bourgeois conquérant* was dominated by Italian singers who visited Buenos Aires, much as the
*golondrinas*, circuses and touring theatrical companies did during
the European winters. In the Teatro Colon, the world's largest opera
house, completed in 1906, Italian opera ruled and although compulsive attendance by the elite was dictated by social snobbery creating
the most brilliant spectacle that even Clemenceau, used to the Paris
Opera, had ever seen, the galleries were packed with enthusiastic
Italians whose critical acclaim could make or break singers — as on
one occasion they nearly broke Caruso. In 1910 verbal abuse and
enthusiastic claques were eclipsed by the impact on public opinion of
the bomb hurled into the stalls by anarchists. This was the most
graphic illustration of widening social divisions and the threat to
political stability, which were attributed to the influence of immigrants and their radical European ideas.[50]

The British were not perceived as a threat in this way but although
the few loafers round the stations hoping for tips from their wealthier
compatriots could be ignored, down on the waterfront it was different.
Twice as many British as any other nationality were apprehended by
the police for drunkenness and disorderly conduct — not surprising
given the preponderance of British ships in the port and the propens-
ity for the British to take to drink.[51] The Mission to Seamen had been
established in the port area to steer sailors away from the red light
district and console them with tea, biscuits and hymn-singing, but
probably the commonest image of 'BA' among seamen remained that
of bordellos and bars. More British subjects would have seen the

underside of Buenos Aires than the glitter of the Colon Theatre or
the fashionable parades of the Palermo racecourse.

Interestingly, though, seamen seem to have been impervious to the
tango. It was not they who introduced it into Britain from the
dockside bars but aristocrats who learnt it from their French peers
at Le Touquet and other fashionable resorts. Today, the popular
perception of the tango in Britain is derived from the acrobatics of
dance competitions where it has been drained of dangerous erotic
content and bears no relationship to the original. As with many other
countries bemused by the example of Europe, so also the tango did
not become reputable in Argentina until it had received the imprima-
tur of the British and French elite.[52]

Buenos Aires' reputation as a centre of the white slave trade can
be related to the sex imbalance caused by the *'golondrinas'* — tran-
sitory workers who crossed the Atlantic from Southern Europe in the
off-season at home to work on the harvest. Few British girls seem to
have taken the 'road to Buenos Aires'[53] — the girls were recruited in
the slums of Mediterranean ports and the ghettoes of Eastern Europe. Nevertheless, in the memory of one English nanny, girls did not
go out alone for fear of being abducted.

The English nanny was a stern figure and symbol of rectitude —
nothing could have been further removed from the alluring image of
the French cocotti — a key weapon in the army of French cultural
imperialism in Lévi-Strauss's view. We badly need a study of those
maiden ladies with pretensions to gentility, the female counterpart
of the remittance man, who were nannies and governesses in many
an elite household. An Argentine Freyre could perhaps assess the
influence of bed-time stories, of toys 'made in England', of dolls with
nordic features, on their charges.[54] Maria Luisa Bemberg found the
experience of having had innumerable English nannies memorable
(or traumatic) enough to make the film *Miss Mary* in which those
above stairs speak English and those below Spanish.

'Miss Mary', she writes,[55] 'was an interesting idea for me because
it had so many different angles'. One of them was just a tribute to
those dear old ladies of whom I knew so many as a child myself, and
with whom one had a love/hate relationship. Even as a child of eleven
or twelve, I was very much aware of the craziness of the lives of these
women, what sad, wasted lives looking after other people's children,
in other people's houses, far away from home, as if very rich but not
having a penny, just as alien from the kitchen as they were from the
living-room, because the servants thought they were traitors. They
were in-between. They all seemed to be carrying their world in their

trunk, under the bed, and they all seemed to mix one into the other, all spinsters, probably all virgins. All drank a little at night, I guess because they were lonely and depressed. They raved about their little princesses. They were very conservative, very Victorian, very repressed sexually, but usually with a sense of humour and tenderness. I was brought up by these English — or rather Irish — women. My mother preferred them Irish because she wanted to be sure that they were Catholics ... I wanted to show through this English governess the influence of the English commercially and culturally on the Argentine upper classes.'

Speaking English was a passport to financial success but French was the language of high culture and Paris was the intellectual capital of Argentina as it was for the rest of Latin America — a posting to an embassy in Paris was the ambition of aspiring writers. Jorge Luis Borges with a Northumbrian grandmother was an isolated figure in his total commitment to English literature which extended even to Anglo-Saxon. But the sensibilities of most Argentine writers were not nurtured on British literature, the influence of which, at best, was fitful. Hudson was unusual in being able to browse in his father's collection of books in the rat and flea infested rancho in which they lived a primitive settler life. There he was to discover through reading James Thompson's *Seasons* and Gilbert White's *Selbourne* that England was 'home' and the 'land of my desires'.

An important philosophical influence had been that of Jeremy Bentham on Rivadavia.[56] They had met each other in London, but Rivadavia's brilliance, his liberal fervour and drive shown in his foundation of the University of Buenos Aires and his economic policies were offset by his cold personality and the shortness of his period of office. If Rivadavia reflects one trend of liberal thought Sarmiento reflects another. He was reputed to have read a novel of Sir Walter Scott a day during a period of his exile in Chile and it may be that his ambivalent view of the gaucho was partly derived from Scott's search for the *volksgeist* among the shepherds of Lowland Scotland in his border novels, and partly from Head who provided a vision of the pampas and the gauchos which Sarmiento did not know at first-hand prior to writing *Facundo*. But Sarmiento was almost unique among Spanish American intellectuals in taking the United States rather than European powers as a model, sensing the comparability of their respective frontier experiences. Fenimore Cooper's heroes were those to emulate, and it would be by applying American educational precepts that Argentina would be redeemed from barbarism and with this end in view sixty-five American school-teachers came by Sarmiento's invitation to teach in Argentine schools.[57]

The other early nineteenth century British literary influence was predictably Byron, particularly among the exiles of the doomed anti-rosista generation of 1837. But behind the Byronic pose of its greatest figure Esteban Echevarría lay the deeper influence of Lamartine, Victor Hugo and the French utopian socialists acquired during a sojourn in Paris.[58] French models also influenced the Zolaesque social realist novels of the closing years of the century.

The British were not concerned to challenge these influences and placed little store on cultural diplomacy. Intellectual pursuits were a leisure-time activity for gifted amateurs — like Sir Woodbine Parish whose curiosity and interest in natural science enabled him to overcome his initial revulsion against Buenos Aires 'that disagreeable and disheartening place'.[59] Hudson, for his part, was to remain the amateur outsider, his sensibilities freed from constricting academic pedantries — an explanation perhaps for his remarkable insights and freshness of vision. Intellectualism was despised although not among the Scots who were cultural pacemakers, prominent in the foundation and staffing of British schools and as writers. Cunninghame Graham, Walter Owen and William Shand were all Scots. Walter Owen — a poet and translator of *Martín Fierro* the Argentine epic — kept quiet about his literary interests for fear of embarrassing his stockbroker employers and perhaps reducing his chances of advancement. The notion of cultural attachés and cultural missions, an integral part of French diplomacy, was alien to the British, for whom culture followed commerce not vice versa.

The French case, however, shows that it did not follow that a strong cultural presence would necessarily strengthen economic ties. Philip Guedalla, much impressed by the French cultural effort in Argentina, thought that it probably did.

> There is no evidence that grateful audiences place orders for French woollens after a lecture on Molière. But national prestige is powerfully aided by such stimulants and it cannot be doubted that they lead to something more than tourist traffic.[60]

He went on to point out that of 27,980 books taken out of the Medical Faculty Library, 13,716 were French and only 53 English, observing that 'this disparity would be reflected in French exports of instruments and drugs'.

On his visit to Argentina in 1910 Georges Clemenceau could not reconcile himself to the way the French lagged behind the British economically in spite of their community being twice the size. He saw his mission to assert the primacy of French civilisation and to '*porter haut le drapeau français*', and to alert the French to economic possibilities as was the purpose of the various visits of British royalty, (Prince George in 1880, the Prince of Wales in 1925 and 1931 and the Duke of Edinburgh in 1962 and 1966). Especially galling to Clemenceau had been the missed opportunity of France dominating the railway system by having turned down an Argentine approach and allowing the British to take it up.[61] He also believed that Franco-Argentines were severely disadvantaged by being liable to military service in both Argentina and France — unlike the British. It was a constant complaint too that the French were denied privileges granted to the British by the 1825 Treaty. One of the purposes behind the French intervention in the River Plate in the 1840s — apart from wishing to break Rosas's blockade of Montevideo (where 30 per cent of the population was French) was to squeeze similar concessions out of Rosas.[62]

With the discrediting of Spain and Spanish culture after independence French diplomats had sensed an opening for cultural influence, capitalising on the Revolutionary and Napoleonic mystique and on more tangible influences like that of the Code Napoléon. Clemenceau was following in the well-worn Pan-Latin tradition of Louis Phillipe and Napoléon III (to whom the phrase 'Latin America' can be credited) in asserting that France was the natural leader of the Latin nations. He discounted German, English and North American influences as of secondary importance in comparison with France's cultural presence in a country 'which has preserved integrally its Latinity'. In his determination to endear Argentines to France, he even regarded Carlos Pellegrini, president from 1890-93, as a Frenchman on the strength of his parents having been born in Nice. German writers were predictably unimpressed by French pretensions. 'The educated Argentine,' one had written in 1888, 'has long understood that the true light of science beams up on him more brightly and purely from the treasure houses of the German intellect than from the trumpery baubles of the Gallic spirit'.[63]

In this battle for cultural supremacy the British were mere skirmishers. Whether because they believed effortlessly in their superiority or because they did not care about cultural matters is a moot point. Culture like commerce was a matter of laissez-faire. The best British writing on Argentina in the nineteenth century was travel writing but this was largely an offshoot of the search for commercial or farming opportunities. So long as Argentina was a land of the future and a field of enterprise it attracted a stream of writers, but there is a falling off in quality and quantity after the First World War. Once the promise faded there was nothing exotic to attract the travel writer comparable to Mexico or Peru; no ancient monuments or mysterious hieroglyphics to decipher. It is symptomatic that the two classics of English writing after the 1920s, Lucas Bridges' *Uttermost Part of the Earth* (1948) and Bruce Chatwin's *In Patagonia* (1977) were set in the periphery peopled by eccentrics, bandits such as Butch Cassidy and the Sundance Kid, political exiles or doomed tribes.[64] No leading British writer's imagination has been fertilised by the Argentine landscape or its peoples. It needed a W.H. Hudson — as much Argentine as British, to discover a world in the emptiness of the pampa which became his 'parish of Selbourne'. Even Graham Greene with his nose for sniffing out the underside of Latin America whether in Mexico, Cuba, Haiti, Paraguay or Panama was not attracted to Argentina, in spite of his popularity in literary circles there: only V.S. Naipaul, but in his case *The Return of Eva Perón* was another exercise in his misogynist's vision of the world.[65]

Cunninghame Graham is perhaps the one imaginative British writer on Argentine themes who lives in the Argentine memory.[66] The same can hardly be said of the Poet Laureate John Masefield two of whose long poems have an Argentine setting and whom as a young writer Graham had encouraged.[67] His tramp steamer with its 'salt-caked smoke stack' would have been a familiar sight unloading coal in the Buenos Aires docks but although he had only visited Chile and not Argentina he had nevertheless heard of the famous case of Camila O'Gorman's love affair with a Catholic priest and their execution by Rosas which he was to make the central theme of a 828-line poem in which the dead lovers are revenged on Rosas at the battle of Caseros:

> But from the sworn attackers came a shout
> Remember those poor lovers and their charge
> Scattered the gaucho lancers in a rout
> And chased their remnant to the river marge.
> Then Rosas turned his horse and rode alone
> To some mean dockyard where he was not known

He was then secreted away in a British frigate to a twenty-five year exile:

He died in England many a year ago
His daughter too: both lie in English soil.
They say that great moon daisies love to grow
Over Camila, and with loving toil
Soldiers who dwell there train the rose boughs
Over the daisies on their narrow home

Whatever the hidden merits of Masefield's poem and exaggeration
of the horticultural skill of Argentine soldiers it did at least acknowledge Rosas's existence and bring to the attention of British readers
the lord of half a million acres, who spent the last twenty-five years
of his life in a thatched cottage as a tenant farmer on the outskirts of
Southampton where the locals acquired a taste for yerba maté and
pumpkins and where his body was condemned to lie in British soil
until the repatriation of his remains in 1989.

It is a curious paradox that the man who was to become the symbol
of anti-imperialism for the ultra-nationalist writers of the twentieth
century should have been so anglophile, leaving British merchants
unmolested even as British warships bombarded his army during the
blockade of the 1840s and whose daughter was courted, albeit unsuc-
cessfully, by a British ambassador, dressed in gaucho garb. Without
British connivance at Rosas's escape after Caseros he would surely
have been strung up like a common criminal. It is difficult to reconcile
British accounts of him, or indeed the historical record, or the portrait
of him with his English looks and whom Parish described as being
'very like an English country gentleman with a benevolent countenance and very polite manners' with vitriolic anti-rosista polemic —
the 'Nero of South America', the 'Tiger of Palermo' — until it is
remembered that he is a symbol representing, as he did for Sarmiento, the savagery of the untutored mind and the unrestrained
instincts of the mob, while for *rosistas* he represents the virtues of
*criollismo* untainted by corrupt foreign influences.[68] For Sarmiento,
Buenos Aires symbolised civilisation which would redeem the barbarism of the empty desolate interior, but this antithesis starts to be
reversed with the growth of *criollismo* at the end of the century. Now
Buenos Aires is the *cabeza de Goliat*,[69] a monstrous growth draining
the countryside of its talent and wealth, a source of festering corruption and of a cosmopolitan, denationalising ethos in which the materialism of immigrants and the race for profits eclipsed spiritual
values.

At intervals since the 1880s a number of Germans concerned with
*Kultur*, unlike most Britons, acidly made this point describing

Buenos Aires as 'the most desolate metropolis on this earth. It exists for only one wretched purpose: to make money', and another was to comment in the 1920s 'It has a history but no tradition. It came from outside: it has no roots in the land ... it is European commercial and North American commercial ... a chessboard of stone ... tasteless parks and villas, all bedecked in kitsch'.[70] These words might have been written by any Argentine nationalist writer of the twentieth century who exalts the traditional rural virtues represented by the gaucho *Martín Fierro* of José Hernández's epic poem as the symbol of *argentinidad*.

Significantly, the four foremost nationalist writers were from the provinces, Manuel Gálvez, Leopoldo Lugones, Ricardo Rojas, and the scourge of the British, Raul Scalabrini Ortiz whose study of the railways is a frontal attack on that instrument of destruction of the old freedoms and traditional ways.[71] The railway — which played a minor social role in most Latin American countries — is in Argentina as important and as ambivalent a symbol as in the United States. In both countries the railway was the major modernising force, facilitating rapid transport of cattle and grain to Atlantic ports, integrating settlement frontiers into the international economy and promoting settlement schemes.

However there was an adverse side. In the United States the 'machine in the garden' destroyed the pastoral idyll of Jeffersonian agrarianism — the 'middle ground' of Crevècoeur's vision — peopled by those independent farmers whom the Founding Fathers saw as the backbone of the American democratic tradition.[72] In Argentina there was no garden to destroy — only hunting grounds disputed between Indians and gauchos but as in the United States' railway monopolies also fixed freight charges, controlled grain elevators, represented the power of banks and corporations, and by enhancing land values led to speculative fever and political corruption. In the United States, resistance took the form of agrarian populism which was the closest Democrats and Republicans ever came to facing a challenge to their dominance, but in Argentina the fragmentation of rural society removed the social basis on which to build even an unsuccessful protest movement.[73] In any case issues could not be resolved by domestic politics alone as the railway system, with only minor exceptions, was foreign-owned with policy decisions taken in European board-rooms. Thus the British-dominated railways became the visible symbol of foreign domination and had to bear the thrust of radical nationalism in the 1930s and 1940s.

It was not only the changing social and political milieu or the rival challenges from other European persons which signalled the decline of British influence so much as the creeping reality of American power and efficiency. The United States took a remarkably long time to break into Argentina but by the 1920s the challenge could not be ignored.

At the beginning of the nineteenth century the triangular trade of flour and timber to Argentina in return for jerked beef to Brazil and Cuba and then sugar and molasses back to the United States was a promising portent for an inter-American trading system but the Argentine market was too limited and American resources too committed to the expansion of the internal domestic frontier to challenge the British who could provide the expertise, the capital and the market for Argentine exports. The Americans were powerless to prevent the economic puncturing of the Monroe Doctrine in spite of persistent attempts to do so.

From the earliest days of independence despatches from the U.S. chargé in Buenos Aires gave vent to indignant frustration and querulous complaints about British dominance. In the 1840s one wrote that he found

the extraordinary partiality, admiration and preference for the English government and English men ... unaccountable and strange, in view of the arrogant and selfish policy, and the meddlesome and sinister influences, which the British Government and peoples have always endeavoured to exercise in these countries.[74]

The United States had become involved diplomatically with Argentina over the Falklands issue when Louis Vernet an adventurer of French origin was appointed Governor of the islands by Buenos Aires.[75] But with the British re-assertion of what they considered their rights in 1833 and the expulsion of Argentine settlers American interest lapsed. So for the present did Argentina's. Rosas was not prepared to challenge Britain at a time when France was perceived to be a more serious threat.

Once the United States had ensured equality of treatment with Britain and France for its shipping in the treaty of 1853, diplomatic and commercial involvement in Argentina was to remain low-key until the end of the century except for the interlude of the Paraguayan war (1865-70) which raised the contentious issue of Paraguay's independence, and the freedom of river navigation.

With the growth of the Western Hemisphere concept and its crystallisation in the Pan American Conference of 1889 United States interest in Argentina took on a new significance but the Pan American ideal so ardently pursued by the Americans was wrecked on the growing rivalry between Brazil and Argentina, reflected in an arms race, which was to bedevil the foreign policies of both powers up to Perón and beyond. In 1907 the Brazilians ordered three Dreadnoughts from Britain which prompted the Argentines to buy two battleships from the United States. Battleship diplomacy was one aspect of American industry's need to find new markets.[76] Another was the supplying of farm machinery and meat packing plants. By the late 1920s the United States controlled 66 per cent of meat exports through its meat packing houses compared with the British share of 19 per cent and the Argentine of 15 per cent.[77]

The First World War was a turning point for the British, not so much because of any threat from import substitute industrialisation as from the United States commercial and financial challenge. In 1914 their legation in Buenos Aires was raised to embassy status and in 1919 the British monopoly of cable communication was at last broken by the inauguration of a direct line between Buenos Aires and New York thus breaking British access to American commercial information. American firms, often represented by underemployed Anglo-Argentines, made inroads in German and British companies, although it has been estimated that in the 1920s some 75 per cent of American business in Argentina was in supplying consumer goods such as refrigerators and cars which an inflexible British industry could not provide. This commercial drive was paralleled by the cultural impact of Hollywood which the British were unable to counter.

Film was not the only area where the British did not or could not compete. With their shipping and rail interests, they did not appreciate the future importance of air and motor transport. It was left to Germans and Americans to compete for control of airways whilst the American support for road construction prepared the way for their overwhelming domination of the automobile market which was to drain away passengers and freight from the railways.[78] The British failed to appreciate the extent to which the deterioration of transport stock would foster mass anti-British feeling among a long-suffering public.[79]

However, the very extent of the American drive, culminating in the visit in 1928 of president-elect Herbert Hoover with his interest in and experience of Latin America, may have been counterproductive by alerting the British. The next year the d'Abernon mission was sent to Argentina (more serious than the outwardly lavish visit of the Prince of Wales in 1925), to dispel any impression that Latin America had a low priority in Britain's foreign policy.

The Argentines were also alerted. The British appeared the lesser of two evils and the ambassador could report that the government was more favourably disposed to them as they were 'less aggressive and domineering' than the Americans. But however aggressive the Americans might wish to be, they were always constrained by the inhibiting fact that the American and Argentine economies were competitive and not complementary. An entrenched farm lobby was able to influence Congress to place high tariffs on imports of Argentine wool and cereals (except linseed) and by strict sanitary regulations to limit the import of Argentine meat.

There was, therefore, an imbalance in U.S.-Argentine trade. The Americans' share of the market rose from 15 per cent to 24 per cent between 1913 and 1929 while the British share fell from 30 per cent to 19 per cent but Argentine imports into the U.S. rose only from 6.3 per cent to 9.3 per cent in the same period.

Europe remained Argentina's best customer, receiving some 85 per cent of its exports, and even though Argentina bought relatively less from Britain, exports to Britain rose from 26.1 per cent before 1914 to some 32 per cent at the end of the 1920s.

The British and Argentine economies still appeared to be complementary, expressed in the slogan 'buy from those who buy from us' but this was largely illusory as British exports continued to be those traditionally supplied and not those capital goods which a nascent Argentine industry required.

Argentine-British trade relations came to a head with the Ottawa Conference of 1932, convened in the aftermath of the Great Depression at a time when laissez-faire was being replaced by protectionism. Imperial Preference threatened to discriminate against Argentine beef in the British market but the importance of the Argentine market to British industry — especially coal, iron, tin plate and textiles — was still sufficiently important for there to be a positive response to the Argentine request for preferential treatment. As no Dominion could replace Argentine beef and so ensure cheap food the Argentines were treated, for trade purposes, as the 'Sixth Dominion' although:

...in a different and inferior category to the British Dominions. Continued access to the British market would cost Argentinians more than it cost the Dominions. The real sense in which Argentina was 'special' was in the British prospects for winning fresh concessions for its trade.[80]

Arguments have raged over the Roca-Runciman Treaty of 1933 which was to regulate trade relations into the 1940s. The concessions for British imports in that agreement were attacked by nationalists as a sell-out of the wider national interest by a small group of cattle barons who only controlled 11 per cent of Argentina's total exports. Through their contacts, limited to the elite and the Anglo-Argentine community, the British seem to have been convinced that the politicians of the Concordancia were the guarantee of political and social stability and so were natural allies who should be supported. This was a miscalculation as in the long run by seeming to favour a narrow elite which lacked a social conscience, and to support an economic system where wealth did not automatically trickle down to the impoverished lower classes, the treaty sharpened anti-British sentiment, leading eventually to Perón's access to power and the final end of the British connection. In the short term, however, it had the effect of slowing down the growth of American influence.

A comparison with Brazil is instructive: there the 1930s and 1940s saw an accelerating 'Americanisation'. Brazil was not dependent on the British market and so the decline of British influence was more rapid than in Argentina,[81] as it was in every other Latin American country, throwing into relief the importance of the Argentine connection. Meat supplies which had always been central to the relationship became an obsession with a population deprived of meat during and after the war until the end of meat rationing in 1953. It was the only period in this century until the Falklands conflict that British-Argentine relations intruded into British domestic politics whereas since the mid 1930s they had never been far from the centre of political debate in Argentina. As the British presence declined so the benefits from the relationship, except to a small ingrown minority of landowners, became less attractive. Nationalism since the 1930s was no longer a preserve of the Right as the integration of second and third generation immigrants weakened residual loyalties to their forefathers' country of origin. The anglophilia of the small increasingly discredited landowning minority enabled Perón to articulate a new mass nationalism which culminated in the nationalisation of British-owned railways in 1947, when the railway code of 1907 came up for renewal.

Disagreements over the valuation of the railway's assets were resolved partly through the US ambassador's intervention. The visible symbol of British economic power was finally sold for £150 million, a sum which the British considered less than the railways were worth (although higher than the Stock Exchange valuation of them). Given the decrepitude of much of the rolling stock many Argentines considered they had the worst of the deal.

The nationalisation of the French-owned railways in the previous year had nothing like the same resonance. Nationalisation not only strengthened Perón's political standing with the unions but indirectly hastened the replacement of British by US economic influence.

For six years during the war Argentina had amassed sterling reserves in London which Britain was reluctant to unfreeze. However, when it was finally compelled to do so under pressure from the Americans whose loans to assist Britain's post-war recovery were dependent on blocked sterling balances being released, creditor nations were now able to buy the goods which only the United States, with its industry intact, could provide.

After 1947 there were still banks, bequeathing in the case of the brutalism of the BOLSA building a belated and, for some, a baleful architectural legacy. There were also insurance companies, some industrial firms, subsidiaries of British multinationals, the *Buenos Aires Herald*, the British schools and, for a brief moment, BMC cars built under licence, but with their replacement by US and European models, with the demise of the railways and the decline of shipping the British presence withered and the Anglo-Argentine community reduced to under 20,000 were left to come to terms with Peronism and its legacies, nostalgically recalling an Edwardian vision of a mother country which no longer existed.

After the war Argentina's frustration grew as the perception of itself as the undisputed leader of South America was challenged by Brazil as the continent's potential Great Power, courted by the United States and benefitting from having been its ally in the war against the Axis. In particular, the Argentine military felt threatened by a modernised and expanded Brazilian army.

In contrast to Brazil's participation in the war, Argentine neutrality brought few benefits apart from the meat and cereal boom. Yoked to a declining imperial power, distrusted for flirting with the Axis, the sense of nationalist exasperation was further compounded by the failure of Perón's ambitious foreign policy, based on establishing Latin America as a Third Force in international politics under Argentine leadership.

Argentina's post-war lukewarmness towards Britain was recipro-cated by a decline of British interest in Argentina once the problem of meat supplies ceased to be so pressing. Argentina was downgraded in the list of Foreign Office priorities together with the rest of Latin America as British diplomacy wrestled with decolonisation in Africa, Asia and the Middle East. For the first time Britain accepted the *fait accompli* of United States hegemony throughout Latin America. The slide in official British interest caused concern to those firms tradi-tionally involved in the region as it was apparent that not only the United States but European powers were capturing traditional Brit-ish markets. The Cuban Revolution and the extension of the Cold War to Latin America provided the catalyst for changing attitudes. The Parry Committee was established to examine ways in which British interest in the region could be revived. The implementation of its recommendation to establish five centres of Latin American Studies marked the beginning of a new professional academic involvement in the region. Although the Parry recommendations did not wholly achieve the major purpose of reviving commerce, it created for the first time a corpus of expertise in the universities. British academic interest in Latin America boomed and especially in Argentine history where attention focussed on the puzzling decline of Argentine pro-minence and on the little understood phenomenon of Peronism, centring on the question of British responsibility or otherwise for its rise and on the long-term effects of the British connection on Argen-tina's economic decline. British academics shared the fascination of Argentines for the cause of that decline as it mirrored, although for different reasons, Britain's parallel decline from pre-eminence. By focussing on this aspect of the relationship, with a prescriptive dimension, other aspects of the relationship tended to be overlooked. It is the purpose of the essays which follow to contribute towards redressing the balance.

## Notes

1. David Rock, *Argentina, 1516-1982*, Tauris, London, 1986: James Scobie, *Argentina: a city and a nation*, Oxford University Press, New York, 2nd edn. 1971. Eduardo Crawley, *A House Divided, Argentina 1880-1980*. C.Hurst, London, 1984. An older but very readable history is Ysabel Rennie, *The Argentine Re-public* 1945, Greenwood reprint, 1975. The chapters on Argen-tina in Vols. III and Vol. V of the *Cambridge History of Latin America* ed. L. Bethell, Cambridge University Press, 1985 and

1986 by John Lynch, Roberto Cortes Conde, Ezequiel Gallo and David Rock respectively. An introduction to the Anglo-Argentines is Andrew Graham-Yool, *The Forgotten Colony: a History of the English Speaking communities in Argentina*, Hutchinson, London, 1981. H.S. Ferns, *Britain and Argentina in the Nineteenth Century*, Oxford, Clarendon Press, 1960 is a standard account for the nineteenth century and Roger Gravil, *The Anglo-Argentine connection, 1900-1939*, Westview Press, Boulder and London, 1985, is a challenging economic analysis.

2. For Buenos Aires by far the best book in English is James Scobie, *Buenos Aires: from plaza to suburb*, Oxford University Press, New York, 1974, and his 'Buenos Aires as a commercial-bureaucratic city, 1880-1910: characteristics of a city's orientation'. *American Historical Review*, 72:4; October 1972. One of the best evocations of Buenos Aires in the 1920s is Francis Korn, *Los huéspedes del'20*. Editorial Sudamericana, Buenos Aires 1974. For an immigrant autobiography showing the underside of the immigrant myth see Juan F. Marsal, *Hacer la América: autobiografía de un inmigrante español en la Argentina*, Instituto di Tella, Buenos Aires, 1969.

3. The 'mystery' of the reduction of the black population of Buenos Aires to some 8,000 by 1900 is discussed in George Reid, *The Afro-Argentines of Buenos Aires, 1800-1900*, University of Wisconsin Press, Madison, 1980. For Rosas's support among blacks and mulattos in the 1830s see Lynch *infra*. pp. 119-24. Many gauchos were black but whether as many as the fifth who comprised the cowboy population of the American West would be impossible to quantify. The Indian appearance of many of the poorer inhabitants of Buenos Aires may seem strange to those who believed Argentina was the 'whitest' South American country. It may be partly explained by the cross-frontier migration of Bolivians and Paraguayans.

4. For 'informal empire' see H.S. Ferns, 'Britain's Informal Empire in Argentina 1806-1914', *Past and Present*, 4, 1954.

5. For railways see Colin Lewis, *British railways in Argentina: 1857-1914: a case study in foreign investment*. Athlone Press, University of London, 1983 and W.R. Wright, *Foreign-owned railways in Argentina: a case study of economic nationalism 1857-1947*, University of Texas Press, Austin, 1974.

6. Retailing is covered in R. Gravil, 'British retail trade in Argentina 1900-1914', *Inter-American Economic Affairs* 24, Autumn 1970.

7. A good pictorial evocation of pre-First World War Buenos Aires are the photographs in R. Lloyd (ed) *Twentieth Century Impressions of Argentina, its People, History, Industries and Commerce, London, 1911 — a remarkable mine of information. One of the earliest pictorial representations of Buenos Aires was by the British naval officer Emeric Essex Vidal, Picturesque Illustrations of Buenos Aires and Montevideo, Ackerman, London, 1820.*

8. For the Baring crisis see Ferns *op. cit.*

9. Both wars made inroads on the Anglo-Argentine community. Only about a quarter of the 4852 who volunteered in the First World War returned to Argentina (Graham Yool *op. cit.* p. 232), 2280 volunteered for the Second World War of whom nearly a tenth died (*ibid.* 242). The latest study of the impact of the First World War is Bill Albert, *The First World War and Latin America*, Cambridge, 1987. For the Second World War see R. A. Humphreys, *Latin America and the Second World War* Vol. 1, 1939-1942, Vol. II, 1942-1945, Athlone Press, London, 1981 and 1982.

10. D.C.M. Platt, *Latin America and British Trade, 1806-1914*, A. & C. Black, London, 1971 is the best overview on British trade relations with Latin America, based largely on the rich sources of the Parliamentary Papers and travellers' accounts.

11. Sir Woodbine Parish, *Buenos Aires and the Provinces of Río de la Plata*, 2nd edit. 1852, p.362 and Nina K. Shuttleworth *A life of Sir Woodbine Parish*, London 1910, p. 235. Parish was passed over through lack of influence in spite of the fact that he probably did more than anyone else to forge the link between Britain and Argentina. His services to the new Republic were recognized by his being made an Argentine citizen and his family given the right to bear the arms of the Republic which they still do in the family crest. Parish refused to return to Argentina when pressed to do so in the 1840s saying that he felt ashamed to show his face there again after the blockade had undermined his work. His son and grandsons made careers there.

12. Quoted in Graham Yool, *op. cit.* p.101.

13. Parish, *op. cit.* For the best discussion of this bifurcation see Miron Burgin, *The Economic Aspects of Argentine Federalism*, Cambridge, Mass., 1946.

14. Sir Francis Bond Head, *Rough notes taken during some rapid journeys across the Pampas and among the Andes*, ed. with an

introduction by C. Harvey Gardner, Southern Illinois Press, Carbondale, 1967 p.72 (originally published 1826). Head was important as an influence on Sarmiento and as a precursor of the championship of the pampas against Buenos Aires. See also J.A. Beaumont, *Travels in Buenos Aires and the Adjacent Provinces,* London, 1928.

15. For this see J.P. & W.P. Robertson, *Letters on South America,* London 1843. British colonies are discussed in D.C.M. Platt, 'British agricultural colonies in Latin America', *Inter American Economic Affairs.* 18:1964.

16. Head *op. cit.* p.72.

17. For Darwin's visit to Rosas's camp see Charles Darwin, *Journal of Researches into the Natural History and Geology of the countries visited during the voyage of H.M.S. Beagle around the world.* London, 1896, pp. 93-6. See Alan Moorehead, *Darwin and the Beagle*, Penguin Books, Harmondsworth, 1971.

18. Cedric Watts and Laurence Davies, *Cunninghame Graham: a critical biography*, Cambridge University Press, 1979, p.20.

19. The *frigorífico* a refrigerated ship or freezing plant was named after *LeFrigorifique* a French refrigerated ship which made its first journey in 1876. Pioneered by the French, the British inaugurated shipments from Argentina in 1883, 3 years after from Australia. By 1900, 278 refrigerator boats were carrying frozen and chilled meat from Argentina to Britain.

20. William MacCann, *Two Thousand Miles' Ride through the Argentine provinces*, 2 vols., London, 1853 is the best source for mid-century British *estancias*. For sheep see Wilfrid Latham, *The states of the River Plate: their industries and commerce*, London, 1866.

21. For the Lafone affair see Ferns, *op. cit.* pp. 237-9.

22. Mark Jefferson, *Peopling the Argentine Pampa*, American Geographical Society, New York, 1926.

23. In 1868 when president, Sarmiento made a speech at Chivilcoy (where he had been responsible in 1855 for establishing a model agricultural colony) envisaging the spread of similar settlements elsewhere. This was to be frustrated by the development of large-scale cattle and cereal estates.

24. See Chapter 6.

25. Gladys Adamson and Marcelo Pichon Rivière, *Indios e inmigrantes: una historia de vida*, Editorial Galerna, Buenos Aires, 1978. Nueva Australia is discussed in Gavin Souter, *A Peculiar*

*People: the Australians in Paraguay*, Angus and Robertson, Sydney, 1968.

26. See Chapter 8.
27. Oscar Bayer, *Los vengadores de la Patagonia trágica*, 3 vols., Editorial Galerna, Buenos Aires, 1971.
28. Lloyd *op. cit.* p. 110,113.
29. R.A. Seymour, *Pioneering on the Pampas*, London, 1869.
30. Richard W. Slatta, *Gauchos and the vanishing frontier*, University of Nebraska Press, Lincoln, 1983, pp. 169-74.
31. Lloyd, *op. cit.* p.108,118. For Sir Horace Rumbold, the British ambassador, 'the Englishman must come last on the list and take rank after his fellow-subjects of the sister kingdoms'. In *Far away and Long Ago*, London, Dent, 1940, p.183, Hudson referred to a Mr Blake who 'had no intimates and was one of those unfortunate persons, not rare among the English who appear to stand behind a high wall and whether they desire it or not, have no power to approach or mix with their fellow-beings.' This was to be a stereotypical view expressed by many other foreign observers.
32. J.A. Hobson, *Imperialism: a study*, Allen & Unwin, London, 1962, p. 151. See Tom Nairn, *The break-up of Britain*, Verso, London, 1981 for the most pungent analysis of intra-ethnic stresses and tensions in Britain.
33. See Chapter 7.
34. Carl Solberg, *Immigration and nationalism*, University of Texas, Austin, 1970, p.62.
35. Korn, *op. cit.* p. 161.
36. Sir Horace Rumbold, *The great silver river: notes of a residence in Buenos Aires in 1880 & 1881*, London, 1890, p.366.
37. Eugenia Scarzanella, *Italiani d'Argentina: storia di contadini, industriali e misionari italiani in Argentina 1850-1912*. Marsilio Editore, Venice 1983, pp. 25-71. See Thomas C. Cochran and Ruben E. Reina, *Entrepreneurship in Argentine culture: Torcuato di Tella and SIAM*, University of Pennsylvania Press, 1962 for one of the most successful industrial enterprises.
38. W. H. Hudson, *Purple Land: being the narrative of one Richard Lamb's adventures in the Banda Oriental, in South America, as told by himself*, London 1922, pp. 48-65.
39. G. Yool, *op. cit.* p.144.
40. R. Newton, *Germans of Buenos Aires 1900-1933: social and cultural crisis*, Texas University Press, Austin, 1977. This is a superb study. We badly need an equivalent for the British.

41. As the British-run subway and tramway was dependent on electricity, British and Germans tacitly co-operated during the First World War (Newton *op. cit.* p. 48).
42. Quoted in Newton *op. cit.* p. 105.
43. G.D. Owen, *Crisis in Chubut: a chapter in the history of the Welsh colony in Patagonia*: Swansea (1977)
44. Sir David Kelly, *The Ruling Few: or the Human Background to Diplomacy*, Hollis & Carter, London, 1952, chapters IV & XIV, pp. 109-135, 287-314. British schools in Argentina (and in Latin America) are fundamental in transmitting British ideas and attitudes but still no adequate study of them exists, nor a comparative study assessing their importance *vis-à-vis* other foreign schools. Were French Lycées the most prestigious academically? Were British schools admired more for their character building qualities than for academic achievement? Once in the 'tram-lines' of a particular national mode of thought it is difficult to break away. This aspect of the sociology of knowledge merits closer attention than it has received. Universities in Britain have more influence today on Argentines whereas up to the 1930s public schools would have been more important.
45. *The Memoirs of Cordell Hull*, Hodder and Stoughton, London, 1948, Vol. II pp. 1377-1426.
46. The majority of travellers' opinions on Argentine Catholicism were 'unsympathetic, prejudicial and entirely critical' — W.S. Trifilo 'Catholicism in Argentina as viewed by early 19th century English travellers.' *Americas* Vol. XIX 1962-3.
47. Lloyd *op. cit.* p. 338 and cf. Rumbold op. cit. pp. 104-5. The image of the British in novels tended to be more positive than other nationalities. See Evelyn Fishburn, *The Portrayal of Immigration in 19th century Argentine fiction (1845-1902)* Biblioteca Ibero-Americana No. 2 Colloquium Verlag, Berlin 1981.
48. Anna Cara-Walker 'Cocoliche: the art of assimilation and dissimulation among Italians and Argentines.' *Latin American Research Review*, 22 No. 3, 1986.
49. W.H. Koebel, *Argentina: Past and Present*, London 1910, p.90.
50. A useful analysis of growing radicalism is David Rock, *Politics in Argentina, 1890-1930: the rise and fall of radicalism*. Cambridge University Press, 1975. A recent general analysis is Ronald Munck with Ricardo & Bernado Galitelli, *Argentina: from Anarchism to Peronism*, Zed Books, London & New Jersey, 1987.

51. Julia Kirk Blackwelder and Lyman L. Johnson, 'Changing criminal patterns in Buenos Aires 1890-1914'. *Journal of Latin American Studies*, 14.2 Nov. 1982 show that for arrest rates per 1000 males in 1910 for public drunkenness the British head the list with 172.7, followed by the French 75.1, Uruguayans 72.9 and the much maligned Italians 33.9. For public disturbances the British again headed the list with 98.6, followed by Uruguayans 88.5 and French 76.9. For criminal offences the British came after Uruguayans and Spaniards.

52. See Chapter 13.

53. See A. Londres *The Road to Buenos Aires*, London, 1930. According to Korn *op. cit.* p.142, the British were not absent from women arrested for 'contravención escándalo' although a very low percentage — on a level with Germans. Manuel Gálvez's novel *Nacha Regules*, Buenos Aires, n.d., was an exposé of the white slave trade and well reflects the view of the corrupting influence of foreigners, especially Jews. There is a virulent anti-semitic strain in Right-wing Argentine nationalism.

54. See Gilberto Freyre, *Order & Progress*, Alfred Knopf, New York. 1946.

55. Quoted from J. King and N. Torrents (eds) *The Garden of Forking Paths: Argentine Cinema*, British Film Institute London, 1988, p.118

56. For Bentham's interest in Spanish America see Miriam Williford *Jeremy Bentham in Spanish America: an account of his letters and proposals to the New World.* Louisiana State University Press, 1980.

57. Sarmiento had visited the United States. See his *Travels in the United States in 1847*, trans. & edited by M.A. Rockland, Princeton University Press, 1970. When in Europe he spent only a few days in England, was unimpressed by France and Spain although French policy in North Africa seems to have impressed him. The experience of travelling from Liverpool to Boston in an immigrant boat must have reinforced his feelings about the superiority of the United States over Europe.

58. Echevarría's short story *El Matadero* translated and edited by Angel Flores as *The Slaughterhouse*, New York, Las Americas Publishing Co. 1959, crystallises the imagery of barbarism by fusing the blood-lust of the mob with the blood-stained cattle-killing grounds on the outskirts of Buenos Aires which so horrified foreign visitors.

59. Among his interests were collecting fossils and geological specimens. He also published an 'Account of the East Falkland Islands'. *Journal of the Royal Geographical Society*, III, 1833, pp. 94-8. He died in 1882, aged 87.

60. Philip Guedalla, *Argentine Tango*, London 1932, pp.163-4.

61. Georges Clemenceau, *South America To-Day*, London 1911, pp. 137. Given what has since become France's superior rail technology, perhaps the Argentines made the wrong choice. The new Buenos Aires metro today is French-equipped. The Argentines certainly chose the right missiles before 1982. For a contemporary account with a contrasting lack of emphasis on culture, see James Bryce, *South American Observations and Impressions*, London, 1912, pp. 315-46.

62. John F. Cady, *Foreign Intervention in the Río de la Plata, 1838-50: A study of French, British and American policy in relation to the dictator Juan Manuel Rosas*, Philadelphia, 1929. The actions of the Great Powers then bears some similarity to the situation in the Persian Gulf in 1988.

63. Quoted in Newton *op. cit.* p. 5.

64. Lucas Bridges, *Uttermost Part of the Earth*, London, 1948, has been reprinted in 'The Century Travellers' series (1987). A too little-known classic which chronicles the devastating effect on Indian tribes (which have now disappeared) of well-meaning missionaries. For the saga of Jeremy Button sent to England and then returned to Tierra del Fuego see Moorhead *op. cit.* Another area of British missionary activity was among Chaco Indians in the North.

65. V.S. Naipaul, *The Return of Eva Perón*, Penguin, Harmondsworth, 1981.

66. See Watts and Davies *op. cit.* pp. 286-7. The crowds following his funeral cortège in Buenos Aires in 1936 included the President of the Republic and Ministers.

67. John Masefield, *Collected Poems*, London 1923, *Rosas* and *The Daffodil Fields*.

68. J.M. Taylor, *Evita Perón: The myths of a woman*, Basil Blackwell, Oxford, 1979 is a stimulating and original analysis of the *rosista* and *peronista* myths and their links. For *rosismo*, see Clifton B. Kroeber 'Rosas and the revision of Argentine history 1880-1955. *Revista Interamericana de Bibliografía* 11.1.1960. For the extreme pro-Rosas position see Manuel Gálvez, *Vida de Don Juan Manuel de Rosas*, Buenos Aires, 1940, and Carlos Ibarguren, *Juan Manuel de Rosas, Su Vida, Su tiempo, Su*

*drama*. Buenos Aires, 1930. By 1965 the latter had gone through 15 editions. See also Julio and Rodolfo Irazusta, *La Argentina y el imperialismo británico*, Buenos Aires, 1934.

69. The title of a book by Ezequiel Martínez Estrada whose *Radiografía de la Pampa* (1933) trans. by Alan Swietlicki as *X- ray of the Pampa*, introd. Thomas McGann, University of Texas, Austin, 1971, is one of the most pessimistic analyses of the Argentine national character warped by lop-sided development.

70. Quoted in Newton *op. cit.* p. 93.

71. For Scalabrini Ortiz see M. Falcoff, 'Raul Scalabrini Ortiz: the making of an Argentine nationalist' *Hispanic American Historical Review* 52:1, 1972. See especially Raul Scalabrini Ortiz, *Historia de los ferrocarriles argentinos*, Buenos Aires, 1940 which argued that the British fraudulently acquired railway concessions. He was to spend some time in Nazi Germany and Perón admitted his intellectual indebtedness to him. From an anarchist youth Leopoldo Lugones became a leading cultural nationalist arguing in *El payador*, Buenos Aires 1961 that the *payador* represented the national spirit. He wrote of the *montonero* guerrillas of North West Argentina as independence heroes in *La guerra gaucha*, Buenos Aires, 1946 . The word *montonero* was significantly adopted by the Peronist guerrillas (now urbanized) of the 1970s — see Richard Gillespie *Soldiers of Perón: Argentina's Montoneros*, Clarendon Press, Oxford, 1982. *Ricardo Rojas La restauración nacionalista*, Buenos Aires, 1909 was the book in which Rojas's ideas were first formulated. For studies of conservative nationalism, see David Rock, 'Intellectual precursors of Conservative Nationalism in Argentina, 1910-27' *Hispanic American Historical Review* 67:2, May 1987 and Sandra McGee Deutsch, *Conservatism in Argentina, 1900-32: the Argentinian Patriotic League*, University of Nebraska, Lincoln, 1986. A useful collection of essays is Mark Falcoff and Ronald H. Dolkart, *Prologue to Perón, Argentina in Depression & War 1930-1943*, University of California Press, 1975.

72. Leo Marx, *The machine in the garden: technology and the pastoral ideal in America*, Oxford University Press, 1964 reprint 1970 and St. John de Crevècoeur *Letters to an American Farmer (1782)* — but in fact the Homestead Law of 1862 which Sarmiento and others took as a model was partly negated by legal fictions and the influence of railroad speculators and 'boosters'.

73. Compare Lawrence Goodwyn *Democratic promise: the Populist Moment in America*, Oxford University Press, 1976 and Ezequiel Gallo, *Farmers in Revolt: the Revolutions of 1893 in the province of Santa Fe, Argentina*. Athlone Press, University of London. 1976.

74. Quoted in Lynch *op. cit.* p. 293.

75. The complexities of the legal position of the Falklands are exhaustively discussed in Julius Goebel, *The struggle for the Falkland Islands*, with a preface and introduction by J.C.J. Metford, Yale University Press, 1982 (originally published 1927).

76. Seward W. Livermore, 'Battleship diplomacy in South America' *The Journal of Modern History* XVI, March 1944. Harold F. Petersen *Argentina and the United States, 1810-1960*, State University of New York, 1964 is a thorough survey.

77. R. Gravil, *op. cit.* pp.151.

78. The granting in 1958 by the British Motor Corporation of a licence to SIAM to manufacture its models in Argentina — the first company to be granted such a licence outside the Commonwealth was not to be the forerunner of similar deals. It is almost impossible now to find British cars, buses or lorries in Argentina — or Latin America for that matter.

79. The appearance of *colectivos*, privately-run mini-buses, in the 1930s, was the response of enterprising Argentines to the general frustration with the inefficiency of the under-capitalized tramway system. See Rennie *op. cit.* pp. 230-8 'The British Octopus'.

80. Gravil, *op. cit.* p. 213. There is a good discussion of Roca-Runciman on pp. 184-197.

81. See for this A.K. Manchester, *British pre-eminence in Brazil: its rise and decline*, Octagon Books, New York, 1964.

# 2

# Argentina: Part of an Informal Empire?

## *H.S. Ferns*

In the years between 1806 and 1986 Argentina and Britain have played four games of violence with each other. The score stands at 'two all'. The Argentines have won both their home games: in 1806-7 and 1845-9; the British their off-shore matches in the Falkland Islands in 1833 and again in 1982.

The effects of victory in Argentina have been curious. After their victory in 1806-7 the Argentines disposed of their Spanish managers, and after that of 1845-48 they soon dispensed with Juan Manuel de Rosas, the architect of triumph. In the British case the victory of 1833 had no discernible effects in Britain and in 1982 victory served to confirm the British management in its power at home.

If Anglo-Argentine relations are described in military terms there would not be much to tell, but nonetheless, the league tables of war underline an important fact in the once intimate and mutually advantageous relations of the two communities, *viz* that neither have been able to dominate politically the other, and that political violence has been a zero-sum game for both players. That neither seem adequately to recognise this fact is part of the data of the relationship.

Studied in terms of British experience until the Great Depression of the 1930s, Argentina can be classed with Australia, Canada and the United States (and also with New Zealand and South Africa) as a frontier of enterprise; a source of raw materials and foodstuffs, a market for capital and consumer goods, and an area of investment opportunities which yielded profits from enterprises and rents from property holding. Argentina differed from Australia, Canada and the United States in that Argentina never received British immigrants on a scale capable of seriously modifying the Latin and Mediterranean character of the community, nor of its political culture.

This absence of a significant volume of immigration leading to permanent settlement is a point worth noting when one speaks of British political power in the international community of nations. In Australia, Canada, New Zealand and South Africa, British immi-

grants and their descendants constituted significant political interests which served the British Government well when Britain was
challenged by other states seeking to increase their power in world
politics. This was not the case in Argentina. The relatively small
number of British residents and their descendants in Argentina had
no power to influence significantly the decisions of the Argentine
Government in international politics, and such assistance as they did
render Britain in war was limited to private initiatives.

In both the great imperialist wars of the twentieth century, Argentina remained outside the contest. Australia, Canada, New Zealand
and South Africa contributed large numbers of effective fighting men
to the British war machine, abundant raw materials, training facilities and in the Canadian case, in the Second World War, munitions
and financial gifts greater in per capita terms than the much better-
known American lend-lease aid to the Allies.

Argentina, of course, contributed to the Allied cause in both world
wars, but theirs was the supply of food and raw materials on commercial terms generally of advantage to themselves. In the Second
World War they agreed, however, to accept payment from Britain in
the form of blocked sterling balances: in fact, a large-scale loan to
Britain which differed from their cash sales to the United States for
gold.

The statement of these general facts which differentiate Argentina
from Australia, Canada *et al*, serves to clarify the nature of Anglo-
Argentine relations. They were primarily economic, market relationships from which political power was absent. Very early, in fact, while
the British were losing their first military contest in the River Plate,
the British Government defined its objective in South America.
Viscount Castlereagh in a Memorandum for the British Cabinet
dated 1 May 1807 [1] argued that the attempts to conquer territory in
South America was a mistake, and that commercial penetration in
cooperation with the people there was the only way forward.

Although Castlereagh eschewed the promotion of revolution by the
British Government, save as an answer to Napoleonic domination of
Spain, autonomously generated revolution against the Spanish
Crown during the years 1808-26 created the circumstances which
made it possible to establish a legally-based commercial and financial
intercourse between Britain and the new states of Latin America. In
that part of the River Plate which emerged as Argentina, the revolution against Spain was never in doubt once independence was
declared in 1816 and this revolution brought to the fore the ranching
interests which, under the *ancien regime* of Spain had occupied a

subordinate place in the political and administrative structure of the sometime Viceroyalty. The ranchers — *estancieros* — had a natural interest in international free trade, both as producers and consumers for, being engaged in the production of a large output with low inputs of capital and manpower, their profits were increased by market expansion, provided they could keep control of the political process in their own community and find trading partners capable of responding to their necessities. They found in Juan Manuel de Rosas — business man, rancher and meat-processor — a politician and soldier capable of controlling the community in their interest, and in the British Government a power willing and able to provide access to wider markets, not just in Britain but wherever they might be found.

This Anglo-Argentine relationship was founded upon and developed within the legal framework established by the Treaty of Friendship, Commerce and Navigation negotiated by representatives of the governments of the United Kingdom and the United Provinces of the Río de la Plata and ratified in 1824 in both London and Buenos Aires by the constitutional sovereigns of both communities. Thus, there came into being very early in the relationship between the two communities, a legal instrument which was part of international law and not of the domestic legislation of either power. This was an arrangement vastly different both legally, politically and practically from those which connected Britain with Australia, Canada *et al* until after the First World War and, indeed, until the establishment of the United Nations in 1945 made the separateness of Britain and its former colonies unambiguously manifest to and accepted by the international community.

The Anglo-Argentine Treaty of 1824 was an early example of the 'new liberalism' which began to develop in Britain and in Argentina after the close of the Napoleonic Wars. In the first place it was an 'equal treaty' by the terms of which Britain and Argentina were equally guaranteed access to the territories of the contracting powers, and once resident, no matter for how long, British subjects were bound to abide by the laws of the constitutional authorities of Argentina and to accept the jurisdiction of its courts in the same way as Argentines in Britain were equally subject to the laws and courts of the United Kingdom. This meant that British residents in Argentina could make contracts, own property and move about freely on the same terms as Argentines in Argentina, and Argentines could do the same in Britain. The only special guarantees accorded to Britons in Argentina concerned exemption from compulsory service in the Argentine armed forces and freedom to practise their own religion in their own churches and to bury their dead in their own cemeteries. There was nothing unequal in these provisions inasmuch as conscription in the armed forces did not exist in Britain then nor at any time until 1916. As for religion, the revolution in Argentina diminished but did not extinguish the power of the Roman Catholic Church to exercise control over marriage, burials and the activities of heretics. In order to ensure practical freedom in Argentina for people, many of whom were Protestants, a legal assurance of religious freedom was given. Later the British Government acted informally to prevent Protestant enthusiasts from proselytizing among Catholics, and they formally refused to countenance any defiance by British subjects of Argentine laws concerning marriage between Catholics and Protestants without the sanction of the Catholic Church.[2]

In the 1840s the meaning, if not the formal provisions of the Anglo-Argentine Treaty of 1824 was seriously prejudiced by the unwise and unsuccesful endeavours of the British and French Governments to bring 'peace' to the River Plate, i.e. to prevent Juan Manuel de Rosas from imposing his solution on the relations between Argentina and Uruguay. The Anglo-French intervention involved the blockade of Buenos Aires, the seizure of the island of Martin García in the estuary of the River Plate, the landing of British troops in Uruguay and a British naval expedition which forced its way up the River Paraguay as far as Asunción. The only reason that war was not declared seems to have been the realisation by Brigadier Rosas that a full-scale war would have been disastrous for both Argentina and Britain and that he understood Britain's long-term interests in Argentina better than the British did themselves.

When the government of Sir Robert Peel, the perpetrator of this nonsense in the River Plate, fell in 1846, the new Foreign Secretary, Viscount Palmerston, studied the situation and concluded that the actions of his predecessors in collaboration with the French was a 'bad business... (and) ... piracy'.[3] He then ordered the negotiation of a new Treaty of Friendship and Navigation. This treaty acknowledged the wrongs done by Britain, compensated Argentina for losses suffered, returned the island Martin García to Argentine possession, and gave an undertaking that British ships of war would salute the Argentine flag in the River Plate as acknowledgement of Argentine sovereignty in the estuary of the great river. In fact, this last provision meant the abandonment by Britain of naval blockade as a method of bringing pressure to bear on the Argentine government.

Subsequently in 1852 Argentina negotiated with Britain a treaty ensuring free navigation of the Plata-Paraná river systems, and similar treaties with the United States and the principal maritime states of Europe. The intention was further to 'open up' Argentina and to improve connections with international markets. More was expected of these treaties than they achieved because within another ten years railways began to prove themselves more effective agencies for pastoral, agriculture and commercial expansion.

The men who negotiated the Anglo-Argentine treaties of 1824 and 1849 were predisposed to a liberal view of the ideal relationship between government and productive enterprises, which had found its best expression in the writings of Adam Smith. Governments fixed the framework of laws, but private property owners and free workers determined in markets the course of economic development. In the British case private enterprise broadened out, and by 1846 Britain became a free trading economy in which government had a minimal part in matters of industry, agriculture, commerce and finance. In the Argentine case the role of the government was otherwise. The policy of the Argentine liberals who negotiated the treaty of 1824 was to stimulate economic, social and political development by the government borrowing in the international capital market large sums of money to finance the building of what, nowadays, is called 'the infrastructure' of the community. British investors were drawn into this plan of development and Baring Brothers & Company became the agents for the flotation of a bond issue with a face value of £1,000,000 in the London market. Both the plan and the British response involved a massive misjudgement of possibilities. The Baring loan was in default from the moment the money was received, but not before the promoters had taken their cut and the British investors had bought the bonds. Other British investments in mining and similar enterprises failed. The quite considerable development which took place under Rosas, however, produced a sound balance of payments on trading account. This was the work of expanding activity by cattle ranchers, meat processors, sheep farmers and commercial enterprises, without the stimulus of government funds.

Nonetheless, the development plans of Rivadavia and his collaborators in the 1820s were to establish the pattern of Argentine development after the overthrow of Rosas in 1852. When the federal and provincial governments of Argentina recommenced borrowing in the international capital markets of Europe in order to finance railways, harbour works and necessary municipal development, some were privately-owned enterprises, but many of those not directly owned and operated by governments had their profits guaranteed by government. Thus, there was an asymmetry in Anglo-Argentine finan-

cial relations, if not in the sphere of commerce and property ownership. In the Argentine case government played a positive role in
inducing investment whereas the British government had nothing to
do with the investment of British capital in Argentina.

When British investors in Argentine government loans ran into
difficulties, as they did in the instance of the first Baring loan and
again during the defaults which brought on the Baring Crisis of the
1890s, there were naturally appeals to the British government 'to do
something'. The British government always refused to do more than
call the attention of the Argentine authorities to the problem. This
refusal was but a particular application of a policy on debt collection
started in general terms by Lord Palmerston in a 'Circular addressed
... to her Majesty's Representatives in Foreign States, respecting
debts due by Foreign States to British Subjects' dated January 1848.
While asserting that the British government had an undoubted right
to engage in diplomatic negotiations about any grievances of British
subjects anywhere, Lord Palmerston stated that:

> It has hitherto been thought by successive Governments of Great
> Britain undesirable that British subjects should invest their capi-
> tal in loans to foreign Governments instead of employing it in
> profitable undertakings at home, and with a view to discouraging
> hazardous loans to foreign Governments who may be either unable
> or unwilling to pay the stipulated interest thereupon, the British
> Government has hitherto thought it the best policy to abstain from
> taking up as international questions, the complaints made by
> British subjects against foreign Governments ... For the British
> Government has considered that the losses of imprudent men who
> have placed mistaken confidence in the good faith of foreign
> Governments would prove a salutary warning to others, and would
> prevent any other foreign loan from being raised in Great Britain
> except by Governments of known good faith and of ascertained
> solvency ... [4]

There are several examples of the British Government's refusal to
apply pressure to Argentina to facilitate the collection of money owing
to bondholders and to intervene in Argentine economic and financial
decision-making. When, in 1856 for example, the government of the
Province of Buenos Aires was negotiating with a representative of
Barings about the repayment of the loan of 1825, the British Minister
in the capital of the Argentine Confederation at Paraná thought it
might help matters along to send a naval force to Buenos Aires, the

British Foreign Secretary absolutely refused. Perhaps the most emphatic of all instances of the British government's policy of non-intervention in the affairs of Argentina occurred during the Baring Crisis
of the 1890s, and this in spite of popular support for imperialism
which was beginning to rise rapidly in Britain towards its culmination in the Boer War.

When the crisis in the affairs of Baring Brothers and Company, on
account of their incapacity to liquidate the Argentine securities in
their portfolio of assets, reached the stage of catastrophe in November
1890, Lord Rothschild, the banker, called on the Marquis of Salisbury, who was both Prime Minister and Foreign Secretary of the
British Government, to discuss the problem. Salisbury reported his
discussion with Rothschild to his political and personal friend, the Rt
Hon W.H. Smith, First Lord of the Treasury and Leader for the
Government in the House of Commons. After much discussion Rothschild turned to the fundamental question of Argentina's financial
policies. 'He (then) ...', Salisbury reported, 'made his proposal for the
supervision and inspection of the Argentine debt by the three Powers
(Britain, France and Germany). I said that, if this were done with the
full consent of the Argentine State, and involved no responsibility,
either to advance money or use force, I saw no objection at first sight,
but the matter was too much out of my ordinary line for me to give
any definitive opinion before I had seen the scheme in detail and been
able to consult over it with others...' [5]

This suggestion was never further considered, but in July 1891 a
delegation of British bankers in Argentina had an 'informal' inter-
view with the Permanent Under-Secretary of the Foreign Office in
which they proposed an intervention in Argentina, either by the
British government directly or by the United States government. The
Under-Secretary reported this interview to the Marquis of Salisbury.
Salisbury wrote in the margin of the report in red ink 'Dreams!'.[6]
Then, a few days after this episode Salisbury made a speech at the
Mansion House in which he declared for all to hear, 'We have been
earnestly pressed ... to undertake the regeneration of Argentine
finance. On (this subject) Her Majesty's Government (is not) in the
least degree disposed to encroach on the function of Providence'
(laughter and cheers).[7]

This public declaration by Salisbury of a determination on the part
of the British government not to become involved politically in Argentina, or indeed anywhere in Latin America, in the way that it had
in Africa, the Middle East and in Asia was but a general expression
of a policy which was applied in detail. The British Government

consistently worked to diminish the sources of pressure which might be employed to push it towards involvement. Mass immigration to Argentina from Britain was discouraged, and British diplomatic agents in Argentina tactfully avoided, for example, any response to the agitation among Welsh colonists in the Chubut to extend the protection of the British government to them.[8] The Anglo-Argentine Treaty of Friendship, Commerce and Navigation was employed to contain the complaints of the British banking community in Argentina about taxation of deposits in foreign-owned banks in Argentina. The law officers of the Crown found in this instance that Argentine taxes had been levied equally on all foreign banks and not on British banks alone and, therefore, there was no legitimate grounds for taking up the matter with the Argentine authorities.[9]

The Baring Crisis of 1890-95 called in to question the entire financial relationship between the Argentine Government and the financiers of the City of London. The British Government did nothing to resolve the crisis except to promise assistance to the Bank of England if it got into difficulties in mobilising the resources of the British banking community in order to liquidate Baring Brothers and Company. The crisis was resolved by a business deal between the bankers themselves and the Argentine authorities. The first stage of the resolution involved the bankers lending money to enable the Argentine government to pay defaulted interest and sinking fund charges. This policy of pyramiding the Argentine debt was recognised in Argentina as a bad policy from its point of view. In the second stage of the resolution, the Argentine Government took the initiative; demanded that further negotiations be opened in Buenos Aires by a British representative who had some real appreciation of Argentine circumstances,[10] and in the end secured a reduction of interest and a suspension of sinking fund payments for a sufficient time to allow the Argentine economy to grow and by this means to maintain an independent control of the size, nature and purpose of its foreign debt.

A major theme in the history of Anglo-Argentine relations is the replacement of power by law as a *modus operandi*. But the possibility of a reversal of this theme was always in the minds of Argentine political leaders. The unsettled grievance of the Falkland Islands was never a significant element in Argentine political consciousness until the dawn of radical nationalist agitation in the 1920s, but it was not a forgotten issue. The Argentine Government refused always to recognise the British seizure of the islands, and they were always scrupulously careful never to prejudice their legal case for possession of the islands by doing anything which might be construed as acceptance of British sovereignty in the islands. They always, for example, refused to accept mail bearing a Falkland Islands postmark, or permit ships to enter Argentine ports which had cleared from the Falkland Islands, nor was trade with the islands permitted. Strictly speaking it was always illegal to print, publish or circulate in Argentina any map which indicated the Falkland Islands to be a British possession. The Falklands issue was always on the agenda of Anglo-Argentine politics, even though the item never reached active discussion until the 1960s. That it was allowed to fester for another fifteen years is the root cause of the tragedy of 1982.

In the international political atmosphere from the 1880s to the outbreak of the First World War, there was much to suggest that power, not law, determined the fate of nations and peoples. The Argentine response to the growth of imperialism in Africa and Asia and, closer to home, in the Caribbean and Central America, was to seek to strengthen international law and to extend its protection to more aspects of the activities of independent nation states. In 1902, for example, the British, German and Italian governments joined forces to blockade the ports of Venezuela in order to assert the rights of foreign residents in Venezuela to the equal protection of the laws, including the right to collect money owing to them by Venezuelans. The rights of bondholders of the Venezuelan government were not part of the European grievance, but nonetheless the Argentine government embarked upon a long campaign for the acceptance of the Drago Doctrine, which took its name from its initiator, Dr Luis Drago, the Argentine Foreign Minister. This doctrine embraced the principle that it is illegal for one nation to use force on behalf of its creditors in order to collect debts from a sovereign government. Dr Drago never succeeded in establishing his Doctrine as a principle of international law, but he projected the problem into the international arena to the extent that the second International Conference at The Hague in 1907 accepted a rule proposed by the United States and seconded by Argentina that the use of force in collecting debts is illegitimate except when a government refused to negotiate or arbitrate. Interestingly, the American resolution was opposed by a Swedish delegate named Hammerskjold because it gave an indirect sanction to the use of force.

The British Government never supported Dr Drago. Although they never were, in practice, willing to support bondholders in their efforts to collect debts from foreign governments, they were as unwilling in the twentieth century as Lord Palmerston had been in 1848, to bind themselves never to intervene on behalf of British subjects whose rights might be prejudiced by a foreign power.

Until the First World War the separation in Anglo-Argentine relations between politics on the one hand and economics and finance on the other — non-intervention and distancing in the first, and an intimate and abundant interconnection in the second — was in accordance with a liberal understanding of the separate and autonomous spheres of government and business. Developments after the First World War changed all this, slowly at first but with greater rapidity as time passed. Before the First World War, Europe was Argentina's best market, and the supplier of capital and consumer goods, as well as investment funds. After the First World War the United States entered the Argentine as a supplier of farm machinery, consumer durables, entertainment and as a source of investment funds. But the United States was not a good Argentine market. Not only were the principal Argentine products competitive with American wool, wheat, other cereals and meat, but the tariff barriers to competitive selling in the United States were very great. In the case of chilled and frozen meat, there was an absolute ban on the grounds that Argentine animals were infected with foot and mouth disease. No notice was taken of the fact that there was no foot and mouth disease in Britain in spite of the high British imports of Argentine meat. The Americans were great sellers and investors, but not buyers; in fact, old-fashioned mercantilists whose idiocies had been exposed by Adam Smith at the time of the American Revolution.

One of the results of the increasing penetration of the Argentine market by the Americans was that Britain's share of that market began noticeably to decline and the balance of trade between the two countries began to change. At first the British were inclined to rely on *laissez-faire* solutions — no tariffs, a stable gold currency and free competition, but problems developed and the answer to them was encapsulated in the slogan addressed to Argentina, 'Buy from them who buy from you'. This could only mean participation by the two governments in economic and financial policy making, if the Argentine were prepared to respond. The Prince of Wales was sent to visit Argentina, and then in 1929 a government mission led by Viscount D'Abernon, sometime financial adviser of the Egyptian government. The radical government of President Hipolito Yrigoyen responded to the mission. An agreement to block Argentine receipts from sales in British markets and devote them to the payments for British goods and services would have been signed had it not been for the fall of Yrigoyen in a military coup in 1930. When depression deepened and the British dominions, led by Canada, began to press for a more secure market in Britain, the Argentine place in the British market began to look as threatened by the British self-governing dominions as the British share of the Argentine market was by the USA.

Following the signature of the Ottawa Agreements of 1932, Argentina joined the queue at the Foreign Office in London along with the Scandinavian countries and the Netherlands to negotiate a share in the British market. The result was the Roca-Runciman Pact, which ensured Argentina a share in the British market and an undertaking by Britain to assist British cereal farmers with subsidies and not by means of quotas and tariffs on cereal imports. The implementation of the pact was facilitated by the existence in Argentina of a new means of controlling international trade and finance. *La Comisión de Control de Cambios* was set up in 1931. Argentine earnings abroad were brought under control, and were spent in accordance with a list of priorities, which ensured that Argentine balances were used for debtor service abroad, and fuel and raw materials for national industries. The liquidation of private commercial debts was given the last place on the list. Free international trade was at an end except trade with Uruguay, Paraguay, Chile and Peru. As a result of the Roca-Runciman Pact and the working of the Exchange Control Commission, the British share of the Argentine market began to grow and the share of the United States to diminish.

When the Second World War broke out the Argentine Government agreed with the British Government to accept sterling balances in the Bank of England as payment for Argentine produce, secured on British assets in Argentina. The liquidation of the Argentine debt abroad commenced. The Argentine sterling balances became one of the means by which Perón, when he came to power in 1946, was able to buy out the British and French proprietors of Argentine Railways and the various foreign-owned public utilities, such as the telephone system and part of the energy industry.

The intrusion of governments in the Anglo-Argentine economic relationship ended the arrangements which had produced a massive British presence in the Argentine economy. Britain ceased thereafter, and bit by bit, to be Argentina's best market and source of capital funds, and both countries became of only marginal importance to each other.

Much intellectual and emotional energy has been expended in Argentina in discussion and agitation about British imperialism and neo-imperialism. In fact, Britain and, particularly, the British Government, has never been able to force Argentina to do anything the

Argentine Government and Argentine politicians have not wanted to
do. Both parties to the Anglo-Argentine relationship were moved by
self-interest and this interest was always commercial, economic and
financial. Britain had the capital resources and the market opportunities which Argentina needed for development. Argentina had the
resources and found the manpower needed to develop their economy,
and to create a wealthy society which, by 1930, was one of the richest
communities in the world. If neither Argentina nor Britain is any
longer in the top ten, say, in terms of wealth they have no one to blame
but themselves, and nothing is owed to one trying to get the better of
the other. Imperialism as an explanation of the Anglo-Argentine
relationship is a nonsense, and fighting each other about the
Falklands/Malvinas is an irrelevant exercise in nostalgia.

Recently (1989) the remains of Juan Manuel de Rosas were disin-
terred from their resting place in a cemetery near Southampton,
where they had reposed for 112 years, and were shipped to Buenos
Aires for reinterment in a national shrine. This repatriation after so
long a time of the dust of a dead politician touches upon and, in some
degree, illuminates the long history of Anglo-Argentine relations. On
his tombstone in a Hampshire cemetery he was described as a
'Brigadier' and a 'Captain-General of Buenos Ayres'. But, though he
answered to the description of a dictator and was for many years an
officer of the militia and a frontier Indian fighter, Rosas was never a
professional soldier nor a military dictator *tout court* like, say,
Generals Farrell and Onganía, who were Argentine presidents in this
century. Rosas was a business man and a rancher, who wrote a book
on ranch management. Dealing with Indians both by fighting and
diplomatic negotiation was an aspect of ranching, and so was his
handling of gaucho ranch workers, urban political interests and
foreign merchants and money lenders. Given the social chaos brought
on by the revolution against the Spanish Crown Rosas had a tough
time creating a viable social order in the River Plate, and he was a
tough man. Nonetheless he was an agency of civilisation, and this his
many liberal critics in Argentina and Europe would never allow him.
He was labelled a barbarian, and certainly the activities of the secret
society of his supporters, the *Mazorca*, anticipated in their barbarity
and lawlessness the suppression only a few years ago of the *Montoneros* and the indiscriminate slaughter of the *desaparecidos*.

Unlike the modern military dictators of Argentina, of whom Galtieri is the final example, Rosas was a rational politician with rational
objectives. For example, he proposed a rational solution of the Fal-
klands/Malvinas problem. He was willing to give Britain a clear title

to the Falklands in return for a cancellation of Argentina's defaulted debt.[11] Similarly he refused to declare war on Britain although Argentina was subjected to the invasion of its rivers by a naval expedition and troops were landed in neighbouring Uruguay. He fought the battle with the Earl of Aberdeen, who was responsible for the armed intervention in the River Plate, with a propaganda campaign, which he won. Although he yielded for a time to protectionist interests in Argentina, he scrapped hindrances to international trade as soon as he possibly could, and when he was overthrown Argentina was as much a doctrinaire *laisser faire* commercial state as Britain was at that time. Rosas was never a romantic nationalist like Perón and his imitators, who have converted a wealthy, civilised nation into an average Third World country. Rosas was much misunderstood in his native land, and it has taken 112 years to rehabilitate him. Perhaps this presages better days for Argentina and Anglo-Argentine relations.

## Notes

1. Castlereagh, *Correspondence*, v11, pp 314 f.f.
2. See an account of the Lafone marriage case in H.S. Ferns, *Britain and Argentina in the Nineteenth Century*, Oxford, Clarendon press 1960, pp 237-9.
3. H L Bulwer-Lytton, *The Life of Henry John Temple, Viscount Palmerston*, London, 1870-74, 111 pp 324-6.
4. D C M Platt, *Finance,Trade and Politics: British Foreign Policy, 1815-1914* Oxford 1968, Appendix II, pp 398-99.
5. Hatfield House MSS, 3M/Class E. Salisbury to Smith, 12.11.1890.
6. Public Record Office, FO6/20 Ferguson to Salisbury, 24.7.1891.
7. *The Times*, 30 July 1891
8. See G D Owen, *Crisis in Chubut: a Chapter in the History Of The Welsh Colony in Patagonia*, Swansea, 1977.
9. FO6/421 Opinion of Sir Ernest Hertslet and of the Law Officers Webster and Clarke.
10. Baring Archives, H C, 4.1.115.
11. H.E. Peters, *Foreign Debt of the Argentine Republic* Baltimore, 1984, p.20.

# 3

# British Capital in Argentine History: Structures, Rhetoric and Change

*Charles A. Jones*

Looking back over the whole of Argentine history the British may plausibly be cast either as progressive partners in the development of Argentina or as the creators of insuperable obstacles constraining economic life and public policy: engine or brake. There has always been a rich variety of contradictory evidence available to fuel debate; but the intriguing thing about all such debates is the ease with which each side finds it possible to dismiss contradictory evidence as uncharacteristic or anomalous. Two processes of interpretation guided by different images at the start, though ultimately constrained by the same body of evidence, will yield radically incompatible accounts and may even tend to diverge from one another over time by generating unrelated research programmes. [1]

Indeed, the facility with which historians seem able to accommodate uncomfortable evidence poses a problem. Why should people ever change their minds about the past given this talent for massaging the facts? What triggers transformations of public opinion about the contemporary significance of history? How do such changes take place? How, in short, is one to account for a change of paradigm, of the bundle of images and ideas that governs any historical interpretation?

An analogy may clarify what follows. If a dam breaks, part of the explanation will surely be that the weight of water retained by it caused it to break. The other part of the explanation has to do with the dam itself. Why did it fail when and how it did? Material interest and social class may now be substituted for the water; the language in which history is expressed, for the dam.

Back, then, to Argentina, where public sentiment underwent an abrupt change in the last quarter of the nineteenth century, passing from enthusiastic support for the British to scarcely veiled hostility. British capital quite rapidly ceased to be perceived as an ally of liberalism and progress, and became instead, for the dominant current of opinion, a symbol of the denial of effective nationhood and autonomy. Once a source of support and prestige for the landed oligarchy who still ruled the country, the British connection now became an embarrassment and a point of vulnerability as the oligarchy reluctantly adapted itself to a new style of populist politics. [2]

At first, the answer to this question seems obvious. It had rained hard. The lake above the dam was full. The international financial crises of the mid-1870s and 1890-91 brought severe fluctuations in the prices of primary products, labour and credit which upset the plans of businessmen, workers and politicians alike, bringing distress, failures, emigration and enormous transfers of property. Of firms operating in Argentina it was, on the whole, those based in Europe which survived and grew by acquisition of the assets of failed local ventures. This produced ill-feeling directed against foreign capital, expressed in a variety of ways, constitutional and otherwise. But why did not more Argentines, finding themselves in this predicament, shrug resignedly and admit that their creditors were only doing their job as instruments of the natural force of competition: that, in the words of President José Battle of Uruguay:

... Our population may be divided into those who have received more than they deserve and those who have received less; but this does not mean that a man is either exploited or an exploiter. The inequality is not deliberate on the part of the more fortunate'. [3]

The economic liberalism of a majority of educated and powerful Argentines of the 1860s and 1870s would certainly have permitted, even dictated, such a reaction. Alternatively, one may attempt an explanation in terms of social class. The steady accession of mercantile immigrants into the Argentine landed oligarchy was interrupted as the development of corporate capitalism sucked Anglo-Argentine business leaders back into the City of London, depriving the oligarchy at one and the same time of fresh blood to cope with the advent of populist politics fuelled by immigration, and of direct channels of regular communication with some of the most powerful controllers of the national economy. This approach, adequate as far as it goes, looks to long-run tendencies in class formation and their consequences for state and economy to account for an abrupt change of heart towards the British. This does not matter too much, as it can easily be integrated into the economic interpretation, with economic crisis acting as a catalyst for changing social attitudes. [4]

But tinkering and elaboration do not touch the fundamental question. Why should a convinced economic liberal take the plunge and adopt nationalistic interpretations of economic and social events? It is not the events themselves which force the decision, because the decision is precisely about how to construe them. Events do not exist until they are described; but to describe is already to interpret. In any case, it is easy to write the economic history of Argentina in a liberal style, stressing the remarkable material success of the country in the early twentieth century, attributing this in part to foreign investment and the relatively liberal policies of major trading partners, and blaming the subsequent catastrophe on mistaken public policies rather than (as in the nationalist version) on entrenched interests, inappropriate infrastructure, assymetries of market strength, and the like. [5]

So while not wishing to argue that one interpretation is as good as another, I am equally resistant to the notion that the facts speak for themselves. Into the space between those two radically divergent methodological positions, a plea may be inserted for recognition of spontaneity: the ability we have suddenly to see things differently or, as in those pictures beloved of Gestalt psychology where what looks like a rabbit is suddenly seen as a duck or a goblet transforms into two human heads in profile, to alternate between interpretations. This ability is not mysterious; but it is deep-seated, and is invoked in language, rhetoric, and, quite specifically, in imagery. In what follows, a sketch of the history of British capital in Argentina and of attitudes to it is drawn, in which more than customary attention is paid to a cluster of nature-based metaphors. It is necessarily no more than a sketch since, like many historians, I have until recently been inclined to view the imagery used by the businessmen and politicians whose correspondence I read as something superficial, hardly noteworthy.

The British first appear in Argentine history as rebels, attacking Spain's monopoly over trade with her empire in the Americas by smuggling manufactured goods. It is true that for a brief period in the early eighteenth century the British South Sea Company was given a legal right to supply slaves to Spanish America. The contract allowed the company to trade in several ports, Buenos Aires among them, to store goods other than slaves, and to travel and trade in the interior. But so blatant and comprehensive was British abuse of these priveleges that the national image of malfeasance, established by Drake and his generation, was hardly damaged. [6]

This bourgeois beard-singeing, in which fire and sword had given way to hardware and calicoes, was as unreflective as it was unofficial. There is no evidence that its object was anything more than unalloyed profit. But it was rapidly mythologised and ennobled by both British and Argentine liberals, who found in it a legitimation of the substantial part British merchants soon came to play in the trade and finances of the post-independence period. Samuel Wilcocke, in his *History of the Viceroyalty of Buenos Aires*, published on the eve of independence in 1807, discovered in the utter inability of the Spanish mercantile system to suppress clandestine trade clear evidence that 'necessity, more powerful than any statute, defeated its operations, and constrained the Spaniards themselves to concur in eluding it.' [7]

When he came to write his history of the independence movement, Bartolomé Mitre, the first president of the Argentine Republic following the reunification of 1862, adopted much the same interpretation. Looking back at the role of the illicit trade of the eighteenth century in which British goods had figured so largely, he declared it to have been 'a normal function of the economic organism a circumstance superior to the power of the King of Spain.' He went on to conclude this same commerce that 'in the struggle of vital interests, natural law is bound to prevail, as did in fact happen.'[8] For both Wilcocke and Mitre, and for liberals throughout the period spanned by their two histories, smuggling 'conjured up a picture not so much of rogues criminally defying authority, as of authority criminally denying the benefits of legitimate trade to its subjects.' [9]

The British in general — and Sir Francis Drake in particular — played the same revolutionary role in the early work of Vicente Fidel López, an Argentine intellectual who will appear again later in this account in the guise of director of an English bank and, later still, as Argentine minister of finance and scourge of British capital. In *Betrothed to a Heretic (La Novia del Hereje)*, which he wrote as a political exile in Chile during the dictatorship of Juan Manuel de Rosas, López went so far as to symbolise the looked for triumph of toleration over the Inquisition, miscegenation over Spanish racism, and private enterprise over state monopoly by marrying Drake to the fictional *mestizo* daughter of an Inca princess.[10]

It is worth pausing for a moment to wonder at this gross and implausible idealisation of the gang of socially and economically marginal adventurers who constituted the vulgar reality of the clandestine trade. For one thing, a big lie boldly told commands attention simply as spectacle. For another, the place of imagery in economic discourse has been wrongly neglected.[11] Consider, for a moment, two views of the economic crises of the late nineteenth century. In one, from the pen of an English bank manager working in Argentina, the imagery is an epidemic disease, picking out weak individuals but strengthening the aggregate of survivors.[12] The other, written by an Argentine publicist, compares economic crises to storms. 'As with great hurricanes,' he writes, 'one can detect their symptoms, assess their severity, and alleviate their effects even though one cannot prevent them.'[13] Here is a more organic view of society. The storm does not pick on the weak, who somehow deserve to suffer because of a fatal individual flaw. It affects the whole economy, and this justifies ameliorative state policies which, on the other model, would be counter-effective. So, in the case to hand, both authors are once again united by images of nature as an inevitable force, but in the British case this is articulated through 'necessity', agent-like, standing outside the economy and acting upon it, while in Mitre's text competitive trade is a condition, internal to or constitutive of the 'economic organism', against which agency is therefore powerless. Differences of this sort in the working out of essentially similar myths (throughout there is agreement on a metaphorical identity of market and nature open the door to variations in policy and rationalisation).

There is also a third, or more specific, reason for considering the idealisation of clandestine trade. It was a powerful lie. For almost a century it would provide a moral shroud to protect British entrepreneurs. Yet at the same time, because of the kinds of alternations, variations, and substitutions which it permitted, it was also a treacherous lie which would later be turned against the British and employed as a legitimation of the very thing it had originally been directed against: greater state intervention in the economy.

In this mythology, commerce is characterised as tranquil or *doux*; it is set against violence. Yet at the same time it is necessary and irresistible; it constrains; it is superior to the power of kings. The resolution of this apparent contradiction is that coercive or violent power, exemplified in the behaviour of prices, is to be seen as arbitrary, personal, passionate, and inconstant. By contrast, the power of the market, because it is grounded in voluntary exchange and natural law (which is after all nothing more than moral order immanent in the world), is at once regular, universal, impersonal and hence authoritative. The place of firms is clearly as ministers of the market. They are not autonomous moral actors. They are instruments of destiny or members of an organism. As generators of taxable funds they provide an essential prop for the state. But this makes the state dependent upon merchants, who became masters in consequence, and lose legitimacy. The tension is perfectly expressed in a passage from the eighteenth-century economist, Quesnay, which uses both images: master/servant and organism.

> The wealthy merchant, trader, banker, etc. will always be a *member* of a republic. In whatever place he may live, he will always enjoy the immunity which is inherent in the scattered and unknown character of his property ... It would be useless for the authorities to try to force him to fulfill the duties of a *subject*: they are obliged, in order to induce him to fit in with their plans, to treat him as a *master*, and to make it worth his while to contribute voluntarily to the public revenue. (my stress)[14]

Nevertheless, it was from this tension that individual liberty and peace between states were to flow. As Immanuel Kant put it, concluding an argument on the relation of commerce to peace almost identical to that of Quesnay and dating back at least to Montesquieu:

> ... if the citizen is deterred from seeking his personal welfare in any way he chooses which is consistent with the freedom of others, the vitality of business in general and hence also the strength of the whole are held in check. For this reason, restrictions placed upon personal activities are increasingly relaxed. And thus ... enlightenment gradually arises.[15]

The beauty of the interplay of nature, market, state, and firm is that it provides, first, a way of ennobling and legitimising British merchants in Argentina, and then, later, a ready-made rhetorical structure in which to pillory them as false ministers, overmighty nobles, denatured dregs, guilty of the unnatural act of revolt against the market. So, by 1890, British firms — the banks most of all — would be cast in the part formerly taken by the Kings of Spain, charged with having 'strangled government and the country, made gold rise and fall ... and made themselves *masters of the market,* impoverishing the country and producing crises.' (my stress)[16] In their place, as true ministers to the market, guardians of natural order and the commonwealth, would stand the state, no longer unnatural, because transformed by the gaining of independence from Spain and from princes into a rational expression of the popular will. The stage was set for economic nationalism.

It must be said that alternative interpretations had always been available and consensus was never more than partial. One need only recall the proto-romantic attacks upon commerce at the end of the eighteenth century by William Roscoe, that most cultivated of Liverpudlian bankers, whose biblical and classical imagery contrasts quite sharply, as does the content of his verses, with the natural law tradition. He wrote, attacking the idealisation of commerce:

But why with foolish fondness would you strive
To dress a devil in an angel's garb,
And bid mankind adore him? — Can it be,
that he, the foulest friend that ever stalk'd
Across the confines of the suffering world;
He, the dread spirit of commercial gain,
Whose heart is marble, and whose harpy hands
Are stain'd with blood of millions; can it be,
That he should personate the form divine
Of soft compassion, and perform the task
To her mild cares and lenient hand assign'd?

And this rhetorical tradition was continued in the works of Carlyle and Marx. It is clear, then, that the choice made by Wilcocke or Mitre was a real one, to be freely decided in historical circumstances. For liberals of Mitre's generation — men who had resisted the rule of Juan Manuel de Rosas and experienced persecution and exile before securing military victory in 1852 — empirical determination of a grandiose and beneficent image of British capitalism seems to have drawn upon the support afforded to the revolution by North American privateers (little distinction was made between Yankees, Britons and North Germans) and, more pertinently, the practical assistance which they and their kind had received from United States and British merchant houses in Buenos Aires during the Rosas years.

When Juan Manuel de Rosas launched a campaign of terror against his political opponents in the wake of the unsuccessful rebellion of 1840, a number of wealthy Argentines transferred their properties to British merchants.[18] In May 1842, while the dictator's personal security force ran riot in Buenos Aires, many sought shelter in the houses of foreign merchants. There they 'were stored away for days, weeks, even months ... until they could be smuggled off to sea in disguise.'[19]

The Yorkshire-born merchant, Edward Lumb, will serve as an example of this symbiosis of foreign merchants and Argentine liberals. Among Lumb's closest acquaintances in the country of his adoption was Alvaro de la Riestra, a former captain in the personal bodyguard of Fernando VII of Spain. When the estates of the de la Riestra family were seized and the son, Norberto de la Riestra, became a fugitive, Lumb was able to secure him a partnership in the Liverpool house of Nicholson Green & Co., a firm in which he was himself Buenos Aires managing partner. Taking de la Riestra into the Liverpool house was, moreover, roughly consistent with the tradition of international exchange of personnel which had long prevailed among the cosmopolitan merchants of this period. It was customary for the sons and nephews of merchants to be placed as clerks in friendly houses overseas not only to learn languages and acquire other practical skills, but to renew the basis of trust and affection which underlay the whole system of trade through the friendships and marriages they contracted. De la Riestra, though no trainee, could scarcely have seemed out of place in the cosmopolitan and liberal world of Liverpool commerce. Following the fall of Rosas, Lumb assisted another member of the new generation of politicians, the impecunious Bernardo de Irigoyen, providing capital for his pioneering investments in Santa Fe Province.[20] These collaborations bore fruit. De la Riestra occupied the finance ministry in the province of Buenos Aires under three successive governors. He retained his links with British capital, serving for a time on the local board of directors of the London and River Plate Bank, and acting as a most effective negotiator with British merchant banks concerning the external debt.[21] Irigoyen was national minister for the interior, twice foreign minister, national senator for Buenos Aires and twice governor of the Province during a long and eminent political career. Moreover, as foreign minister he proved himself sympathetic to British interests during the diplomatic crisis surrounding the Rosario branch of the London and River Plate Bank in 1876.[22]

For Lumb and many of his compatriots, therefore, friendship, politics, and business had become inextricably intertwined by the third quarter of the century. Although absurdly pompous and patronising, the account of another British merchant, Wilfred Latham, would have been substantially conceded by men like de la Riestra, Yrigoyen, or Sarmiento.

'The fall of Rosas', he wrote;

> ... readmitted into Buenos Aires the political exiles, men of intellect and education, who had been obliged to fly from their country during the Dictatorship. During their exile they had come into contact with a more advanced civilization and learned in adversity to appreciate constitutional order and industrial development.

Henceforth they exercised a marked influence in forming and modifying public opinion. They predisposed large numbers of their countrymen to defer to, and to a certain extent take tone from, the intelligent portion of the foreign residents whose interests had been engrafted into those of the country'.[23]

This engrafting was vitally important. The original Argentine concessions, out of which grew the Great Southern Railway Company or the London and River Plate Bank, were given to men like George Drabble and Edward Lumb: known and trusted by those in power; owners, like themselves, of great *estancias*. The new companies were to be one more facet of a developing partnership: indeed, a continuation of the partnership principle with just that minimal concession to corporate organisation needed to secure the unprecedently large sums required for the new projects. So de la Riestra became a modest shareholder in the London and River Plate Bank as well as being actively engaged in its affairs as a member of the local board.[24] As for the British, the balance of the somewhat fragmentary evidence on marriage, land ownership, and continued residence indicates a smooth and progressive integration of the British mercantile elite into the Argentine governing class up to the 1870s, justifying the anticipation of Michael Mulhall, editor of the local English language newspaper, that the beginning of the next century will perhaps see a preponderance of English ideas, as well as the elevation of men of English descent to some of the highest posts in the public service.[25]

Then came the economic crisis of the 1870s and 1880s. Taken in conjunction with long run tendencies in the social organisation of firms, they appear to have catalysed a transformation and subversion of the liberal ideology which underlay the British presence in Argentina, producing resentment of and opposition to the British. But just how was this ill-feeling produced? British firms in Argentina had to be conceived of as culpable, not merely instrumental; no longer mediators of the power of a sovereign and natural market, but subversive of it. The change in moral attitude required a change of interpretation; indeed, the division betwen Argentine and Anglo-Argentine, or more correctly, between economic nationalist and liberal, required a bifurcation of the original enlightenment imagery which had up to now smoothed over the cracks. The chronological source of the bifurcation is to be looked for in divergent perceptions arising out of the changing structure and development of foreign firms. Leading firms were growing in size and market power. More and more were adopting corporate form in preference to partnership. This had a number of effects. Managers on the spot were to be bureaucrats, constrained by rules enunciated by directors in Europe which, even when disobeyed, set the moral parameters of business. 'The most essential duty of a manager is to do what he is told', thundered the directorate of the London and River Plate Bank.[26] The managers, for their part, grumbled at business lost through their lack of autonomy or else quietly disobeyed.[27] In outright policy disputes between local and London boards it was generally London that triumphed.[28] Vicente Fidel López, for example, soon left the Montevideo local board of the London and River Plate Bank after a disagreement with head office over lending policy.[29]

To make matters worse, there had been a steady move of foreign capital from international trade into activities which had a more obviously public character, either because, as in the case of banking or insurance, they brought into the open a clash of private and public interest over the proper investment of large accumulations of funds, or because, as with railways and urban utilities, they brought quasi-monopolistic capitalists into conflict with large groups of consumers and workers. So, at precisely the moment when the British were acquiring unprecedented objective market power in Argentina because of the dramatic concentration of capital brought about by the two successive international crises and their shift into more public undertakings, the subjective experience of managers was of diminishing or of illegitimate power, while directors, too, idealising their own pragmatic codes of practice into timeless commands of the market and recognising the disobedience of their subordinates, experienced a loss of power.

Ironically (and lest it should be thought at this juncture, any more than in the earlier period, there was any neat match of ideological, economic, and social divisions) even some leading Argentine officials and politicians of the 1890s were won over to the British view. Accepting the implausible thesis that it had been obedience to rule which had brought success to the British banks rather than good contacts, superior financial resources, and the kind of innovative local management that all those rules had been designed to eradicate, they turned their back on the expansionary style of the old official banks, and created, in the Banco de la Nación and the Caja de Conversión, an ultra-conservative system of monetary and financial management, more British than the British.[30]

But to others, economic nationalists really, though they did not use the term themselves, evidence of corporate power seemed incontestable, and the fact that they were now often dealing with salaried managers, ambiguously responsible to boards of directors in London, instead of, as in the old days, principals with a personal stake in the country, only exacerbated the situation.

Take just one emblematic instance of the new policies of foreign investment. In 1891, in the depths of the most severe economic crisis yet experienced by the Republic, a last ditch attempt was made to save the two great official banks: The Banco de la Provincia de Buenos Aires and the Banco Nacional. The national government appealed to the private banks in Buenos Aires to subscribe to a new internal loan to be known, by a macabre twist typical of the time, as the Popular Loan. The power of the leading English bank, the London and River Plate Bank, is evidenced in the price it exacted for participation in this futile exercise. A telegram despatched to London enunciated one element in the agreement. It read: 'If loan successful promise has been given by Argentine President of Republic to cancel deposit tax.'[31] The second element appears to have been withdrawal of long-standing government opposition to a proposed acquisition by the London Bank of one of its major Argentine competitors, the Banco Carabassa, a purchase completed shortly after the conclusion of the popular loan agreement.[32] This merger, together with the suspension of the official banks, which followed apace in spite of the government's efforts, made the London Bank far and away the biggest bank in Argentina.

Shortly before these events of March 1891, Vicente Fidel López, estranged local director of the London Bank and now national minister of finance, had already had occasion to attack the English banks during the Senate debate on the 2 per cent bank deposit tax. The main thrust of his attack was to emphasise the power both of individual managers and of the banks as corporations, both of which he deemed improper. He drew attention to the 'omnipotence of a few subordinate managers, hungry for profits, who come and live here as progenitors of rich speculations.' But his real objection concerned the public status of the banks:

> These banks, which call themselves private, strangle the government when it suits them, and most of all at moments of crisis, carrying on and speculating like agencies of the state: and all the public authority and a firm hand will be needed before they can be reduced and controlled as they ought to be by the authorities and the laws of the country. [33]

Contrast the words chosen by Rodney Fennessy, Buenos Aires manager of the London Bank, opposing the current tendency to state intervention in his Memorandum on the Situation, of December 1890: 'I firmly believe [he wrote] that no pressure from however powerful a government can control the natural laws which govern business.' [34]

Here is the impasse: López, convinced of the need for state action to defend legality, order, and the market itself against the banks; the banks, convinced that they alone, as bastions of the market, stood between economic order and the encroaching state: López, convinced that the power of the banks, expressed through speculation was subverting the nation and the market by precipitating crises; the British, still seeing themselves as powerless instruments of the market, blaming the repeated runs on the banks on politically inspired manipulation.

One critical moment in 1891 nicely illustrates the ambiguity of the Anglo-Argentine economic relationship by this point. Outwardly, it appears as a celebration, even a ceremony, of cosmopolitan liberalism, an affirmation of identity of interests. Towards the end of a day of panic in the Buenos Aires stock market and runs on the banks, when the worst was over, '... the then president of the Stock Exchange Council, Sr. Francisco Uriburu, with Srs. Anderson, Fennessy, and Boutell, managers of the leading Anglo-Argentine financial institutions), went up to the gallery overlooking the banking hall (of the London and River Plate Bank), and as a sign of triumph shouted with one voice: "Viva la República Argentina; Viva el Banco de Londres y Río de la Plata."'[35] But that the two vivas should be uttered together at such a moment could not but be seen by López or President Pellegrini as an ominous token of dependence. Yet how were they, astute politicians and, in their different ways, learned men, to resolve this clash of mind-set through conversation with banks who thought that to be innocent of political entanglement it was enough that they make no donations to party funds and decline to subscribe to a pension fund for a widow of their former colleague, de la Riestra? [36]

The original pretext for all this dwelling upon detail and imagery was the inadequacy of any purely structural explanation of Argentina's rather sudden falling out of love with Britain towards the end of the nineteenth century. But it would be quite wrong to make the fragments of evidence about imagery and mind-set presented here the foundation of yet another causal structure centring now upon the creation and decay of liberal ideology, whether this was to be regarded as merely complementary or as basic to the economic, the social, and the political. Multiplication of structures provides no salvation from structuralism; in particular, it offers no solution to the frequently noted inability of structuralistic social theory to provide convincing explanations of change. The study of rhetoric and metaphor in history may, however, foster incredulity and restore strangeness to lived experiences trapped in the rigid and predictive structures of economic, social, and political explanation,'this perfectly sealed circle of facts and interpretations'.[37]

The point of the parable is, then, that the transition from economic liberalism to economic nationalist perception in Argentina, with all it entailed, was achieved within a single rhetorical structure based on the metaphor of market as nature. For nationalists this structure was inverted by the transformation of state as prince (unnatural) to state as nation (natural), firm as servant of the market (natural) to firm as rebel (unnatural), and market as rebel (against the unnatural, princely state) to market as regulator (of the ordered rational state). The switch, precisely because it involves a transformation of old imagery rather than the invention of genuinely new imagery, was not epoch-making. It has left opposed groups divided by a common discourse and helps account for the internecine character of subsequent Anglo-Argentine relations. But above all, it seems in some degree spontaneous, a creative act which rises above and is not fully determined by mechanistic causes, suggesting historical change partly constituted by rather than simply imposed upon actors. It allows, in a manner evocative of the physicists' definition of chaos, the genesis of infinitely large variations in outcome from infinitely small variations of initial conditions.

## Notes

1. See Thomas S. Kuhn, *The Structure of Scientific Revolutions*, 2nd ed., University of Chicago Press, 1970.
2. See, for example, Charles A. Jones, 'Personalism, Indebtedness and Venality: The Political Environment of British Firms in Santa Fe Province, 1865-1900', *Ibero-Amerikanisches* Archive, N.F. Jg. 9 H.3/4 (1983).
3. S. G. Hanson, *Utopia in Uruguay*, Oxford University Press, New York, 1938, p.28.
4. This idea is more fully developed in Charles A. Jones, *International Business in the Nineteenth Century*, Wheatsheaf, Brighton, 1987, p.4 and passim.
5. Laura Randall, *An Economic History of Argentina in the Twentieth Century*, Columbia University Press, New York, 1978.
6. L.E.M. Batchelor, 'The South Sea Company and the Asiento', University of London, unpublished dissertation (1924), espe-

cially pp. 137,181, 227-8; George H. Nelson, 'Contraband Trade under the Asiento, 1730-1739', *American Historical Review*, LI (1954) p.55.

7. Samuel Hull Wilcocke, *History of the Viceroyalty of Buenos Aires*, London, 1807, pp.506-7.

8. Bartholome Mitre, *Historia de Belgrano y de la independencia argentina* (4th ed., Buenos Aires, 1887), I, p.50.

9. Lord Palmerston, quoted in Brian Inglis, *The Opium War*, London, 1976, p.218.

10. Vicente Fidel López, *La novia del hereje o la inquisición de Lima* (1854) La Cultura Argentina, Buenos Aires, 1971.

11. Though see Donald McCloskey, *The Rhetoric of Economics*, University of Wisconsin Press, Madison, 1985.

12. Archives of the Bank of London and South America (BOLSA), University College, London. D.35, 15 March 1890.

13. Angel J. Costa, *El Banco de la Provincia decapitado por el Banco Nacional*, Buenos Aires, 1873, p.10.

14. Quoted in Albert O. Hirschman, *The Passions and the Interests: Political Arguments for Capitalism before its Triumph*, Princeton University Press, Princeton, N.J. 1977, p.94.

15. Immanuel Kant, 'Idea for a Universal History with a Cosmopolitan Purpose', in Hans Reiss, ed., *Kant's Political Writings*, Cambridge University Press, Cambridge 1970, p.50.

16. Records of the English Bank of the River Plate, formerly in the Archives of Mandatos y agencias del Río de la Plata S.A., now destroyed.

17. From William Roscoe, The Wrongs of Africa (Part 1, 1787), in George Chandler, *William Roscoe of Liverpool, 1753-1831*, Batsford, London, 1953, p.356.

18. Wilfred Latham, *The States of the River Plate*, 2nd ed., London, 1868, p.356.

19. Ibid., pp.260-1.

20. José Bianco, *Don Bernardo de Irigoyen, estadista y pionero 1822-1906)*, Buenos Aires, 1927, pp.136-47.

21. D.M. Joslin, *A Century of Banking in Latin America*, Oxford University Press, London, 1963, pp.31-2.

22. PRO FO 6/345 St.John to Derby, 1 June 1876; BOLSA D.35, 11 October 1876, Behn (Rosario) to Head Office; (This volume of Rosario letters was misplaced in the D.35 series in the original cataloguing).

23. Wilfrid Latham, *States of the River Plate*, pp.317-8.

24. Return to the Registrar of Companies, file 2854 (1864).

25. M.G.Mulhall, *The English in South America*, Buenos Aires, 1878, p.598; on social integration there is, of course conflicting evidence, but see Vera Blinn Rèber, *British Mercantile Houses in Buenos Aires 1810-1880*, Harvard University Press, Cambridge, Mass.,1979, pp.47-9.
26. BOLSA, London and River Plate Bank, Head Office to Valparaiso, 26 August, 1914.
27. Charles Jones, 'The Transfer of Banking Techniques from Britain to Argentina, 1862-1914', *Révue Internationale d'Histoire de la Banque*, 26-7 (1983), pp.255-61.
28. Charles Jones, *International Business in the Nineteenth Century: The Rise and Fall of Cosmopolitan Bourgeoisie*, Wheatsheaf, Brighton, 1987, chapter 5.
29. BOLSA D.75 Fennessy to Ross Duffield, 30 January 1891. De la Riestra encountered similar problems, referred to in Jones, 'Transfer of Banking Techniques', p.255.
30. Jones, 'Transfer of Banking Techniques', pp.261-3.
31. BOLSA D.75 8 March 1891.
32. BOLSA D.75 1, 5, 9 March 1891.
33. Camara de Senadores de la Nación, Diario de Sesiones, 17 January 1891, pp. 76-84.
34. BOLSA D. 35 7 December 1890
35. *La Nacion*, 7 January 1895.
36. BOLSA D,1, 3 December 1879; see also D.1, 23 October 1878.
37. J.F. Lyotard, *The Postmodern Condition: a report on knowledge*, Manchester University Press, Manchester, 1984, p.12.

# 4

# End of Empire : the Decline of the Anglo-Argentine Connection 1918-1951

## Callum A. MacDonald

In 1925 Argentina celebrated the centenary of the treaty of friendship, commerce and navigation with Britain, an occasion marked by the state visit of the Prince of Wales, later Edward VIII to Buenos Aires. In a speech to the opening session of the Argentine Congress, President Alvear hailed the visit as evidence of Argentina's international importance and emphasised the value of the Anglo-Argentine connection to national progress. According to Alvear, the Prince was 'the representative of a glorious dynasty' and 'of a government which is a model of good sense and efficiency'. He hoped this his royal visitor would be 'afforded unquestionable proof that the people of the Argentine appreciate the value of British friendship, a friendship shown in vigorous contribution to the progress of our country ever since the days of our emancipation ...'[1] 'The press was similarly effusive. According to *La Nación* the visit was a manifestation of the marked preference for Argentina displayed by Britain, that 'noble nation', since the days of Canning, while *La Prensa* emphasised the role of British capital and markets in establishing the economic basis of the republic.[2] Smart society in Buenos Aires awaited the Prince's arrival with eager anticipation. When his ship docked on 17 August, he was greeted by a massed gun salute from the Argentine fleet and proceeded to the Casa Rosada with President Alvear through cheering crowds throwing flower petals.[3] The British accepted this reception as little more than their due and congratulated themselves on what they had done for a republic which represented civilised European values on the South American continent. According to the special correspondent of *The Times*, the popular enthusiasm for the Prince reflected not only affection for himself but also for his country. He was a representative of 'the might and majesty of Britain'.[4]

Within thirty years of this celebration, however, the Anglo-Argentine connection was all but dead. Britain had become the symbol of a foreign economic domination which Argentina was determined to escape. At a far different ceremony in March 1948, a 21 gun salute marked the nationalisation of the British-owned railways, an occasion greeted by President Perón as an assertion of national independence. The British ambassador, Sir Rex Leeper, complained bitterly that in 'all the torrent of words, official and unofficial, written and spoken' which accompanied this demonstration there appeared 'no tribute, however conservative or indirect, to those who, with their own capital, skill and drive, built in Argentina the finest railway in Latin America and laid the track along which this country advanced to prosperity'. [5] By 1950, the two countries were locked in a bitter dispute about trade and the political climate had been transformed to the point where Buenos Aires was regarded in the foreign service as on a par with Moscow for the icy quality of relations with the ruling elite. The embassy had become almost a punishment post. [6] As the British ambassador, Sir John Balfour, left Argentina for Spain in January 1951 his departure was greeted in the *New Statesman* with a piece of doggerel entitled 'Frozen Out'.[7]

> Deadlock in the Argentine;
> No meat upon the Plate!
> Failure of a mission to a foreign Fascist State!
> Buenos Aires beef chief's their frozen shipments stop
> Diplomatic temperatures down to zero drop.
> (Haggling is proceeding on the Foreign Office plane)
> But Britain's chilled ambassador is on his way to Spain!

This verse accurately conveyed the qualities of political distaste and economic tension which characterised the British relationship with Argentina after the Second World War. The collapse of the old Anglo-Argentine connection, whose centenary was celebrated in 1925, was the product of British decline and social and economic change in Argentina, fostered by the coup of 1943 and the rise of Peronism. [8] It was a transformation which the British, long accustomed to a favoured position, were ill-prepared to understand when they suffered 'the vilification inevitably directed against a dispossessed colonial power'. [9]

The Anglo-Argentine connection was created as part of the British free trade empire of the nineteenth century. This depended on a world division of labour in which Argentina provided meat and grains for the British industrial metropolis, whilst Britain provided Argentina with industrial goods and the capital necessary to develop the pampas. In the 1880s there was a surge of British investment in the

Argentine. In the peak year of 1889 Argentina absorbed between 40 and 50 per cent of all British funds invested outside the United Kingdom. [10] Despite the Baring crisis, British investment continued into the twentieth century and had reached £290 million by 1911, much of it tied up in the railways and the *frigoríficos* which provided the infrastructure for the chilled meat trade with the United Kingdom.[11] Along with British investments came British immigrants to manage and run the new enterprises. By 1910 the British community had reached 30,000 and supported two English language newspapers.[12] The boom in the agricultural economy enriched the Argentine landowners who embraced the Anglo-Argentine connection as the key to economic progress. An exclusive group of 400 families, with interests revolving round the meat trade, the *estanciero* oligarchy controlled the levers of political and economic power. [13] Its organisation, the Rural Society, 'enjoyed remarkable representation in government. Between 1910 and 1943 ... over half the chief executives were prominent ranchers'. [14] Under this group there was no tendency to question the world division of labour. The British buttressed their position with a 'highly extensive system of semi-institutionalised direct linkages with the elite. They had important allies at cabinet and congressional level, and an influential voice ... in many of the ... leading press organs ... The British lobby ranked with the cattlemen's association as the most powerful in country'.[15]

A quiet word of advice where it mattered from a prominent banker such as Sir Hilary Leng, was enough to influence proposed legislation. The British community introduced the Argentine elite to the joys of golf, rugby and polo although it was unable to export cricket. A British governess was considered essential in smart society. [16] In this atmosphere British officials enjoyed a privileged position. During the First World War the British minister, Sir Reginald Tower, was a popular figure at the sumptious parties held in the vast town houses of the aristocracy while in 1919 even a junior diplomat like David Kelly enjoyed an entrée into the exclusive fencing club. As he later recalled: 'Our social relations (apart from the British colony) lay entirely with the Argentine plutocracy, and inevitably so; just because they still controlled everything ...' Kelly himself married into an *estanciero* family. [17] The British were comfortable with an enlightened aristocracy dedicated to free trade, whose clubs and landed interests to an extent replicated the background of the Edwardian elite which ran the pre-war Empire. It is hardly surprising that in these circumstances the British believed that they had created Argentina and expected the Argentines to be duly grateful. In fact the Anglo-Argentine connection was an alliance of convenience. It worked smoothly only while Britain remained the leading industrial power and Argentines did not question the world division of labour. This in turn required the continuing dominance of the *estanciero* class and its identification of the national interest with chilled beef exports. When the Prince of Wales visited Buenos Aires, the connection was already in decline, eroded by the growth of import substitution in Argentina and the displacement of Britain by the United States at the centre of the world economy after the First World War. [18] As early as 1919 the *Economist* remarked: 'It would be folly to ignore the hold Argentine manufacturers have secured in the Argentine market ... locally manufactured goods are in a position to compete in many directions in which British merchandise was supreme only a few years ago'. It also noted the impact of American competition, a matter which seemed 'to demand the attention of the British Board of Trade'. [19]

In addition to these factors, the British were faced with political change in Argentina. In 1916 the oligarchy conceded a share of political power to the rising middle classes, led by the Radical Party. Despite their nationalist rhetoric, the Radicals had no quarrel with the export economy, demanding only access to posts in the bureaucracy and the professions. The *estancieros* retained a powerful influence in the party and produced in Alvear a President who was an Anglophile and a member of the Rural Society. [20] The atmosphere, however, was clearly changing and Kelly compared the situation unfavourably with the privileged British position before 1914:

> Already ... all the British public utilities ... were being subjected to an ever-growing cold war of niggling and obstruction which during the next twenty-five years led to their gradual expropriation ... the growing spread of nationalism, which in practice usually boiled down to jobs for the boys, led to the gradual restriction of immigration and of openings in the professions and finally in business, for new arrivals, which dried up at source recruitment of new blood for the foreign colonies. [21]

The Anglo-Argentine connection only survived into the thirties because of changes in British trade policy and the effects of the Argentine military coup of 1930 which overthrew the Radicals and ushered in a decade of renewed *estanciero* dominance. In 1932, to meet the global US economic challenge and protect its position during the depression, Britain abandoned its traditional policy of free trade at the Ottawa Conference and went over to a system of protection and imperial preference. The government was able to use continued access to British markets as a lever to protect its threatened position in Argentina. By the terms of the Roca-Runciman Agreement of 1933, Argentina guaranteed favourable treatment to British trade and investments in return for the continuation, on a reduced scale, of Argentine chilled beef exports to Britain. London was in a strong bargaining position since the oligarchy was faced with ruin. Already excluded from US markets by a series of sanitary and tariff measures promoted by the American farm lobby, Argentine ranchers had to hold on to the British market at almost any price. [22] In fact the pact symbolised the weakness of both parties. The British position could not hold up against the Americans on the old basis of free trade while the social and economic power of the estancieros was uniquely dependent on British goodwill. In these circumstances it is hardly surprising that London was well satisfied with the treaty which was also approved by 'most groups connected with beef production'. [23] The real losers were Argentine manufacturers and consumers and of course the United States which complained long and bitterly about its effects on American interests. Between 1930 and 1936 the US share of the Argentine market dropped from 22.1 to 14.4 per cent, a reduction which was blamed on the Roca-Runciman Agreement.[24] On the surface the Roca-Runciman Agreement seemed to restore the old basis of the Anglo-Argentine connection. The British ambassador, Sir Neville Henderson, recalled his posting to Buenos Aires as a period of calm before his controversial mission to Berlin and clearly enjoyed good social relations with an Argentine elite which still deferred to Britain. According to Henderson, Buenos Aires was 'a purely economic post ... There is ... one political question at issue between us, namely the Falkland Islands ... It was, however, never mentioned to me during the whole time that I was there. Our good or bad relations seemed to depend entirely on the import duty which was levied on chilled beef ... a penny less or a penny more made all the difference to the prosperity or the reverse of the great Argentine industry and its cattle breeders'. He remembered clearing up some controversial points during the renewal of the Roca-Runciman Agreement in 1936 with the Minister of Agriculture, Carcano, 'one of the best types of Argentine landowners and politicians'. He had similar words of praise for the Minister of Marine who was 'a useful friend ... especially when it was a question of contracts for warships for the Argentine Navy'. [25] The Argentine leaders were public-spirited gentlemen, unlike the elite with which he had to deal on his next posting to Nazi Germany. In contrast to this picture of harmony,

Argentine relations with the United States were bad throughout the 1930s when an economic cold war prevailed. The US Secretary of State, Cordell Hull, characterised the Argentine Foreign Minister at this time, Saavedra Lamas as an 'outstanding and irrepressible' opponent of the United States, while his deputy, Sumner Welles, regarded the oligarchy as the reactionary tool of British interests. [26]

Britain continued to enjoy a privileged position after the outbreak of war. Argentina supplied meat on favourable terms, accepting blocked sterling, essentially a British promise of future payment, in return. The Argentines also promised not to take advantage of British difficulties to press the Falklands/Malvinas question. In these circumstances London, while irritated by Argentine wartime neutrality, was not inclined to confront Buenos Aires on the issue in contrast to the United States which regarded Argentina as a pariah in the Pan-American system. [27] As Sir David Kelly, now ambassador, remarked in December 1942, in view 'of the great importance which British trade and investments in Argentina must necessarily hold in our own postwar recovery' it would be impracticable to risk a quarrel with the Argentine ruling class. Kelly did not regard neutrality as a serious threat arguing that most members of 'smart society were thoroughly ... pro-British in their personal sympathies'. [28] Some officials, including Kelly, saw Argentine neutrality and the continued dominance of the oligarchy as a safeguard against the renewal of the US economic challenge and had no objections to the system of electoral fraud which had kept the *estancieros* in power since 1930. As one Foreign Office official remarked in March 1943: 'From our point of view the older generation are definitely an advantage at the head of affairs, the Meatgrowers of Buenos Aires Province especially. So I see no need to wish matters were otherwise as regards elections; though just now Neutrality seems more strongly than ever in the saddle'. According to another the *estancieros* had good reasons for 'keeping in with us' and represented 'quite the soundest section of the Argentine ruling class'. [29]

While the British position steadied under the protection of strict bilateralism in the 1930s, fundamental weaknesses remained. The clock could not be turned back to 1914. Local industry continued to grow in Argentina, partly represented by US corporations circumventing trade and exchange controls by founding local branches. In textiles in particular, local industry was a 'most formidable competitor'. [30] The British industrial performance itself remained indifferent with exports concentrated on old staples such as coal rather than consumer goods or modern industrial equipment. As the Department of Overseas Trade complained in 1937, Argentines wanted articles like fridges, radios and electrical machinery but 'either we do not make them or we do not market them, at least not on a scale worthy of our position as an industrial and exporting nation', a situation which had prevailed since the 1920s. [31] Britain was thus vulnerable to any renewal of American competition, a possibility which became very real when British involvement in the Second World War reduced British exports and put the continued existence of Britain itself in doubt. In these circumstances the oligarchy split and one group considered building a new relationship with the United States, the main victim of the Roca-Runciman pact. While this was never consolidated, it remained an attractive proposition to many *estancieros* as it became increasingly clear that the US and not Britain would emerge from the war as the dominant power in the international system. [32] As Kelly emphasised, Britain could not rely on a sentimental attachment to the past to protect its position. Whatever their past quarrels with the US, the *estancieros* would leap at any offer to admit their products to the American market. [33]

If the Roca-Runciman Agreement failed to guarantee the British long-term position, it also made the Anglo-Argentine connection an issue in domestic politics. Britain had allied itself with a group which maintained its position only by force and electoral fraud rather than consent, excluding other social and economic groups and producing an inherently unstable political system. In pursuing its own interests at the expense of consumers and manufacturers, the oligarchy could be seen as the tool of a foreign power and was so regarded by a new generation of Argentine nationalists. The Roca-Runciman Agreement became the symbol of the 'infamous decade' and the betrayal of national interests. This was particularly dangerous in a period of growing economic nationalism throughout Latin America where the depression had pointed up the dangers of relying on exports to the industrialised world and had provoked demands for economic diversification and greater controls on foreign capital. In Argentina this feeling was particularly prevalent in the officer corps which brought the period of *estanciero* dominance to an end with the military coup of June 1943. [34] The displacement of the oligarchy and the appearance of a new elite took the British by surprise. As the Foreign Office remarked in September 1943, power now appeared to be wielded by 'a group of mysterious army officers who are led by a Colonel Perón (of whom we know nothing)'. [35] The rise of Perón and the new social

and economic forces which he represented was the death knell for the
Anglo-Argentine connection.

The British were suspicious of Perón from the start and watched
his rise in the wartime military governments and his election in 1946
with fascinated horror. The promotion of economic nationalism which
emphasised industrialisation, financed by high prices for Argentine
meat and grains, posed dangers for British postwar recovery. As the
British ambassador, Sir Rex Leeper, remarked in 1946 when Perón
published his Five Year Plan for industrialisation: 'In these pages
there is no sign of dawning recognition that the traditional customers
for Argentine primary produce may be estranged or impoverished by
these selfish designs, or that the costs of these unsound enterprises
must eventually impede the republic's ability to maintain her agricultural costs at competitive levels'. [36] At the same time the British
recognised that while an agricultural Argentina might be more to
their taste, they were powerless to stop these new developments.
Dependent on Argentine food supplies for their own recovery, the
British could not afford to quarrel with Perón. Instead it was hoped
to put the old Anglo-Argentine connection on a new footing.

After 1945 Britain abandoned traditional forms of capital investment such as the railways, nationalised in 1948, and chose to em-
phasize a trading relationship based on the supply of capital goods
and industrial raw materials in return for Argentine food. [37] From
the beginning the problem about this strategy was that Britain,
undergoing its own economic difficulties as a result of the war, was
incapable of supplying Argentina with the goods it required. The lines
available from Britain, apart from armaments, were often those
which Argentina could manufacture itself and which it wished to
protect from foreign competition. [38] As the head of the new state
trading organisation IAPI, Miguel Miranda, complained in January
1947; 'What he wanted was coal and raw materials such as caustic
soda and soda ash. Argentina could not live on whisky and lipstick'. [39]

In a free market, Argentina would have turned to the US for its
requirements but Britain was saved from the full impact of American
competition by sterling inconvertibility in 1947 and the continuing
influence of the US farm lobby which blocked the expenditure of
Marshall Plan dollars on Argentine foodstuffs. [40] As for Argentina, it
was progressively less able to supply the meat Britain required in
sufficient quantities and at an acceptable price: 'Partly as a result of
the government's policy with regard to agriculture, the effects of
industrialisation, and natural disaster, virtually every sector of agri-

culture witnessed a decline in economic activity and a falling-off in production'. [41]

The result was to lock together two powers which were no longer natural trading partners. The bilateral relationship forced on Britain and Argentina after 1947 did not function in the manner of the Roca-Runciman Pact. The Argentines made continual difficulties about licencing 'inessential' imports and used meat as a lever to secure a quota of scarce dollar items like oil. At the same time, as Argentina entered its own postwar economic crisis, deliveries of agricultural goods became unreliable. The three trade agreements concluded between 1946 and 1950 were plagued by controversy as each side accused the other of bad faith. In August 1949 the British ambassador, Sir John Balfour, complained: 'The Argentines seem incapable of drafting an agreement themselves but they are finished experts at twisting contractual terms in such a way as to derive all, and more, of their own benefits, while depriving the other side of their share of advantage as far as possible'. [42] Argentina was regarded as an increasingly dubious trading partner and steps were taken to diversify British sources of supply. [43] In 1950 there was a complete economic deadlock when the government refused to submit to further Argentine 'blackmail'. These complaints overlooked some legitimate grievances on the Argentine side. Argentina found itself tied to a declining power which not only declared its currency inconvertible in 1947 but devalued in 1949 changing the framework within which economic agreements had been concluded. Nor could Britain any longer supply what Argentina required. [44] The deterioration of economic relations was parallelled in the political sphere when Perón's government renewed pressure over the Falklands/Malvinas and laid claim to a section of the Antarctic. The conduct of Argentine warships in the area was considered provocative enough to justify the despatch of HMS *Nigeria* in 1948. [45]

The British saw only their own side in the trade dispute and blamed the Argentines for their problems. The regime was universally unpopular. The Labour government elected in 1945 was initially sympathetic to the rise of Argentine trade unions. In May 1946, Bevin ordered the embassy to pay particular attention to labour problems and recommended that British companies in Argentina grant their workers the same conditions of service as the best local firms. [46] As the regime slid towards totalitarianism and state control of unions this early sympathy evaporated particularly when high Argentine meat prices threatened the living standards of British workers. [47] On the left of the party, Perón had always been unpopular and was condemned as a fascist. The permanent officials at the Foreign Office, who dealt directly with Argentina, continued to be drawn from the establishment and found social contacts with the Peronists distasteful. The regime was corrupt, inefficient and 'drunk with the adulation of the mob'. [48] The role of the former acrtress, Evita Perón, who was regarded as no friend of Britain, was singled out for particular criticism. According to Sir John Balfour, who suffered repeated frustrations at Argentine hands, government by elightened grandees had been replaced by an irrational system 'where ministers trailed through the corridors of the Casa Rosada after the petticoat of the first lady of the land — transacting business with her on the principle of the Mad Hatter's tea party'. [49] Evita called off her trip to Britain during the 'Rainbow Tour' of 1947 when it became clear that she would not be invited to stay with the Royal Family at Buckingham Palace. Indeed the King and Queen would not be in London during her projected four day visit, a fact which she justifiably regarded as a snub. [50] Miranda, who as head of IAPI was at the centre of repeated economic rows with Britain, was as unpopular as Evita. He was variously described as a 'crook' and a 'quick-witted, unprincipled ... horsetrader, who gabbled Spanish with an atrocious Catalan accent' and had 'the manner and appearance of an animated toad'. He and his like had reduced the country to a state of financial and moral ruin. It was a far cry from Henderson's cosy chats with the Minister of Marine in 1936 about naval contracts. As the British commercial attaché concluded, it was 'not pleasant to do business with such people'. [51] Even the Foreign Minister, Bramuglia, regarded as a 'reasonably sensible man for an Argentine' because of his intervention against Miranda in two sets of trade negotiations, was not spared a sneer. According to Sir Evelyn Shuckburgh, the head of the South American Department, he was 'insignificant and feather-headed'. His entourage made an even less favourable impression. [52]

If the regime consisted of crooks and incompetents, its policies were regarded as a selfish attempt to capitalise on Britain's shortage of food. From the British perspective, Argentina's role was to subsidize the recovery of Britain with supplies of cheap foodstuffs, postponing its own modernisation in the process. In effect, despite a verbal acceptance of change, London was attempting to turn the clock back and freeze Argentina in its nineteenth century position. As Leeper remarked as early as September 1946: 'It is ... important that these people should be stopped in their present course in order to put them in their proper place in the world and in our interests as a country considerably dependent on the purchase of their products during the next two years'. [53] The refusal of the Argentines to fall easily into this role any longer accounted for much of the bitterness of British comment. Perón's regime was both venal and totalitarian but the oligarchy had hardly been a model of either moral rectitude or democratic practice. Its failings in this respect had always been overlooked because of its dependent relationship with Britain. Despite the changes since 1943, Britain continued to believe that it was somehow natural for Argentina to serve British interests, if only out of gratitude for the services of British trade and capital in the past.

A barely concealed anger ran through official comment at Argentina's sheer ingratitude and failure to reward past friendship with current concessions. This was clear in Leeper's description of the ceremony marking the nationalisation of the railways in 1948, which complained that Perón had not a word of praise for the historic achievements of British capital and went on to talk of a 'ragged' twenty-one gun salute and of a blue and white flag 'straggling out' in the breeze. [54] His successor, Balfour, was even more scathing, denying that Argentina, a nation of immigrants, had any right to claim a genuine nationalism. Anti-foreignism sprang instead from 'a kind of perverse group conciousness which is not nationalism'. Incapable of building a functioning nation on their own, the Argentines blamed their misfortune on others. Balfour later connected this national immaturity with the appeal of Evita Perón: 'In many ways Evita Perón was an ambitious, self-willed, self-seeking schoolgirl who had never grown up. Argentina ... was still an adolescent country. The youth, glamour, and uninhibited eloquence of Eva Perón were the embodiment of this adolescence and as such made a strong popular appeal'. [55] Behind such statements lurked the assumption that Argentina had been created by British capital and skill and could not exist without them.

Although the embargo ended in 1951 and meat shipments resumed on a reduced scale, the old Anglo-Argentine connection did not revive, killed off by the changed conditions which followed the Second World War. Britain's role as Argentina's major trading partner was 'irretrievably lost'. [56] In retrospect the period of stability which followed the Roca-Runciman Agreement proved to be an illusion which failed to solve the weaknesses which had underlain the British position since 1918. Britain was able to capitalise on the desperation of the oligarchy to guarantee foreign markets during the depression, only to fall victim to their displacement by a new coalition of social and economic groups after 1943. As for the Argentines, despite Perón's declaration of economic independence both he and his successors

were finally forced to come to terms with the power which had begun
to dominate the international system after the First World War and
completed the process after the Second World War — The United
States. [57] As Kelly had predicted, one kind of informal empire was
rapidly replaced by another. By the time of his fall in 1955 'Perón had
established a pattern of further industrialisation which involved a
large-scale participation of multi-national corporations in manufacturing and the production of industrial raw materials and intermedi-
ate goods ... In fact ... the key points in the Argentine economy were
less in Argentine hands than they had been in the days of the
oligarchy'. [58] It was perhaps no consolation to Argentine nationalists
that the erstwhile imperial power, Britain, was itself being integrated
into the postwar US empire as the American Century dawned.

## Notes

1. *The Times*, 16 May 1925, 14
2. Ibid, 11 December 1924, 13
3. Ibid, 18 August 1925, 12
4. Ibid, 28 September 1925, 12, 15 August 1925, 9
5. Leeper to FO. 5 March 1948. AS179012 FO371/68089
6. Interview, Sir John Balfour, 5/4 81
7. Sir John Balfour, Unpublished Memoir Notes
8. C.A. MacDonald, 'The United States, Britain and Argentina in
   the Years after the Second World War' in Guido Di Tella and
   D.C.M. Platt (eds), *The Political History of Argentina*, London
   1986, 183-281
9. Andrew Graham-Yool, *The Forgotten Colony*, London 1981,
   244-45
10. H.S. Ferns, *Britain and Argentina in the Nineteenth Century*,
    Oxford 1960, 397
11. Ibid, 486
12. Graham-Yool, 228-32
13. David Rock, *Politics in Argentina*, London 1975, 2-3
14. Peter H. Smith, *Politics and Beef in Argentina*, New York 1969,
    48
15. Rock, *Politics in Argentina*, 6
16. W.H. Koebel, *Modern Argentina*, London 1907, 33, Sir David
    Kelly, *The Ruling Few*, London 1953, 110
17. Kelly, 109-35

18. Roger Gravil, 'Anglo-US Trade Rivalry in Argentina and the D'Abernon Mission of 1929'in David Rock (ed), *Argentina in the Twentieth Century*, London 1975, 41-66
19. *Economist*, 29 November 1919, David Rock, *Argentina 1516-1982*, 197-99
20. Rock, *Politics in Argentina*, 271, Graham-Yool, 236
21. Kelly, 115
22. Rock, *Argentina*, 224-5, Smith, 126-7, 139-47
23. Smith, 146
24. Colin Lewis, 'Anglo-Argentine Trade 1945-1965', in D.Rock (ed) *Argentina in the Twentieth Century*, 115
25. Sir Nevile Henderson, *Water Under the Bridges*, London 1945, 205-6
26. Cordell Hull, *The Memoirs of Cordell Hull*, London 1948, Volume 1, 322-23, Sumner Welles, *Where Are We Heading*, New York 1946, 191-2
27. R.A. Humphreys, *Latin America And The Second World War* London 1982, 138-42, Kelly 287
28. Kelly to FO, 7 April 1943, A3903/11/2 FO371/33511, Kelly 287
29. FO Minutes on Hadow to Perowne, 12 March 1943, A3015/11/2 FO371/33511 Mario Rappaport, *Gran Bretaña, Estados Unidos y las clasas dirigentes argentinas*: 1940-1945, 96-146, Buenos Aires 1981.
30. Department of Overseas Trade *Report on the Financial, Commercial and Economic Conditions of the Argentine Republic*, London 1937, 33
31. Ibid, 30-32
32. Rock, *Argentina*, 240-45
33. Kelly to FO 7 April 1943, A3903/11/2, FO371/33511
34. Rock, *Argentina*, 232-34, 245
35. Minute by Henderson, 27 September 1943, A8973/11/2 FO371/33516
36. Leeper to FO, 2 December 1946, AS7799/22/2 FO371/51778
37. Leeper to FO, 24 September 1946, AS6228/22/2 FO371/51778, Leeper to FO, 18 September 1946, AS5965/2/2 FO371/51766, Perowne to Hooper, 20 February 1947, AS960/16/2 FO371/61124
38. MacDonald. 'The US, Britain and Argentina', 184-86
39. Ibid, 190
40. Ibid, 191-92
41. Lewis, 'Anglo-Argentine Trade', 122-23
42. Balfour to FO 24 August 1949. AS4648/11578/2 FO371/74375

43. Minute by Jackling, 19 May 1948, AS3146/248/2 FO371/68124
44. MacDonald, 'The US. Britain and Argentina', 192-3
45. Balfour to FO 24 May 1949, AS2867/10ll/2 FO371/74288
46. Bevin to Leeper, 16 May 1946, AS2588/235/2 FO371/51813
47. Balfour, Unpublished Draft Memoir
48. Balfour to Attlee, 5 December 1949, AS6084/10119/2 FO371/74299
49. Balfour, Unpublished Draft Memoir
50. Joseph Page, Perón: A Biography, New York 1973, 194-5
51. Balfour, Unpublished Draft Memoir, Minute by Shuckburgh, 15 September 1948, AS65289/248/2 FO371/62186, Labouchère to Shuckburgh, 12 September 1948, FO371/68126
52. Sir Evelyn Shuckburgh, Descent to Suez, London 1986, 16
53. Leeper to FO, 8 September 1946, AS5460/2/2 FO371/51764
54. Leeper to FO, 5 March 1948, AS1790/1/22 FO371/68089
55. Balfour to FO, 24 May 1949, AS2867/10ll/2 FO371/74288 Balfour, Unpublished Draft Memoirs
56. Lewis, 'Anglo-Argentine Trade', 132-34
57. C.A. MacDonald, 'The US. the Cold War and Perón', in Christopher Abel and Colin Lewis (eds), Latin America: Economic Imperialism and The State, London 1984 405-413
58. H.S. Ferns, The Argentine Republic, London 1973, 162-63

# 5

# The Denigration of Peronism

*Roger Gravil*

*I cannot understand why the Argentines did not shoot this dangerous man* [1]

Nearly all the literature on Peronism takes the form of indictment. Except in Party hagiography, the general line is so unremittingly hostile that the reputation of Juan and Eva Perón is notorious rather than famous and their movement is denigrated rather than admired. The charges levelled range from fascism to sexual misconduct, from tyranny to mass deception, from monumental misgovernment to personal corruption, from jingoism to selling out the Republic of Argentina. In *Out of Africa*, Count von Blixen says to his forgiving wife, Karen, 'Accuse me of anything: I have surely done it.' That has been the attitude of critics to Peronism with no trace of forgiveness. The denigration has reached a scale that historians must resist accepting it at face value and pose instead the scholarly question 'why is it there?' Most of the time Argentina is not central to the world's concerns, so how has it come about that on one of the rare occasions that an Argentine politician became globally well-known, it took the form of rabid vituperation? After all, some of the charges prove surprisingly easy to refute. Allegations of fascist dictatorship, for instance, crumble with the slightest reference to professional psephology,[2] which shows that President Perón's electoral support in 1946 was firmer than that of, say, Clement Attlee or Harry Truman.[3]

Perón's political debut, in fact, placed Argentina in the vanguard of the post-1945 restoration of world democracy rather than in the rearguard of international fascism. Moreover, without resort to cheating, the Peronists soundly won every election, from which they were not debarred by their opponents, for the next forty years.[4] This record merited the envy of many Western statesmen, if there had been any unprejudiced enough to deem the comparison fitting. Certain other anti-Peronist charges are best left in the scurrilous sub-literature where they originated. But the accusation that is most persistent and hard to dismiss is that Peronism wrecked the potentially rich country of Argentina, or more specifically, that a promising national economy was ruined by Peronist mismanagement. In the 1900s Argentina was forecast to surpass the United States and even as late as 1942 Colin Clark, in his famous book, *The Economics of 1960*,[5] predicted that Argentines would soon enjoy living standards second only to those of the North Americans. The challenge of Argentina was long viewed apprehensively by the British Dominions, who pressed energetically to blackball this Latin American imposter from the 'imperial club'.[6] Yet, in the event, Argentina has fallen far short of even the most humble expectations and the republic's recent economic history is even less inspiring than that of Britain. In consequence, exuberant forecasts for the future have been supplanted by accusatory invocations of the past and a prime suspect for causing national decline is the decade or so of Peronist rule ending in September 1955.[7] On this view, economic growth, of the last eighty years, was so maladroitly dissipated that Argentina continues to suffer the consequences in the 1980s.

Against this background of historiographical condemnation, the present study offers a handful of tentative propositions. First, Argentina's earlier development (1862-1930) is grossly flattered in the standard account. Secondly, *Concordancia* rule (1930-43) merits a worse reputation than Peronist government (1943-55) if the concern is with the general well-being of the Argentine people. Thirdly, Argentina's ambitions were to a major degree thwarted by Great Power politics in the post-war years. Fourthly, there were admittedly grave errors in Peronist rule. Fifthly, the recall of Juan Domingo Perón in 1973 bears elements of comparison with that of Winston Churchill and Charles de Gaulle in their nations' hour of need.

It is well-known that Argentina shared a number of the characteristics of British Dominions. British capital investment there had reached a possible £600 million by 1930,[8] British enterprise was prominent in transport, banking and business, while the Argentine economy depended heavily on exporting meat and cereals to the United Kingdom market. Increasingly, from the later nineteenth century Argentina's wealth had grown briskly on this basis, for though commodity prices had rarely been high, export growth was simply attained by incorporating new land. Around 1900 land in use amounted to 6.5 million hectares while a generation later it stood at 25.8 million hectares.[9] Such a period in primary-exporting, however, corresponded to industry's import- substitution phase, being a spell of easy growth to be enjoyed with foresight and preparation rather than assumptions of permanence.

In the second decade of the twentieth century ominous features were already appearing in the Argentine economy. By 1914 most worthwhile land had been brought into use so that productive intensification was unmistakeably indicated, but met little response from Argentina's frequently absentee landlords. The habit of easy earnings from casual land exploitation was hard to break. Marketing rural produce, once an initial local interest had faded, was increasingly dominated by North American, German and British companies and a growing volume of complaint accrued about their pricing policies. Once the post-1918 boom was over, primary commodity prices weakened as decades of high overseas investment resulted in excess world output, so that Argentina encountered stiffening international competition in exporting grain and meat. Under such conditions the republic's future development, assuming retention of the export-import model, depended on Britain adhering to free trade and multilateral payments. The British were Argentina's indispensable customers, while North Americans were increasingly the republic's preferred suppliers. By the late 1920s the Argentines were clearing up to £20 million a year from their British trade, which they spent mainly on the technically superior products of United States industry.

Recent studies[10] have played down the significance of 1929. Yet in prompting Britain to abandon the gold standard and adopt imperial preference, the Wall Street Crash certainly concentrated Argentine minds wonderfully, if only in a determination to preserve the status quo. Possessing the economic circumstances, but not the political claims, of a British Dominion, Argentina sought to outbid her competitors by offering Britain a seductive package of low cost, refined foodstuffs, along with an export market for British manufacturers, in which competition from local industry and that of the United States would be minimised. In practice, though, improvement of rural production proved much harder to accomplish than the restraining of national industry. In 1928 one imported tractor cost an Argentine farmer 47 tons of cereals; by 1933 the same vehicle cost 102 tons.[11] The disadvantage of a late start was so debilitating that even at the end of the 1940s Argentina had only one tractor for every 880 hectares compared to the North American statistics of one for every 80 hectares.[12] Impeding Argentine manufacturing to favour British industry was child's play by comparison. Contradicting a congenial scenario for national industrial advance, in the shape of export decline and foreign exchange scarcity, was a battery of concessions granted to Britain, which held back Argentine manufacturing progress to no more than 1920s levels, when German and North American competition had also been in full swing. Even at the end of this sometimes vaunted period in 1939 the traditional foodstuffs and beverage trades still accounted for 25 per cent of all industrial establishments, employed 21 per cent of all industrial labour and produced 34 per cent by value of all industrial output. Textiles trailed far behind with 13 per cent, 15 per cent and 14 per cent respectively, while 84 per cent of capital goods used in Argentina were still imported.[13]

A much higher government priority than manufacturing promotion was counter-inflation,[14] which in the context of the 1930s was an absurdity. Yet this (not purely local) obsession led the *Concordancia* to drastic cuts in public spending and a 10 per cent wage reduction for state employees eagerly imitated by the private sector. Argentina was a welfare-less state contrasting starkly with Uruguay across the River Plate, which had developed a welfare system roughly contemporaneous with that of Lloyd George in the United Kingdom.[15] The *Concordancia's* inflammatory combination of transparent collaboration with Britain and indifference to general welfare meant that the regime could never have survived free elections. Instead, control of an electoral machine[16] underwrote a grand design for self-perpetuation so detailed that forthcoming presidents could be named in advance as far ahead as 1950.

The coup of 1943 definitively stopped rule by oligarchy and ultimately produced a revolution which fundamentally transformed the political economy of Argentina. This regime originated in a political cell labelled the GOU and it is typical of the ambiguity surrounding all things Peronist that even the meaning of the acronym is disputed. Some said *Gobierno! Orden! Unidad!* insinuating an echo of the slogans of Franco's Spain. Others said, '*Grupo de oficiales unidos*' implying a narrow military clique. Another rendering was, '*Grupo, obra de unificación*', indicating a definite policy objective, which Peronism most certainly had.[17] Yet Colonel Juan Domingo Perón did not rush to the fore:[18] rather he gradually accumulated the Ministry of War, the Vice Presidency and the dogsbody job of Secretary of Labour, which he proceeded to inflate, much as Joseph Stalin elevated the insignificant Secretaryship of the CPSU. Premature seizure of leadership by Perón would have meant early loss, for purely military regimes generally rest on clique alliances which prove short term. His objective was not to remain a purely military figure; on the contrary, he achieved a more complete civilianisation than any comparable statesman. His metamorphosis was certainly more complete than that of Nasser in Egypt or Ataturk in Turkey, while Fidel Castro, whom the exiled Perón claimed to have pre-empted by fifteen years, actually performed the opposite feat of a transformation from law graduate politician to irregular military president.

Perón's capture of the Presidency was a personal accomplishment which owed nothing to Maria Eva Duarte. Tradition, prompted by her book, *La razón de mi vida* and vastly embellished by pure malice, film and folk opera, portrays Evita as the vital force in Peronism and reduces Juan Perón to an indolent child molester perpetually planning early retirement. The insinuation is that as she rallied the faithful on 17 October 1945, forcing his release from prison, he was obliged to reject an appealing exile and gird himself for a leadership bid with Evita as the power behind the throne. The trouble with this tradition is that contemporary accounts of these momentous events allocate no role to Eva Duarte. Scrupulous reports[19] by Britain's outstanding ambassador, Sir David Kelly, to Ernest Bevin make no mention of Evita in the entire October saga. *The Times*, the *Manchester Guardian* and *Daily Herald*[20] all covered these hectic days of the Peronist Movement without so much as catching sight of a glamorous film star in the swirl of events. Seasoned male reporters could hardly have failed to appreciate the newsworthiness of a stunning blonde actress in the thick of things. The meticulous Spanish scholar, Marysa Navarro,[21] says that reports of Evita's dramatic intervention first appeared only in 1951 after she had achieved some importance in Perón's entourage. Even so, British officials were unanimous that her death in July 1952 was an unmixed political blessing for President Perón. There is no serious doubt that as Head of State he was in command of affairs and policy in Argentina.

Calm, rational assessment of what Juan Perón stood for was rare for many years and, more typically, the subject was approached with the kind of hysteria later prompted by contemplation of Fidel Castro, Salvador Allende and Daniel Ortega. Denigration was officially solicited, while sympathisers were sanctioned. The standard British view of Peronism, for instance, stemmed primarily from the prejudices and resentments of some 40,000 UK passport holders, who were deemed authoritative on the strength of their residence in this remote and little-known country. Even the exceptional diplomat, Sir David Kelly,[22] relied heavily on his Anglo-Argentine wife. Peronist economic and social policies undermined the British community and spawned the politics of sour grapes rather than dispassionate analysis of Argentina's breakaway regime.

When the veteran head of the River Plate firm, Pendle and Rivett, offered some mildly sympathetic comments on the fall of Perón[23] in Royal Institute of International Affairs and BBC talks, it was hard to judge who was the more furious, the Aramburu Government in Buenos Aires or the Foreign Office in London.[24] By that time George Pendle had already published his masterly little trilogy[25] on the River Plate countries with Chatham House and surely rated among Britain's top dozen authors in the field as it stood thirty years ago. Yet when Perón's opposition complained, the Foreign Office, far from defending a British author's right to speak his mind, moved to placate the regime, which was soon to break with previous, including Peronist, traditions by carrying out the first wave of political executions in twentieth century Argentina.[26] The British Embassy in Buenos Aires was ordered to give Mr Pendle no further assistance, he was accused of ignorance and of 'la trahison des clercs', while the BBC and Chatham House were pressed to terminate his employment. Similar sanctions were adopted against the Anglo-Polish writer, George Bilainkin for befriending Perón and calling Anglo-Argentine businessmen effete.[27] Though the Plate-based correspondent Hinkson, met the canons of impartiality exacted by his employers, *The Times*, he was constantly criticised by the Foreign Office for refraining from blanket hostility to Peronism.[28] Significantly, there was delight in Whitehall with four articles in the *New York Times*, in which Spanish Republican veteran, Herbert Matthews, made Perón resemble Spain's *caudillo*, General Franco. [29]

But the most outrageous piece of denigration, which put Britain's derogatory campaign deeply into the shade, was the extraordinary episode of the Blue Book[30] perpetrated by the one-time US ambassador to Argentina, who was subsequently recalled to high office in Washington. Spruille Braden was the son of a Montana mining engineer, who made a fortune from Chilean copper, though his unusual name actually came from his father's elder brother, who worked in African mining as consultant to Cecil Rhodes. When approaching eighty, Spruille Braden admitted that he had always feared failure in the eyes of his uncle, which still followed his progress from the portrait over the mantelpiece. The only other person, whose approval seemed permanently indispensable, was his wife for forty-seven years, the Chilean aristocrat, Maria Humeres Solar. When Ernest Hemingway was well over forty he was reduced to a 'timid little boy' in her presence and on her death in 1962, Spruille Braden begged God to take him too. But he was intimidated by nobody else. As Simon Hanson said, Braden took on anybody and everybody if the situation seemed to demand it. He called his memoirs *Diplomats and Demagogues*,[31] though he was certainly no diplomat. Thomas McGann[32] and Hugh Thomas[33] judged him as the best US ambassador ever sent to Cuba, yet 'our man in Havana' said

> Neither he nor his wife has been the success which was anticipated. He is considered to interfere too much in Cuban internal affairs ... The Cuban Government recently asked unsuccessfully for his removal ... he appears to be extremely inconsistent in his utterances; almost abject flattery of the Cuban government in public, together with biting criticism in private, which of course leaks out.[34]

On his service in Colombia, at a time when the security of the Panama Canal was vital to war strategy, Pan American Airways judged that 'Braden is the best god-damned ambassador we ever had in Colombia or anywhere else ...'[35] though the company's vice-president admitted that he finished up hospitalised as a result of conflict with Braden. Looking back on the turmoil in Argentina, all concerned found it incredible that Spruille Braden spent a mere four months there from 19 May to 23 September 1945 before his recall to Washington as Under Secretary of State for Latin America. He was a man who made a fabulous life out of his interest in Latin America and Simon Hanson said of his autobiography

> This is easily the most important book on Latin America and US policy towards Latin America to have appeared in the past thirty years.[36]

His assistant, some would say accomplice, was a Spaniard called Gustavo Durán Martínez,[37] who was a story in himself as creative writers quickly realised. He was a principal informant for Simone Terry in *Front de la liberté: Espagne 1937-1938* (Paris, 1938), the model for the communist, Manuel, in André Malraux's *L'Espoir* and appears by name in Ernest Hemingway's *For Whom the Bell Tolls*. It was intended that Paramount Pictures should employ him for the film version of Hemingway's classic novel with Gary Cooper and Ingrid Bergman. But when they were cautious Hemingway introduced him to Spruille Braden. Much more could be told about Gustavo Durán though what is most relevant here is that he is generally credited with part-authorship of the *Blue Book* on Argentina. Robert Potash wrote that:

The complete history of the Blue Book episode from its conception through its preparation to its release deserves a separate mono-graph.[38]

A considerable task force was appointed by James Byrnes to research the study and Braden claims that it rested on five tons of documentation for 130 pages of text.[39]

Its precise origins and purpose still require further research but here is a powerful hint of how Spruille Braden arrived at the method adopted for launching it. He says:

One day late in October 1945 I attended an urgent and important meeting held in Under Secretary Acheson's office. All the top echelons were there ... On Dean's desk was a book that without exaggeration was six inches thick and nearly a foot long. He said, 'It's all in here ...' The book was to go to the Hill that very afternoon ... He said, 'This is decided upon. If you have any objections they'll be thrown out...'[40]

The matter referred to here is not the Blue Book on Argentina but, more likely, some of the input which went into the creation of the modern CIA. But it is the *fait accompli* technique which probably appealed to Spruille Braden. The document officially called, *Consultation among the American Republics with Respect to the Argentine Situation* was issued without discussion with any Latin American government. The editor of the Argentine newspaper, *El Dia*, Hugo Stunz, suggested to Braden that it should be published to influence the elections by then scheduled for 24 February 1946 and Dr Enrique Mosca, running mate of Perón's opponent, José Tamborini, said he would welcome it.[41] Whether Braden had resolved to use it in the elections without such prompting from others is still not known. All supporters of the Blue Book hoped that it would discredit the group-ing made up of Nationalists, Conservatives, some Radicals, Labour, Army and Church, who were following Perón, though as yet, there was no Peronist Party as such, and influence voting in favour of José Tamborini's loose *Unión Democrática* made up of other Radicals, Socialists, Progressive Democrats and Communists. The expectation was that the vote would be turned decisively by revelations that Juan Domingo Perón had conspired to assist a victory of Nazi Germany in the Second World War.

The heart of the story was simply that Argentina had tried to purchase weapons from Germany during the war. An Argentine national of German origin, Oscar Hellmuth, had been engaged to conduct the negotiations. He was arrested in Trinidad with papers showing that Perón had arranged his travel and been a part of the arms deal. Perón was in the GOU which was, therefore, an arm of the German Secret Service. If Perón became president, Argentina would be a transplant to the New World of the Axis so recently defeated in Europe. The republic would be an international pariah seeking to draw other countries into a Fascist bloc threatening the democratic ideals for Latin America of the USA.[42]

Far from succeeding in its aims, some well-informed people, including President Perón, judged that the Blue Book intervention attracted a sympathy vote to the cause which won him the presidency. In subsequent elections, Perón always cleared about 10 per cent more than the 1946 vote of 52.40 per cent without backlash from direct US intervention, but against a continuing barrage of denigration. For the truth is that Braden's influence persisted longer in the academic sphere than in practical politics. While such authors as Robert Alexander,[43] George Blanksten,[44] Arthur Whitaker[45] and Jeanne Kirkpatrick,[46] slavishly expounded what could be called 'Bradenism', US Government policy established accommodation with Perón's regime. From May 1952, Ambassador Albert S. Nufer was developing a personal friendship with Juan Perón[47] and the visit of Milton S. Eisonhower in 1953 confirmed more cordial relations between Washington and Buenos Aires.[48]

The British also proved capable of combining a derogatory public line with private actions and policies which were more accommodating towards President Perón. For instance, it was known to the Foreign Office that Perón owned a large country house at Berkhampsted in Hertfordshire, which was kept up by Argentine Embassy staff from London.[49] The house was probably used by visiting friends and relatives such as Hector Campora and Juan Duarte.[50] There is no record of a visit to Britain by Juan Perón, but the prospect of an official one was discussed in Whitehall and it is intriguing to recall that Perón was known to travel incognito. Furthermore, when Perón was deposed in 1955 a senior member of the Foreign Office commented '... from a political point of view there would be no disadvantage and perhaps some advantage in our relations with Argentina to agree to give asylum if it is asked for.'[51]

The precedent of Juan Manuel Rosas[52] was cited and an ancestral link to Britain established through Perón's Scottish antecedents. Clearly, informed officialdom did not regard Peronism as a spent force, for the motive of this generosity was to earn the gratitude of a future Perón regime. To offset derisory gossip of a president sunk into dissipation from mid-1952 onwards, Whitehall had the awestruck reports of Sir Henry Mack that Perón '... arrives at his office from Monday to Friday at 6.20 a.m., remains there until after 12 noon, rests after luncheon and works in his house, if he has no speeches or public functions until 9 or 10 p.m. when he retires. He claims by this programme to make two days work out of the 24 hours'.[53]

A workaholic president is more convincing in accounting for the record 65 per cent won in congressional, provincial and municipal voting in 1954. The function of Lonardi's coup was not to depose a hopelessly discredited figure; it was the sole remaining means of preventing yet another resounding Peronist triumph in the coming presidential elections of 1957. That surely makes more sense in explaining why, despite the unexpected prolongation of exile into an eighteen years span, Juan Perón remained Argentina's most powerful politician, recalled as a last resort to tackle the national emergency of the 1970s.[54]

## Notes

1. Grateful acknowledgement is made to the University of Natal Research Fund for financing a field trip to Argentina, spent at the Instituto Torcuato Di Tella, Buenos Aires. For the first quotation see FO 371/114025, Rio de Janeiro to F.O., 8 Nov. 1955. A comment by an unidentified hand in the Foreign Office, London.
2. Dario Canton, *Materiales para el estudio de sociología política en la Argentina*, (Buenos Aires, 1968), 2 vols: Peter H. Smith, 'Las elecciones de 1946 y las inferencias ecológicas' in Manuel Mora y Araujo e Ignacio Llorente (eds) *El voto peronista: Ensayos de sociología electoral argentina*, Buenos Aires, 1980, 165-89.
3. F.W.S. Craig (ed.) *British Electoral Facts 1885-1975*, London, 1968, 2nd ed., 20; *Congressional Quarterley's Guide to United States Elections*, Washington, 1975, 293.
4. Lars Schoultz, *The Populist Challenge: Argentine Electoral Behaviour in the Post-War Era*, North Carolina, 1983; For a first class popular history see Felix Luna, *Perón y su tiempo*, Buenos Aires, 1984-6, 3 vols.
5. Colin Clark, *The Economics of 1960*, London, 1942.

6. Roger Gravil and Timothy Rooth, 'A Time of Acute Dependence: Argentina in the 1930s', *Journal of European Economic History* (Rome), 1978, 337-78.

7. Carlos F. Díaz Alejandro, *Essays on the Economic History of the Argentine Republic*, London, 1967, is the most technically sophisticated elaboration of this view. Not all of his readers realised that the late Professor Diaz was actually Cuban and much criticised by Argentine scholars for his unfamiliarity with the details of their country's history. See, for example, H.S. Ferns, *The Argentine Republic*, London, 1973.

8. British Economic Mission to the Argentine, Uruguay and Brazil: The D'Abernon Report (1929); Certain recent research proposes a drastic downward revision of such estimates see D.C.M. Platt, *Foreign Finance in Continental Europe and the USA 1815-1870*, London, 1984; D.C.M. Platt, *Britain's Overseas Investments on the eve of the First World War*, London, 1986.

9. Guido Di Tella and Manuel Zymelman, *Las etapas del desarollo económico argentino*, Buenos Aires, 1967, draws out the significance of this process. More generally see Alistair Hennessy, *The Frontier in Latin American History*, London, 1978.

10. Rosemary Thorp, *Latin America in the 1930s*, London 1984.

11. Most of the E.C.L.A. Reports on Argentina stress the technically retarded character of Argentine agriculture.

12. Though Alexander Gershenkron stresses the advantages of a late start, they have never been apparent in Latin America.

13. Jaime Fuchs, *Argentina: su desarrollo capitalista*, Buenos Aires, 1965, 227.

14. See Raul Prebisch's discussion Guido Di Tella and D.C.M. Platt (eds), *The Political Economy of Argentina 1880—1946*, London, 1986.

15. M.B.J. Finch, 'Three Perspectives in the Crisis of Uruguay' *Journal of Latin American Studies*, Vol. 3.

16. On earlier Radical use of this machine see David Rock, 'Machine Politics in Buenos Aires and the Argentine Radical Party 1912-1930', *Journal of Latin American Studies*, Vol. 4., November 1972.

17. In the enormous literature on the nature of Peronism two penetrating studies are Eldon Kenworthy, 'What Peronism Wasn't, *Comparative Politics*, 6,1, Oct. 1975, 17-45; Eldon Kenworthy, 'Interpretaciones ortodoxas y revisionistas del apoyo inicial del peronismo' in Manuel y Araujo and Ignacio Llorente (eds) *op. cit.* 191-218.

18. Joseph Page, *Perón: A Biography*, New York, 1983, is the most recent major study of his life and career.
19. FO 371/44714, Kelly to Bevin, 26 Oct. 1945, *The Times*, 17 Oct. 1945; *The Times*, 19 Oct. 1945.
20. FO 371/44714, Kelly to F.O. 12 Oct. 1945, makes clear that the *Manchester Guardian* and *Daily Herald* had reporters present in Buenos Aires.
21. Marysa Navarro and Nicholas Fraser, *Eva Perón*, London, 1980; Marysa Navarro, *Evita*, Buenos Aires, 1981. Albert Ciria, 'Flesh and Fantasy: The Many Faces of Evita (and Juan Perón)'. *Latin American Research Review*, 18, 2, 1983, 150-65, is a helpful guide to this untrustworthy literature.
22. David Kelly, *The Ruling Few*, London, 1952. However, Perón was so pleased with the two Argentine chapters in Sir David's memoirs that he had them translated into Spanish and published in Argentina as a booklet called *La traición de la oligarquia*. See Arthur P. Whitaker, *The United States and the Southern Cone*, Camb. Mass., 1976, 442.
23. George Pendle, 'The Revolution in Argentina' *International Affairs*, 32, 2, April 1956, 166-172 is the printed outcome of various talks which Mr Pendle was giving in 1955-6.
24. F.O. 371/119864, A.S. Fordham to Morgan Man, 4 June 1956 and various comments by Foreign Office staff.
25. All three of them went through several editions. George Pendle, *A History of Latin America*, London, 1963, was also a success.
26. F.O. 371/119865, A.S. Fordham to Selwyn Lloyd, 23 June 1956 includes a printed account of the abortive rising in Argentina on 9 June 1956; *The Times*, 12 June 1956; Robert Potash, *The Army and Politics in Argentina 1945-1962: Perón to Frondizi*, London, 1980, especially 230-236.
27. F.O. 371/114028, Memo by Mr Wilde, who attended an Anglo-Argentine Society lecture by George Bilainkin called 'Ushuaia to Iguazu' on 2 Mar. 1955; F.O. 371/114064, Memo by Mr Leadbitter, 27 May 1955, complains about anti-British articles in *La Prensa* by George Bilainkin. Ernest Bevin in 1947 ordered an investigation of this writer's activities in criticising British foreign policy. *Buenos Aires Herald*, 1 Nov. 1955.
28. *The Times* for 27 Aug. 1955, 5 Oct 1955, 6 Oct. 1955, 9 May 1956, 18 May 1956, 12 June 1956. The Foreign Office took particular exception to a two part article by Mr Hinkson called 'Balance Sheet after Perón', published in the first week of Oct. 1955. It attempted what might be called an 'evenhanded' treatment and

on this occasion the Embassy tried to counter Whitehall's disapproval.

29. *New York Times*, 10, 11, 12 and 13 April 1955. They were all datelined from Santiago in Chile, though it is said that Herbert Matthews spent two months of intensive study in Argentina. His conclusion was that Perón could not be overthrown, just as Arthur P. Whitaker had said in *Argentina and the United States*, New York, 1954. See Arthur P. Whitaker, *Argentine Upheaval: Perón's Fall and the New Regime*, New York, 1956, VII-IX.

30. Gary Frank, *Juan Perón vs Spruille Braden*, Lanham, 1980, is a compact account, though based entirely on secondary sources and one interview with Mr Braden given on 18 Feb. 1975.

31. (New York, 1971).

32. J. Lloyd Mecham, *A Survey of United States-Latin American Relations*, Texas, 1965, 399.

33. Hugh Thomas, *Cuba or the Pursuit of Freedom*, London, 1971, 730.

34. F.O. 371/33829, George Ogilvie Forbes to Mr Eden, 14 July 1943.

35. F.O. 371/25909, Paske Smith to Mr Eden, 1 March 1941 Simon G. Hanson, 'Diplomats and Demagogues: The Memoirs of Spruille Braden', *Inter-American Economic Affairs*, 25, 1971-2, 67-71. This testimonial is quoted on page 67.

36. Hanson, *ibid*, 70. But see Samuel L. Baily, *The United States and the Development of South America*, New York, 1976, 62-64.

37. David Caute, *The Great Fear*, New York, 1978, 330-8 has an account of Durán's experiences based on Durán's own files as detailed on p.599 footnote 12. See also Carlos Baker, *Ernest Hemingway: A Life Story*, New York, 1969, Penguin edition, 1972, 528-33, 543-4, 560-8, 571-7 and 682.

38. Potash, *op. cit.* 39.

39. Braden, *op. cit.* 356.

40. Braden, *ibid*, 350.

41. Potash, *ibid*, 41.

42. Albert P. Vannucci, 'The Influence of Latin American Governments on the Shaping of United States Foreign Policy: The Case of U.S. — Argentine Relations, 1943-1948'. *Journal of Latin American Studies*, 18, 2 Nov. 1986, 355-382; Callum A.MacDonald, 'The United States, Britain and Argentina in the years after the Second World War' in Guido Di Tella and D.C.M. Platt, *The Political Economy of Argentina*, London, 1986, 183; Callum A. MacDonald, 'The U.S., the Cold War and Perón' in Chris-

topher Abel and Colin Lewis (eds) *Latin America: Economic Imperialism and the State*, London, 1986, 405-413; The best Argentine works are Carlos Escudé, *Gran Bretaña, Estados Unidos y la declinación argentina 1942-1949*, Belgrano, 1983; Mario Rapoport, *Las relaciones anglo-argentinas; aspectos políticos y económicos: la experiencia del gobierno militar 1943-1955*; Buenos Aires, 1979, Mario Rapoport, *Gran Bretaña, Estados Unidos y las clases dirigentes argentinas 1940- 1945*, Buenos Aires, 1980: See also *Desarrollo Económico*, 23, 92, enero-marzo 1984, 627-636 for a debate between Escudé and Rapoport.

43. Robert Alexander, *The Perón Era*, New York, 1951; Robert Alexander, *Juan Domingo Perón: A History*, Boulder, 1979.

44. George I. Blanksten, *Perón's Argentina*, Chicago, 1953.

45. Arthur P. Whitaker, *Argentine Upheaval: Perón's Fall and the New Regime*, New York, 1956; and *The United States and Argentina*, Camb. Mass., 1954.

46. Jeanne Kirkpatrick, *Leader and Vanguard in Mass Society: A Study of Peronist Argentina*, Camb. Mass., 1971.

47. F.O. 371/114019, Buenos Aires to F.O., 18 Aug. 1955.

48. *New York Times*, 12 April 1953 lists the senior figures on this visit which took place 18-20 July 1953; F.O. 371/103118, P. A. Wilkinson to G.S. Jackson, 14 Aug. 1953.

49. F.O. 371/114060, F.O. Minute by I.F.S. Vincent, 23 Sept. 1955.

50. It was thought that the purpose of their visits was to check the loyalty of the embassy staff to the Perón regime and to adjust Evita's overseas investments.

51. F.O. 371/114060, F.O. Minute by I.F.S. Vincent, 23 Sept. 1955.

52. The full story of Rosas' British exile is told in John Lynch, *Argentine Dictator: Juan Manuel de Rosas 1829-1852*, Oxford, 1981, Chapter IX. Perón's Sardinian great-great-grandfather married a Scottish woman.

53. F.O. 371/108791, Sir Henry A. Mack to Sir Winston Churchill, 10 Sept. 1954.

54. Guido Di Tella, *Argentina under Perón: the Nation's Experience with a Labour-based Government*, Oxford, 1983; Felix Luna, *Argentina de Perón a Lanusse 1943-1973*, Buenos Aires, 1984; Jorge Luis Bernetti, *El peronismo de la victoria*, Buenos Aires, 1983.

# THE BRITISH EXPERIENCE
## IN ARGENTINA

# 6

# Neither Welsh nor Argentine; the Welsh in Patagonia

*Glyn Williams*

## Rationale of the settlement

In many respects the founding of the Welsh settlement in Patagonia, although it did not occur until 1865, was the product of a more general emergence of dissatisfaction among the various stateless nations of Europe. The break-up of multi-national political units, together with the new social formations which emerged within emerging industrial capitalism, contributed to dissatisfactions which were often expressed in terms of the desire among stateless nations to develop independent political units. Although Wales was enmeshed in the discourse of Britishness and Empire during the nineteenth century there were undercurrents of nationalism. Although the latter might be implicit in the former there was a tendency for the two to polarise.[1]

It was felt that the economy of Wales was disadvantageous to the Welsh and that English dominance was accompanied by cultural oppression which was expressed in terms of linguistic, educational and religious discrimination. As elsewhere in Europe emigration to the New World provided an escape. However, emigration to North America involved the rapid assimilation of Welsh immigrants. As a consequence there emerged a movement to find a location where Welsh emigrants could achieve political autonomy and establish a society where the Welsh language and culture could flourish.

While the initial impetus for this movement derived from Welsh immigrants in the USA the idea was quickly established among members of the new Welsh petit-bourgeoisie, numerically a small but important class in Wales and in Liverpool and Manchester. The majority of the early activists in the movement were young idealists who eventually left for Patagonia where their enthusiasm, dedication and ability were important in the development of the settlement. The patron of the movement was Michael D. Jones, one of Wales' most prominent and respected non-conformist ministers of the second half of the nineteenth century. Not only did he lend credence and respectability to the project, but he also sponsored it financially through his wife's modest inheritance. Indeed, most of the 3000 or so who joined the settlement between 1865 and 1915 were recruited and vetted through the chapels which were under the care of Jones and his associates.

## The early years

The initial group of 165 Welsh settlers arrived in the Lower Chubut Valley in July 1865 and for ten years their numbers scarcely increased. It was a period of considerable difficulty and hardship during which the survival of the settlement was often in doubt.[2] The Argentine government had made it clear that political autonomy was in no way possible but the promise was held out for some sort of political independence. The precise form of this independence was never clarified and the relationship between the Argentine government, the British Consul in Buenos Aires and the Welsh settlers revolved around this particular issue. For several years the settlers administered themselves by their own constitution drawn up before they left Wales. It involved a legal framework which allowed for political autonomy. It has been heralded as the first example of political democracy within South America and within its terms everyone, both male and female, over the age of eighteen was guaranteed a vote by secret ballot.

Most of the initial group of settlers were drawn from industrial centres but they had participated in earlier rural/urban migration and were familiar with the agricultural practices of rural Wales. It was these practices which they sought to emulate in the Lower Chubut Valley. The original intention was to practice a mixed economy involving the cultivation of wheat and sheep rearing together with guano extraction for export, and the cultivation of vegetable crops, dairy farming and fishing for domestic consumption. The Lower Chubut Valley is marginal for non-irrigation farming and although the settlers did raise crops almost to fruition the scarcity of rainfall prevented harvesting. Consequently during the early period of economic adaptation survival depended to a large extent upon trade with the native Americans and the hunting skills which they taught the settlers.

The settlers were cut off from Wales and dependent on the good will of the government for supplies. They had no choice but to accept the authority of the Argentine state. On the other hand the government was dependent on the Welsh to substantiate their claim to the whole of Patagonia. Not only was the settlement subject to practical constraints but the relationship with the British was ambivalent. The embassy at Buenos Aires kept surveillance over the settlers who were British subjects and over Patagonia in general where other British settlers, mostly Scottish sheep farmers, were to settle further south. Officials both in London and in Liverpool from where the settlers sailed unannounced were perplexed by the departure of the *Mimosa* in 1865 and went out of their way to rectify their ignorance. Once the settlement had been established the British government and the consulate in Buenos Aires were obliged to offer assistance if it was requested. During the early years of hardship units of the British navy from Montevideo were called upon to render aid and after 1869 naval vessels called in regularly at Puerto Madryn while on exercise.

Between 1865 and 1869 the leaders of the settlement skilfully manipulated British officials in their attempts to extract advantages from the Argentine authorities, exploiting their rights as British citizens. The contradiction between Welsh and British identity was not regarded as a problem even though to many settlers the very existence of the settlement was a means of escaping from British tutelage. At times they even enlisted the aid of various Welsh MPs with the aim of goading the Home Office into pressuring the Foreign Office and ultimately the British consul in Buenos Aires to take action on behalf of the settlers.

Nevertheless, it is clear from their reports that consular officials at Buenos Aires viewed the Welsh settlers with a mixture of arrogance and disdain, regarding them as ignorant peasants who had blundered into a part of the world where no one in their right mind would venture. Through their reports an erroneous picture of the settlement was formed in London. However, attitudes were modified once the settlement was recognised as a success and contacts had been made with the leaders of the settlement whose ability, knowledge and sense of purpose came to be reluctantly admired.

In Wales the organisers of the settlement had gone out of their way to recruit emigrants with a range of skills needed in the settlement as well as experienced farmers. During the early years much of the work was conducted on a reciprocal basis with craftsmen involved in construction and the farmers working their land in return. From 1869 much of the labour input involved the construction of canals by which water was drawn from the Chubut to irrigate the land which had to be levelled. This work was also undertaken on a corporate basis.

This was the process of immigration during the years 1865 to 1915 with one flow of immigration from Wales being followed by a period of consolidation and adaptation necessary to facilitate economic expansion and to accommodate further immigration. Waves of immigration occurred in 1865, 1874-6, 1881, 1885 and 1910 although immigration did not cease between these dates. In Wales the settlers were recruited through the non-conformist chapels and the Welsh language press. The wave of 1885 was somewhat distinct in that it involved the largest contingent of close to 500 recruited to construct a railway link between the Lower Chubut Valley and Puerto Madryn some forty miles to the north. This group consisted mainly of labourers who hoped to obtain land after the completion of the project. The original settlers had received 100 hectares of land but by 1885 all of the irrigable land had been allocated while some of the land which had been under cultivation since 1865 had deteriorated. This prompted the settlers to intensify their efforts to extend the settlement to the Andes. This was accomplished before 1890 and much of the immigration thereafter involved the recruitment of Welsh shepherds to pioneer the sheep-rearing units in the Andes and another agricultural offshoot at Sarmiento. Other features of the immigration process worthy of note was the tendency for single men, once established, to return to Wales in search of a spouse and the tendency for the majority of the immigrants to leave Wales in the autumn after the harvest there, arriving in Chubut in time for its harvest. Although many of those who sailed in 1865 were drawn from the lower middle class, fired by the political and cultural nature of the venture, the majority of the subsequent immigrants were proletarians seeking mobility to petit-bourgeois status.

Once a lucrative export economy based upon wheat cultivation had been established it became evident that a large part of the profits of this economy was falling foul of the price-fixing practices on the Buenos Aires-based merchant houses which held a monopoly on transportation to and from Chubut. Thus, at the end of the 1870s, the settlers established a Cooperative Society with individual producers marketing through this institution. Vessels were purchased and profits at the market maximised through choosing the appropriate time to sell. Trade links were also established further afield. Such profits were employed to purchase goods at wholesale prices in Buenos Aires which were 'sold' to the members at retail prices against credit in the stores which were established in Chubut. The profits were returned to the members in the form of an annual dividend. In a short time the 'Co-op' became an important credit agency as well as an economic advisory service for the entire community.

Within the settlement the immigrants were organised into chapel-based communities consisting of between 200 and 300 people living within a radius of about five miles of the respective chapels. Seventeen chapels were constructed in the Lower Chubut Valley and for functional reasons denominationalism was abandoned. Within these communities the social and spiritual life of the settlers was catered for and the diaries of the settlers at the turn of the century indicate that only on very few occasions were the majority of the population drawn out of their community. These communities were endogamous in nature with most of the marriages contracted being between members of the same or adjoining communities. Indeed the social relationships were so centripetal in nature that even though the settlers were drawn from a variety of dialect areas in Wales, these communities were beginning to develop their own unique Welsh dialects.

The future now seemed to be guaranteed but success removed some of the constraints on the Argentine government and a period of antagonism ensued. The ambiguity over the rights of the settlers had never been clarified as the settlement had never been integrated into the constitutional framework of the Argentine state. At times local antagonism between Argentine officials and the settlers verged on open conflict and various mediators of standing in Buenos Aires were drawn in to resolve the situation. They included such figures as the Chief of Police in Buenos Aires, an ex-Minister of the Interior, the Sub-secretary of Agriculture, the Administrator of Lands and Colonies and others. When these contacts failed to produce results the British authorities were also drawn in. One of the most significant episodes occurred during the Conquest of the Desert between 1879 and 1880.[3]

The Conquest of the Desert marked a crucial phase in the expansion of the frontier in response to land-hungry cattle barons and the need to reward political followers with land grants. But there were wider international implications. The insecurity of foreign settlements on the Pampas, where they were exposed to raids by the native Americans on whose lands they were encroaching, prompted the British, French and German governments to threaten to suspend further immigration unless the native Americans were exterminated. Faced by both domestic and international pressure, President Roca launched a genocidal campaign, reminiscent of, but even more drastic than the Indian wars of the United States. In the course of the

campaigns the majority of the indigenous population was slaughtered
or used as virtual slave labour.

During the first half of the nineteenth century, the Tehuelche had
been integrated into an unequal exchange economy based at Viedma
on the Rio Negro. A central feature of this integration was the
creation of an alcohol dependency among the Tehuelche in order to
entice them to trade. By the time the Welsh settlers settled further
south alcoholism was rife among the Tehuelche and this led them to
develop seasonal migratory patterns covering hundreds of miles in
order to reach the Rio Negro. Although it was not entirely adhered
to, the settlement's Council adopted a policy of not giving the native
Americans access to alcohol and they also established fairer trading
terms with them. The Argentine government had entered into a
treaty with the Tehuelche with reference to the lands occupied by the
Welsh but even so the settlers were aware of their trespass on
Tehuelche territory. At first they were paranoid about them to the
extent that it was agreed that should any of the Tehuelche approach
the settlement they would be killed in order to prevent their spreading knowledge of the settlement to their kin. Fortunately, this did not
occur and friendly relationships were established to the benefit of
both groups.

With the onset of the Conquest of the Desert the Tehuelche
*caciques* chiefs turned to the Welsh for assistance asking them to
intervene on their behalf. This they did, writing not only to the
Argentine authorities but also to the British Consul in Buenos Aires.
A similar protest to the latter was made by the Bishop of the Falkland
Islands. In turn the Welsh were accused of treason by the military,
of arming the Tehuelche, thereby impeding the 'pacification' of the
pampas. Nor did the settlers receive much sympathy from the British
Consul who wrote to London that there was little reason for reversing
the genocidal policy of the Argentine state since native Americans
were little better than animals and were holding up the progress of
the nation. This was one occasion when the British and the Argentine
state found themselves united in opposition to the Welsh settlers.

## The Law of the Territories

The Law of the Territories granted local self-government to localities
with a population in excess of a thousand. Such localities had the
right to formulate local laws, to collect taxes and to oversee public
works and local education. The law had been applied to Italian,

Basque and French groups but none of them had taken advantage of it. However, it was denied to the Welsh on the grounds that none of the settlers spoke Spanish and that the settlement had more schools and chapels than any other similar group in the Republic. In practice there was a gulf between the expectations and aspirations of the Welsh and official state policy which resulted in indecision and conflict over the role of the Welsh settlers and state officials throughout the Lower Chubut Valley, focussing on education, the legal system and local administration. State officials expected conformity in institutional matters at a time when the Welsh were in competition with these officials over legal and administrative control. Indeed, the community drew much of its strength from resisting the power of the state which was seeking to control it and enforce conformity to state norms. In Buenos Aires it was felt that the time had come to despatch civil and military officials to the settlement: 'in order to establish respect for the Argentine authorities.'[4] When this was attempted a British warship was despatched to oversee the situation.[5]

Much of the tension focused on the distinctive qualities of Welshness. The Welsh looked down on the Argentine educational system claiming that it was preoccupied with rote-learning while the state claimed that at least 200 of the Welsh settlers were illiterate.[6] Objection was also made to schoolbooks which contained such statements as: 'we Welsh of this colony came here to keep our language and customs'.[7]

In 1882 the settlers once again petitioned the government to be included under the Law of the Territories but not only were they refused but were accused of heresy and of promoting armed conflict. The military stationed in the region were instructed to 'take arms to defend the Argentine flag'.[8] The Welsh, in turn, refused to sign a document to the effect that they respected and accepted national authority in the area under the control of Argentine officials.[9] In these conflicts we can see the suspicion of the Argentine government of British motives and the fear that they might have designs on Patagonia — a view which was not entirely fanciful given the proximity of the Falkland Islands.[10]

## Nation equals state

In October 1884 the Law of the Territories was finally applied to the settlement and Chubut was made a Territory under a diplomatic and sympathetic governor. The next year a local council, Welsh in composition, was elected. The Welsh in Chubut were, in fact, the first group in Argentina to elect a local council under this law. They now had control over taxation, registration, education and public works and had the right to pass local laws. For the next fifteen years Welsh aspirations and the interests of the state were harmonised and conflict subsided.

However, the appointment of a new governor in 1895 who was a devout Roman Catholic and resented the numerical and economic superiority of the Welsh in the Lower Chubut Valley, generated a new series of conflicts. Latent tension surfaced over the issue of military training on Sundays which struck at the settlers' deeply held Sabbatarian beliefs. Over the next seven years, feelings over Sunday drilling were so intense that many of those affected were prepared to be imprisoned or left for Wales in order to avoid being drafted.[11] A mission was sent to Britain to solicit the aid of the government, and plans were even drawn up to remove the entire settlement to South Africa. Finally, President Roca was forced to intervene which he did in favour of the settlers. However, the basic conflict was more deep seated than that represented by the whim of an individual governor with religious prejudices.

Under the Law of the Territories, local government was subordinated to the Territorial level of administration. The territorial governor could intervene in local politics and could over-rule lesser bodies and officials. The municipal level of government was dominated by the Welsh settlers and this was resented by the non-Welsh:

> ...we have the formation of eminently Welsh municipalities whose sessions are held in a foreign language, and which completely forget their common interests by busying themselves in opposing all available means of assimilation of the foreign elements to the motherland that gave them bread for their children and that from pariahs converted them into free men sheltered by the glorious shade cast by the flag of May.[12]

This attitude, together with the recognition that most of the private sector of the regional economy was monopolised by the Welsh antagonised many local and regional administrators.

The case of the municipality of Gaiman illustrates the nature of the conflict at local level. No non-Welsh speaker was elected to the council before 1918 but in that year a retired military officer was sent to the village to organise the hitherto unorganised non-Welsh population. As a result, for the first time, non-Welsh speakers were

elected. The *Centro Progresista* was established which met every
Sunday to act as a forum for the non-Welsh population. In these
meetings the Welsh were criticised for their insularity, conservatism
and lack of patriotism in contrast to the 'progressive and patriotic
Latins ...'[13] In 1919 the *Liga Patriótica*, with its headquarters in
Buenos Aires, established branches throughout the Lower Chubut
Valley. These institutions represented the reaction of Argentine
politicians to non-patriotic threats to the state.

The Welsh response to these developments was through *Camwy
Fydd*, an obvious play on words of the *Cymru Fydd* nationalist
movement in Wales.[14] The non-Welsh lost their majority in the
Municipal Council in 1921 and only regained it twice prior to the
military government of 1943 — in 1927 and 1938. Control of this
council was important to the Welsh as it enabled them to safeguard
their economic interests as well as the sanctity of the Sabbath. The
Municipal Council also mediated between the Welsh population and
higher authorities in all disputes.

By the end of the century, the settlement had become economically
successful and an infrastructure laid down which enabled the Welsh
to control a large part of the rudimentary Patagonia economy. Fourteen branches of the 'Co-op' were opened in Chubut and Santa Cruz
and its activities extended to include the franchise of the Ford Motor
Company in the south. Little wonder that the Welsh settlement
became the most highly mechanised and one of the most successful
agricultural settlements in South America.

As the settlement's economic security increased, with its interests
now extending to the whole of Patagonia, so the state sought to
intervene more actively in its affairs. Whereas those engaged in
agricultural production, marketing and transport were Welsh, the
state bureaucracy was non-Welsh. The conflict that ensued thus had
a class, ethnic and economic dimension. Within Argentina there was
a new urgency as the pace of immigration from Europe quickened in
the 1890s posing new and acute problems of assimilating large
numbers of immigrants of Italian and non-Hispanic stock few of
whom became Argentine citizens. Among them were numerous anarchists and socialists who were active in the emerging labour movement. In response the state began to place more emphasis on patriotic
loyalty, claiming that the threat derived from the unwillingness or
inability of the immigrants to assimilate into national society. This
was held to be the reason why the state was not fulfilling its economic
potential. Patriotism held priority over ethnicity and thereafter anyone wishing to express their ethnic standing had first of all to declare

themselves as loyal Argentines. Education and the school system were seen as the instruments of nationalisation where the state was consolidated in the name of nation. To challenge this discourse was to challenge the whole concept of nation and to be labelled unpatriotic. In practice it reached the point where, among school children, to speak Welsh was unpatriotic. Welsh children were cruelly punished for speaking what for many, was the only language known to their parents. The situation was reminiscent of that which their fore-fathers had experienced under the English in Wales, a situation on which they had turned their back in favour of Patagonia. Similarly, to wish to sustain private sector ethnic institutions in the face of state appropriation was unpatriotic. Little wonder, therefore, that at the turn of the century, the government interpreted the conflicts in the Lower Chubut Valley in terms of the unwillingness of the Welsh to assimilate. To make the point Welsh teachers were removed to remote parts of the territory and were replaced with monoglot Spanish speakers.

## Institutional collapse and state intervention

The problems of conflict at the local level between the conflicting claims of the state and ethnicity were further exacerbated by the economic crisis of the 1920s and 1930s which severely affected the agricultural economy of the Chubut settlements as well as of Patagonia as a whole.

A collapse of wheat prices had led to a shift of emphasis to alfalfa production linked to expanding ranching activities in Patagonia. However, poor harvests, caused by bad weather and the *isoca llindys* plague in which caterpillars devoured the wheatcrop affected production. Wool prices also declined disastrously. These factors, coupled with mismanagement, resulted in the collapse of the Co-operative Society which was the mainstay of the Welsh economy as it controlled marketing and was the only source of credit.

The second key institution was the *Companía Unificada de Irrigación* (The Unified Irrigation Society) which in 1910 had brought together several irrigation societies on which agriculture depended. As in the Co-operative Society, officials were elected from among the community. The third institution was the English-owned railway company which was administered by members of the Welsh settlement.

During the inter-war years ethnic conflict centred on the local administrative bodies and on these economic institutions. Attempts to break the Welsh monopoly of the private sector were fiercely resisted but the collapse of the Co-operative Society during the Great Depression, and the expropriation of the Irrigation Society and the Railway Company under Perón undermined the institutional basis of the Welsh settlement and removed the backbone of their ethnic organisation.

During the Peronist period between 1943 and 1955 the municipalities did not function and so could not fulfil their mediating role. Administration was carried out by centrally-appointed commissioners who in every case were non-Welsh. It was this which facilitated the nationalisation of the Irrigation Society and the Railway Company during the 1940s. Since 1955 and the fall of Perón a new factor appeared as national political parties became active at Territorial and local levels. Local elections coincided with elections of the national President and Vice-President and of territorial representatives to Congress. The Welsh vote was thus split between the various national parties as none of them showed any concern to represent specifically Welsh interests.

For several generations the chapels had served as the focus on community life. It was through the chapels that social, cultural and religious activities were organised. Medical insurance was also organised through the chapels with members undertaking the day to day work of their sick neighbours who, through the insurance scheme, received free medical treatment at the British Hospital in Buenos Aires. With all of its activities conducted in Welsh the chapel was an important agency of language reproduction once the Welsh language had been abolished in state schools. This was all to change within a single generation and the main cause was the Perónist intervention in welfare matters. Compulsory medical insurance for the self-employed was introduced making the chapel's welfare activities largely irrelevant. Chapel attendance fell off abruptly.

Clearly with the collapse and nationalisation of the hitherto controlled economic institutions, the Welsh language was of little value for social mobility into private sector administrative posts. Also its agencies of reproduction were undermined: it was abolished in the schools. School officials not only punished children for using Welsh but also placed considerable pressure on their parents not to use the language in the home. Participation in chapel activities also declined. This, together with the stigmatic influence of peer group activities led to a rapid decline in Welsh language ability and use. Thus while most of the Welsh descendants over the age of forty still speak the language, the number of people under that age who speak it can be counted on two hands.

The collapse of the Co-operative Society deprived the Welsh not only of their only credit facilities but also of their only source of capital investment. Most members lost their savings and some even lost their farms. For the Welsh farmer, who, at the turn of the century, had been described as the most highly mechanised in South America, the possibility of capital investment in the enterprise rapidly disappeared, and for many self-sufficiency was essential in order to reduce overheads. At the end of the 1930s and during the 1940s much of the best agricultural land was sold to Italian and Spanish immigrants. A cultural division of land-use developed.[15] The Welsh cultivated alfalfa for the transhumant sheep rearing of the Patagonian plateau and livestock rearing on large enterprises. The Latins, on the other hand, practised a lucrative but risky market gardening on small plots of land. It was lucrative in terms of income per unit of land but less lucrative than the Welsh system in terms of income per unit of labour. The risk derived from the effects of produce imported from the Rio Negro upon local market prices. The Latins were able to overcome these risk elements because of the availability of reserve capital and credit from Spanish and Italian banks to tide them over the catastrophic years.

The two forms of agricultural practices involve different patterns of labour investment. The intensive practices involve an even annual distribution of labour which can be undertaken by family labour. Welsh farming practices, on the other hand, required heavy labour input at key times in the annual labour cycle. Originally this was satisfied by casual and migratory seasonal labour but the industrialisation of what is a sparsely populated area during the 1960s has pushed up the cost of labour beyond the reach of the Welsh farmer. As a consequence there has been an intensification of mutual aid practices involving near neighbours and near kin among the Welsh producers.

It is not surprising that these developments have witnessed a reassessment of the nature of the Welsh community among members of the out-group. The Welsh are no longer seen as an ethnic group marked by linguistic and religious features. Rather, they are seen as an occupational group with distinctive agricultural practices which involve close reciprocal ties based upon mutual aid.

# Conclusion

Since 1958, two important events have occurred to undermine the situation of the Welsh settlers in the Lower Chubut Valley. In that year Chubut became a province and a programme of regional development was initiated. One feature of this programme was the opening of the Fiorentino Ameghino dam two hundred miles upstream from the Lower Chubut Valley. This was heralded as of great benefit to the farmers in the Lower Valley since it would eliminate the periodic threat of floods. While this was indeed the case it also had the effect of raising the water table as well as the salt level in the soils to an extent that much of the land became sterile and most of the rest lost its previous level of productivity.[16]

The industrialisation of the Lower Chubut Valley was similarly heralded as of great advantage to the local farmer by increasing the local population and thereby extending local marketing potential. Again, the converse was the case since the opening up of road transportation to the north involved a reduction of transportation and other overheads to competing producers in the Rio Negro Valley. Consequently, the local market was flooded with produce from outside the area which undermined the local price structure.

Thus, in a short period of time, what was an agricultural landscape hewn from the hard work of the pioneers into a productive garden has become a virtual wasteland. The descendants of the Welsh pioneers are obliged to abandon their holdings or to live their life out on the little that their farms can produce. The majority leave the farms to work as a proletariat for a meagre wage in the new factories which have entered the area. It is the sad legacy of a rich culture and past.

The often tempestuous history of the Welsh in Chubut has left a generation of descendants who regard themselves first and foremost as Argentines. The recent acknowledgement of the role of the pioneers in securing the whole of Patagonia for Argentina and the interest shown by Welsh tourists in Chubut, has strengthened the identity of the Welsh descendants. Regular visits are made in both directions and attempts are made to stimulate interest in the Welsh language and elements of culture. Perhaps the tragedy of it all is that this re-awakening, as always, is too late and there is now a growing awareness that now the struggle for the survival of the Welsh language and culture lies not in Chubut but in Wales itself.

# Notes

1. Williams, Glyn; 'The Ideological basis of Nationalism in 19th century Wales: The Discourse of Michael D. Jones.' In G. Williams ed. *Crisis of Economy and Ideology*. B.S.A. Sociology of Wales Study Group, Bangor, 1983, pp.180-201.
2. Williams, Glyn; The Structure and Process of Welsh Emigration to Patagonia'. *Welsh History Review*. Vol. 9, No.1, 1976, pp.42-74.
3. Williams, Glyn; 'Welsh settlers and Native Americans in Patagonia'. *Journal of Latin American Studies*. Vol. 11, No. 1, 1979, pp.41-67.
4. *La Nación*, 28th March, 1979.
5. Public Records Office, Manuscript No. Adm. R O 147/1.
6. National Library of Wales, Manuscript No. 12200A.
7. Library of the University College of North Wales, Bangor, Manuscript No. 7623.
8. *Ibid*, manuscript no. 12280A.
9. *Ibid*, manuscript no. 7623.
10. Public Records Office, Manuscript No. Adm RO 147/1.
11. Williams, Glyn; *The Desert and the Dream: The History of the Welsh Colonization of Chubut*. University of Wales Press, Cardiff, 1975. Interestingly, a small Boer colony was established in Argentina to escape control by the British in South Africa.
12. *Avisador General de Chubut*, August 17 1898.
13. *Avisador Commercial*, August 3 1918.
14. Camwy is the Welsh name for Chubut and 'Camwy Fydd' translates as the 'Welsh settlement will be victorious'.
15. Williams, Glyn; 'Differential Risk Strategies Among Farmers in the Lower Chubut Valley, Argentina'. *American Ethnologist*. Vol. 3, No.2, 1976, pp.65-84.
16. Williams, 1978. 'Industrialisation and Ethnic Change'. *American Ethnologist*. Vol. 5, No.3, 1978, pp.618-32.

# 7

# Argentina and the Falklands (Malvinas) — the Irish Connection

*Dermot Keogh*

Some people attending the Eucharistic Congress in Dublin, in 1932, may have come into possession of the booklet, *A Short History of Irish Catholic Action in Argentina.*[1] It was one of the many publications which appeared at the time to celebrate the biggest home coming of the Irish Catholic diaspora in recent history. Irish-Argentines were strongly represented. In 1975, the *Southern Cross* published a centenary edition which told the popular history of the Irish in Argentina. Other similar publications on the same topic could be cited. This genre of commemorative immigrant literature is familiar to the student of the Irish diaspora in Canada, the United States, Britain or Australia. While the history of the Irish in Argentina has been well served by a number of fine studies,[2] the country still remains relatively unexplored by scholars.

A diplomatic report, written by T.J. Horan at the Irish Embassy in Buenos Aires in the late 1950s, stresses economic stagnation in Ireland and the growth of the wool industry in Argentina as twin factors which encouraged emigration to South America in the nineteenth century. In 1823, Colonel John Thomond O'Brien, a County Wicklow man, who had distinguished himself in the wars of independence and had been the *aide-de-camp* of General San Martín, was given a commission to bring out colonists from Ireland. The scheme was not successful but O'Brien was said to have opened offices in Dublin and elsewhere — making the existence of Argentina known in certain parts of Ireland. The Irish diplomat reported:

> In 1824 the Argentine Government with a view to improving the native breed, imported 100 marino (*sic*) sheep and these were purchased by an Irishman named Sheridan who was in partnership with an Englishman named Harret. Here we have evidence that the Irish were already in the sheepfarming business ... Since they (the emigrants) came mainly from such midland counties as Meath, Westmeath, Longford and Monaghan and also from Wex-

ford. Perhaps a fillip to their emigration was the policy of the
landlord aristocracy which in that part of Ireland was then beginning to concentrate on the destruction of the small farm and the
creation of the great cattle ranch. If that is so, it is one of history's
little ironies that our emigrants came to Argentina to assist in
building up a system and a class the creation of which in Ireland
has led to their own emigration'.[3]

One contemporary source cited in the Irish diplomatic report, gave
the number of Irish in the area of Buenos Aires by 1848 as 4,500 —
but that figure may be too high. The Irish Hospital was founded in
Buenos Aires in 1848 to help tend the immigrants who arrived ill
after the hardships of the sea-journey to the River Plate which
sometimes took up to four months. Within a year, the hospital had
dealt with 156 cases. In 1856 the hospital was taken over by seven
nuns from the Irish Sisters of Mercy.

### Irish and Irish-Argentine Population in Argentina (1895)

| Province | Irish | Irish-Argentines | Total |
|---|---|---|---|
| Capital fed. | 915 | 1937 | 2852 |
| Buenos As. | 3778 | 9654 | 13432 |
| Catamarca | 1 | 6 | 7 |
| Córdoba | 42 | 216 | 258 |
| Corrientes | 24 | 127 | 151 |
| Entre Rios | 78 | 315 | 393 |
| Jujuy | 16 | | 16 |
| La Rioja | 1 | | 1 |
| Mendoza | 4 | 37 | 41 |
| Salta | 2 | 22 | 24 |
| San Juan | 4 | 44 | 48 |
| San Luis | 2 | 36 | 38 |
| Santa Fe | 504 | 719 | 1223 |
| Tucuman | 8 | 35 | 43 |
| Chaco | 17 | 11 | 28 |
| Chubut | 5 | 2 | 7 |
| Misiones | 5 | 11 | 16 |
| Neuquen | 1 | | 1 |
| La Pampa | 15 | 8 | 23 |
| Rio Negro | 2 | 13 | 15 |
| **Total** | **5407** | **13210** | **18617** |

Eduardo Coghlan estimated that there were about 18,000 Irish-Argentinians by 1895. He has compiled the table on p. 124 which shows the distribution by provinces.[4]

Coghlan's industry has helped provide a wealth of data and answers to a number of questions.[5] He has shown that the great influx of Irish emigrants came in the post-famine period, the majority of whom settled either in Buenos Aires or in the surrounding province. It would appear that some were quite successful in securing a good living. Many of the prosperous Irish owed their success to the growth of sheep-farming. Professor Rock has argued:

Wool exports rose accordingly, from 300 tons in 1829 to 7,600 tons in 1850, then more than doubled to 17,000 tons in 1860, and increased threefold in the next five years to 55,000 tons. Subsequently the pace of expansion slackened, but continued its upward course, with wool remaining the largest export earner until after 1900 ... The expansion of the wool economy led to substantial changes in pampas rural society. Such tasks as shearing, carting the fleeces, and constructing fences and sheds attracted a larger population onto the land. Sheep farming was also more suitable to family labour than cattle ranching and thus helped augment the rural female population. In some measure the rise of sheep farming helped break up the largest of the *estancias*, as the luckier shepherds — the Irish being the best example — gathered the capital to set themselves up as landowners, usually on small plots under 1,750 hectares in size.[6]

Post-famine emigrants from Ireland, although they only formed 2.47 per cent of foreigners registered in the country in 1869, moved to the land — unlike the vast majority of their fellow countrymen in North America — and established themselves as an economic force. The diplomatic report already referred to quotes from *La Nación Argentina* of September 1862:

On Saturday last sold by auction .... about three-fourths of a square league of land for the sum of $1,010,000 m/c ... the largest price ever known in this country. It is unnecessary to state that the purchaser was an Irishman. Who can pay $1,010,000 for three-fourths of a league except an Irishman? ... The fact is that Irishmen pay for land what no one else can afford: and hence are becoming owners of some of the best lands of the Province. There are whole counties in the north belonging exclusively to Irishmen.

At this rate no one can compete with them. Persevering and laborious, their aspiration, their leading passion is a flock of sheep and after that a piece of ground whereon to feed them. Thanks to this the Irishmen for ten years back have been working an incredible revolution in the country. In the midst of wars, in spite of disturbances, drought and depreciation of produce they have kept up the value of land and gradually increased the figure up to an amount which the most sanguine could never have expected ... We hope they will continue to buy land by the Million'.[7]

In the first edition of the Hiberno-Argentine paper, the *Southern Cross*, on 16 January 1875, an editorial commented on the progress of the Irish community:

In no part of the world is the Irishman more respected and esteemed than in the province of Buenos Aires; and in no part of the world, in the same space of time, have Irish settlers made such large fortunes. The Irish population in this Republic may be set down at 26,000 souls. They possess in this province Buenos Aires 200 leagues of land (and our calculation is rather under the mark), or 1,800 miles, or 1,500,000 acres. Almost all the land is of the very best quality. They own about 5,000,000 sheep and thousands are worth 600,000,000 m/c or 5,000,000 L. sterling. This vast fortune has been acquired in a few years.[8]

By the end of the nineteenth century, Korol and Sabato estimate that between 10,000 and 15,000 Irish had arrived in Buenos Aires. Most had settled in the same province where they became shepherds, farmers and landowners and transformed themselves into a rich, powerful and stratified community. By 1890 some formed part of 'the rural bourgeoisie of Buenos Aires'. About one hundred families of landowners were fully integrated into the bourgeoisie, thus leaving behind many of their fellow countrymen and women. Others remained middle range landowners — farmers — who are described by Korol and Sabato as part of the petit rural bourgeoisie. Future research will examine the degree of stratification within the Irish communities. But Horan's report pointed to the significant social cleavage that existed between Irish landowners and Irish labourer:

These Irish landowners, who devoted themselves to sheep-farming and at a later stage to cattle-raising, needed labour. Where were the new land-owners to get labour? Not in Argentina itself where there was no supply of labour, cheap or dear; where the countryside was in any event thinly populated and where the 'gaucho' would work for nobody ... The new Irish landowners were thus forced to turn elsewhere for the labour which they needed. Naturally enough they turned to the country from which they themselves or their fathers had come, and particularly to counties such as Meath, Westmeath, and Longford, where doubtless so many of them once had their homes. From these places they brought out to Argentina the workers they needed. As one oligarch put it to me his father and grandfather brought them out 'by the shipload...'[9]

The Irish diplomat felt there was some substance to that latter view. Horan reported that in January 1889, a ship called the *City of Dresden* sailed from Cork for Buenos Aires with 1,800 passengers aboard: 'These had been rounded up and induced by the specious promise of two agents of the Argentine Government with Irish names', wrote Horan, 'to try their fortune under the Southern Cross'. But when the vessel arrived in the River Plate the immigrants discovered that no arrangements whatsoever had been made by the authorities for their reception. The majority wound up in the south of Buenos Aires among the very poor of the city.

Did a shared nationality mitigate the social distinction between 'oligarch' and Irish peon? The *estanciero* was top of the social scale. Horan was convinced that the majority of those who came out between 1840 and 1870 'were destined to be the hewers of wood and drawers of water for their more fortunate brethren who had emigrated a generation or two earlier.' He concluded:

The result of this mass immigration from Ireland, while it was an excellent thing for Argentina inasmuch as it helped to populate and develop the pampa, was the creation in the Irish community itself of something like a feudal society composed of landowners, and that means the owners of very vast tracts of land indeed, so vast that land is measured not in acres and not in hectares but in square leagues, and their labourers. The vast bulk of Irish immigrants to the Argentine were thus landless peasants who normally could never hope to be anything else but farm labourers on an *estancia*.

Horan argued that the majority of the immigrants went into sheepfarming on the *estancias* and were given little huts for their families, called *puestos* or posts, where their task was to look after a

certain tract of land and the sheep on it: 'The big majority of these
*puesteros* and their children could, in the normal course of events,
never hope to be anything but farm labourers.'[10] The large numbers
of Irish in Argentina created a significant pastoral problem for the
Catholic Church. English- and Irish- speaking priests were required
to minister to them. Happily, the records of the missionary effort in
Argentina provide a very rich source for the study of the Irish
community in that country.

The evolution of the Irish community in Argentina during the
nineteenth century was influenced by a number of major personalities. Admiral William Brown, 'an Irish-born deserter from the
British Navy', is very well known.[11] But perhaps the single greatest
influence on the way in which the Irish emigrant community developed in Argentina was exercised by an Irish Dominican, Anthony
D. Fahy, from Loughrea in County Galway who came to Buenos Aires
in 1842 where he ministered until his death in 1871.[12]

Fahy was not the first Irish priest to work in Argentina. Thomas
Field SJ came to the River Plate area in 1587. A number of other Irish
names can be found in the missionary history of the area for the
seventeenth and eighteenth centuries. The son of an Irish doctor
working in Manchester, Thomas Falkner SJ, is among the better
known. He ministered in the River Plate area from his ordination in
1740 up to the expulsion of the Jesuits in 1767, in Córdoba and in
other states. In the nineteenth century a Dominican called Burke was
working in the area from 1802 until the time of his death in 1828
when the Irish population in Buenos Aires was about 500. Patrick
Moran SJ was sent by Archbishop Murray of Dublin in 1829. He died
within a year and was succeeded in 1831 by Patrick O'Gorman who
worked in the city as Irish chaplain until his death in 1847 at the age
of forty-six. Fahy, who was a friend and supporter of Juan Manuel de
Rosas, had been educated at San Clemente in Rome and had spent
ten years working in Kentucky and Ohio before coming to Buenos
Aires. He set up an Irish chaplaincy in St Roch's church in Buenos
Aires and that was an 'interim' Irish church for more than thirty
years.[13] While the Irish remained in or near the small towns on the
plains of Buenos Aires, Fahy arranged to visit the centres at specific
times. With the influx of Irish after the famine, Fahy actively discouraged settlement in Buenos Aires. 'Do not hang about the port or the
city' Fahy advised Irish emigrants but 'Go out into the camp and get
work on a sheep-run'. While Fahy cannot be held solely responsible
for the Irish drift to the land, he has been popularly given the credit
for it. Horan, in his diplomatic report, accepted that view:

It was Father Fahy who was mainly responsible for making the Irish settle in the 'camp' in large numbers. In this he was farseeing. Quite clearly those who took his advice in those days did well for themselves and acquired land, wealth and social position. But his foresight had other results, unfortunate results, which he could hardly have foreseen. His policy resulted in the creation of a large population of landless serfs, an Irish rural proletariat, and thus had consequences which affect to this day the status of the Irish in Argentina. From the Irish colonization in Argentina no middle class developed.[14]

Unlike the Welsh, who settled in Chubut in the south, the Irish diaspora was very scattered. That made the task of the Irish chaplains all the more difficult. 'Stations' and 'Mass houses' were set up and they were visited by either Fahy or his assistants. Fahy paid for the education of a number of priests at All Hallowes Seminary in Dublin.[15] In the 1850s and 1860s about eleven came and were posted to various parts of what became known as the Irish Chaplaincy in Argentina. The first was at Capilla del Señor and the second at Lobos. Others were established later at Lugan, Mercedes, San Antonio de Areco, Carmen de Areco, Santa Lucia, Rosario and Navarro.[16]

The Falkland Islands (Malvinas) were part of the Irish Chaplaincy and Fahy felt obliged to take particular interest in looking after the spiritual welfare of the Irish there although — contrary to the folklore — he never visited the area himself.[17] There is no doubt that the islanders stood in need of pastoral guidance. Governor Rennie reported in 1849:

It is scarcely possible to conceive a greater state of apathy, destitution, and drunkenness, than is found among the lower classes more particularly the English and Scotch. The Irish and foreigners are less addicted to intemperance; but equally devoid of industrious habits generally. A few creditable examples are, however, to be found, and it is upon this small minority, with fresh emigration, that I must rely'.

By 1865, there may have been as many as 300 Irish on the Falklands (Malvinas).[18]

Christofer Murry[19] wrote to Archbishop Paul Cullen of Dublin on 2 September 1853: 'There are upwards of three and four hundred Catholics settled on this island and a probability of a greater number in a short time.' He stated that 'as we have no clergyman of our faith to administer the consolation of religion we have taken into consideration the necessity of applying for one.' Murry outlined the islanders terms:

> Your Grace we consider the best person to apply to as head of the Irish church. We will pay the passage and send home fifty pounds to pay the outfit of any clergyman that may be approved by Your Grace. His salary here would be one hundred pounds exclusive of other sums arising from marriages and christenings. In the course of time the salary would naturally be increased by the increase of population. The government will pay one half of the salary and the people the remainder.

Murry warned that there was a 'protestant clergyman' coming 'here in a short time and, unless we get out a priest, I fear he will pervert a great many of our people'. He told the Archbishop that they had a stipendary magistrate — E. Montaga — 'who is a Catholic and he is very anxious to have a priest here also.' Murry said that they would forward the money if it could be arranged for a priest to reside on the island: 'The island is very healthy — provisions are cheap and we acquire our letters from Europe every two months. The rapid communication by steam brings us much nearer to Europe than formerly.'[20]

In 1857, Fr. Laurence Kirwan, an All Hallowes student who had been ordained in Montevideo, was placed under the authority of Fahy. He was sent to the Falkland Islands a year later. Kirwan arrived on St. Patrick's Day. The islanders passed a vote of thanks to Fr. Fahy for sending them a priest. A committee was formed to raise money to build a church in Port Stanley; it was made up of Thomas Havers, treasurer, P.D.Lynch, secretary and Patrick Maguire and Murry. The committee addressed an appeal to the Governor of the islands, Colonel Thomas E.L. Moore. The governor stated that before a site could be granted for a church and cemetery the committee would have to raise £500. The committee then wrote to Fahy who appealed to Cardinal Wiseman of Westminster. But it was not until 1861 that a grant was made of half an acre to Thomas Havers, his wife Maria Clara and Fahy. They were given permission to build a church and have a Catholic graveyard. The property was vested in Havers who was a British citizen. When Havers and his wife left the islands very soon afterwards, the property passed to the Archbishop of Buenos Aires who named Fahy and James Carroll — both British citizens —

as trustees. The islanders had, however, to wait for over a decade
before a permanent structure was erected.[21]

The Catholics on the island proved to be very persistent. They were
less than satisfied with the occasional visit of priests and for over ten
years they corresponded with the Cardinal Secretary of Propaganda
in Rome, the Archbishops of Dublin and Westminster and the Bishop
of Southwark. The Catholic islanders wrote to Cardinal Barnabo in
late 1858. He referred their inquiry to the Archbishop of Dublin in a
letter dated 10 February 1859:

> I have received a petition of the Catholic inhabitants of the Fal-
> kland Islands to the Congregation of *Propaganda Fide* the object
> of which was to obtain the necessary aid to the spiritual wants of
> the Catholics established there. In reference to the said Petition I
> am very happy to state that letters have been already directed to
> the Representative of the Holy See at Buenos Aires, in order that
> a Priest may be sent by him to the Falkland Islands to administer
> the Sacraments and to give the consolations of religion to the
> Catholic people.

Barnabo wrote at the same time to the Bishop of Southwark
requesting him to make

> an application to the English Government, that a Chaplain may
> be established in the Falkland Islands to assist the Catholic
> Soldiers, who are there stationed. The Priest from Buenos Aires
> will offer to the Holy See an exact report of the conditions of religion
> in the Islands, and after that I hope your wishes will be entirely
> satisfied. If before the arrival of a Priest in the Falkland Islands,
> any children should require to be baptised, you are aware that any
> layman or woman may administer that sacrament according to the
> form laid down in the Catechism, and I pray that God may bless
> you.[22]

On 11 February 1859, the Bishop of Southwark, Grant, wrote to
Woodlock looking for information about the Falkland Islands. He
wanted to know whether there was anything in his correspondence
to 'show the number of Catholic (Irish) inhabitants'. He mentioned
that the number of soldiers on the islands was about thirty. Grant
asked Woodlock whether he had any priest for the islands 'if we can
get means to support him?'[23] Grant wrote to Woodlock again on 30
March 1859: 'The Propaganda seems disposed to follow your sugges-

tion about placing the Falkland Islands under Buenos Aires and has sent to ask the Bishop of the latter about it.'[24] But on 30 March 1859 — the same day as Grant had written to Woodlock — Fahy wrote to Woodlock regarding the Falklands:

> It would be necessary to apply to the English Government for support for a priest as the people there are mostly old pensioners. It is a wretched climate as neither tree or plant can grow there for the continuous blast from the South.[25]

On 28 May 1859, Fahy explained to Woodlock that he had received a letter from the apostolic nuncio 'asking me to go to the Falkland Islands to give a mission but I sent him an apology as I cld. not abandon this mission on any account.' He told the President of All Hallowes that 'the English government should be asked for an Irish chaplain for the islands especially as all the old pensioners are mostly Catholic.' He warned however, that it was 'almost impossible' to live there 'and I am sure unless a priest gets a good salary it will be difficult to get one to continue there.'[26] On 28 June 1859, Fahy warned Woodlock against sending anyone young and inexperienced to the Falkland Islands: 'I hope you will not think of sending anyone of our young men to the Falkland Islands. That place will require a person of some experience and a strong constitution.'[27]

Fahy wrote to Woodlock on 28 October 1859 reporting that he had received a letter from Havers of the Falkland Islands:

> 'I received a letter some time since from the Nuncio — stationed up the Parana, asking me to go — or to name some priest that I cd. recommend for that mission. I replied that it was absolutely impossible for me to leave, nor did I know any suitable person here that wd. go there. It wd never answer to send any young man there, nor can any priest live there unless supported by the government or the Propaganda. I have spent a large sum of money already on the priest who visited that Island and I am too much involved in difficulties to attempt more. I will send some prayer books and catechisms by next packet to J.W. Havers whose zeal and chris-tianity is deserving the sincere thanks of the ecclesiastical amt. to about two hundred including several Spanish farmers — the voyage from here is generally about three weeks — the climate is dreadful and the soil more barren than the Bog of Allen — unless a priest can get a good salary I don't see what inducement can be held out on the part of the people there for all are poor.'[28]

Fahy wrote to Woodlock on 28 December 1859 requesting that Propaganda Fide send prayer book and catechisms to the Falkland Islands as he had 'sent all I could spare there lately.'[29]

Woodlock had written to Havers explaining that they did not have a priest for the Falklands. He urged him to get in touch directly with Fahy whose bishop had jurisdiction for the islands. He felt sure that if they could get one Propaganda Fide it would help pay for the upkeep of a priest.

Woodlock wrote to Fahy that he had received a 'most saddening' letter from 'good Mr Havers of the Falkland Islands' and asked 'what can we do for the poor man and the other poor souls there?' Woodlock told Fahy:

I wrote to him by this mail — but I scarcely know what to say — I have had a conversation on the subject with our good archbishop ... He agrees with me that the best course practically would be: that you should send a priest to visit them once or twice a year — you might do so at the beginning and towards the end of your good season.[30]

Woodlock wrote to Fahy again: 'By this mail I have had a letter from good Mr Havers of the Falkland Islands — The sad state of the poor Catholics there pierces all our hearts: but what can we do? I do not see any way to help them.' He suggested to Fr. Fahy that his local bishop should press Propaganda Fide for a special grant for the support of a priest on the islands. In making his application, Woodlock warned, that the bishop should 'be carefull to explain, how the Falkland Islands, although under his jurisdiction, are in circumstances totally different from B. Ayres, which is supposed to be a Catholic country, while they are Protestant.' But on 28 July 1860, Fahy wrote to Woodlock that the Bishop of Buenos Aires was not in a position to undertake the chaplaincy work of the Falklands. He, too, was not in a position to do it either. Fahy recommended that since the islands were under British civil authority they were better attended from an English or Irish diocese.

Fahy was finally forced to take responsibility for the pastoral work of the islands. All efforts to get support from either Propaganda Fide or the British government had failed. Patrick Dillon, the founder of the *Southern Cross* newspaper, went to the islands on 27 November 1864 where he remained for three months. Dillon who came from Ballyhaunis in County Mayo was a brilliant preacher. He was an adviser to the Argentine bishops at the First Vatican Council and was elected to the Argentine Senate. Dillon, however, did not spend any more time on the Falklands. The islands were visited irregularly during the late 1860s by Irish chaplains and the Falklanders had to wait for their church. The first permanent church on the island was opened by Fr. James Foran at Port Stanley in 1875 and was dedicated to Our Lady, Star of the Sea. He had taken over from William Walsh who had been sent to the Falklands in 1872. Foran also opened the first Catholic school on the islands. He served there for almost fifteen years, returning to the mainland during the winter to preach missions for the Irish communities in the Province of Sante Fe. (But he had spent five consecutive years on the islands before he began the practice of going to the mainland during the winter months.)

Foran has left the following account of his mission in the Falkland Islands (Malvinas):

When I took charge of the mission ten years ago, I hoped to make its real state known at Rome and thereby secure a permanent supply of priests for the Catholics of those islands. I received my powers direct from Rome. My Bishop was requested by the Sacred Congregation of Propaganda to place no obstacle in the way of my departure. When I had been five years on the islands, making very slight progress, I requested to be allowed to remove for a portion of each year to this archdiocese. After some delay the favour was granted, and I was requested to send a report of the state of the mission. In doing so, I urged in the strongest terms I could command the importance of uniting the Falkland Islands and the southern portion of this continent in a Vicariate. I stated that myself and another priest at Punta Arenas in the Straits of Magellan were the only Catholic priests south of the Rio Negro. Two years later I learned that steps were being taken to place those regions under the care of the Salesian Fathers, who had already charge of Patagones. I am glad now to know that a Bishop is appointed, and that he will soon visit the Falklands and place the islands under the care of his priests.[31]

In 1888, the Salesians took over the mission. But that was not the end of Irish involvement. Priests were needed who could work in English. One of the first Salesians sent to Port Stanley was Patrick Diamond. He was accompanied by Mgr. Fagnano. After two years, Diamond was replaced by a Fr. Mignone who remained until his death in 1937. He was succeeded by an Irish priest called Drumm who was replaced by a Fr. Kelly. However, very few of the original

Irish remained on the Falklands (Malvinas). They seem to have regarded the place as providing an opportunity to accumulate capital before moving on to the mainland.

Meanwhile, on the mainland, a number of Irish clergy served the scattered Irish communities. In 1863, Fr. Michael Leahy from Co. Kerry, arrived in Argentina. A year later he was posted to Carmen de Areco in the Northern part of the Province of Buenos Aires. He spent much of his time visiting the scattered Irish community on horseback. He built four chapels two of which still stand, one at San Patricio called St Michael and Mel's and the other, Kilallen Chapel, at Castilla. He opened a boarding school in Carmen de Areco and ran libraries stocked with books brought from Ireland. Leahy's brother, John Baptist, was also ordained for Argentina and arrived there in 1869. He worked in the same area until his health broke and he died at sea, off the coast of Spain. Michael Leahy died in Mendoza in 1884.

Father William Gannon arrived in 1863 and worked at Capilla del Señor. He worked through the great cholera epidemic of 1867. He went to the United States in 1881 and returned to Capilla a few years later. He died in 1888. Three other Irish priests, Patrick Lynch, Samuel O'Reilly and Thomas Mulleady came to Argentina in 1867. Lynch worked at Mercedes and died in 1880. O'Reilly worked in Lujan and transferred to Mercedes in 1880. He moved to Chivilcoy where he was chaplain for thirty years. Mulleady was appointed to San Antonio de Areco after a short time in Chascomus and remained there for thirty years. He died in Ireland in 1909. Edmund Flannery from Cork went to Argentina in 1869 where he was appointed chaplain of San Pedro in the northern part of the Province of Buenos Aires. He built a church at Santa Lucia. He died in 1923.

In the 1860s Joseph Kirwan, who had ministered on the Falklands (Malvinas) was also chaplain at Lujan. He was succeeded by Thomas Carolan and then by Samuel O'Reilly. In 1879, an Irish Vincentian, Henry Gray, was made chaplain to the district. He spent over thirty years in the region. He died in 1928.

In the province of Santa Fe, the Irish community was also quite numerous and at one time the district of Venado Tuerto was predominantly settled by the Irish. The city of Rosario was also a centre of activity for the Irish chaplaincy.

Most of the credit for the work of the Irish chaplaincy in this period must go to the indefatigable Fahy. From shortly after his arrival in Buenos Aires on 13 June 1843 until his death on 20 February 1871, the Dominican was 'the effective ruler of the community'. Horan found that, as late as 1958, 'to this day his name is a legend among them'. He was 'evidently a dominant personality and this allied to his clerical status gave him a position of preponderating influence in the community such as no one has ever had since'. Fahy had not only been pastor to the Irish community 'but he was also their friend and counsellor, their financial adviser and even their marriage broker'.[32]

The Archbishop of Buenos Aires, sent a petition to Rome after Fahy's death looking for help to provide chaplains for the Irish community. He told the Vatican that there were about 28,000 Irish in the Province of Buenos Aires settled over about 7,400 leagues. 'The future of the Irish is sad', he wrote, 'unless a timely remedy is brought to them'. It was necessary to establish missions in the countryside 'in order that the people may be instructed in the faith, and taught to practice its most holy precepts'. [33] Largely as a result of that appeal, the interim arrangements established by Fahy to educate men in All Hallowes for Argentina have ended. The Passionist and Pallottine Fathers took over the chaplaincy work and education of Irish immigrants. The Irish Sisters of Mercy continued their work in Argentina and ran a hospital and an orphanage in Buenos Aires. They also ran a school in the capital and schools in Mercedes and Chascomus. After a brief period when they were forced to go to Australia, the Irish sisters returned and expanded their work in the country. The Irish Christian Brothers also opened schools in Argentina.

By the beginning of the twentieth century, the successors of Fahy

### Irish Emigration to Argentina, 1925-1946

|           | Arrivals | Departures | Balance |
|-----------|----------|------------|---------|
| 1925-1930 | 938      | 259        | 679     |
| 1931-1940 | 1006     | 157        | 849     |
| 1941-1946 | 80       | 10         | 70      |
| **Total** | 2024     | 426        | 1598    |

had built up a strong pastoral and educational structure for the Irish diaspora in Argentina. But the fall-off in emigration placed fewer demands on those services. There was a resurgence between 1925 and 1940 but since the end of the Second World War emigration has slowed to a trickle.

When the Province of Buenos Aires changed over from sheep-farming to cattle-raising and the growing of grain crops, many of the Irish who had been engaged as shepherds began to drift away from the

land. Whole areas once known to have been exclusively Irish, no
longer had many Irish names in the region. The Italians had usually
become more numerous. The Irish diplomat, Horan, suggests another
reason why the Irish in Argentina did not remain an exclusively rural
community:

> The Irishman who immigrated to the Pampas did not leave all his
> native characteristics behind him in the plains of Westmeath. We
> Irish are not exactly a provident people and are unworldly enough
> by comparison with other peoples. While many of our people were
> successful in amassing wealth, they were not always equally
> successful in holding on to it. They were more interested in getting
> the enjoyment out of spending it. Hence many of the landed
> aristocracy and many others not belonging to that class are not
> today as well off as their grandparents. Many of them let their land,
> or a good deal of it, go, though others who arrived late in the last
> century when land had to be well paid for had the ability, thrift
> and foresight, to buy land and keep it. In contrast to the 'happy-
> go-lucky' Celt, the allegedly pleasure-loving Latin is a much more
> thrifty, hard-working and hard-headed individual and better
> equipped to hold on to what he had worked hard for.[34]

Notwithstanding that judgement, Horan reported that there was
still a lot of very good land left in the hands of the Irish in the 1950s.
Despite the obvious successes, Horan concluded that the Irish community might have made better use of their opportunities if it had
been less exclusively rural in the nineteenth century.

As regards the political involvements of the Irish in Argentina,
certain sections of the community were very nationalistic. Irish
support in Argentina for the politics of the homeland dates from at
least the 1820s when prominent members of the community in
Buenos Aires — including Admiral Brown, supported Daniel O'Connell's fight for Catholic Emancipation. A Repeal Club was formed in
Buenos Aires at a later date. During the famine in the 1840s, Fahy
helped establish an Irish Relief Fund. In 1848, a fund was set up to
erect a statue in honour of Daniel O'Connell. Fr John Large Leahy
established a Fenian Prisoners Fund in 1867 and the same priest
made another effort to collect for the same purpose in 1880. That year
a Land League was set up in Salta to collect funds for the Irish
agrarian struggle. A branch of the Gaelic League was set up in Buenos
Aires in 1889. There were demonstrations in the Plaza de Mayo in
Buenos Aires following the execution of the 1916 leaders. In 1920

protests were lodged with the British following the death of Terence MacSwiney. A Dail Eireann envoy, Lawrence Ginnell, visited the capital in 1921 recruiting support for Sinn Fein.[35]

But sympathy among the larger landowners for Irish nationalism was difficult to find. Many of their children would have been educated in Ireland, in colleges like Rockwell, up to the First World War. The tradition since then is to use English colleges like Stoneyhurst and Downside. But they also used the fine schools run by Irish religious orders in the capital. Horan noted that 'with the landed oligarchy Ireland counts for very little, if at all. Indeed one has the impression that as a class that section of the community would almost prefer to pass as British and not Irish.' While that view would not pass unchallenged in Argentina, Horan recorded that the group in question would not have had 'any sympathy with Argentina's own policy of neutrality' which was maintained, despite pressure from the United States, up to 26 January 1944. Argentina then broke off diplomatic relations with Japan and Germany but did not declare war on those powers until March 1945. 'No doubt they would have taken the view', reported Horan, 'that our neutrality was similar to that of Argentina, which was, on the whole, Anti-Ally and pro-Axis'. Irish policy was, quite emphatically, the reverse.

In 1947, the former Irish Minister to Spain, L.H. Kerney, visited Buenos Aires when the memory of the war was still fresh and, according to Horan 'gave great offence to those people by his public utterances in which he defended our policy of neutrality and laid the blame for Partition on Britain'.[36] The memory of that visit did not make the task of the Irish envoy Murphy any easier when he arrived later in 1947 to set up a diplomatic mission in Buenos Aires. Argentina remains Ireland's only embassy throughout the whole of Latin America. It is a measure of the importance of the Irish community in Argentina that that remains the case.

## Notes

1. Anon. *A Short History of Irish Catholic Action in Argentina*, Buenos Aires, 1932.
2. Among the best books on the subject, are: Juan Carlos Korol and Hilda Sábato, *Como fue la immigración Irlandesa en Argentina*, Editorial Plus Ultra, Buenos Aires, 1981, Thomas Murray, *The Story of the Irish in Argentina*, P.J.Kennedy and Son, New York, 1919, Eduardo Coghlan, *Fundadores de la Segunda Epoca: los irlandeses*, Buenos Aires, 1967, M.G. Mulhall, *The English in*

*South America*, Buenos Aires, 1878, M.G.Mulhall, *Handbook of the River Plate Republics*, London/Buenos Aires, 1875, Mons. Santiago Usher, Father Fahy, *A Biography of Anthony Dominic Fahy O.P. Irish Missionary in Argentina 1805-1871*, Buenos Aires, 1951 and *Los capellanes irlandeses en la colectividad Hiberno-Argentina*, Buenos Aires, 1951. The newspaper *Southern Cross*, which was founded in 1875 is also a valuable source.

3. Horan, Report from Horan to the Dept. of Foreign Affairs, Iveagh House, Dublin, Copy in author's possession.

4. Eduardo A. Coghlan, 'Orígenes y evolución de la colectividad hiberno-argentina' in *The Southern Cross* (Numero del centenario), 1975. This table has been condensed and reproduced in Juan Carlos Korol and Hilda Sábato, *Cómo fue la inmigración Irlandesa en Argentina,* Editorial Plus Ultra, Buenos Aires: 1981, p.52.

5. Up to 1870, Korol and Sabato have calculated that there were 7,080 emigrants from Ireland and 3,592 between 1870 and 1895. That gives a total of 10,672 many of whom remained in the city and Province of Buenos Aires. (pp. 48 and 194); Some of the original Irish to come to Argentina may have been deserters from the armies of generals Whitelocke and Beresford in the years 1806 and 1807. Horan, *op. cit.,* p. 3.

6. David Rock, *Argentina 1516-1982 – from Spanish Colonisation to the Falklands War*, University of California Press, Berkeley, 1985, p. 134.

7. Horan report, *op. cit.,* 9 and 10

8. *Southern Cross*, 16 January 1875; the first editor was Monseñor Patricio J. Dillon from Connaught. He was ordained in Dublin 1863 and left for Buenos Aires the following year. Dillon, who was to spend some time ministering on the Falklands, returned to Ireland in 1881 with a government directive to attract emigrants to Argentina. But his mission did not prove very successful.

9. Horan report, *op. cit.,* pp. 11-12.

10. *Ibid.,* pp. 8 and 12

11. Rock, *op. cit.,* p. 91

12. Born Loughrea, Co. Galway, in 1804, he entered the Dominican Order and was ordained in Rome. He was sent to the United States in 1832 where he spent seven years before returning to Ireland. He was in the Black Abbey, Kilkenny when he was asked by Archbishop Murray of Dublin to go on the missions to South America. He went to Argentina in 184 and died there on

20 February 1871. See also Monseñor Santiago M. Ussher, *Father Fahy. A Biography of Anthony Dominic Fahy O.P. Irish Missionary in Argentina (1805-1871)*, Buenos Aires: 1951.

13. *Catholic Action in Argentina, op. cit.*, pp.17-19.

14. Horan report, *op. cit.*, p. 16.

15. See my study: 'Ireland, Argentina and the Falkland crisis'.

16. *Catholic Action in Argentina, op. cit.*, p. 19 and Argentina files, (All Hallowes Archive, Dublin).

17. *Catholic Action in Argentina, op. cit.*, p. 19, see also Anon. Misioneros Irlandeses en Las Islas Malvinas, *Southern Cross* (centenary number) pp. 32-33; see also Monseñor James M. Ussher, *Father Fahy – a biography of Anthony Dominic Fahy O.P.*, Irish missionary in Argentina (1805-1871), Buenos Aires, 1953, pp. 81-85; He rejects the idea that Fahy visited the islands.

18. Rennie to Earl Grey, 27 January 1849 (received 15 May 1849), letter accompanying1848 report, *State of Colonies,* 1849(1126), Vol. xxxiv; Rennie reported that he was convinced, notwithstanding the problems, that the islands were worth colonising. He reported: 'Of European males there are 101, whilst there are only 44 females; of strangers and aliens there are 58 males and 25 females; coloured race 5 males and 4 females. Any comment on so serious a disproportion is unnecessary; nor is there any probability of the evil being remedied by the desultory arrival of single men from the River Plate, or of sailors shipwrecked or leaving their ships, which are, I may say, the only description of emigrants that come here. Independently of the moral and physical evil attending this inequality, it prevents those of the population who are unmarried and of industrious habits from identifying themselves with the colony, and they no sooner realise a moderate sum of money than they go elsewhere.' *Ibid.*; The estimate of 300 Irish on the islands can be found in Anon. 'los Irlandeses en la Argentina', *Southern Cross*(Centenary Number), 1975 p. 24.

19. In the article 'Misioneros Irlandeses en las Islas Malvinas', *Southern Cross* (centenary number), 1975, there is a reference to Cristobal Murray, Tomas Harves, Patricio Maguire and P.D. Lynch who were active in the community about the mid-1850s. The same article, quoting Fr Juan Santos Gaynor, states that when the British took the islands in 1833 the externals of Catholicism disappeared and the islanders were not visited by a priest for twenty years.

20. Cristofer Murry, merchant, Fort Stanly, Falkland Islands, September 1853 (Cullen Papers, Latin American File, Dublin Archdiocesan Archives, Drumcondra).
21. *Irish Catholic Action in Argentina, op. cit.,* p. 21 and *Southern Cross* (centenary number),1975 pp. 32-33.
22. Barnabo to Archbishop of Dublin, 10 February, 1859, (trans.), Dublin Archdiocesan Archive (Latin American file).
23. Grant to Woodlock, 11 February 1859, Southwark 24 (All Hallowes Archive, Drumcondra Dublin).
24. Grant to Woodlock, 30 March 1859, Southwark 24 (All Hallowes Archive).
25. Fahy to Woodlock, 30 March 1859, Buenos Ayres 19 (All Hallowes Archive).
26. Fahy to Woodlock, 28 May 1859, Buenos Ayres 20, (All Hallowes Archive).
27. Fahy to Woodlock, 28 June 1859, Buenos Ayres 21 (All Hallowes Archive).
28. Fahy to Woodlock, 28 October 1859, Buenos Ayres 26 (All Hallowes Archive).
29. 28 December 1859, Buenos Ayres 28 (All Hallowes Archive).
30. Woodlock to Fahy, 7 February 1860 Ms. i 262 (Woodlock Ms., All Hallowes Archive).
31. *Catholic Action in Argentina, op. cit.,* p. 21.
32. Horan, *op. cit.,* p. 14.
33. *Catholic Action in Argentina, op. cit.,* pp. 26-27.
34. Horan, *op. cit.,* p. 22.
35. *Southern Cross* (Centenary number), 1975.
36. Horan, *op. cit.,* p. 22.

# 8

# Peasants or Planters? British Pioneers on Argentina's Tropical Frontier[1]

## Oliver Marshall

*The frontier is the line of most rapid and effective Americanisation. The wilderness masters the colonist. It finds him a European in dress, industries, tools, modes of travel and thought ... It strips off the garments of civilisation ... Before long he has gone to planting Indian corn and plowing with a sharp stick ... In short, at the frontier the environment is at first too strong for the man. He must accept the conditions which it furnishes, or perish.[2]*
Frederick Jackson Turner

Although Britain by 1930 still claimed the greatest proportion of foreign capital invested in Argentina, British immigration to the country had never amounted to much more than a trickle. During the 1920s there were approximately 40,000 Britons living in the Argentine, the largest such community after Argentina's Italian, Spanish and German colonies. Most Britons were concentrated in Argentina's cities overseeing Britain's considerable investments but, in contrast to other Europeans, they tended regard themselves as mere sojourners even if Argentine-born and not ever having set foot in the United Kingdom — rather than as genuine immigrants. Amongst those Britons who would admit they were laying roots in Argentina were *estancia* owners and managers scattered throughout the Pampas and Patagonia where English, Scots, Welsh and Falklanders had done much to open up frontier territory to wider settlement. However, because they were spread over such a wide expanse of territory, isolated in single family units, employing mainly non-British personnel and dependent on outside centres for many essential services, they rarely succeeded in developing a complete community structure.

Though there have been numerous attempts at planned British group settlement in Latin America, only the Welsh of Chubut can claim to have achieved a degree of success.[3] Time and again, failure was met for similar reasons. Both before departure from Britain and on arrival in Latin America, planning was poor and information on the destinations limited or inaccurate. Emigrants were usually totally unsuited for the conditions in which their isolated, and generally tropical or sub-tropical new homes were located, and markets for their produce were virtually non-existent. With most of the British colonies being comparatively small, few preserved their British identities for more than, at the very most, a few years, by which time the settlers were overcome by illness, hunger, internal squabbles, home sickness and alcohol abuse. Nevertheless, while the history of British group settlement has been one of abject failure, on the whole the colonies did not perform markedly worse than neighbouring non-British colonies established simultaneously.[4]

Colonia Victoria[5] was the last attempt at establishing a wholly British settlement in Latin America, one of the most enduring of colonies and, for a short time, one of the largest. As with other British settlement schemes on the continent, Victoria ultimately failed, but that very failure was all the more conspicuous as it contrasted with successful colonies inhabited by northern and central Europeans established in the north-east Argentine territory, now province, of Misiones at around the same time. During the early decades of the twentieth century, Ukrainians, Poles, Germans, Swiss and Scandinavian homesteaders formed the bases of some of Latin America's most successful colonisation schemes with only Finns meeting complete failure. By 1932, when the first British settlers arrived in Victoria, Misiones, a sub-tropical strip of Argentina sandwiched between Brazil and Paraguay, had progressed from being not merely a geographical aberration but, given the minimal Hispanic presence and an economy based on the productive capacity of European peasant small-holders, into a social anomaly.[6]

El Dorado has long been upheld as the great success story of European settlement in Misiones. Located in the Upper Paraná River some 1,200 kilometres north-east of Buenos Aires and 120 kilometres up the river from Posadas, the capital of Misiones, El Dorado was founded in 1919 by Adolf J. Schwelm, a German-born naturalised Briton. The colony's first settlers were Danish, but later it attracted mainly German-speaking immigrants from Brazil and Europe. By 1930, only six years after settlement seriously got under way, El Dorado's population had reached 7,000, growing yerba maté[7] and engaged in mixed farming.[8] An American sociologist who visited El Dorado in 1942 commented that the Spanish language was still rarely to be heard and described the colony as 'a complete community, with all the agencies and services necessary for community life ... Its settlers range from Ph.Ds to illiterates and its social life from family and neighbourhood visiting to contract bridges and highly intellectual discussion.[9]

With the apparent success of El Dorado behind him, Schwelm's *Compañía El Dorado: Colonización y Explotación de Bosques Ltda. S.A.* took over two further Misiones colonies, Puerto Rico and Monte Carlo, that were experiencing financial difficulties. In 1931 Schwelm founded the *Victoria Compañía de Colonización S.A.* (Victoria Colonisation Company)[10] to create a further settlement, this time inhabited by Britons who, it was intended would develop yerba maté plantations on land adjacent to El Dorado.[11] Intensely vain, Schwelm enjoyed being compared to Cecil Rhodes and, as a fervent Anglophile, named his new colony, 'Victoria' in homage to the era he wished to emulate.

With influential British connections, developed during years employed by a London merchant bank, a period spent extracting *quebracho* wood for Argentine Southern Railways and as a Director of Western Telegraph and Associated Companies (later Cable & Wireless) in Buenos Aires, and having married into a wealthy Argentine family, Schwelm succeeded in attracting distinguished individuals to serve on the company's boards of directors and advisors in London and Buenos Aires[12].[13] From his suite in London's Ritz Hotel and offices in the Haymarket, Schwelm set out to recruit men and women to his new colony, mounting a sophisticated advertising campaign based on his previous successes in Germany and Switzerland in support of settlers' conditions 'before' and 'after' their arrival in Misiones.[14] Handsomely illustrated booklets were distributed featuring photographs of healthy looking Nordic families, plantations stretching far into the horizon, graded roads, churches, schools, attractive houses and well-tended lawns and gardens[15].[16] The 'before' scenes of the film were specially created in a friend's farmyard near Buenos Aires, while the attractive scenes in both film and prospectus were largely from Schwelm's lush park or so-called 'model farm' in El Dorado.[17] Advertisements were placed in the personal columns of British quality newspapers specifying that no previous experience in agriculture was necessary to farm successfully in Misiones, while glowing articles — sometimes signed, sometimes not, but never indicating the author's close connections with the company nor that identical words and pictures formed the basis of the company brochures — appeared in *The Times*, the *Daily Telegraph, The Illustrated London News* and *Country Life* explaining that Victoria had all the potential to be as successful as El Dorado. In 1931 and 1932

Schwelm visited England where his lectures on settlement to the
Royal Institute for International Affairs[18] and The Royal Empire
Society[19] were received with considerable attention by people concerned with migration.[20] Never did the British media utter a single
word of caution regarding Victoria.

The question 'what shall we do with the boys?', the second, third
or other son not staying on to look after the family estates, had long
occupied the minds of upper class families and a traditional solution
was to send them overseas with a remittance of some sort to establish
a ranch, plantation or farm and pursue the life of a landed gentleman.
But the days of land-operating in India, Ceylon, Malaya and Africa
were either over or closed to all but those with very considerable
amounts of capital. In the midst of economic depression and suffering
high unemployment, many people in the 1930s dreamt of emigration,
oblivious to the fact that the economic situation of the rest of the world
was no better than Britain's. The romance of Empire-building still
remained strong and now many members of the middle class, anxious
parents, unemployed young men and families, were only too eager to
hear that in a part of Britain's informal Empire there was an expanse
of sub-tropical forest awaiting settlement and development at a price
that they could afford. The remoteness of Misiones was not an issue,
in fact it was even seen as a virtue, contributing to the fulfillment of
ideals of manhood and that of leading a highly romanticised planters's life, of inspecting crops and labour force in the morning, hunting
in the afternoon and evenings spent gossiping (and drinking) on their
verandas or at the club. In the company's publicity material, as if to
underline the type of colonists that Schwelm wished to encourage to
be his new neighbours and who would welcome additions to Anglo-
Argentine society, much was made of the Victoria's 'unrivalled free
fishing' and hunting, and it was stressed that 'efficient native labour
at a moderate wage ... (was) ... easily obtainable'.[21]

On applying to purchase land in Victoria, applicants were interviewed by a representative of the company in its London office. When
available Schwelm was in attendance where, eager to impress his
associates, he would be at pains to point out that a pioneering life
would not merely be one of romance and riches and, according to
Kenneth Lindsay, honorary secretary of the company, applicants for
land were sometimes rejected.[22] Schwelm was deliberately keen not
to be too firm on the capital requirements for prospective settlers, as
his experiences of El Dorado were that there were those who could
settle in Misiones with no more than a couple of hundred pounds,
while others needed considerably more.[23] In general though, English

settlers were required to place twice the down payment that Swiss, Danish or German colonists were asked, while the Silesian-Germans' down payments were still less. The company's view, as explained by an El Dorado administrator, was that the willingness to make necessary sacrifices was in inverse ratio to the colonist's previous European standard of living and the English were most able to consider the luxury of failure, still having, at the very least, a country to return to which could provide an alternative future.[24]

Victoria's colonists came from a wide variety of mainly middle class backgrounds.[25] There were numerous retired army and navy officers and their wives with little in the way of savings and eager to avoid the prospect of cold and damp, Cheltenham attic flats, all that their savings and meagre pensions would have supported in England. There were also former Malayan rubber plantation managers seeking land of their own, a Ceylon tea planter, a Shanghai policeman and a number of people with experience of farming in South Africa. However, the majority of the settlers were single young men sent out by their parents, in time-honoured upper class style, though with only a few hundred pounds. Apart from the former planters, previous agricultural experience varied considerably. A few colonists actually came from genuine farming backgrounds, while others had tended allotments of fruit and vegetable gardens in England. But for many settlers knowledge of the land was limited to the mowing of lawns and the cultivation of sweet peas. However, the background of most of the settlers were probably no less relevant to sub-tropical pioneering conditions encountered in Misiones than those of El Dorado's and Monte Carlo's settlers, 60 and 80 per cent respectively came from highly urbanised areas of Germany and whose 'farming' had been limited to small allotments.[26] In all, several hundred English-speaking men, women and children made their way to Victoria, remaining for periods varying from a few weeks to over four decades. At its peak in about 1938, Victoria's population approached two hundred, divided into over fifty family or individual holdings and whose determination to remain, and their ability to succeed, bore no obvious correlation to their previous experience.

From Victoria's very inception, doubt was cast on the wisdom of locating a British settlement in Misiones. While coverage in the British press was exclusively glowing, Anglo-Argentine opinion, for social, rather than economic reasons, was at best sceptical, at worst hostile. This was partly due to genuine memories of earlier failed British settlements, particularly the disastrous Australian utopian socialist colony in Paraguay, but mainly out of a sense of social snobbery, that what might be acceptable for Germans should never be expected of British in Argentina.

Edward Every, Anglican Bishop of Argentina and Eastern South America, was one of Victoria's most vociferous critics. Even by the standards of the often arrogant and inward-looking Anglo-Argentine community, Every's view on such issues as 'mixed marriages' caused some to blush slightly, but his passionate outpourings regarding 'our sturdiness of character and racial superiority, or perhaps, a less offensive way of putting it, the superiority of our civilisation',[27] still expressed a strain of opinion beyond simply that of one particular bigoted old man. Bishop Every had no doubts that South America was quite unsuited to British settlement and warned parents to hesitate before sending out their sons because of what he termed the continent's 'debased moral atmosphere', manifesting itself in terms of a low level of sexual morality, dishonesty, lawlessness, gambling and cruelty to animals. In Every's opinion, while Spaniards and Italians were easily able to adapt to such lax moral conditions, Argentina and the rest of the continent would never be suitable for the only true 'white men', the British.[28] At a time when Victoria was no more than a dream of Schwelm's, Every warned that the continent's prevalent amorality, the 'natural' result of South America being both Spanish and Catholic, ought to be taken into grave account by the misguided people who plan colonies of Anglo-Saxon or other northern folk in the lands.[29] Every felt that Britons abroad had a duty to 'maintain the race' difficult at the best of times given the 'hostile' social conditions of South America, but well-nigh impossible in the more remote and tropical regions of the continent.[30]

Every held out a bleak vision for the Victoria's future, an exaggerated reflection of Anglo-Argentina's generally held sense of social superiority, but also a view which ultimately proved correct. 'It is fallacious to suppose', wrote Every shortly after Victoria was founded,

> that because El Dorado Colony may be a conspicuous success, therefore, Victoria, which is to be built up on the model of it out of British public school boy material, is sure to be a success also. Only on a superficial view, either by those that do not know the country or those that fail to understand the peculiar characteristics and traditions of our race, is such a conclusion possible ... Such a colony needs as settlers men who are prepared to throw in their lot with the country and ultimately become citizens of it, like El Dorado; Englishmen, especially of the type desired, most emphatically will not do that. Again, the settlers needed must themselves work the

land when cleared and live mainly on what it produces; educated Englishmen will not be content to do that for long, because it holds no future; when they realise what the life is, they will almost certainly be dissatisfied and take the first opportunity of leaving'.[31]

The first four settlers disembarked at 'Puerto Victoria', in fact no more than a small clearing on the river bank, in April 1932. The Argentine and British flags were ceremonially hoisted and, to commemorate the event, the 'four young Englishmen of just the right type' (as they were described in *Country Life* by Christopher Turnor, a member of the company's advisory committee, who accompanied the group) were photographed beside a large board with the colony's motto inscribed in Latin.[32] Housed in *ranchos* (thatched huts) and facing conditions none of the men had ever experienced in Buenos Aires, on Pampas *estancias* or at Eton, they set out to master the dense forest and cope with the natural elements with little in the way of protection. Isolated, homesick, disillusioned and unwilling to await the arrival of 'some hundreds of families' who Turnor, writing in *The Times* of 30 May 1932, confidently expected to make Victoria their home, three or four men abandoned Victoria in a matter of months, ill and in despair.[33 34]

Over the following five years, a steady flow of slightly better prepared colonists made their way to Victoria. Land holdings varied in size between 20 and 200 hectares, most being nearer the smaller. The cost of purchasing 30 hectares of land, clearing 7 hectares (enough for initial planting), building a comfortable house and sinking a well typically came to about 7,500 pesos or, say £450.[35] Some settlers though, were unable to invest even that much money, but a few sunk considerable sums for much larger properties, expressing blind confidence that Victoria would hold a bright future. Houses ranged from mere *ranchos* with perhaps a vegetable patch along side, to an enormous mansion-type house complete with baronial hall, servants' quarters, immense formal flower gardens, tennis court and swimming pool.

In part, the later arrivals' lot was eased simply because there were more of them, so reducing the impact on the colony's morale should some opt to leave, and better able to offer mutual support during the difficult initial months and years, and also because general conditions were improving. Saw mills were introduced and carpenters arrived to build houses and make furniture. The company opened a comfortable hotel where the settlers were able to stay until their houses were ready for occupation (or until their savings ran out) as well as a butchers' shop, a general store and telegraph and postal services linking Victoria to the outside world. The *picados* (trails) along which the homesteads were located developed into routes passable (when dry) by trucks and a launch made the 12-kilometre trip to El Dorado every day providing access to essential services not available in Victoria, such as a doctor, and offering settlers a chance to simply escape from the claustrophobic atmosphere of a small community. An active social life developed that had much more in common with the Home Counties than the South American jungle. Formal dinner parties and dances were held regularly, a gymkhana was organised, amateur dramatics were staged and a jazz combo, 'The Mandioca Boys', was formed.[36] At Christmas, mince pies were baked and groups of carol singers toured the homesteads, while twice a year Anglican and Presbyterian ministers would travel up from Buenos Aires. *Dorado* ('the salmon of South America') fishing was superb, while in the forests there were tapir, wild pigs and turkeys, deer and jaguar to be hunted.

Despite improving conditions and the development of a community spirit, the turnover of settlers was high. Though the company made it clear both in press releases and prospectuses that it would welcome single girls, either unaccompanied or in small groups, to grow fruit and vegetables, the publicity campaign was aimed at a middle class audience and it was unsuccessful in attracting them (see, for example, *The Illustrated London News*, 23 July 1932).[37] With such a lack of female companionship, bachelors, who made up the bulk of Victoria's population in its early years, sometimes found solace in wine and caña and, occasionally, other men's wives. A few, to the embarrassment of fellow Victorians, took to drinking more and working less, neglecting their plantations and being content to continue living in *ranchos*, 'turning native', as their decaying lifestyle was patronisingly termed.

Allegations of being deceived by the company about the conditions of Victoria were many, and were awarded front page attention by Argentina's English language newspapers. Fighting a bitter circulation battle and attracted to the home-grown human interest story, the *Standard* saw the settlers as representing the British thirst for fortune and adventure, while the attitude of the American-oriented *Buenos Aires Herald* was one of criticism couched in terms of faint amusement by the entire affair. Reasons offered by colonists for leaving Victoria were insects 'revolting and repulsive things for a refined woman, such as come to live in the colony, to endure', an entomologist having spent six months in Misiones told the *Buenos*

*Aires Herald* (16 April 1934) and 'most offensive to the sensibilities', a settler told the same newspaper (17 June 1934), were the constant presence of sores on settlers' bodies, occasional malaria outbreaks, lack of a resident doctor, the two periods of exceptionally heavy rainfall per year (not even interspersed with genuine dry seasons), flash floods, fires sometimes burning out of control while preparing land for planting, dramatic temperature changes and general doubts regarding the possibility of future prosperity. Responding to the criticisms, the *Standard* accused their rival of 'journalistic dishonesty' and 'canting humbug' (20 June 1934) and argued that only fools could be deceived into believing that the South American jungle could be insect-free and, in any case, in time the settlers would gain immunity from what were non-virulent species, that the experience of El Dorado had proved that the climate was essentially healthy and suitable for European habitation, that in an emergency El Dorado and a doctor could be reached by launch and truck in less than an hour. Only toil, sacrifice and persistence, it was often argued, would lead to success and therefore attract further settlers from England. (The *Buenos Aires Herald* and the *Standard*, various issues, 1933-35.)

Anyone who had troubled to examine a map of South America before venturing out to Victoria should have imagined that they were likely to experience certain discomforts of nature. What none of the colonists could have been expected to have been aware of, but which Schwelm and the company certainly were, was that by 1932 the era of 'green gold', as yerba maté was termed, had come to an end. But as the 1930s progressed, the claims featuring prominently in all the company's publicity material for the existence of 'an unlimited and assured market' for Victoria's produce, gradually changed from being merely exaggeration to outright lies.

Since the turn of the century, the Argentine government required that settlers in Misiones should plant yerba maté on a set portion of their properties with the result that within thirty years Argentine producers had reached the point of being capable of satisfying home demand. Realising that without immediate action the Argentine market would be lost to foreign yerba maté, Brazilian producers took to 'dumping' action in 1926-7 by increasing their own collections of the commodity, lowering its price, and resulting in the closure of 40 per cent of Argentina's yerba maté mills.[38] Fearing that Argentina's traditional exports, wheat, flour, beef and wine, would be excluded from the important Brazilian market should action to curtail imports of yerba maté be taken, and mindful of the political importance of

Misiones' smallholders, legislative action was taken in 1935 virtually terminating the extension of yerba maté cultivation and imposing limits on the extent that these could be cropped. At the same time, agreements were made with Brazil to curb 'dumping' but effectively guaranteeing Brazilian producers to 40 per cent of the Argentine yerba maté market.[39] The yerba maté crisis was a severe blow to all Schwelm's colonies in Misiones and, as the 1930s progressed, all attracted fewer and fewer new colonists.

Many of the disgruntled bachelors drifted away from Victoria without remaining long and most of those remaining were able to depart, without having to admit defeat, in 1939 to go to war.[40] Other settlers, their capital fast depleted and either too proud or without the necessary ability and energy, would not consider, even temporarily, descending to the level of peasants, living from the production of subsistence crops, also chose to abandon Victoria before they found themselves completely trapped. One such colonist, an unidentifiable Scot, writing to the British Embassy in Buenos Aires in 1934, explained that farming in Misiones was only possible 'if a man has a horde of brats, as have most of the Huns in El Dorado, they spawn like rabbits to get cheap labour'. Selling their land holdings to remaining settlers, departing colonists made their way to Buenos Aires, either in search of regular employment elsewhere in Argentina or to move on to Canada, South Africa or, as was the case with one family, the Seychelles, to continue their search for their dream frontier or tropical paradise.

With the hope of returning to Victoria once their trees had reached maturity, some of those who had arrived in Victoria before restrictions were imposed became absentee landowners, leaving their plantations in the care of friends who, by choice or force of circumstances, remained and to whom they paid a management fee. As it took about four years before trees could be first cropped, an alternative income of about £100 a year was required in the meantime. Settlers were dependent for their sheer survival on a combination of part-time employment provided by the company or Schwelm personally, or by more fortunate fellow colonists, and on remittances sent from England. Later, when yerba maté trees had reached maturity and while other crops were being contemplated to supplement the unreliable price paid, for yerba maté, two or more years after being cropped, an alternative income of some kind was all the more essential in order to pay for the extras considered essential if 'standards' were to be kept up, such as the expenses of importing most food consumed in Victoria and paying fees for the older children's Buenos Aires or Córdoba boarding schools. These were hardly 'luxuries' for the off-spring of aspiring planters, but the payment of fees was a source of much soul-searching to some parents: would their self-respect permit the acceptance of bursaries towards the cost of their children's education that were offered to underprivileged members of the Anglo-Argentine community? There were also the high fares to and from Buenos Aires for the children during vacations and the adults when they felt it was time to go on 'leave'. The colony suffered enormous capital drain with the colonists requiring incomes far in excess to that which their plantations might ever be capable of providing.

When the whisky ran out, the English left, this is how Victoria is unfairly remembered by many in El Dorado.[41] Unaccustomed to isolation and without experience of agricultural and climatic vagaries, certainly some settlers found their only way of coping with a failed harvest was to turn to alcohol and, in the resulting economic crises, by selling up. It very quickly became apparent to British settlers arriving in Victoria that it was impossible to survive, let alone thrive, on the basis of yerba maté, an alternative produce was sought by the more determined. Tung proved extremely successful as, eventually, did citrus fruit, but little in the way of advice was available. They also required the persistence and experimentation of farmers, not romantics, before success could be contemplated.

During the 1940s and 1950s Victoria struggled on, not receiving any further settlers from England but still retaining a distinct British character. Some of the settlers simply had no alternative but to remain, growing old, their savings exhausted, bridges burnt. Others had developed a genuine fondness for Misiones, even achieving a measure of prosperity by purchasing the properties of departing Victorians, so extending their yerba maté quotas and generally reducing plantation overheads, or by turning towards commerce, linking their fortunes, paradoxically perhaps, with El Dorado.

As Victoria's population declined, so did the sense of physical security of those remaining. With increasing distance between inhabited homesteads, there was a constant fear of robbery, and the murder in 1956 by Paraguayan bandits of one of their number on an outlying *chacra* was cause for much alarm, precipitating further departures. Over the following decade Victoria's population continued to fall as older Victorians passed away and others, growing too old to live alone and manage their properties, left for the security of El Dorado or to join their children elsewhere in the world who had long seen no future for themselves in the colony. The last British

Victorians finally departed for Buenos Aires in the early 1980s and today Victoria is no more than an extension of El Dorado.

## Notes

1. Thanks are due to the following former 'Victorians' for much valuable information: Basil Burrage, June Duthie, Martin Garsed, Bernard Jackson, Edward Lawrence, Jack McKenzie, Lisa Mockler, Marjorie Scovel, Eileen Thornton, Marjorie Vandersluys and John Winder.
2. Turner, Frederick Jackson, *The Frontier in American History*, New York 1921, p.4.
3. 'Success' here refers to the development of a self-sustaining community.
4. Platt, D.C.M.'British Agricultural Colonisation In Latin America', *Inter-American Economic Affairs*, vol. 18, no.3, 1966. Platt, D.C.M. 'British Agricultural Colonisation in Latin America', Part II, in *Inter-American Economic Affairs*, vol. 19, no. 1, 1965.
5. Also called 'Puerto Victoria'; thereafter referred as 'Victoria'.
6. Eidt, Robert C. *Pioneer Settlement in Northeast Argentina*, University of Wisconsin Press, Madison 1971.
7. Yerba Maté is a South American tree, the leaves of which, having been dried and ground, are used to make a tea-like beverage which is widely drunk in the River Plate republics.
8. Lindsay, Kenneth, *Eldorado: an Agricultural Settlement. A Brief History of its Origin and Development*, Kinoch Press, Birmingham 1931.
9. Taylor Carl, C. *Rural Life in Argentina*, Louisiana State University Press, Baton Rouge, 1948, p.344.
10. Hereafter referred to as 'the Company'.
11. Victoria Colonisation Company, *Victoria — A New British Agricultural Settlement on the Upper Paraná River, Misiones, Argentina*, Victoria Colonisation Company, London 1932.
12. Kenneth Lindsay, interview 1986.
13. VCC *ibid.*
14. Micolis, Marisa, *Une Communuaté Allemande en Argentine; Eldorado*, Centre Internationale de Recherche sur le Bilinguisme, Quebec 1973, *pp.14-8.*
15. Lindsay, Kenneth, *Eldorado: an Agricultural Settlement, ibid.*
16. VCC *ibid.*
17. Marjorie Clements, personal correspondence, 1986.

18. Schwelm, Adolph J. 'The Forest Land of Misiones, Where Opportunity has not ceased to call'. Lecture delivered at the Royal Institute of International Affairs, Chatham House, London 14 December 1931.

19. Schwelm, Adolph J. 'Some Thoughts on Colonisation'. An Address delivered to the Royal Empire Society, London, June 1932.

20. Lindsay, Kenneth, interview *ibid.*

21. Victoria Colonisation Company Ltd., *Victoria in its Fifth Year*, Victoria Colonisation Company Ltd., London c. 1937.

22. Lindsay, Kenneth, interview, *ibid.*

23. Schwelm, Adolph J. 'Some Thoughts on Colonisation', *ibid*, pp. 14-6.

24. Taylor, Carl C. *Rural Life in Argentina*, *ibid.* p.343.

25. A list, drawn up from memory fifty years after the period refers to, supplied by Bernard Jackson mentions 104 colonists by name.

26. Eidt, *ibid.* pp.161-2.

27. Every, Edward F. *South American Memories of Thirty Years*, Society for the Promotion of Christian Knowledge (SPCK) London 1933, p.42.

28. Every, Edward F. *Twenty-five Years in South America*, Society for the Promotion of Christian Knowledge (SPCK), London 1929, p.15.

29. *Ibid.* p.15.

30. Every, Edward J. *South American Memories of Thirty Years*, *ibid.* pp.37-49.

31. *Ibid.* p.48.

32. VCC *ibid* (1932) p.1.

33. The fourth remained in Victoria, working as an assistant to Schwelm, and now lived in Eldorado.

34. Marjorie Clements, personal correspondence 1986.

35. Thompson, R.W. *Voice from the Wilderness*, Faber and Faber, London 1960.

36. Under the circumstances, it would have been easy to have mistaken them for the fancy-dress events that were also organised.

37. VCC 1932, *ibid.*

38. Eidt, *ibid.* pp. 144-7.

39. Storey, R.N. *Report on Economic and Commercial Conditions in the Argentine Republic*, Department of Overseas Trade, London 1939, pp.106-7.

40. Five were to lose their lives. Only one eventually returned to Victoria.

41. Not least unfair simply due to the inaccuracy of the statement: wine and cana were the drinks most widely consumed, whisky being a luxury for all but a few. The colony's one-time wealthiest inhabitants, said to have arrived in Victoria with £30,000 gave up whisky when his capital ran out but remained in the colony until his death in the late 1940s; Micolis, *ibid.* p.48, n.12.

# THE CULTURAL
# CONNECTION

# 9

# The Influence of British Culture in Argentina

*John King*

*They would have been friends, but they met only once face to face
on some too famous islands, and each one was Cain and each one
was Abel.
They buried them together. Snow and corruption know them.
The events to which I refer took place in a time that we cannot
understand.* [1]

This poem, 'Juan López and John Ward', a commentary on the
Falklands/Malvinas war, was written by Argentina's most famous
man of letters, Jorge Luis Borges. It tells of two young men, from
Britain and Argentina, well versed in each other's literature, who die
needlessly on a remote island. In a life that spanned the century and
in a writing career of seventy years, Borges referred constantly to the
close relationship between British and Argentine culture. He himself,
he often remarked, was brought up in 'a garden, behind speared
railings and in a library of limitless English books'.[2] In his view, the
war was a result of autarchic nationalist sentiment and a negation
of that heterodox spirit which he felt should inform Argentine culture.
At a time when there is a danger of becoming entrapped in simple,
Manichean, definitions of 'otherness', Borges' words encourage us to
look at the complexities of Anglo-Argentine cultural relations. This
essay offers an analysis of the impact of British culture in Argentina.

   In 1845, an Argentine politician in exile, Domingo Faustino Sarmiento, wrote an essay entitled *Facundo: Civilization and Barbarism*
which was to become one of the vertebral texts of Argentine cultural
history. It was written at a time of crisis, when the Federalist dictator
Juan Manuel de Rosas was attempting to organise the province of
Buenos Aires under his exclusive rule and shut it off from outside
influences. In broad terms, Sarmiento expressed the views of a sector
of the Argentine elite which opposed Rosas and sought to promote a
dynamic export economy linked to the expanding British Empire. The
export traffic would pass through the city and port of Buenos Aires

and yield a high revenue which would benefit the whole country. The central city of Buenos Aires would thus control a process which would encourage foreign investment, technology and immigration. Refracted through the Romantic prose of Sarmiento, this struggle between liberalism and autarchy was expressed in terms of a war between civilisation and barbarism. Barbarism was equated with the backward interior, local *caudillos* or strong men, the gaucho as an inferior social type and introverted nationalism. Civilisation could be found in adopting European patterns in the political, social and cultural spheres. Argentina had to open its trade to the rest of the world, attract European immigrants and acquire at the same time values of sociability and respectability which would lead the country out of fragmentation caused by excessive individualism, into a well-organised social system. The models were Northern Europe and North America and Sarmiento placed a great emphasis on education: education through schools and through books, and to know how to read in other languages. In an interesting hyperbolic passage in his *Recuerdos de provincia* (1850), he informs us that he spent half his salary for one and a half months on English lessons, after which time he read 'a volume each day of the sixty novels in the complete works of Walter Scott'.[3]

Sarmiento's liberal contemporary Juan Bautista Alberdi, one of the main architects of the constitution of 1853 and the leader of that generation's support for European immigration, is well-known for his famous phrase '*gobernar es poblar*', 'to govern is to populate'. He had a very clear idea, however, of the necessary 'stock' required in Argentina. 'Put the bum, the gaucho, the peasant, the basic element of our population, through all the transformations of the best systems of education; in one hundred years you won't make of him an English worker, who works, consumes and lives in dignity and comfort'. Alberdi considered the British 'the most perfect of men' and argued that English, 'the language of liberty, industry and order' be taught in all Argentine schools. Argentina, he felt, was really a European country: 'We who call ourselves Americans are nothing more than Europeans born in America. Cranium, blood, colour, it's all from abroad.'[4]

The ideas and prejudices of liberal intellectuals such as Sarmiento and Alberdi were to be important in the development of the nation-state in the second half of the nineteenth century. Indeed, as several essays in this volume point out, the state was consolidated very much according to Sarmiento's vision: the great landowners of the Littoral Provinces, working through the city of Buenos Aires, controlled the growth of the export economy which became enormously profitable when allied with British capital and technology. It was in the period from 1880 to 1929 that the influence of Britain was at its height. I will analyse certain cultural manifestations in this period, before going on to describe the relative decline of Britain in Argentina after 1930.

The most obvious place to begin is with education, Sarmiento's most insistent concern. We find the influence of Britain at every stage in the Argentine elite's education process. The nanny appears in a number of memoir accounts. The writer María Rosa Oliver, referring to her childhood in the 1890s, speaks with affection of a Scots nanny, Lizzie Caldwell, and paints a picture of a whole community of British women working as nannies, meeting in their employmer's houses or in the parks and squares.[5] The British governess was also an integral part of the upper-class family, especially for the education of women. Victoria Ocampo, cultural Maecenas and writer, talks of her governess, the redoubtable Miss Ellis and remarks that her first incursion into writing was a protest letter against Miss Ellis' severity. 'I wrote the letter of protest accusing Miss Ellis of being a coward for "telling on me" to my parents ... I wrote that the English were cowards because they wanted to destroy the poor Boers... I wrote that I offered up prayers for the overthrow of the British Empire. Finally I pointed out what the British had done to Joan of Arc ... I discovered that writing offered me a great sense of relief'.[6] Later, as we shall see, Victoria Ocampo was to be a great promoter of British culture in Argentina. She was brought up with French and English as her first languages and did not feel comfortable writing in Spanish until she was in her thirties. Another recent vision of the British governess is offered in María Luisa Bemberg's film *Miss Mary* (Argentina, 1986), when Julie Christie is sent down to teach the children of an upper-class family in Argentina in the late 1930s.

In terms of a formal education, the sons and daughters of the Argentine elite could attend the British schools that appeared in Argentina in the nineteenth century. The first English-language school, St. Andrew's Scots School, was founded in 1838. Perhaps the most famous British school, the Buenos Aires English High School, was opened in 1884. 'The founder was a Scot, Alexander Watson Hutton, who arrived in Argentina two years before with the appointment of headmaster at St Andrew's School. Watson Hutton's entry to British education in Argentina was revolutionary because he brought with him school customs and teaching methods used in Britain. Not least of them was the introduction of sport into the curriculum'.[7] Some were also sent to public schools in Britain. The Martínez de Hoz family, for example, regularly attended Eton, as Sir David Kelly (the British Ambassador in Argentina in the 1940s) noted approvingly in 1919. Kelly had been accepted into a 'young men's club called the Huegen which had just been started by the Etonian sons of Don Miguel Alfredo Martínez de Hoz for gilded youths who were too young for the Círculo de Armas; Martínez de Hoz had been a well-known character in Edwardian London with his race horses and his coach and four and in 1919 was a leading social figure in Buenos Aires. He paid £40,000 for his horse '"Botafogo"' and tried to breed pheasants at his English-style country seat at Chapadmalal'.[8] We will return to Botafogo and the 'turf' later in this essay. It is also likely that an analyst of the archives of the Catholic public schools such as Ample-forth, Downside and Stoneyhurst would reveal a constant presence of Argentines. The novelist Manuel Mujica Láinez, also states that he attended summer schools in England, where Argentines regularly rented a school in Sussex for the education and entertainment of their sons.[9] These contacts stimulated a knowledge of British culture, especially of literature: countless memoir accounts talk of constant reading in English, in Borges' library of limitless English books. Emphasis was also placed on spoken English, something that Sarmiento could never master. The acquisition of language was a constituent part of 'civilised' society.

These contacts were also stimulated by frequent visits to Europe. The 'journey to Europe' has been analysed in a series of witty and acerbic essays by David Viñas, the Argentine novelist and cultural critic, published in the populist-nationalist climate of the early 1970s, when the critique of liberalism was at its height.[10] He seeks to expose the assumptions and prejudice of generations of Argentine politicians and men-of-letters as they drank at the fount of European culture. Interestingly, the main focus for these travellers is almost invariably Paris rather than London, as the travellers were attracted by the ideas of the Enlightenment, the Revolution and the ability of the French to produce artistic movements with precise philosophies and practices.[11] Parisian architecture was a dominant style in the development of the city of Buenos Aires in the late nineteenth century. It was French writers and artists that influenced the first 'professional' group of writers in Latin America, the *modernistas* — Ruben Darío always referred to Paris as 'la ciudad del ensueño' — and stimulated modernist movements in Buenos Aires in the 1920s. It was to Paris that Argentines flocked, renting apartments and hotels in the most fashionable areas, Neuilly, Passy and L'Etoile. It is in the late

nineteenth century that the phrase 'riche comme un argentin' begins
to appear in the French vocabulary. London was often part of the
itinerary, but not the main reason for the visit. If Paris could nurture
the spirit, only the wealth of the pampa could be relied upon to
nurture the body. Victoria Ocampo records that when her family left
for Europe, they would take not only the household servants and
tutors, but also cows and chickens to provide food during the long boat
journey and the subsequent stay.[12]

Paris was a more attractive city than London, and the French were
always much better than the British in directly 'marketing' their
culture in Argentina. From the nineteenth century, the French had
treated cultural diplomacy, the 'mission civilisatrice', as an important
part of foreign policy. For example, the Alliance Française was
founded in 1880, to set up schools, libraries and arrange lectures and
exhibitions. In Britain, on the other hand, as Frances Donaldson
points out, attitudes were different. 'The British would not, and in
the event did not, embark on any programme of this sort until they
were convinced that it was materially damaging to their interests not
to do so. Their scepticism about the value of spreading such intan-
gibles as language, literature, the arts and civilised values was
almost as complete as the French belief in it ...'.[13] It was, in fact, partly
a reading of the gloomy report of the D'Abernon trade mission to
Argentina in the late 1920s that was to prompt the Foreign Office to
found the British Council in 1935. D'Abernon wrote that ... 'we have
not been sufficiently active in the exercise of British cultural influence' and added: 'To those who say that this extension in influence has
no connection with commerce, we reply that they are totally wrong;
the reaction of trade to the more deliberate incalculation of British
culture which we advocate is definitely certain and will be swift'.[14] Of
course D'Abernon was attempting to revive flagging British trade in
the Argentine, which was suffering from increased competition with
the United States. His strictures pointed to the need to reverse that
attitude which assumed that the value of British culture was self-evident.

If Britain up to the 1930s was unprepared to market the 'self-evident' civilisation of the country, it was certainly prepared to emphasise the physical, mental and perhaps even spiritual value of sport.
Wherever the British went they took sport with them and, in the
Argentine these practices were taken up eagerly. Sir David Kelly
wrote with some irritation:

The ease with which the plutocracy has acquired wealth and political influence was paralleled by a patient determination to wait until a foreign community had done the spade work in building up some institution and then quietly absorb it. Thus the British community had ... introduced cricket, tennis, golf, polo and football and started and built up all the first clubs; but already in 1919 all these, with the exception of cricket (which, as in most countries remained a purely British amusement), are being absorbed by the Argentines.[15]

An irritation perhaps that the British would soon be suffering at the feet of Di Stéfano or at the hands (or head) of a Maradona.

Andrew Graham-Yooll has traced a reference to the formation of the Buenos Aires football club in 1867[16] and football must have been played by the workers that built the railways in Argentina. Most accounts of organised football, however, begin with Alexander Watson Hutton, who included football in the curriculum of his school. In a few years after this date, 1884, a dozen clubs had been formed in Buenos Aires, with predominantly British membership. Hutton was elected President of the Argentine Football Association and his school team, the English High School (later to be called the Alumni), won an early championship. In fact the Alumni, who in the early years fielded a team containing five brothers — the Browns — carried all before them in the first decade of competitions. Yet, if the British resident, teacher and migrant worker first established the game, 'it was the British touring team and the British football coach who consolidated the game's position. The touring team showed what could be achieved and the coach came to help the local players achieve it. British football teams went everywhere in the years 1900-1914.'[17] The amateur team of ex-public school boys, the Corinthians, toured Latin America, but increasingly the professional clubs set the standards abroad. Before the war, Everton, Nottingham Forest, Southampton and Tottenham went on tour in Argentina and Everton played Tottenham in two exhibition games in Buenos Aires in 1909. The President and various ministers attended the games, thus offering important patronage in these early days. Later leaders would also realise the symbolic importance and popular appeal of football: Perón regularly attended the matches and liked to be known as the 'primer deportista' (the 'first sportsman' — a reference to his skiing prowess) and Videla tried to make political capital out of Argentina's success in the 1978 World Cup, staged in Argentina during the infamous recent military regime. By 1930, football had a firm hold in Argentina and the national side met with considerable success. In 1953 Argentina beat England for the first time in an international match. 'We beat them, like in the English Invasions of 1806 and 1807', wrote an enthusiastic journalist. 'We recently nationalised the railways. Now we have nationalised football', commented euphoric politicians.[18]

If football soon became an important part of popular culture, the same is true of horse-racing which was institutionalised in 1849 with the foundation of the Foreign Amateur Race Sporting Society.[19]There was a brisk trade in English thoroughbred horses, and owners such as Martínez de Hoz set up stud farms (the magnificent stud-farms in Chapadmalal remain to this day). Horse-racing became a regular feature of Buenos Aires popular culture, and there have been some legendary horses like 'Botafogo', cheered to victory by such cult figures as the tango singer Carlos Gardel who, like many of his compatriots, was addicted to the 'turf'.[20]

Other sports such as rugby, cricket and polo moved predominantly into the hands of upper-middle class Argentines. The Argentine team performed well in the recent rugby world cup and Buenos Aires must be one of the few places in the world outside Britain where a morning newspaper, the *Buenos Aires Herald*, publishes daily the English County Championship cricket scores. Polo (first played on the *estancia* of Mr David Shennan in the 1870s), took a firm hold and by the 1920s, the Argentines were pre-eminent in the world, an ascendance they maintain to this day. Argentine polo ponies have always been in great demand in Britain and the British royal family have played on several occasions in Argentina. Sport, therefore, has been one of the most important British contributions to Argentine elite and popular culture.

The British and their values held an important position in the largely immigrant society that developed in Argentina in the late nineteenth century. What of the other communities? Sarmiento had decried the indigenous population and had argued for immigration as a means of developing the country's resources and improving its stock. Massive immigration did take place between 1870 and 1930, filling the country in the main with men and women from Southern Spain and Southern Italy. Although the immigrants were a necessary economic input, their value in social and cultural terms was not viewed as wholly positive by the Argentine elite. As an abstraction, the idea of mass immigration was attractive. In reality, however, it seemed to fill the country with morally and socially inferior beings from Southern Europe, who brought with them dangerously egalitarian or anarchist ideas. A number of novels and articles written in the late nineteenth century reflect this anti-immigrant feeling. Interestingly, as Evelyn Fishburn has shown, British characters in these texts are always exemplary, hard working and civilised.[21] The novelists could shape the destiny of the immigrants in the pages of fiction, but it was less easy to modify the text of history. Substantial working-class and lower-middle class sectors emerged, which provided a market for more popular forms of cultural expression, the theatre, music-hall, tango, the serialised novel and the political newsletter. It can be argued that in the early twentieth century Argentine society was becoming more pluralist and democratic, yet there was little contact between elite culture and the more popular forms of art, which were considered beyond the boundaries of civilisation. In the last instance, 'high' culture was liberal and European: it reflected the cosmopolitan taste of a small group which shared its *cénacle* control over writing, distribution and consumption. The Prince of Wales visited this cosmopolitan society in 1925. A typical day in his visit was described in a local newspaper (*La Razón*, 28.8.1925): '10 a.m. St Andrew's College. 11 a.m. British Hospital. 12.30 p.m. Lunch with the British Chamber of Commerce. 2.30 p.m. Polo at the Hurlingham Club'. He was entertained by the sizeable British community, but he could also be found relaxing with the Argentine elite, playing his Hawaiian guitar at the home of society hostess, Victoria Ocampo. As Argentina lived through a period of prosperity between 1880 and 1929, few saw any reason to question its economic and cultural dependence on Europe.

These years of harmony were to give way to the Great Slump, a military coup in 1930 and the advent of what is known as the 'infamous decade' of Argentine history, during which a small group of conservative landowners maintained its power through falsifying elections and banning other political parties. Liberalism could no longer be equated with democratic values, and other, more populist and nationalist political groupings were to emerge in opposition to these governments, and were to gain power under Perón in the elections of 1946.

A critique of elite, liberal, European values began to emerge in the 1930s, though it had little influence in the wider society. Liberalism was seen as a system which had allowed a landowning elite and foreign interest group to run the country. In opposition to this, nationalist critics began to rewrite their own history and revive wilfully barbarous symbols such as the dictator Rosas, or the gaucho literary hero, Martin Fierro, who represented the popular struggle against an effete European aristocracy. The dominant cultural groups were not greatly distrubed by such criticism (which often came from within the dominant class: the scourge of British imperialism, Julio Irazusta, was educated in Oxford and spends many pages of his autobiography talking about meetings with famous British men and women of letters).[22] In 1931, a cultural magazine *Sur* founded by Victoria Ocampo began to appear, which sought to combine the best of Argentine and European writers. Many writers and intellectuals travelled to Argentina and those who could not make the journey were translated in the pages of the magazine. *Sur* helped to set the standards for quality and for scope in translation. Argentina has always been very conscious of the need for translation as part of a process of cultural modernisation. If *Sur* sought to be a bridge between the cultures, the traffic was largely one way: of the Argentine writers only Borges would later be taken up enthusiastically abroad. Latin America would remain for European intellectuals a largely unknown continent, on which they could project their fantasies. Virginia Woolf, a model for her Argentine contemporaries, who sought to establish Bloomsbury in Buenos Aires, could speak of Argentina as 'those immense blue and grey lands with the wild cattle, the pampas grass and the butterflies'.[23]

Certain Argentine writers also helped to disseminate such utopian fantasies. Benito Lynch's *El inglés de los güesos* (The English Man of the Bones) is structured around the clash between an educated and cerebral Englishman and the beauty and instinctual behaviour of the inhabitants of the virgin continent of America. Mr James, a paleonthologist, seeking clues to the origins of man in remains found in the Argentine pampa, is bewitched by a beautiful girl. His 'Britishness' comes into conflict with the 'reality' of Argentina.

> That unique, doleful and ignorant virginal heart that in an obscure ranch of a remote land, made him experience the deepest emotions that he had felt in his life and allowed him to glimpse at the marvels of a New World, in whose existence he had never seriously believed, despite having the repeated guarantee of his wise teachers and the extraordinary libraries of Cambridge and Oxford.[24]

Yet this relationship between the 'intellect' of Britain and the 'body' of Argentina cannot be harmonious — the pressures of class and background are too great.

Aside from the idealist, pastoral vision of Lynch, many intellectual groups still tried to maintain their faith in cosmopolitanism, in a world that was falling under the sway of authoritarian and nationalist regimes in the 1930s and early 40s. Borges wrote at the outbreak of the Second World War: 'To be a nazi (to play at energetic barbarism, at being a viking, a Tartar, a sixteenth century conquistador, a gaucho, a redskin), is, in the long run, a mental and moral impossibility'.[25] The fall of Paris was seen as the eclipse of civilisation, and despite the Argentine government's official policy of neutrality in the war (which incurred the wrath of the United States), intellectual groups, in the main, supported the Allies, celebrating with a large demonstration the liberation of France.

While the forces of barbarism had been defeated in Europe, it seemed to many intellectuals that the cancer of totalitarianism had spread to Argentina, with the increasing power of Perón. A bitter debate is still raging as to the true nature of the Peronist regime. For the purposes of this discussion, it is sufficient to say that the ten-year period of the first *peronato* can be seen as a deliberate assault on aristocratic and liberal, European, values. Peronism claimed for itself a new synthesis of democracy, nationalism, anti-imperialism and industrial development and railed against the undemocratic, dependent Argentine oligarchy. Whilst Perón's aggression remained at the level of rhetoric — he stopped short of class confrontation — his use of symbolism and mythology was deliberately populist. The image of Evita, the studiously cultivated resemblance of Perón to the tango singer Carlos Gardel, the *descamisado* and the *cabecita negra* (terms used to describe Perón's working-class supporters), the rhetorical manipulation of Perón's speeches and his use of radio and the press, all made up a new style which was anathema to liberal groups. These sectors in turn built up a Manichean picture of Perón as another Rosas, supported by lower-class, gross and stupid people who were outside the boundaries of civilisation. Since the growing gap between culture and civilisation could not be bridged, the masses should be ignored as far as possible, with meaningful dialogue maintained among the few who could maintain standards. Peronism, for Borges, was literally bad art, organised for mass consumption: 'There were thus two stories: one of a criminal variety, made up of prisons, tortures, prostitutions, robbery and fires; the other, more theatrical, made up of ridiculous events and plots for the consumption of louts'.[26]

Peronism could not so easily be dismissed as a working-class cabaret. From the downfall of the regime in 1955 until Perón's return in 1973, every government had to come to terms with a party which still maintained mass popular support. After a brief period of military repression, power was handed back to a civilian government led by

Frondizi, which seemed to embody progressive democratic ideals that could steer the country away from the excesses of populism and militarism. The country had remained culturally cloistered under Perón, almost entirely cut off from the scientific and artistic development that had taken place in other parts of the world. After 1955, a large number of people were eager to renovate Argentine culture by opening the country up once again to Europe and the United States. At this time, the older elite groups were partially replaced by new middle-class politicians: the 'winds of change', it was felt, would blow away the remaining vestiges of traditional Argentine society.

The rhetoric of 'modernisation', however, could not become a reality in a country which was stagnating economically and was politically volatile. There was a brief period of optimism between 1958 and 1965 when Buenos Aires seemed to reflect a number of characteristics associated with modernisation, not just of goods, but of many different aspects of culture. This was the time in which considerable sums were spent on advertising, visits to the psychoanalyst became an integral part of middle-class Buenos Aires life, people flocked to the films of Ingmar Bergman and helped to create a 'boom' in Latin American fiction, by buying fictional works in tens of thousands. The recent Nobel Prize winner, Gabriel García Márquez first published *One Hundred Years of Solitude* in Buenos Aires. The publishing house expected small sales, but the book sold hundreds of thousands of copies in the first months. News journals grew up to reflect and direct these new tastes, and fashion in all its aspects became extremely important.

Yet despite some superficial similarities, Buenos Aires was not London and the 'swinging sixties' were curtailed by another military coup in 1966. The military had firm ideas as to how the country should be run, but little expertise in the cultural field. It intervened in the universities, closing down many faculties, seized magazines, closed theatres on the grounds of morality, ordered imported political textbooks such as works by Marx and Engels to be burned by the Post Office, closed radio news services and television shows. A number of artists and intellectuals reacted to these conditions by leaving the country, but many others became politicised and fought the government in all areas of cultural activity. Their analyses varied in sophistication, but the dominant strands of thought were nationalist, populist and, in many cases, Marxisant. Perhaps for the first time in Argentine history, young middle-class intellectuals were predominantly nationalist and anti-British (for it should be remembered that Peronism in the 1940s attracted little support among intellectuals).

The European 'universalist' model was called into question for having distorted national development. In a number of research institutes in Argentina and Latin America, work began to appear on the nature of economic and cultural dependency, which explored the links between dependency and underdevelopment, and provided theoretical justification for rejecting the old tradition of assimilating uncritically the latest European trends. Concepts such as 'the people', the 'nation' and 'the Third World' were given a new positive value, and the word *extranjerizante* became widely used as a term of abuse to describe those who followed without question ideas from abroad.

Working-class unrest and student radicalism in the late 1960s and early 1970s eventually caused the military to stand down in favour of Perón. The return of Perón was initially greeted with euphoria and led to an increase in all aspects of 'popular' culture, a rather vague term used to describe many forms of anti-elitist art, from street theatre to open air concerts. It was a confused and confusing time, but it soon became clear that Perón had not returned to a social revolutionary. With Perón's death, the regime was torn by internal feuds and degenerated into violence and near anarchy. There was a purge of left-wing intellectuals, many of whom left the country to avoid death threats.

The military intervened once more to restore order in 1976, and waged a campaign of systematic murder under the guise of a war against terrorism. (It took another six years for Britain to 'recognise' the nature of this regime.) Virtually all forms of cultural activity were silenced and even old liberal intellectuals such as Borges could no longer even share in the optimism that military rule would restore the value of civilisation. The six years between 1976 and 1982 represented something of a cultural vacuum, in which no dynamic cultural groups could operate. The Falklands/Malvinas War altered this situation by discrediting the military, who had to permit elections at the end of 1983. Under the six term democratic term of the Radical Party President Alfonsín and recently, under the newly elected Peronist president, Carlos Menem, a country that had been mute for so long is finding its voice, and intellectual and cultural matters are once again being discussed freely. Argentine culture has always developed through dialogue. The reception of foreign movements and tendencies, including those of Britain, which have been the subject of this essay, is an integral part of Argentine culture and instead of interrupting the purity of improbable autochtonous developments, it stimulates debates (like that of cultural dependency) and adds a dynamic element in the development of artistic creation. It is to be hoped that this process will continue and that Britain and Argentina can maintain and strengthen those cultural exchanges which are as old as the Nation-State itself.

# Notes

1. J.L.Borges, 'Juan López y John Ward', *Los conjurados,* Buenos Aires, 1985, p. 95.
2. J.L.Borges, *Evaristo Carriego* 2nd ed, Buenos Aires, 1955, p.9.
3. D.F. Sarmiento, *Recuerdos de provincia*, Centro Editor, Buenos Aires, 1979, p. 164. See the discussion of this text in Carlos Altamirano, Beatriz Sarlo, *Literatura / Sociedad*, Buenos Aires, 1983.
4. J.B. Alberdi, *Bases y puntos de partida para la organización de la República Argentina*, Buenos Aires, 1952, pp. 31, 33, 38. I am using George Reid Andrews translations of Alberdi from his *The Afro-Argentines of Buenos Aires, 1800-1900*, University of Wisconsin, Madison, 1980, pp.103-104.
5. Maria Rosa Oliver, *Mundo, mi casa*, Buenos Aires, 1965. For an analysis of the British nanny see J. Gathorne-Hardy, *The Rise and Fall of the British Nanny*, London, 1972.
6. Victoria Ocampo, *Autobiografía Vol.1, El archipélago*, Buenos Aires, 1979, p. 113.
7. Andrew Graham-Yooll, *The Forgotten Colony: A History of English-Speaking Communities in Argentina*, London, 1981, p.130.
8. Sir David Kelly, *The Ruling Few*, London, 1952, p. 122.
9. Manuel Mújica Laínez, *Los porteños*, Buenos Aires, 1979, p.77.
10. David Viñas, *De Sarmiento a Cortázar*, Buenos Aires, 1974.
11. See Gerald Martin, 'The Literature, Music and Art of Latin America, 1870-1930' in L. Bethell, ed., *The Cambridge History of Latin America*, Vol. IV, Cambridge 1986, p. 461.
12. V. Ocampo, *Autobiografía Vol. II: El imperio insular*, Buenos Aires, 1980.
13. Frances Donaldson, *The British Council: The First Fifty Years*, London, 1984, p.12.
14. Quoted in Donaldson, p.18.
15. Kelly, op. cit., pp. 114-115.
16. Graham-Yooll, op. cit., p. 194.
17. Tony Mason. 'Some Englishmen and Scotsmen abroad: The spread of world football', in A. Tomlinson, L. Whannel, eds. *Off the Ball*, London, 1986, pp.67-82.
18. Graham-Yooll, op. cit., p. 191.

19. Quoted in the recent Argentine film, *Fútbol Argentino*, produced by GEA Cinematográfica
20. See Simon Collier, *The Life, Music and Times of Carlos Gardel*, Pittsburg, 1986.
21. E.Fishburn, *The Portrayal of Immigration in Nineteenth Century Argentine Fiction, 1845-1902*, Berlin, 1981.
22. Julio Irazusta, *Memorias*, Buenos Aires, 1974.
23. Virginia Woolf, *The Sickle Side of the Moon: The Letters of Virginia Woolf, 1932-1935*, ed. N. Nicholson, London, 1979, p.439.
24. Benito Lynch, *El inglés de los güesos*, 8th ed., Buenos Aires, 1960, p.253.
25. J.L. Borges, 'Anotación al 23 de agosto de 1944', *Sur* 120, October, 1944, pp.25-6.
26. J.L. Borges, 'L'illusion comique', *Sur* 237, November-December 1955, p.9.

# 10

# Charles Darwin and W.H.Hudson

*Jason Wilson*

Recovering from an illness W.H.Hudson (1841-1922), the Argentine-born naturalist and writer, recaptured sudden intense images of his wild childhood in Quilmes, near Buenos Aires. He then wrote the autobiography of his first eighteen years and published it as *Far Away and Long Ago* (1918) though he himself was already seventy-seven years old. It has deservedly become a classic. It has also been often used as a documentary source for farm life in the middle of the nineteenth century, without questioning the accuracy of Hudson's memory. Though this autobiography evokes the grain of lived experience it does build up to a plot that suggests a sense of betrayal. In his eighteenth year the combination of the death of his beloved mother (1859) and a casual but compulsive reading of Charles Darwin's *The Origin of Species* close the book hinting at a kind of spiritual death. It is Hudson who inextricably links the two events to a crucial date.

Hudson's mother was a devout Christian who shared a passion for wild flowers with her son. In his autobiography Hudson interprets her adoration: wild flowers are little voiceless messengers and divine symbols. Fifty-eight years later Hudson still vividly remembered that his mother died leaving her son with a 'distressed mind'. Though his mother never openly questioned what caused her son's distress, it was clear that Darwin's undermining of the Christian order in terms of a materialistic or natural one was to blame. A reading of Darwin caused the deathbed rift.

Like countless others Hudson found Darwin's incredible compilation of facts concerning speciation quite obvious and convincing. He has twice referred to this book that changed his life and became a grudging 'evolutionist' despite his mother but not without a struggle. He confessed he was 'able to resist its teachings for years, solely because I could not endure to part with a philosophy of life, if I may so describe it, which could not logically be held if Darwin was right, and without which life would not be worth living'. *If* Darwin was right: this was the doubt his mother bequeathed him.

One of Hudson's brothers brought Darwin's *Origins* back from England with him, but here we cannot rely on Hudson's memory. His mother died on 4 October 1859 and Darwin's *Origins* was published after in November, and sold out very quickly. Could Hudson have even read the second edition of 1860? We will never know for his copy has vanished. What counts in Hudson's life plot is not immaterial chronology, but the emotional yoking together of Darwin and mother. Between Hudson's mother's death (1859) and his journey to England (1874), never to return to Argentina, we can only imagine how he assimilated Darwin's theory against his mother's pleas. Little documentary evidence survives those fifteen years which included military service and years of sheep farming amassing enough money to travel to his beloved England. But what emerges from some letters that Hudson sent to London is an aggravation of his resentment with Darwin and a thorough reading of Darwin's earlier *The Voyage of the Beagle* (1839, 1845). And during those intervening years Hudson's ambition to become a naturalist like Darwin grew to become one of the prime motives for abandoning his native land.

The evidence for Hudson's further reading of Darwin and for his scientific ambitions comes from his assiduous collecting of birdskins, sent on Dr. Burmeister's recommendations to both the Smithsonian and the London Zoological Society, accompanied by notes that led to his first publications as an ornithologist from La Plata in the *Proceedings of the Zoological Society*. His letters have been republished and his work with Dr. Sclater well recognised. But the most interesting insights into Hudson's continuing resentment with Darwin surface in an exchange of letters with Darwin himself published in the Zoological Society's Proceedings.

In an understandably naive way, for Quilmes was far removed from the polemic over evolution in London and Oxford, Hudson penned an 'insolent' letter (Alicia Jurado's phrase) criticising Darwin's description of a local ground woodpecker (*Colaptes campestris*). In this open letter of March 1870 Hudson attacked Darwin's 'erroneous' and 'careless' description of this treeless woodpecker, blaming his hasty passage across the pampas and by inference contrasting his own permanence there, on the spot. He further suggested that Darwin had 'purposively wrested the truth in order to prove his theory', arguing that this *carpintero* did inhabit the *ombú*, a tree adapted to the pampas. His letter concluded that this very woodpecker 'affords an argument against the truth of Mr. Darwin's hypothesis' for 'natural selection has done absolutely nothing for our woodpecker'.

On 1 November 1870 Darwin answered Hudson's charges. With Hudson Darwin 'departed from his rule' — in his son Francis Darwin's words of not stooping to counter the many criticisms he suffered after publication of the *Origins*. In his letter Darwin cited another authority — Felix de Azara — and insisted that a slight modification had occurred in the ground woodpecker's habits. He denied inventing anything and admitted his only mistake had been to claim that this beautifully tree-adapted bird found without a tree had never climbed trees. And he modified the eloquent passage about this ground woodpecker in a later — the sixth — edition of the *Origins*. But it was the ending of Darwin's letter that had fateful consequences for Hudson: 'I should be loath to think that there are many naturalists who, without any evidence, would accuse a fellow-worker of telling deliberate falsehood to prove his thesis'. For in these words Darwin denied Hudson his greatest ambition, that of being considered by Darwin as a fellow-worker. Hudson had broken the rules of the scientist's/gentleman's code of conduct and had been dismissed. Hudson was never to know that far more lurked behind Darwin's example of this ground woodpecker and that this involved Darwin's own private debunking of Paley (I have studied this further in a forthcoming book). We cannot assess whether Hudson even read Darwin's reply. We can only assume that Dr. Sclater — with whom Hudson later wrote *Argentine Ornithology* (1888) — sent him a copy. But this matter did not end in 1870.

By the sixth edition of *The Origin of Species* (1872) Darwin found the incident with Hudson faintly amusing. By the 1870s the whole debate over natural selection had been won by the Darwinists. In 1870 Darwin had interrupted his work on *The Descent of Man* (1871) in order to answer Hudson. Darwin was airing newer theories like sexual selection and dealing with Man, so glaringly absent from his *Origins* and he had more formidable enemies like Mivart to cope with. Yet Darwin bothered — such was his concern for honesty — to refer to a 'Mr.Hudson' in the re-edition of his *Origins*. He allowed Hudson's disclaimer about the woodpecker to stand, but referred to it with an exclamation mark. But Hudson's name re- appeared later in the book — 'the scientific event of the century', in D.E.Allen's words — where Darwin praised Hudson as an 'excellent observer' then damned him in terms of the scientific community as a 'strong disbeliever in evolution'. And that phrase in 1872 was enough to snuff out Hudson's scientific ambitions. Whether Hudson read this 1872 edition before leaving for England in 1874 or read it on arrival in London, without contacts and with very little money, has not been recorded. Whatever, he must have blushed with shame.

The closest we can approach Hudson's gaffe is to look at the way he deals with the ground woodpecker in his *Birds of La Plata* (1899) where he repeats Darwin's descriptions of this ground-feeding, river-bank-nesting, atypical woodpecker. Hudson also cites Azara and adds that this bird's habits are 'exceedingly curious' as if he Hudson was the first to alert his English reader to this anomaly, without mentioning Darwin at all. This absence of recognising his debt after nineteen years (the 1870 polemic) is eloquent of Hudson's hurt.

Over the next decade of Hudson's life in London (1874-85) we can only interpret his fiction to catch his moods and thoughts. That he could not make it as a scientist must have been obvious to him. Science had moved into the laboratory and the universities beyond the old-fashioned naturalists like Gilbert White of Selborne, amateurs with whom Hudson identified. In his impecunious situation Hudson turned to fiction to earn some money and wrote anonymously, under pseudonyms, even under a woman's name. The first of his novels *The Purple Land that England Lost* (1885) concerns us because he wrote it while Darwin still lived, though it took him some years to find a publisher and Darwin died in 1882.

*The Purple Land* has become, after the later *Green Mansions* (1904), one of Hudsons' most edited books. There is no doubt that this novel can be read as a flimsy fictionalisation of a naturalist's probable wanderings and observations in Uruguay in the 1860s. But Hudson's original impetus in writing the novel has been buried in the past. A clue arises from the title *The Purple Land that England Lost* for in subsequent editions, after Hudson had acknowledged authorship, he quickly and guiltily suppressed 'that England lost'. Why? Because the British Empire was at its most dominant and London its busy, thriving centre. Hudson did not want to offend imperial pride as he sought to become 'English'. 'That England lost' clearly refers back to England's failure to colonise Argentina and Uruguay in 1806-07. After the English were evicted from Buenos Aires, they returned under General Whitelocke with 12,000 men in a revenge task force, easily taking Montevideo but not Buenos Aires. General Whitelocke surrendered rather than see his troops pointlessly massacred, but was later court-marshalled. The whole incident was a minor imperial set-back, quickly forgotten. Sir Samuel Ford Whittingham wrote, though, that this surrender 'appears to me one of the most severe blows that England has ever received'. And Hudson, in his poverty and misery, sought to re-open this wound. But it was the still living Darwin that he hoped to affect: the Darwin who had arrived at the River Plate Republics in 1837 with this imperial defeat still in mind. For under all that Darwin wrote about the River Plate there was a sense of scorn and sarcasm: it was as if the offended patriot in Darwin came to the fore, ahead of the budding scientist. If one adds to this Darwin's thrill at encountering tropical nature in Brazil one can explain, in part, his disappointment that so irked Hudson who found himself in the inverse position of being an Argentine stuck penniless in Gustave Doré's London.

To exemplify Darwin's patriotic contempt for Hudson's 'distant' land I will recall some of his remarks made during the *Beagle* trip. Darwin found his first view of the famous treeless pampas 'one of the most uninteresting I ever beheld.' He described it as 'an undulating green plain and large herds of cattle has not even the charm of novelty'. About the river Plate estuary, from Maldonado where he stayed: 'An enormous brackish river bounded by an interminable green plain ... enough to make any naturalist groan'. So much for the pampa landscape that so gripped Hudson as a naturalist when in London!

When Darwin described the local creole inhabitants he was even ruder. He asked mocking questions about where London was or whether the sun spun round the earth. He struck matches with his teeth and hid his compass as he guided himself about. He joked to his English reader about the creole's ignorance and was disgusted by local medicine ('Many of the remedies used by the people of the country are ludicrously strange, but too disgusting to be mentioned'). When Darwin evoked the politics and revolutions he was frankly contemptuous. As a liberal democrat he was outraged at the tyranny and found the so-called revolutions 'laughable', quite irrelevant. He concluded: 'I am writing as if I had been among the inhabitants of Central Africa. Banda Oriental (Uruguay) would not be flattered by the comparison'. Darwin followed this negative comparison between the Hottentots and Creoles with a withering value judgement as to their morals. This is summarised in Darwin's code language as a total absence of 'gentlemen'. It is well to remember that Darwin travelled as a gentleman-companion to Captain Fitzroy and received no pay on board. Darwin recapitulated: the creoles were 'detestably mean and unprincipled'. He added: 'Sensuality, mockery of all religion and the grossest corruption are far from uncommon'. To him the epitome of the creole's behaviour was the way the Indians were slaughtered. Darwin asked his reader a rhetorical question: 'Who would believe in this age that such atrocities could be committed in a Christian civilized country'.

These traveller's perceptions led Darwin to try and re-write history, especially the 1806-07 set-backs. He exclaimed: 'How different would have been the aspect of this river if English colonists had by good fortune first sailed up the Plata! What noble towns would now have occupied its shores!' Later, on arriving in Australia, Darwin measured the difference between British colonialism and Spanish, at a glance. Australia 'is a most magnificent testimony to the power of the British nation. Here, in a less promising country scores of years have done many times more than an equal number of centuries have effected in South America'. And Darwin felt proud: 'My first feeling was to congratulate myself that I was born an Englishman'. He enumerated the benefits of this birth-mark: 'To hoist the British flag, seems to draw with it as a certain consequence wealth, prosperity and civilisation'.

All the details that I have quoted concerning Darwin's imperial superiority and its concomitant scorn were digested by Hudson and exorcised in his novel about Uruguay. His prime intention, evident from the first full title, was to thank heaven that the Banda Oriental had never been conquered, made decent, democratic and civilised. The liberal progressive myths of the 1840s had become empty for Hudson himself suffered the negative consequences of the British flair for 'wealth, prosperity and civilization'. The barbarity of Uruguay became a paradise for Hudson from the 'civilities' of Paddington. *The Purple Land* is a compensation novel, an exorcism of Darwin's power.

This plot, then, in Jorge Luis Borges's words, explores the male typically English protagonist's (Richard Lamb) *acriollamiento*; how his rough life as a horseman (gaucho) on the undulating plains slowly turned a quintessential Englishman, a Darwin, into a violent creole. The true Englishman discovers the thrill of reverting to savage life. He wakes up. Notice how Richard Lamb opens the novel as a patriot who wishes to transform the backwardness of the Banda Oriental: 'We are here gentlemen to infuse a little of our Anglo-Saxon energy and all that sort of thing into this old tin-pot of a nation'. In this novel Hudson subtly reveals the kind of class prejudices that Darwin himself had aired until, unlike Darwin, Lamb becomes South American (like Hudson at the time in London), that is, free, open and in touch with his senses, alive to danger and life. By the end of Lamb's vivid ramblings around the purple land he confesses something that Hudson must have wished Darwin might have said: 'I wished that I had been born amongst them and was one of them, not a weary, wandering Englishman overburdened with the arms and armour of civilization'. In this confession we can see that Hudson was 'one of them' but trapped in London, unable to return home. He was a creole squeezed into a suit of armour, the conventions of dress and social

intercourse. The England of the 1870s cruelly excluded him from
female company so that he had to marry his landlady to find a
companion (she was eleven years older). Hudson contrasts this difficulty in meeting women with how creole women relate to men like
Lamb:

> Could any woman in my own ultra-civilized and excessively proper
> country inspire me with a feeling like that in so short a time? I
> fancy not. Oh civilization with your million conventions, soul and
> body withering prudishness, vain education for the little ones,
> going to church in best black clothes, unnatural craving for clean-
> liness, feverish striving after comforts that bring no comfort to the
> heart, are you a mistake altogether?

Here then is Hudson's direct answer to Darwin. Through his
character he sweeps away the Victorian way of life and moans the
conquering of nature, progress and technology. For Lamb — and
Hudson — civilization had taken the 'wrong way'. Lamb's image of
crowded urban life is that of one vast Clapham Junction 'with human
creatures moving like trucks and carriages on cast iron, conventional
rails'. In 1902 Hudson wrote directly about London: 'I fancy London
is poisonous'. His only antidote had become his memory of the
depopulated pampas.

But what most pained Hudson both in Darwin and his experiences
as an outsider in London was the English class-system, the 'gentle-
manly' code. This was completely alien to the creoles, whether gaucho
or *estanciero*. It was the English class-system that made it so hard
for him to make contact with what lay behind the masks of convention. In a letter he confessed: 'I detest ... the upper class'. He praised
the Great War as a purge of the 'loathsome cursed civilization of
Europe', especially its 'caste feeling' and its 'detestable partisanship'.
In his novel Hudson redeems another way of relating to people. Lamb
is dumb-struck at the absolute classlessness of Uruguay: 'Here the
Lord of many leagues of land and of herds unnumbered sits down to
talk with the hired shepherd, a poor, bare-footed fellow in his smoky
*rancho*, and no class or caste difference divides them, no consciousness of their widely different positions chills the warm current of
sympathy between two human hearts.' And Lamb contrasts this
manner with his own English system: 'What a change to a person
coming from the lands with higher and lower classes, each with its
innumerable hateful subdivisions...'

By the end of the novel Lamb has learned to hate his own English roots, especially his culture's jingoism. He is glad that England lost its chance to colonise Uruguay and that it has remained a savage land. Unlike Darwin, Lamb can purge himself of his 'exclusively British characteristic' which is 'contempt'. He concludes — and here Hudson bore Darwin's actual words in mind:

> and where a few months ago I sang the praises of British civiliza-tion, lamenting that it had been planted here and abundantly watered with blood [ie Whitlocke's failure], only to be plucked up again and cast into the sea. After my rambles into the interior ... I cannot say that I am of that opinion now. I cannot believe that if this country had been conquered and recolonized by England, and all that is crooked in it made straight according to our notions, my intercourse with the people would have had the wild delightful flavour I have found in it. And if that distinctive flavour cannot be had along with the material prosperity [Darwin's word] resulting from Anglo-Saxon energy, I must breath the wish that this land may never know such prosperity.

In retrospect, then, despite his yearning to become English, Hud-son preferred bloodshed and violence as more authentic than any-thing he had encountered in the London of the 1870s. Hudson discovered that vitality, 'cackling laughter', the 'healthy play of passions' were missing. It was as if through his fictional character's liberating meanders around Uruguay that he had imagined a variant to Darwin's *Beagle* narrative: that Uruguay, its revolutionary politics, its seductive, fiery women, its nature had so entranced Darwin that he jumped ship at Maldonado and began to live like a *criollo* or gaucho for the rest of his life, instead of for a few exciting weeks as he crossed the empty pampas on horseback from Bahía Blanca. This heresy, an Englishman preferring abroad, focuses on what was most precious to Darwin and nineteenth-century England, its democracy. Hudson made Lamb choose violence and bloodshed to the hypocrisy of fairplay and what is proper. The way gauchos cut throats in a personal duel seemed almost human compared to how the majority lived under industrialism in urban England. In his novel Hudson wanted to shock his prim reader by defending bloodlust:

> If a murderous brute with truculent eyes and gnashing teeth attempts to disembowel me with a butcher's knife, the instinct of self-preservation comes out in all its old original ferocity, inspiring

the heart with such implacable fury that after spilling his blood I could spurn his loathsome carcass with my foot. I do not wonder at myself for speaking those savage words. That he was past recall seemed certain, yet not a shade of regret did I feel at his death. Joy at the terrible retribution I had experienced when galloping away into the darkness — such joy that I could have sung and shouted aloud...

This fantasy murder becomes a metaphor for the awakening of the 'old, original' instincts that have withered under civilisation. Whether Hudson ever killed anybody or perhaps witnessed a knife fight in the thirty-four years he lived and worked in Argentina is not the point: bloodlust allows Lamb to become a savage and feel alive again.

Hudson's novel ends with a prayer: 'May the blight of our superior civilization never fall on your wild flowers'. The irony is obvious: Hudson has turned Darwin upside down and blight equals disease equals corruption. Wild flowers stand for Christian innocence which for Hudson can be related both to his mother and to his own pre-Darwinian childhood.

But the truth was that few readers bought his novel and most of the early critics dismissed it. Later when Hudson achieved the integration with the English that he yearned for he excised half the title 'that England lost' hoping that the novel would be read as a romance (as it has been by most later critics and readers) and not as revenge on Darwin. And anyhow by the time Hudson managed to find a willing publisher Darwin had died. The novel became a private, fantasy revenge. The fact was that Darwin, perhaps without really intending to, had thoroughly excluded Hudson as a fellow-worker; had so damned Hudson as a 'strong disbeliever' that Hudson's only recourse over his later years was to elaborate another alternative and more primitive strategy to life, work, nature and England. As late as 1920 when he was seventy-nine years old Hudson confessed in a letter to his first biographer, Morley Roberts, that he still supported Samuel Butler against Darwin, for it was Butler 'who smashed the Darwin idol and finally compelled the angels of science to creep cautiously'. Was Hudson aware that he was repeating verbatim Bishop Wilberforce's words from 1857 when he vainly tried to ridicule Darwin's theory? Sadly what Hudson embodied was far from smashing the Darwin idol, for by the 1920s he was quite out of touch with the realities of science.

To conclude, we could situate this one-sided confrontation between Charles Darwin and W.H.Hudson into a greater context so that it becomes eloquent of a historical experience focussing on power and prestige and revenge and fantasy. Darwin and Hudson have been read not along the conventions of either a scientific or a literary discourse but as human documents dealing with a cultural clash in a narrative way, epitomising the unconsciousness of power and the crippling resentment of the powerless. Their relationship becomes a parable.

## Notes

This study was begun in my working paper (no.5) *W.H.Hudson: the Colonial's Revenge* published in 1981 (University of London: Institute of Latin American Studies) and has been considerably enlarged, especially concerning Charles Darwin,in my forthcoming book *Killjoy: an Enquiry into Charles Darwin and W.H.Hudson, ancestors*. Some of the material has been aired by previous critics, especially Alicia Jurado, *Vida y obra de W.H.Hudson*, Buenos Aires 1971 and Ruth Tomalin's second book on Hudson, *W.H.Hudson. A Biography*, London 1982 but all the speculations and interpretations are my own. For a recent view of Hudson's fiction based on literary critical premisses see John Walker 'Home Thoughts from Abroad: W.H.Hudson's Argentine Fiction' *Canadian Review of Comparative Literature*, September 1983, 332-76.

# 11
## British Travel Writing and Argentina

*John Walker*

One of the most interesting features of the development of Argentina over the last two centuries since Independence has been the contribution of the English-speaking community. Although the efforts of the pioneer settlers, the early railway-builders, the skilful engineers and the shrewd businessmen have been well documented, less attention has been paid to the literary efforts of the English-speaking writers of the River Plate region. This is understandable in a way, since many of the works produced were not written by settled members of the new republic, but by birds of passage, usually British travellers who came, saw, made notes, and returned to the homeland. As such they belong to the mainstream of English literature, if what they wrote can be considered to have any literary merit at all.

One must not assume, then, that every book that got into print was a literary masterpiece, of the same calibre as those produced later by R.B. Cunninghame Graham or W. H. Hudson who, although they are important, are only two in a long line that continues into the present day with the poet, dramatist and short-story writer, William Shand. Most of the nineteenth-century works were by-products of travels or expeditions organised for non-literary reasons. They were written mostly by soldiers like Alexander Gillespie whose typically long-winded title, *Gleanings and Remarks Collected During Many Months of Residence at Buenos Aires and Within the Upper Country* (Leeds: Dewhurst, 1818), relates his experience during his imprisonment after the abortive English invasions of 1806-07 (Popham, Beresford, White-locke).

Interlaced with the many military details and matters relating to the army mission, one finds the perceptive comments on the Argentine character and land, a true mine of *costumbrismo*, not to mention Gillespie's personal views with regard to the Spaniards, the Catholic religion, and the suitability of the land for prospective British immigrants. Gillespie's *Gleanings and Remarks* are representative of the military memoir type of literature that one finds later in Millar,

Holland, Craufurd and others like Essex Vidal, whose apt illustrations bring to life what were to be the familiar features of River Plate
history and geography (pampas, gauchos, Indians. etc.).

Amongst the diplomats Woodbine Parish, for example, appointed
chargé d'affaires by Canning in 1823, showed more than a passing
political interest in his monumental *Buenos Aires, and the Provinces
of the Río de la Plata* (London: John Murray, 1839), which is a history
of the Plate region from discovery to independence, a geography,
geology and botany manual, not to mention a compendium of valuable
information on trade and debt supported by up-to-date statistics
(especially in the enlarged second edition of 1852). With the emergence of the new states after the Wars of Independence against Spain,
however, the interest was generally commercial, and a whole procession of mining engineers, metallurgists and mineralogists would
wend their way from Britain to Montevideo, to Buenos Aires and
across the pampas, usually to Chile and Peru, recording their impressions as they went. Peter Schmidtmeyer's *Travels into Chile over
the Andes in the Years 1820-21* (1824), J.A.B. Beaumont's *Travels in
Buenos Aires and the Adjacent Provinces of the Río de la Plata* (1828),
the mining-businessman John Miers' *Travels in Chile and Peru*
(1831), the merchant Samuel Haigh's *Sketches of Buenos Aires, Chile
and Peru* (1831), plus scores of others, are examples of the stuff from
which was created the legend of *los viajeros ingleses* (the English
travellers).

These chronicles, notes, letters and travel stories, although they
may have lost much of their appeal for modern English readers, began
to take on a new interest in Argentina, with the gradual awareness
of the emergence of a new independent country. With a growing
consciousness of Argentine history and the development of new
sciences, these 'mere' travel books became mines of information for
the historian, the political scientist, the economist and the sociologist.
The description of the financial situation of the new republic, the
geography, the climatic, agricultural, commercial and industrial aspects (cf. Woodbine Parish) of the young states, not to mention the
unstable political situation, became the basis of modern studies of the
nineteenth-century Argentine *modo de ser*. In the absence of national
research material, since the natives were too close to their own life
and customs to consider the documentation or recording thereof to be
of value, the twentieth-century scholars turned to the works of the
aforementioned British travellers, plus many others like Andrews,
Bonelli, Brand, Elwes, Hadfield, Hibbert, MacDowell, Mansfield,
Proctor, the Robertson brothers, Scarlett, Snow, Temple, Thomson,

Webster, Weddell and others, whose apparently casual comments, notes and observations on Argentine life and customs became a treasure trove for Argentine scholars. Enrique de Gandia, José Luis Busaniche, Carlos Aldao, Luis Baudizzone *et al*, in their critical introductions to the Solar-Hachette, Emecé and Claridad editions and in individual studies on *los viajeros ingleses*, not only absorbed and produced penetrating studies of the now invaluable narratives, but also had them translated into Spanish editions which were then ploughed back into the field of Argentine literary and historical criticism. Solar-Hachette and Editorial Universitaria de Buenos Aires continue to produce works in this area, whilst one can still find occasionally rare works published under the Emecé, La Cultura Argentina, and Claridad seal.

One of the rarest, earliest and most interesting examples from a literary point of view is that published in 1918 in the Biblioteca de la Nación series, *Las Pampas y los Andes*, known in its original English title as *Rough Notes Taken During Some Rapid Journeys Across the Pampas* (London: John Murray, 1826) by the soldier-cum-mining engineer, Francis Bond Head, later to become Lieutenant-Governor of Upper Canada at a restless period (1837) in that country's history. Retiring from the army in 1825, he accepted a post supervising the mines of the Río Plata Mining Association in the Southern Andes. *Rough Notes*, is the record of his horse and carriage trips as a mining supervisor. Since his mines were far removed from his Buenos Aires base, where he had left his family, Head had to cross the pampa from east to west four times to study his mines in West Central Argentina. He also had to cross the Andes, touching on Santiago, to investigate his Chilean mines — an odyssey of epic proportions worthy of being chronicled, especially at this important period in Argentine history, immediately after Independence. Long regarded by Argentine scholars as a classic, if less appreciated in English-speaking circles, *Rough Notes*, Head's first literary venture, makes a valuable contribution to pampa *costumbrismo* and places Head high on the list of gaucho apologists of which he is certainly one of the first. In its feeling for the vast expanse of the pampa, *Rough Notes* prefigures the *costumbrismo* of Facundo and the gauchesque poetry of Martín Fierro. No greater tribute could be paid to Head than to have quotations from his work used as introductory tags by Sarmiento in his classic study of Argentine life. In fact, the great Argentine thinker was probably influenced by Head's notes, not only in his painting of the customs, types and geographical characteristics, but also by Head's shrewd commentary on the political scene.

It is, however, in his description of the wonders of nature, especially the immensity, solitude and hostility of the Argentine plains,
that Head best merits the title of *pampa costumbrista*. But Head was
also a social animal, and in his narrative he shows himself to be much
more interested in human attitudes, tending at times to forget, in his
curiosity, the real purpose of his trips i.e. the investigation and
inspection of mines. Several decades before Sarmiento proposed his
gloomy thesis on the struggle between civilisation and barbarism, it
is revealing to find Head's assessment of the gauchos, many of whom
he found to be of good manners and noble sentiments.

Despite his modesty, and given his non-literary reasons for writing, Head has produced a little masterpiece. As a guide for prospective
miners and investment companies, *Rough Notes* was a valuable
enough document, in which he shows a fine grasp of trade and
commerce matters that was to influence greatly British dealings with
the River Plate region. But this dimension of his work is of less lasting
importance than his perceptive remarks as to the physical, moral and
political reasons for his recommendation of non-investment. His is
the stuff of which Sarmiento, Alberdi and Mitre created their repu-
tations as *pensadores*. If Head can be considered a *pensador*, in his
analysis of the (then) present and his concern for the future of a
nation, he also transcends geographical and chronological barriers in
his preoccupation with the human condition. Having thought long
and deep on man's estate, he takes pen to paper in order to criticise
man's inhumanity to man. It is the abuse and exploitation of all
peoples (especially the American Indian) that motivates his reluctant
moralising and his philosophical disquisitions. But a metaphysical
preoccupation remains in the realms of the mind unless there is a
concretisation in literary terms of these philosophical inquiries about
life and death, essence and existence. It is Head's capacity to render
these metaphysical concerns in aesthetic fashion that makes out of
the amateur philosopher a writer — romantic, realist, and apologist
of the gaucho, whose apprenticeship was served on the Argentine
plains. It is no surprise that Head is still treated with some reverence
in Argentina where, with Cunninghame Graham and Hudson, he is
regarded as one of *Los tres clásicos ingleses de la pampa*.[2]

It is no coincidence either that Head's work was cited in many
similar narratives (often of lesser quality) produced by later travel
writers, the miner Andrews (1827), Brand (1828), and the aforementioned Miers (1826), Beaumont (1828) and many more in the late 1820s.
The decade of the 1830s saw the appearance of the narratives of
Temple (1830), Haigh (1831), MacDowell (1833), Webster (1834), Scar-

lett (1838) and, of course, the first edition of Woodbine Parish's work (1839), expanded to mammoth proportions when published in 1852, the year of the birth of probably the most important literary traveller, Cunninghame Graham, and the overthrow of the dictator Rosas. In the decades immediately afterwards travel literature continued to flourish: Bonelli (1854), Elwes (1854), Hadfield (1854), Mansfield (1856), Snow (1857). Industrial investigators like William MacCann, *Two Thousand Miles Ride through the Argentine Provinces* (London: Smith, Elder, 1853), and Wilfrid Latham, *The States of the River Plate: their Industries and Commerce* (London: Longmans Green, 1866), came and narrated their experiences in no mean literary fashion, as did the scientists like Robert Fitzroy, *Narrative of the Surveying Voyages of His Majesty's Ships 'Adventure' and 'Beagle' between the Years 1826 and 1836* (London: Henry Colburn, 1839) and Charles Darwin, *Journal of Researches into the Natural History and Geology of the Various Countries Visited During the Voyage Round the World of 'H.M.S. Beagle'* (London: John Murray, 1890).

When Robert Bontine Cunninghame Graham arrived as a youth in Argentina in 1870, he was neither scientist nor industrial investigator, although his intentions were supposed to be commercial (to earn his fortune) and personal (to seek adventure and escape from a harrowing home life at the hands of his ill soldier-father). Not surprisingly, one can say with hindsight, the ranching venture in the Argentine failed, but it did provide him with the desired adventure, valuable experience, a philosophy of life (and politics), and a great deal of material for his future writing. Apparently he found the life of the gaucho to his liking, and took part in all their activities, breaking in mustangs, throwing the *bolas*, racing horses and participating in ostrich hunts. These activities formed an important part of his literary output over the last forty years of his life, when he produced several hundreds of impressionistic sketches, mostly devoted to the pampas way of life for example 'La pampa', 'Paja y Cielo', 'El Rodeo', 'La Pulpería', 'Los Indios', 'The Captive', 'The Gualichú Tree', 'Los Seguidores', 'La Tapera', 'Un Angelito', 'Facón Grande', 'San Andrés', 'Gualeguaychú' and many others[3], as well as literary essays on the *bolas, lazos, baqueanos, rastreadores*, etc., which represent a valuable contribution to a growing gauchesque *costumbrismo* on what Graham labels 'A Vanishing Race,' in the line of Echeverría, Sarmiento, Hernández, Benito Lynch, Güiraldes and, of course, W. H. Hudson (of the romances and the short story). With the latter, who was born in Argentina but came to England to live, write and die, he was later to share many nostalgic reminiscences in the cold English days of depression, far from the purple land. The gaucho in Graham never died, and in later life he often wore the gaucho belt, even with formal dress, and spent his leisure time throwing the lasso — a skill he learned early in his days in Argentina when he was caught up in the revolution of López Jordán against the government of Sarmiento. Some of the brutality he describes graphically in sketches like 'A Silhouette' (from *Faith*, 1909). In 1873-74 he was off on a 'money-making' trip to Paraguay (where he obtained a concession to grow maté tea), under the dominance of yet another *caudillo*, Francisco Solano López, immortalised by Graham in *Portrait of a Dictator* (1933). It was experiences like this on the pampa that awakened the radical spirit in Graham and laid the foundations for his later socialist liaisons with (given his noble background) apparently unlikely comrades like Keir Hardie and John Burns.

After Argentina, another 'profit-making' adventure took him two years later to Uruguay where he bought horses to sell in Brazil — another project that brought him more excitement and future literary material than financial reward. No wonder he was to spend the rest of his literary life lambasting the monster Commerce. With the end of these adventures in 1878 his active life on the River Plate really came to an end. He was not to return there till the 1914-18 war, and only then on a brief distasteful mission to buy horses for the government (cf. 'Bopicua' from *Brought Forward*, 1916).

After his six-year stint (1886-92) as Radical Liberal M.P. in Parliament, where he plagued even his own party with fiery speeches and progressive ideas that were products of the radical spirit born on the pampas of Argentina, and eventful trips to North Africa (*Mogreb el Acksa*, 1898) and Europe, he settled down in his 'quiet period' to write almost a book a year from 1898 to 1914. Many of these collections of sketches contain some of his best impressions of the pampa, the gaucho and Argentine life in general — *Father Archangel of Scotland* (1896), *The Ipane* (1899), *Thirteen Stories* (1901), *Success* (1902), *Progress* (1905), *His People* (1906), *Faith* (1909), *Hope* (1910), *Charity* (1912), *A Hatchment* (1913), and *Brought Forward* (1916). Although his literary output was to keep him occupied over the next decade, the outbreak of the war in 1914 gave him the aforementioned opportunity to go back to Argentina which he found greatly changed since the halcyon days of his youth. The triple-headed monster, Civilisation/Commerce/Progress, in all the manifestations that he detested— telephones, telegraph wires, fenced trails, machinery — had almost rendered the gaucho extinct and the pampa no more than 'a cultivated prairie cut into squares by barbed wire fences, riddled with railways and with the very sky shaped into patterns by the crossing lines of telegraphs' ('Un Angelito').[4]

His last years in the Scottish family home at Ardoch and in London were devoted to riding, writing and working for the cause of Scottish nationalism. In another productive period he published biographies, histories and more collections of sketches, like *The Conquest of the River Plate* (1924), *Doughty Deeds* (1925), *Pedro de Valdivia* (1926), *Redeemed* (1927), *José Antonio Páez* (1929), *The Horses of the Conquest* (1930), *Writ in Sand* (1932), *Portrait of a Dictator* (1933) and *Mirages* (1936). In 1936, at the age of eighty-four, he decided to make the final, cyclical pilgrimage to his first love Argentina. In his last book Mirages he had narrated the story of the Englishman 'Charlie the Gaucho' who had returned to the pampa to die with his boots on. As if impelled by his own creation, Graham set out for Buenos Aires on 18 January 1936, carrying two bags of oats for the horses of his friend and biographer Aimé F. Tschiffely, whose famous horse trip from Buenos Aires to New York Graham had described in his sketch 'Tschiffely's Ride' (*Writ in Sand*). An emotional visit to Los 25 Ombúes, Hudson's birthplace, was an integral and final part of his pilgrimage. By March he had contracted bronchitis and died in Buenos Aires on 20 March 1936. When the funeral procession, attended by numerous mourners including the President of the Republic, went through the streets of Buenos Aires, Tschiffely's horses Mancha and Gato walked behind the hearse led by two gauchos.

It was fitting that the gauchos should be present to honour Don Roberto, as they affectionately called him. For forty years he had immortalized them against the background of their pampa: 'All grass and sky, and sky and grass, and still more sky and grass' ('La Pampa').[5] If his regret for the changing of the pampas was keen, his nostalgia for the passing of its inhabitants was a veritable lament, echoing Hernández in *Martín Fierro*. A horse-lover all his life, Graham appreciated with unusual perception the role of the horse, without which the gaucho was only half a man: 'No mariner afloat upon the waves, his mainstay but a little boat, was in a worse condition than the man who, from some cause or other, found himself horseless in the vast sea of grass' ('La Pampa'). With his great love of horses went a great knowledge of things equine, historical and technical, for example, 'The Horses of the Pampas' (*Father Archangel of Scotland*). Also his years with the gaucho had increased his knowledge of horse-lore and had sharpened his awareness of the psychological role of the horse in the gaucho mentality, and its link with *hombría*. The details of the round-up, the dangers of panic, the

stampede, the description of the mutilated bodies of the peons when
caught under the hooves as portrayed in 'El Rodeo' cannot be bettered
by native writers: 'The whole impression of the scene was unforget-
table, and through the dust, both of the prairie and the thicker dust
of years, I can still see the surging of the living lava stream and hear
its thunder on the plain.'[6]

Obviously a master of detail with regard to horses, Don Roberto
also had a wonderful ear and a keen eye for the natural phenomena
of the pampa scene. Whether he is describing insects, animals, birds,
or the wonders of nature in general, he paints pictures and recalls
details captured in his mind's eye from thirty years back. In the shade
of the ombú tree he describes 'lizards flattening themselves against
the stones drinking in the sunbeams, reflecting gems of light from
their prismatic backs'; whilst at sunset 'bischachas sat and chattered
on their mounds, and teruteros, flying low, uttered their wailing cry';
and also the armadillos emerging from their holes like survivors of a
pre-historic age, and the fireflies flitting through the trees like spirits
('La Tapera').[7]

As he knew the gauchos and his ways, so too did he know his
half-brother and yet his enemy, the Indian, about whose passing too
he reminisces in 'Los Indios' (A Hatchment) — their attacks, their
capture of Christian women, their brutality, and their superstitions.
Of all his writings about the Indians one picture in particular stands
out, i.e. 'The Captive' (from Hope, 1910), the story of a white woman
captured by the Indians and later rescued by a Belgian — only, after
an idyllic love affair, to return to her abandoned children and her
infidel husband, in the face of irrepressible maternal instincts.

As a costumbrist and painter of the gaucho modo de ser Graham
approaches Hernández, and in a sense surpasses Güiraldes since his
portrayal of the gaucho is not stylised, as in Don Segundo Sombra,
but stems from observed reality for example his realistic description
of 'La Pulpería' (from Thirteen Stories, 1900) with its fights, its
payadores, its convivial but dangerous atmosphere, its chinas or
quitanderas, the prostitutes for whom Graham always had a soft spot,
'sitting like swallows on a telegraph wire' ('Un Angelito' (The Ipane),
1899). He is superb in his portrayal of such strange gaucho customs
as the angelito — a dead child, greenish in the first stage of decom-
position, dressed in its finery, propped up in a chair, and surrounded
by revellers celebrating the passing of its soul into heaven. This pagan
materialism of the gaucho ('a strange compound of ferocity and
childishness, a link between ourselves and the past'), who actually
hires such angelitos to attract customers to the pulpería,is also

portrayed in 'Los Seguidores' (*Success*, 1902), a powerful sketch in which Graham describes two brothers in love with their half-sister. One of the brothers, crazy with jealousy, suddenly rushes to knife his rival, falls on the knife and dies, not before he asks for forgiveness and touchingly pleads with his brother to take care of their sister. This instinctive fascination with violence, this atavistic treachery of the gaucho mentality, as highlighted first in *Facundo*, is shown at both the individual and national level in Graham's sketches. Few scenes are more moving than the pathetic murder of young Cruz, in 'A Silhouette' (*Faith*, 1909), whose assassins cut his throat ('played the violin' or 'did the holy office') in full view of his grief-stricken brother. In his description of the callous slaughter, Graham reaches the classic heights of Echeverría in *El Matadero*.

Graham, then, did not shrink from realism when he deemed it necessary as in the description of death, both human and animal. He also reveals the other side of the coin in his romantic attitude to literature, at times writing with a naturalness, a spontaneity, and a lack of discipline that occasionally marred his style. His attitude towards writing stemmed from a lack of pretentiousness as to his role as an author: 'Still I believe that be it bad or good, all that a writer does is to dress up what he has seen, or felt, and nothing real is evolved from his own brain, except the words he uses, and the way in which he uses them. Therefore it follows that in writing he sets down (perhaps unwittingly) the story of his life.'[8] Although this statement tended to detract from the writer's image, and until recently in Graham's case, to highlight the man, the adventurer, the eccentric, the traveller, the politician to the detriment of the artist, fortunately Graham was appreciated enough by contemporaries like Hudson, Shaw, Ford Madox Ford, Edward Garnett and others with solid credentials, like Conrad, to debunk at least partly this myth, although there is undoubtedly some truth to the self-confessed charge. His friend Conrad, whilst praising his art, constantly chided him for not taking the trouble to correct his proofs properly.[9]

As Graham's massive correspondence reveals, Conrad was but one of Don Roberto's many protegés, one of the scores of writers whom he helped early in their career. Another was W. H. Hudson who, although born in Argentina (1841), came to Britain in 1874 and stayed in his adopted country till his death in 1922. Although technically Hudson is outside of my domain in this study, since in chronological and geographical terms he represents the opposite phenomenon of the so-called *viajeros ingleses* who went to Argentina, there is no doubt that in that country Hudson is considered to belong to that group. In any case, I have commented at length elsewhere on Hudson's work about Argentina written in English from Britain, especially *The Purple Land* (1885), the tales of *El Ombú* (1902), and the autobiographical *Far Away and Long Ago* (1918), not to mention many individual essays in collections like *Idle Days in Patagonia* (1893), which strengthen his reputation as a painter of pampa life and a guardian of gauchesque values — from afar.[10]

Another protegé of Graham was the aforementioned Swiss-Argentine horseman and writer, Aimé F. Tschiffely, author of many travel and adventure books like *The Tale of Two Horses* (1934), *Bridle Paths* (1936), *This Way Southward* (1945), *Bohemia Junction* (1950), *Round and About Spain* (1952). His famous journey from Buenos Aires to New York, commemorated by Graham in his 1932 sketch, was described in detail by the author in *Tschiffely's Ride* (1933). Tschiffely, who was early taken under Graham's wing on arriving in Britain from the Argentine, returned the favour to the master by writing a eulogistic, if inaccurate, biography of Graham, *Don Roberto* (1937), based on (not all of) the family letters and papers, not to mention a few fictions, which Graham had already entrusted to him before his death in 1936. Tschiffely also wrote a little biography about another Anglo-Argentine, *The Man from Wood Creek*, based on the fascinating life of E. Lucas Bridges, who told in detail his own story in *Uttermost Part of the Earth* (1947) about his life amongst the Fuegian Indians as the uncrowned King of Patagonia, that magical, mysterious region in the South of Argentina that has intrigued English writers from Father Thomas Falkner, *A Description of Patagonia, and the Adjoining Parts of South America* (London, 1774), Byron, Darwin up to Hudson and George Chaworth Musters, in *At Home with the Patagonians* (London, 1873).

Most of the travellers who narrated their experiences in the River Plate region either passed through or stayed for a few years before returning to 'civilisation.' One of the few writers to stay was the Scottish emigré, Walter Owen (1884-1953), taken by his businessman-father to Montevideo at the age of six. After having been sent back to Scotland for schooling and business-training, Owen returned to the Argentine as a stockbroker. If commerce was his profession, literature was his love. As early as 1910 he produced his first collection of poems *Amor viri*, and in 1913 *Aurora*, both published anonymously for fear of harming the interests of the staid British businessmen who might not care to have their names linked with a poet. The 1914-18 war inspired *Sonnets to Soldiers* (1918) and in 1940 appeared his best one hundred *Sonnets of GSO* (his pen name being Gauthier de Saint

Quen, a gallicised, whimsical poetic rendering of his own name), republished in 1946 with a gloss.

Already in 1917 he had written his biting prose allegory on the war, *The Cross of Carl*, which was banned by the censors as being too realistic. It was finally published in 1931, with an Introduction by General Sir Ian Hamilton, a noted figure during the war, and it met with great success. Moving more and more towards the spiritual life, as his correspondence increasingly demonstrates in the later years, Owen published in 1938 the sequel, *The Ordeal of Christendom*, to be followed in 1946 by *More Things in Heaven* (London: Andrew Dakers, 1947) in which the occult element is even more pronounced. In this strange and harrowing book, Owen delves into the realms of philosophy, psychology, religion and the natural sciences in a dazzling and at times frightening display of how supernatural forces control the lives of the victims of a curse — ranging through history from Alexander the Great to an obscure Englishman who dies in Buenos Aires in 1936 in such peculiar circumstances that even the police abandon the case as insoluble. There is almost a Borgesian display of knowledge here of other countries and languages, with something of the great Argentine writer's capacity for satire at the expense of the reader in his intellectual jokes, although it is not in any sense a light-hearted book.

It is unfortunate that Owen's creative writing, his poetry and his spiritual prose, have tended to be neglected in favour of his translations which are themselves, however, works of art. Since they are generally translations of the Latin American classics, it is no wonder that they have survived whilst his own poetry and prose have been somethat overlooked by his compatriots. His first major work of translation (1935) was, appropriately, Hernández's great swan song of the gaucho, *Martín Fierro*, which Owen renders, in the words of Sir Eugene Millington-Drake, 'with the raciness of an old Border ballad.' At its best *Martín Fierro* (1872) transcends the regional level and rises to the heights of universal epic in its description of Man in his struggle against Nature and Destiny, which Owen captures beautifully. It is fitting that in this, the culmination of gauchesque poetry, Owen too reaches his peak.

Staying with the gauchesque, in 1943 he translated *El Fausto* (1866) of Estanislao del Campo, published as *Faust*. The pity is that Owen started at the top with *Martín Fierro*, since *Faust* is perforce of lesser quality and interest, being only partly in the gauchesque vein, since it is the tale of a gaucho's reaction to the performance of Gounod's opera in the Teatro Colón in Buenos Aires. Its attraction lies in the meeting of two cultures, in the psychological interest of witnessing a European theatrical presentation rendered in gaucho terms.

The year 1944 saw the translation of Zorrilla's Spanish classic, *Don Juan Tenorio*, to commemorate the centenary of its first presentation in Madrid. However, it was in the field of Latin American epic poetry that Owen achieved most renown. In 1945 he produced the first part of Ercilla's sixteenth-century Chilean epic, *La Araucana*, which renders homage to the fighting spirit of the Araucanian Indians, despite the author's declared intent to write in praise of the Spanish conquistadores. Having paid tribute to Argentina and Chile, Owen then turned his attention to neighbouring Uruguay to complete the trilogy with *Tabaré* (1886) of Zorrilla de San Martín. Unfortunately, Owen's health was deteriorating rapidly, but somehow he rallied and encouraged by the support of Millington-Drake, the British chargé d'affaires, and the blessing of the Uruguayan poet's son, the famous sculptor José Luis, Owen began to recuperate in hospital and turned his efforts again to the tragic tale of the Indian chief Tabaré and his impossible love for the daughter of a Spanish conquistador, which he finished in the first months of 1953. It was, however, to be his swan-song, since he died in the British Hospital in Buenos Aires on 29 September 1953. The work was published in 1956 in a bilingual edition by Unesco and the Organisation of American States, with an introductory note by Millington-Drake. It was also his patron, supported by other friends, who founded the Instituto Cultural Walter Owen and who initiated the 1965 publication of the translation of *The Argentine and the Conquest of the River Plate* by Martín del Barco Centenera (1602). Still unpublished are Owen's renderings of Pedro de Ona's *Arauco Domado* and *The Narrative of the Expedition of Sir Francis Drake to the Indies* by Juan Castellanos. Almost incredibly, the last three translations were done from a hospital bed in the last few months of his life.

Although Walter Owen was a prolific poet and powerful writer of prose, it is as a translator of Latin American (and especially Argentine) poetry that he is best remembered. His motives in translating these masterpieces were a genuine desire to spread Latin American culture to the English-speaking world, and also to provide him with an opportunity for creative work, not merely servile translating: 'My English version of *Martín Fierro* must not be taken for a text book, for which one can find literal equivalents; but is instead intended to convey as near as I found possible the total meaning, effect, and atmosphere of Hernández's epic of gaucho life' (letter to Millington-

Drake, May 1944). In other words, it is a creative adaptation, a transformation, a transliteration, or even a psychological transvernacularization, as he variously called his efforts, rather than a mere translation. Each translation published in Owen's lifetime contains an introduction or a preface explaining in detail his literary and linguistic credo.

Making the Latin American classics available to the English-speaking world was perhaps Owen's greatest achievement. This desire to link nations was one of the recurrent themes of his work, which has not gone unrewarded. It was almost entirely Owen's modesty (as revealed in his correspondence and in his various Introductions) that prevented his writings from becoming better known. No mean poet and prose writer, he preferred to have his translations published privately rather than deal with haggling publishers — and only then at the prodding of appreciative friends, especially Millington-Drake. If his primary aim in doing these translations was 'to strengthen understanding and good will between the Argentine people and the nations which use the English tongue',[11] he also succeeded in raising the status of the translator to a more honourable level, affirming with Carlyle: 'What work nobler than transplanting foreign thought.' Using language as the instrument and common tie of humanity, as Locke would have it, Walter Owen in his role of cultural ambassador has done much to bring together the English-speaking peoples and Argentina, his adopted homeland — no mean achievement for this 'quiet old Scot,' a sadly neglected artist and translator.[12]

Contemporary with Owen for the last fifteen years of his life was another Scottish *viajero inglés* (!) who came to Argentina and like Owen stayed. William Shand (born 1902), resident in Buenos Aires since 1938 and still actively involved in literary circles, has rubbed shoulders with and even outlived some of his great friends, Borges, Mallea and Sábato. Although Shand would modestly brush off any comparison with these giants, it says much for his reputation that his works were often introduced and presented by such masters as the above, and others like Bernardo Canal Feijóo and Ulises Petit de Murat, as well as scholars like Raul Castagnino of the Argentine Academy of Letters — a sure sign that Shand is appreciated in Argentine literary circles if not always by his English-speaking compatriots. This in a sense is not surprising since generally he has published only his poetry in English. Claiming to be most comfortable in his native tongue, during the five decades of his stay in Argentina he has produced several collections of his highly personal poetry of

our time, like *Dead Season's Heritage* (1842), and *Ferment* (1950),
which contains a penetrating prologue by Borges who gets to the root
of Shand's poetry by praising 'su capacidad de crear símbolos para el
glorioso, tedioso y horrible mundo de nuestro tiempo.' ('His capacity
for creating symbols for the glorious, tedious and horrible world of
our time.')[13] With *The Malice of their Clime* (1956), *The Sad Essence*
(1961), *The City* (1967) and *The Final Balance* (1971), Shand has
maintained his high standard of lyrical-tragical poetry, combined
with a concern for the human condition in the face of a corrupt society,
an interfering state, a crumbling world, and an absurd universe.[14]
    Apart from writing his own work, like his fellow Scot Walter Owen,
Shand has also served as a cultural ambassador (but in reverse) by
making the beauties of English poetry available to his Spanish-speak-
ing compatriots. In collaboration with Alberto Girri, one of the finest
contemporary Argentine poets, he has translated *Poemas de Stephen
Spender*, *Poesía inglesa de la Guerra Española*, *Poemas de John
Donne*, *Poesía norteamericana contemporánea*, as well as *Contemporary Argentine Poetry*, an anthology for English readers, and *Poesía
africana de hoy*. Although an English-speaking resident of Buenos
Aires, Shand's interests transcend epochs, national frontiers and
literary genres. In 1971 he had the pleasure of seeing the fruits of his
efforts on the libretto of Alberto Ginastera's opera, *Beatriz Cenci*,
performed at the John F. Kennedy Centre in Washington.
    Although Shand reserves his native tongue for his poetry (lan-
guage of the soul?), his many forays into the field of the short story
have been conducted in Spanish. Shand himself would prefer not to
distinguish between his various genres, since his *visión de la vida* is
reflected in the totality of his work which is inextricably linked.
However, his short fiction does reflect his metaphysical outlook as
well as highlighting the social and political problems of contemporary
Argentina. Shand is not a comforting soap-opera type of writer who
gives his readers happy endings. The hard picture of existence is
starkly portrayed in his short stories, some of which were first
published in the literary supplements of *La Nación* and *La Prensa*
and then collected in *La obsesión de Branti* (1975), *Una extraña
jornada* (1978), and *El cuarto deshabitado* (1985). With a cold, clinical,
economical style Shand has pared his prose down to the bone to give
us a bare picture of life that conjures up images and atmospheres
worthy of Orwell, Kafka and Borges himself. In his fiction Shand
seeks to present a view of life, society and eventually the universe
that is nothing if not realistic — a vision of humanity with all its
defects, reflecting not only the social malaise of his time and place,

but also a strong metaphysical outlook (the absurd) which pervades all his work and transcends chronological and geographical frontiers. In his words of introduction, presenting *La obsesión de Branti*, Borges described it thus: 'Estos cuentos corresponden a la triste realidad argentina de nuestro tiempo.' ('These stories correspond to the sad Argentine reality of our time.')[15]

This same vision of humanity with all its defects is revealed too in Shand's drama. Although not all his performed plays have been published, Shand has been producing drama all his working life — also in Spanish — some of which were performed as early as the 1950s. Some of the collected drama appears in two volumes of *Teatro* published in 1967 and 1976, and two of his prize-winning pieces, *La cultura del látigo* and *Judith y el gangster* were published in 1965 and 1967 respectively. The perennial favourite *La transacción* was also published in 1965 in *Piezas cortas*, whilst another short piece 'El escritor' appeared in the journal *Comentario* in 1966.

Because Shand has been writing dramatic works for at least four decades, there has obviously been some change in his literary, stylistic and even theatrical production. He has honed his craft to produce a drama that represents his growing grasp of the tools of his trade. One remembers, however, that Spanish is not Shand's native language, and his drama, like his fiction, reflects this attitude to his adopted language which is simple and spare, rendered in laconic fashion, with no Gongorostic flourishes. The terse, concise exchanges of his characters, delivered with an economy of words that reduces style to the mere bones, captures precisely the essentials of life, the heart of things, and the basics of the human condition. Thus if Shand's language and style seem austere, even bare and cold, this is aesthetically fitting, since his view of life is equally so.

Since Shand has lived in Argentina since 1938, there is no doubt his drama, at least on the most obvious plane, reflects the Argentine way of life and national values at a crisis period in that country's history — the Second World War, the era of Perón, various military governments, the return of Perón, the period of terrorism and the most recent military dictatorship, with its concomitant problems of politics/literature/censorship. Shand's drama reflects all of these issues, and he has not been afraid to confront them openly. However, he has transcended narrow, parochial nationalism (in time and place) by describing a past (often the barbaric treatment of Jews by Nazi Germany), the present (the opposing phenomena of Peronism and military dictatorship, with the fascist manifestations of both), and the future (his prophetic Orwellian view of a world, not just Argen-

tina, under the yoke of totalitarianism). In this way Shand goes
beyond the regional to touch on matters international, even universal.

Despite his own personal sense of humour, and his facility for
producing also farce and extravaganzas, William Shand is not a
comforting author who writes escapist drama. All his theatrical work
reflects a view of life rooted in the individual, which goes up through
the family to include society and the state, and ultimately embraces
the whole world. Although his dramas are obviously works of art, he
is as much concerned with ethics as aesthetics. That is not to say that
he preaches, moralises or explains. Shand's method, rather, is to
present the individuals and the families as they really are — lacking
in communication, respect, love, morality and values. As they go, so
goes society. Shand does not hesitate to use the scalpel and open up
the cancers to reveal the pus of corruption (drugs, prostitution,
promiscuity, alcoholism, theft, cheating, etc.) at all levels, whether it
be in commerce or in politics.

Shand's literary output, then, is a concrete manifestation of his
vital sensibility. Therefore to know the man and his view of life one
has to go to his writings. Not to have them available denies us
valuable insight into what constitutes an important philosophical
comment — not just on life in Buenos Aires, although one agrees with
Borges that one can feel the *porteño* elements in Shand's work — but
life in general. It is the general concern that places this Anglo-Argentine writer in the ranks of those who go beyond the regional to reach
universal heights.

Almost two hundred years have passed since those first English
invasions of Sir Home Popham and his ilk, which gave the Argentine
people a pretext for snatching independence and the soldier Gillespie
a rare opportunity to observe and comment on a country which was
almost to be a British colony over the next two centuries.[16] Many trips
were made and much ink was spilt by hordes of visiting soldiers,
politicians, missionaries, engineers, miners, businessmen, scientists
and mere travellers. Not many of these literary efforts were to reach
the heights of a Cunninghame Graham, although almost all of them
were eventually welcomed and included in the newly-constituted
republic of Argentine letters and transformed, as Walter Owen would
have said, into valuable contributions to the national *modo de ser*.
Few, not even Cunninghame Graham, were to stay for long periods
of time, except the two twentieth-century expatriate Scots, Walter
Owen and William Shand, the former to be remembered best as a
cultural ambassador for his transliterations of Argentine classics,

and the latter, now a spry octogenarian, for viewing his adopted land through the eye, if not always the tongue, of *los viajeros ingleses*. The ties between Argentina and Britain have always been close. Not even Peronist xenophobia or the most recent pointless little war can destroy completely the centuries-old links. The contribution of the British travellers can never be eradicated, for it has been immortalized in the most lasting way possible, through the medium of literature.

## Notes

1. For detailed bibliographical information on most of the English-speaking writers of the River Plate region, see José Evaristo Uriburu, *La República Argentina a través de las obras de los escritores ingleses*: Compilación Claridad:Buenos Aires, 1948, and S. Samuel Trifilo, *La Argentina vista por viajeros ingleses: 1810-1860* Gure:Buenos Aires 1959. Though not current, complete or accurate, these two compilations provide usual bibliographical details on works published both in English and in Spanish.

2. Title of the brief study of Graham, Hudson and Head by Enrique Espinoza, *Santiago de Chile, 1951*. For biographical details see the disappointing study by Sidney Jackman, *Galloping Head*, Phoenix House, London 1958. For a detailed study of the Argentine episode, see John Walker, 'From the Argentine Plains to Upper Canada: Sir Francis Bond Head', *Norte/Sur*, Vol. V, No. 9 1980 pp. 97-120.

3. All of these pieces, from various books, have been collected and annotated in John Walker, *The South American Sketches of R.B. Cunninghame Graham*. Norman: University of Oklahoma Press, 1978. However, in the footnotes that follow, I refer to the original first editions, although they are now difficult to obtain.

4. *The Ipane*, Fisher Unwin, London, 1899, p.65.

5. *Charity*, Duckworth, London, 1912, p.27.

6. *A Hatchman*, Duckworth, London, 1916, p.68.

7. *Progress*, Duckworth, London, 1905, pp.86-87.

8. *Apologia to His People,* Duckworth, London, 1906, p.x.

9. Letter dated 9 December 1898:'You haven't been careful in correcting your proofs. Are you too grand seigneur for that infect labour? Surely I, twenty others, would be only too proud to do it for you. Tenez vous le pour dit. I own I was exasperated by the errors'. Also reproduced in *Joseph Conrad's Letters to R.B.*

*Cunninghame Graham* edited by C.T. Watts, Cambridge University Press, London, 1969, p.111. See also Watts and Laurence Davies, *Cunninghame Graham: A Critical Biography*, Cambridge University Press, 1979, a more reliable source of information than Tschiffely.

10. John Walker, 'Home Thoughts from Abroad: W.H. Hudson's Argentine Fiction', *Canadian Review of Comparative Literature*, Vol. X, No. 3, (1983), pp.333-76

11. Introduction to *Martín Fierro*, Basil Blackwell, Oxford, 1935, p.xxiv.

12. For biographical details, see Charlotte de Haringh, *Servitor on an Outer Plane*, Buenos Aires, 1966, published by the Instituto Cultural Walter Owen. See also Joyhn Walker, 'Walter Owen: the Latin American Epic and the Art of Translation,' *Latin American Literary Review*, Vol. iii,No. 5, 1974, pp.51-64.

13. Buenos Aires: *Botella al Mar*, 1950, pp.7-10. This quotation is from p.9.

14. For anthologies of his many collections of poetry, see *Selected Poems*, Torres Aguero, Buenos Aires, 1978, the bilingual *Poemas*, Fraterna, Buenos Aires, 1981, and most recently, *Collected Poems*, Torres Aguero, Buenos Aires, 1985.

15. Reproduced as 'Palabras de Jorge Luis Borges sobre la obra de Shand', in *Una extraña jornada*, Rodolfo Alonso, Buenos Aires, 1978, p.11. For a detailed study of Shand's work see John Walker, 'The Real Fictional World of William Shand', *Bulletin of Latin American Research*, Vol.2, No. 1, 1982, pp.43-50, and also 'The Dramatic works of William Shand', *Norte / Sur*, Vol IX, No. 17, 1984, pp. 75-86

16. One remembers that the original title of Hudson's *The Purple Land* (1885) was *The Purple Land that England Lost*.

# 12
# Borges and England

*Evelyn Fishburn*

Jorge Luis Borges was brought up in Argentina at the turn of the century, under the lasting influence of his Northumbrian grand-mother, Fanny Haslam, and the guidance of his British governess, Miss Tick. He learnt the speech and manners of an Edwardian England that was fast disappearing; and, in a sense, it was that image of England which remained with him in the private, though most fertile, world of his imagination. When he died on the 14 June 1986, the last Edwardian gentleman of this century died with him.

Borges was born in 1899, in Buenos Aires, into a household in which two dominant cultures coexisted: the *criollo* one on his mother's side, whose ancestry went back to the earliest Spanish settlers, and the British on his father's side, whose mother was of Quaker and Methodist stock. Borges's grandmother, the redoubtable Fanny Has-lam, had met and married Colonel Francisco Borges in a small garrison town in the provinces, where she courageously brought up her family after her husband's death in battle. Borges often spoke about her, always with affection, and seems to have been deeply impressed by her 'British reserve', best illustrated by her parting words at the age of ninety, when she tetchily declared: 'Nothing special is happening here. I am only an old woman, and I am dying very, very slowly, no reason for the whole house to worry about it. I have to apologise to you all.'

Borges's double lineage, which was not at all uncommon in a land of immigration such as Argentina, was to have a deep effect upon his thinking, and upon his approach to the world. He spoke English almost before he spoke Spanish, and the realisation that the two different words could be used to obtain the same thing taught him to see as arbitrary the relationship between words and the things they designate and to question the 'naturalness' of language for expressing the universe. It also taught him to formulate his thoughts without the heavy rhetoric of the literary Spanish of his time, before, that is, he had freed it from redundancies and pomposity. The economy and succinctness for which his writing is justly famous can be traced back to lessons learnt in childhood.

The connection between Borges and England was important in both directions: he was clearly greatly influenced by English literature but, in a sense, his fictions have also influenced our own reading of English literature. Borges was an Anglophile all his life. His great attachment for England manifested itself most of all in his deep love and knowledge of the English language, or 'verbal music' as he often termed it, and English literature, which he extended in later life to serious study of its Anglo-Saxon origins. Borges also had a great respect for English institutions, which he saw as the result of liberalism and pragmatism, though it was largely the ideas of the English metaphysical philosophers which touched a sympathetic chord in Borges's creative imagination and led him to question, in his fiction, most of the assumptions upon which our lives are based.

English has always held a special attraction for Borges. His first readings were in this language, and they included not only English authors but also many works in translation. English was for him the language of the Bible and also the language in which he first read and loved *Don Quixote*, so that for many years the original seemed to him a less exciting rendering. He recalls having first encountered Grimm's fairy tales in their English version and the *Volsunga Saga* of Icelandic mythology in William Morris's vivid translation. English also opened up for Borges the magic world of the East, when as a young child he read in secret the forbidden *The Thousand Nights and One Night* in Burton's highly explicit translation of 1885. Though he later came to value Burton's predecessor, the Orientalist Edward Lane for his scholarly annotations, he found his expurgated version rather bland, calling it an 'encyclopaedia of evasions', whereas he said admiringly of Burton that he had falsified the original by 'the richness of his English'. In a discussion of the various translations which have been made of the Odyssey, Borges emphasises the abundance and variety of English versions, citing those of Cowper, Pope, Chapman, Lang, Morris and Butler, pointing out the great affinity of English letters with this great epic of the sea. He explains the extraordinary richness of English by pointing to its double etymology, its Anglo-Saxon as well as its Latin roots. While only one word is given in more purely Saxon languages, such as Swedish or German, and in Spanish or other Romance languages, English has, for example, 'dark', 'kingly' and 'brotherly', as more concrete registers of expression, along with 'obscure', 'regal' and 'fraternal' as correspondingly more abstract connotations. The importance of this distinguishing feature for poetry is further enhanced by the wealth of sounds provided by the approximately twenty-two English vowels (as opposed to the mere five of

Spanish). But of course Borges's greatest admiration was reserved
for the canon of English literature, as is clear from his *Introduction
to English Literature (1965)*.[1] In this brief work he discusses mainly
those writers whom he considers most representative of their particular times, drawing on an exceptionally wide frame of reference and
making many unconventional observations and original comparisons
with other works. Though Borges is known for his extravagant praise
of writers more usually considered of secondary importance, this
idiosyncrasy does not bias him against the truly great. Thus, in
talking of Shakespeare, it is not only the poet and playwright he
admires, but the actor and the theatre manager, in short, the creator
*par excellence*. He considers Shakespeare the symbol of all humanity,
the creator whose identity, not unlike that of God himself, is dispersed
in his multiple creation. In an essay entitled 'Everything and Nothing'
Borges illustrates this idea, concluding:

> History adds that before or after dying he found himself in the
> presence of God and told Him: 'I who have been so many men in
> vain want to be one and myself.' The voice of the Lord answered
> from a whirlwind: 'Neither am I anyone; I have dreamt the world
> as you dreamt your work, my Shakespeare, and among the forms
> in my dream are you, who like myself are many and no one.'[2]

I do not propose to expand upon Borges's views on English literature as expressed in his essays and his *Introduction* since these
are recorded in a comprehensive study by Michel Berveiller.[3] I should
like to concentrate instead on those English writers whose influence
has most readily marked Borges's fiction. One of the first writers who
comes to mind is the essayist and historian Thomas Carlyle, with
whom Borges seems to have had a wavering relationship, at first one
of quasi-reverence for one of the most important representatives of
literature, later of condemnation for his cult of heroism, to which
Borges traces the origins of Nazism. Carlyle's *Sartor Resartus*, an
apocryphal biography of a character named Dr. Teufelsdrockh is said
to contain many autobiographical details: Borges used a similar
device in several of his stories, notably in 'Approach to Almotasim',
'Pierre Menard, author of *Don Quixote*' and 'The Gospel according to
Mark'.

Andrés Maurois said that Borges's form often recalls Swift's:[4]
though perhaps he does not quite share in the ferocity of Swift's
satire, certain important similarities may be found. The most salient
is in his use of a 'naive observer', in which a situation is described

from a seemingly uncomprehending point of view, just as the Lilliputians describe Gulliver's watch, in all its particularities without comprehending its essential function. This device, which so radically makes the reader question inherited assumptions, is used to great effect in 'Averroes's Search', a story in which the twelfth-century Arab commentator of Aristotle's work finds difficulty in understanding the meaning of the words 'tragedy' and 'comedy' because they belong to a tradition absent from his own culture. Thus, when distracted by some children acting he describes this as 'playing'; a theatre is 'a house of painted wood where many people who were eating and drinking ... praying, singing and conversing. They suffered prison, but no one could see the jail; they travelled on horseback, but no one could see the horse; they fought, but the swords were of reed; they died and then stood up again.' [5] In 'The Immortal', arguably Borges's most Swiftian tale, the traditional portrayal of immortality as an ideal state is ruthlessly subverted by the picture of a desolate city, whose grey troglodyte inhabitants live meaningless, bleak existences: 'invulnerable to pity ... a man once fell headlong into the deepest of (the ancient quarries); he could not hurt himself or die but he was burning with thirst; before they threw him a rope, seventy years went by.' [6] The presentation of immortality, however, is not left at a crude destruction of Judaeo-Christian myths of paradise, but also involves a classical concept of literature in terms of the immortality of certain essential themes. In this sense, Borges invokes the English dramatist Ben Jonson, whose essays on his contemporaries are derived from Seneca, Pliny and other writers of antiquity. In 'The Aleph', Borges recalls Ben Jonson's contemporary, Michael Drayton, whose famous poem, *Polyolbion*, was an attempt to celebrate all the points of topographical and antiquarian interest in Great Britain, and thus a kind of 'universal poem' like that so brilliantly satirised by Borges in his description of the eponymous, microcosmic Aleph. But also in this story, Borges alludes to Tennyson's moving poem *Flower in the Crannied Wall* '... but *if* I would understand / What you are, root and all, and all in all, / I should know what God and man is'. Thus, Borges should not be thought of as simply ironic about the relationship of the microcosm to the cosmos.

Kipling was a writer greatly admired by Borges, who said that he had learnt from him the most important device of using minute description of circumstantial detail, that is, to give the physical atmosphere of a story in order to convey its metaphysical atmosphere. Borges mentions that in writing 'The Approach to Almotasim' he drew freely from Kipling's short story 'On the City Wall', in which skirmishes between Hindus and Moslems are vividly portrayed. 'The Approach to Almotasim' is set in British India and though it concerns mainly the protagonist's search for God, ultimately to be found within himself, the narrative journeys through largest parts of the Indian subcontinent, evoking many names and places of colonial interest. (One of these is the Anglo-Indian writer Philip Meadows Taylor, whose novel *Confessions of a Thug*, published in 1839, was instrumental in eradicating the practice of thuggee from India.) What is of particular interest here is the identification that may be made between Kipling's marked Englishness and Borges's Anglophilia.

Though of Polish origin, Conrad ranks among the great British writers, acknowledged as a master of the English language. According to Borges he has given it an epic and ceremonial ring such as would be 'proper to French prose'. He pays tribute to him in 'Guayaquil', a story of intrigue and battle between two opponents' wills in which Conrad is referred to indirectly by his original Polish name, Korseniowski, and places and events from his novel *Nostromo*, set in a fictitious South American country are inserted into Borges's story. The effect of this is to counterbalance allusions to a historical event, the famous meeting between Bolívar and San Martín which took place in Guayaquil, with allusions to a work of fiction. In 'The Other Death' the narrator compares the bravery of the gaucho character Martín Fierro (considered to be Argentina's literary hero) unfavourably with Conrad's Lord Jim and Razumov, because he is said to lack the complexity of their behaviour, a mixture of cowardice and nobility.[7]

Complexity is unquestionably a fundamental feature of Borges's work. It is often expressed in the form of paradox, an art Borges claims he learnt from Chesterton, observing that 'Chesterton resorts to paradox and humour in his vindication of Catholicism, thereby reversing a tradition established by Swift, Gibbon and Voltaire who employed such forms of ingenuity and wit in order to attack rather than defend the Catholic church.' Paradox in Chesterton is the result of his deep attraction for the 'order' represented by the church and his equally deep conviction of the 'outrageous implausibility' of its beliefs.[8] This conflict underlies the five *Father Brown* stories, mystery tales for which the author proposes supernatural solutions only to dismiss them in favour of rational conclusions. Chesterton's constant perception of the uncanny and the mysterious, married to the elegance of his reasoning are qualities much admired by Borges, who considered that Chesterton had the ability to reduce any argument to a geometric diagram. The influence of this upon Borges has been emphasised, perhaps unduly, by a number of critics.[9] A geometric pattern is most evident in 'Death and the Compass' where the conflicting worlds of reason and intuition are represented by two detectives differing in their approach to murder. One, rationally prosaic, opts for the obvious solution, but the other seeks a more esoteric explanation. Developing Chesterton's idea that the criminal is the creative artist and the detective only the critic, the adventurous detective, thinking he is the artist in charge of finding a solution becomes the mere interpreter of the artistic work of the master criminal. Thus, in working out geometrically the exact date and location of the last crime in a series, the detective walks into a most ingenious death-trap set for him. This is where Borges differs from his English mentor for his endings offer none of the comfort of optimism of the *Father Brown* tales. The order in his stories is shown to be man-made, there to mask the mysterious but surely chaotic nature of the universe. To convey this paradox he uses the metaphor of the labyrinth, an orderly construct in which man errs, lost and bewildered.

Many of Borges's fictions are concerned with a mystery of labyrinthine construction. One which combines the subject of the detective story and the labyrinth set in an English background is 'The Examination of Herbert Quain'. Though Borges rightly maintained that the genre of detective writing was fathered by the American Edgar Allen Poe, he asserts that it is in England that its classical tradition developed, dispensing with scenes of violence and sexual excesses, emphasising instead the logical progression of the plot and rational solution of the mystery. The way in which Borges subverts the expectations of the genre has already been hinted at. In the lesser known 'Examination of Herbert Quain' he presents a critique of the conceit upon which the traditional thriller, linear in form and unequivocal in meaning, is conceived. Writers mentioned are Agatha Christie and Julian Green. One of Quain's mystery plays is set among the rural gentry of the West Midlands, its elusive caste composed of a society lady whose portrait appears in *Tatler* and in *The Sketch* and who is courted by the Duke of Rutland though loved and admired by a 'dramatic playwright' who turns out also to be a lowly commission agent from Liverpool. Needless to say, this suggestion of domestic social comedy is an inadequate summary of Quain's complex creation in which such philosophical questions as the background flow of time and the illusion of casualty are positioned. As mentioned earlier, Borges drew liberally from philosophy, particularly from the English metaphysical idealists for the elaboration of his fiction. Herbert

Quain's formula where Z is the final chapter of a novel, Y 1-3 the three
preceding possibilities and X 1-9 the ones preceding these may be an
allusion to the philosopher John William Dunne's argument of a
pre-existent future towards which our lives flow. It also recalls the
ideas of Francis Bradley's essay on metaphysics, *Appearance and
Reality*, quoted by Borges not only in this story but also in 'The Secret
Miracle'. In his essay Bradley invites us to doubt and question all
preconceptions and to ponder the extent to which reality can be
known. Though firmly of the opinion that knowledge of the Absolute
is available to us, Bradley maintains that our comprehension is based
on appearance and is therefore partial, imperfect and ultimately
worthless. This questioning of the epistemological limitations of the
human mind is also a constant feature in Borges's writing, and the
particular type of questioning which is suggested in 'The Examination of Hebert Quain' stems from Bradley's discussion on *regressus
ad infinitum*. Denying the existence of causal relations, and indeed
all types of relations, Bradley argues that direction is in appearance
relative to 'our' world but not necessarily an aspect of reality. We can
suppose, for instance, that there are beings who have no contact with
the world we experience whose lives run in a direction opposite to
ours.

Herbert Quain's regressive novel can be seen as an ironic illustration of this point. Looked at from another angle, it can also be seen
to illustrate Hume's questioning of the validity of causation. Hume
speaks of the 'probability' of knowledge, referring to the unreliability
of any notion empirically derived from inferences which, he asserts,
are neither demonstrative nor demonstrable. He claims that we
cannot demonstrate the existence of an objective reality, even though
we naturally posit it; all we can affirm is the existence of 'bundles of
perception'. The possible arbitrariness of the relationship of such
bundles is neatly illustrated by Quain's formula, and indeed the deep
scepticism that underlies Hume's philosophy can be perceived
throughout Borges's work. Though Borges has not written as extensively about Hume as about other philosophers, the undermining
effect of his thought upon all certainties can be perceived as a most
pervasive influence in Borges's fictions. Hume's elegant discarding of
any practical purpose for philosophy, which he regards as nothing
more than an agreeable way of passing the time, is emulated by the
very Borgesian narrator of 'Tlon, Uqbar, Orbis Tertius' who remains
unaffected by the prospect of a disintegrating universe, calmly continuing his revision of a translation (which he does not intend to
publish) of Browne's *Urn Burial*.

Questioning the substantive existence of reality is a philosophical tradition that stems in Britain from the ideas of one of Borges's favourite philosophers, Bishop Berkeley. In *The Principles of Human Knowledge* Berkeley denies the independent existence of matter maintaining, in his famous formulation *esse est percipi* that the world is precisely as we perceive it, and does not exist outside our perception. Objects are sustained by God's continued perception of them. Borges, who asked 'What are all the nights of Scheherezade compared to one argument of Berkeley?' summarizes one such argument with a line from *Alice through the Looking Glass*: 'and if he left off dreaming about you ...' which he uses as the epigraph to 'Circular Ruins'. One of Borges's most chilling stories, this tells of a silent, undistinguished man who wills himself to dream another man, and does so arduously and lovingly over repeated attempts. His one concern is that this other man, his son, as it were, should never find out that he is but a dream, only to realise 'with relief, with humiliation, with terror ... that he too was a mere appearance, dreamt by another'.[10] This is only one example of many in Borges's fictions of reality dissolving into nothingness, as inspired by English idealism.

Locke is the last figure to be discussed in this list of English philosophers whose ideas have inspired Borges's imagination. Belonging to British empirical tradition, Locke believes that though man's understanding falls far short of a total comprehension of reality, human knowledge is sufficient for the purposes and needs of mankind. Following from this premise, Locke is led to consider the relationship between the particularities which make up reality, and man's knowledge of such reality based upon general ideas abstracted from such particularities. Borges has shown a special interest in Locke's deliberations on the nature of language, noting its imperfections with regard to the subjective nature of its categories. He fictionalises Locke's intellectual argument in 'Funes the Memorious'. In this story the eponymous hero suffers an accident and as a consequence is unable to select knowledge or form any general ideas. His memory too becomes totally unselective, so that to remember a day, he needs a whole day; his vision so sharp, that he sees not a grape arbour but all the leaves and tendrils and fruit that make up a grape arbour; his mind so obsessed by detail that he fails to comprehend the generalising workings of language, puzzling that 'the dog at three fourteen (seen from the side) should have the same name as the dog at three fifteen (seen from the front)'.[11] Borges humorously illustrates the abstracting nature of our minds, fed by language which arbitrarily imposes categories upon what is essentially a random universe.

As Locke says, 'the reason for this is necessity since it is beyond human capacity to frame and retain distinct ideas of every particular thing'; fittingly, the hapless Funes dies, overladen by so much particularity. [12]

English characters hold a very special place in Borges's fiction. One of his most venerated creations is Stephen Albert, an elderly sinologist who lives in peaceful retirement in the small town of Ashgrove, pursuing his reflective studies of the riddle of the universe. He seems to have absorbed all worldy knowledge (for which he is likened to Goethe by his admiring assassin), and acquired the quiet wisdom of a Taoist monk. But Borges, typically, avoids falling into the trap of creating a stereotype: Albert, who patiently solved the riddle of a famous Chinese labyrinth, becomes himself the victim of another riddle. His name, reported in the papers when he is senselessly killed by a Chinese visitor, becomes a signword to the Germans that an offensive is imminent near the Belgian city of Albert. Needless to say, the metaphysical atmosphere which pervades the centre of this story, set in rural England, is counterbalanced by its strongly realistic framework, which includes an account of the incident as related in a page of Liddell Hart's *History of World War I*. Each version implicitly questions the validity of the other.

Another two very 'British' characters appear in 'Ibn Hakkan al-Bokhari, Dead in his Labyrinth', a story which brings Middle Eastern intrigue to the remote confines of Cornwall, puzzling the peaceful existences of Unwin, a perceptive young man, drawn to the mysteries of geometry, and his more credulous companion, Dunraven. The former's pipe-smoking habits make the comparison with Sherlock Holmes and Watson inescapable. The mystery which they set themselves to solve is set in Cornwall during the summer of 1914, 'weary of a world that lacked the dignity of danger', a phrase which encapsulates not only the characters' naiveté but also indicates the narrative's restraint and objectivity. The story is one of changed identity surrounding the killing of an Arabian king by his vizir. Of course, there is a labyrinth, but this improbably Cornish labyrinth has been constructed not to prevent anyone escaping from it but in order to attract the victim to its centre. [13] The story is told in several versions, first, as Dr. Watson might have told it, by Dunraven, repeating what he heard from one of the protagonists in the mystery, and secondly, by Unwin, discarding all visible evidence and proposing a typically startling 'solution' based upon the switched identities of king and vizir. 'Ibn Hakkan, Dead in his Labyrinth' is written in the rigorous deductive tradition of a Conan Doyle story, yet reflects Borges's usual preoccupations with philosophical themes. A motive based upon financial greed is replaced by one founded on the metaphysical desire to assume another identity through the power of the will. A third version is given in allegorical form by the rector of Pentreath, Reverend Allaby, through whom Borges could arguably be paying tribute to a now unfashionable writer whom he much admired, Samuel Butler, one of whose minor characters is Rector Allaby in *The Way of All Flesh*. In this version, presented as a sermon and published separately from the main story, a king is said to have constructed a labyrinth in which he entraps another king who, however, manages to escape. The second king takes his revenge by luring the first king to his labyrinth, which turns out to be a desert. There are no walls, towers or corridors, but escape is still impossible and the trapped king is left to die of hunger and thirst.

Whether by use of English literature, philosophy or character, Borges has enriched the heritage from which he lovingly borrowed. But England has not adequately repaid Borges' devotion. He is one of the most respected intellectual figures of this century whose writings are constantly published and re-printed in this country. He is studied not only in Spanish but in English departments in most universities, many of which have given him honorary doctorates (Oxford in 1971, and Cambridge in 1984). Four lectures, given in 1971 in Westminster's Central Hall attracted such large audiences that many were unable to secure admission. His more recent talk at the Royal Society of Arts was a gathering of leading academicians and was an important event in the intellectual calendar of London. But outside academic circles Borges seems to be considered too remote a figure to interest the general public. Unlike France, where his death opened the daily news programmes on both radio and television and whose *Figaro* carried a six-page feature on his life and work, and Italy, where his death was declared 'to have made orphans of us all', the English media were niggardly in their reporting. Full tribute was paid in the literary press, but the bulk of the English population is denied access to a writer who could rightfully be considered part of the English heritage. His understatement, his humour and his originality all witness that distinctive quality of 'Edwardian Englishness' which should not be allowed to disappear unmarked from our memories.

# Notes

1. J.L. Borges, in collaboration with M.E.Vazquez, *Introducción a la literatura inglesa*, Buenos Aires, 1965.
2. *Labyrinths*, p.285. Unless otherwise stated, all quotations by Borges are from *Labyrinths*, Harmondsworth, 1964.
3. M. Barveiller, *Le cosmopolitisme de Jorge Luis Borges*, Paris, 1973.
4. André Maurois, Preface to *Labyrinths*, p.13.
5. *Labyrinths* p.184.
6. *Labyrinths* p. 145.
7. The views of the narrator ought not to be confused with Borges's on this subject. Borges shocked his compatriots by pointing out Fierro's complexity of character, his laziness and cowardice as well as his brave fortitude in *El 'Martín Fierro'*, Buenos Aires, 1953.
8. See J.L. Borges, 'Modes de G.K. Chesterton', in *Sur*, July 1936, Vol.22, pp. 47-53.
9. See my article on '"Algebra y fuego" in the Fiction of Borges', in *Revista canadiense de estudios hispanicos*, Toronto,Vol. xii, No.3 1988.
10. *Labyrinths*, p.77.
11. *Labyrinths*, pp.93-4.
12. J. Locke, *The Essay Concerning Human Understanding*, 1690, Book III, Chap. 1.
13. See S. Boldy, 'Eramos pocos y la abuela: más versiones borgianas', in *Revista canadiense de estudios hispánicos*, Vol. VI, No. 2, 1982. In his stimulating reading of this story, Boldy suggests that the constructed labyrinth represents man-made culture whereas the desert is the divine labyrinth which the first king had tried to imitate and for which he is punished.

# 13

## 'Hullo, Tango!' The English Tango Craze and its After-Echoes

*Simon Collier*

It began very quietly... Later there were some complicated set pieces; then deft swirling and turnings, but on the whole there seemed little stingo in the Tango. It was a trifle Funereal; graceful, no doubt, and complicated...It must require a lot of learning — indeed almost enough brain work to enable you to earn a fortune in the City.

*The Sketch*, 23 July 1913.

Argentina's most famous export to England is not one that has ever been, or could ever be, measured and analysed by economic historians. Yet, unlike the beef and cereals that once flowed so copiously from River Plate ports, the Argentine tango went right round the world, and it continues to amuse and delight people in many different places even today. It belongs to an altogether higher plane than beef and cereals, in the realm Dr Johnson called 'the gaiety of nations'.

The tango's origins (usually dated at around 1880) remain somewhat conjectural. It was first danced in the arrabales, the poorish outer districts of Buenos Aires, and it was an amalgam of various preceding dances and rhythms: the Spanish-Cuban *habanera*, the local Argentine *milonga* (itself partly derived from the *habanera*), and the music-and-dance traditions of Buenos Aires' earlier black and mulatto community. The word itself is probably of black (possibly Afro-Portuguese) origin; it long antedates the dance, and was used to label other dances before the tango came along. The Argentine tango as such, in its initial phase, had a strongly erotic and sensual form, with its *cortes* and *quebradas*, its ostentatious halts and semi-athletic contortions. Thanks to this, and given the semi-delinquent social milieu in which it appeared, the tango was long repudiated by Argentine high society. This remained broadly true until its great triumphs overseas. Nevertheless, its popularity in Buenos Aires and

Montevideo had become considerable by 1910 or so, by which time a strong musical tradition was also developing very fast.[1]

In the international diffusion of the tango, one city above all others holds the key place. In Edmundo Guibourg's phrase, 'Paris universalized the tango.'[2] We cannot establish with any precision the date of the first tango in Paris, but clearly the dance was becoming well known there before 1910. The problem is complicated by the fact that 'at the turn of the century tango was the word used to describe every exotic dance that was introduced'.[3] After that, its conquest of French dance floors speeded up. Argentine dancers and teachers flocked to Paris in their dozens. Tangos swamped all other dances at the fifth world dancing championships, held at the Nouveau Cirque in 1913. These were organised (as were all previous and many future championships) by Camille de Rhynal, an assiduous promoter who also did much to smooth the dance into an acceptable ballroom form. (It was essentially the Parisian tango that triumphed in Europe, as was duly noted back in Argentina.)[4] Tango teas, tango vermouths and tango dinners now became the great French rage, starting on the Riviera and at Biarritz and spreading to the capital in the early months of 1913.

There was now no holding the tango in Paris. The popular cartoonist Sem (Georges Gourat) renamed the city Tangoville. A considerable stir was created in October 1913 when, at the annual gathering of the five Academies of the Institut de France, the well-known author and academicien Jean Richepin (he is now largely forgotten, although the late Georges Brassens set two of his poems to music) selected the tango as subject of his discourse on behalf of the forty Immortals. Richepin suggested classical precedents for the tango; its ancestry, he claimed, could be traced back to the war dances of ancient Thebes. This learned opinion was commented on all over Europe, where it was taken seriously, and also in Argentina, where it was not.

As with Paris, so with the provinces. Among the resorts where the tango was cultivated were Le Touquet, Deauville and Dinard. (Marcel Proust does not tell us whether it was danced at the Grand Hotel in Balbec; it must have been). It was here that English visitors received their first serious exposure to the dance, during the summer season of 1911. That same year the newly-founded *Dancing Times* in London published photographs of the tango being danced. One or two individual contacts can also be traced. The actor George Grossmith, for instance, learned the steps in Paris in the winter of 1911-12. There were no doubt many other ways in which the mania was transmitted.

Having made its giant leap up the Atlantic, the tango was now poised for the much shorter hop across the English Channel.

The English were ready for it. Ever since Tudor times, England had been used to receiving and domesticating new dances from foreign parts. Sometimes the traffic flowed the other way: the English country dances of the seventeenth century had an important international impact. In the nineteenth century, however, the greatest dance fashions once again originated abroad, often arousing controversy when they arrived — as was notably the case with the modern waltz in the 1810s and again with the polka in the mid-1840s. The rest of the century saw little innovation in the social dance, affection for which did not rank high in the scale of Victorian values. Only after 1900 or so did England show signs of reverting to type. Transatlantic influences were now well to the fore — a pattern that was to continue throughout the twentieth century. Just before the arrival of the tango, the Boston (an American waltz variant) became popular for several seasons; so too did the turkey trot, the first of a succession of ragtime-related dances. Englishmen and Englishwomen were evidently prepared once again to experiment on the dance floor.

Into this newly volatile atmosphere there exploded the Argentine tango. 1912 was the year the tango really came to England. The explosion was sparked off in the theatre rather than on the dance floor, as was invariably acknowledged by the press at the time. The 'Sunshine Girl' (by Paul Rubens and Cecil Raleigh), which ran at the Gaiety Theatre in London from February 1912 to February 1913, featured several eye-catching song and dance routines, one of which was a tango danced by George Grossmith (the male lead) and Phyllis Dare, the 'Sunshine Girl' of the play's title. The public's fancy was somehow tickled. Dancers everywhere aspired to recreate the graceful movements of Grossmith and Dare. By the winter of 1912-13 there was every sign of what was coming. From now on, the experience of London was to mirror that of Paris; the fever chart for both cities was essentially similar, though London lagged a few weeks behind.

As in France, the most novel and dramatic sign of the craze was the new institution of the tango tea — and its equivalents for later hours of the day. In the spring of 1913, the *Illustrated London News* reported this latest Parisian fad with a full-page drawing, and the comment: 'The craze, it is said, will assuredly spread to London'.[5] It assuredly did. Hotels and restaurants adopted the fashion with avidity, sometimes organising clubs for the participants. From the summer of 1913 the Savoy Hotel ran regular tango dinners.[6] Other

significant metropolitan locales, by the autumn at least, included the
Carlton Hotel, whose Thé Dansant Club was restricted to one hundred members paying fairly steep fees, and the 400 Club in Old Bond
Street, where the subscription was five guineas.[7] Prince's Restaur-
ant, which had its own Tango Club,[8] and the Waldorf and Cecil Hotels
also ran teas or dinners for tango dancers. The craze quickly spread
beyond the capital: prominent provincial hotels that took up the
fashion included the Metropole at Brighton, the Queen's at Westgate,
and the Grand at Scarborough.[9] Tango teas were also held in
numerous private houses by members of the upper and middle
classes. Meanwhile, of course, the dance had caught on in a very big
way in the ballroom. One occasion where it was especially prominent
was the Roof Garden Ball at Selfridges in July 1913. High society
evidently loved the dance: in December 1913 *The Sketch* published
photographs of nine society ladies who were renowned for their
tangoing — among them we find Lady Randolph Churchill, the
Countess of Pontarlington, the Countess of Drogheda, and Lady
Diana Manners, the last-named being better known later on as Lady
Diana Cooper. (Alas! she does not mention her tango skills in her
autobiography.)

The newspapers naturally took a lively interest in the growing
craze. It was graphically documented in the illustrated magazines. A
typical example is an issue of *The Sketch* in November 1913. Its front
cover displays two pairs of feet supposedly tangoing, over the caption
'Why worry about Home Rule and the Land question when you can
learn the tango?' The cover-story is effusive:

> Everybody's doing the Tango, learning the Tango, talking the
> Tango, watching the Tango. Never, perhaps, has a dance become
> of such universal interest so quickly... To the British stage it came,
> by way of the Continent, from the Argentine, of which it is a
> 400-year old national dance... [The] original dance has at least two
> hundred steps; for ballroom purposes about five-and-twenty are all
> that is necessary.[10]

As can be seen from this, there was a certain amount of confusion
about the precise steps for the tango, and little knowledge of the
previous history of the dance, which was far less venerable than this
report suggested. There were, however, experts on hand to guide the
eager terpsichoreans of London. Instructors, some of them Argentines, came from France. Exhibition dancers, too, were something of
a fixture at tango teas and suppers. Among those whose names have

come down to us were Maurice and Florence Walton (Maurice Walton
was American), Marquis and Miss Clayton, Almanos and Odette, and
Roland and Marion Mitford. All of these were to be seen regularly at
London's principal tango spots. They were also to be seen in the
theatre, for the popularity of the tango was reflected on the London
stage throughout 1913-14. The Waltons danced it to great acclaim in
the revue '8d a Mile' at the Alhambra in the spring of 1913.[11] So did
George Grossmith and Kitty Mason in 'The Girl on the Film' (Gaiety
Theatre, April-December 1913). The revues at the Hippodrome had
a veritable procession of dancers — one of these, a Brazilian called
Antonio Lopes de Amorim Diniz (stage-name: Duque), had already
been highly applauded in Paris and Berlin. Quite a number of
theatres, it seems, felt obliged to include tango routines in their
productions. Two notable examples are 'Marriage Market' (Daly's,
May 1913-July 1914) and 'Pearl Girl' (Shaftesbury, September 1913-
May 1914). One or two staged tango exhibitions during the tea
interval at matinées — the Queen's and the London Opera House
being cases in point. Several of the Christmas pantomimes that
season incorporated comic parodies of the dance. (A good example
is'Sleeping Beauty Reawakened' (Drury Lane).) The English surrender to the Argentine tango was perhaps most concisely symbolised in
the title of a revue that opened on 23 December at the Hippodrome;
it was called, simply, 'Hullo, Tango!' '...the prettiest, gayest, brightest
show in town'.[12]

The tango was the first great English craze of the twentieth
century, the forerunner of many others. As so often with crazes, it
assumed a variety of shapes and forms. As in France, 'tango' became
a colour — a deep shade of orange. Dress-designers soon appreciated
the possibilities. Madame Lucile of Hanover Square devised pretty
tea-frocks and ball gowns for the true devotee. A 'tango trouser' was
marketed.[13] During the winter of 1913-14 there was tangoing on
roller-skates at the Queens and Holland Park rinks. *The Sketch* even
published photographs of suitable exercises to prepare the human
body for tangoing.[14]

English humour rapidly embraced the craze. *Punch's* various
allusions to the topic included several cartoons: in one, an eighteenth
century French aristo says to another, 'Been to many Minuet teas
this season, Duchesse?'[15] Another cartoon touched on one of the great
issues of the day by showing a policeman arresting a militant suffra-
gette in a typical tango posture.[16] A hundred years earlier, the waltz
had elicited a caustic poem from Lord Byron. Nobody of his stature

was on hand in 1913-14 to mock the tango, but *Punch* did manage a
few feeble verses eulogising a spoof-dance called the Dongo:[17]

> It fills, when other diet palls,
> Our restaurants and music halls...
> It shows in an engaging shape
> The antics of the human ape.
> Inkslinging pedants it impels
> To search for classic parallels...
> It spurs dilapidated satyrs
> To tear stale passions into tatters...

Early in 1914 an entire book on the tango appeared. Its author,
Mrs Gladys Beattie Crozier, was an ardent propagandist, and her
opinions are of some interest. In respect of the tango's past, she duly
notes Jean Richepin's views, but herself inclines to the theory that
the tango was originally a gypsy dance, transmitted to Argentina
from Spain. She is well aware, however, of the Parisian modifications,
loyally claiming that 'the real Argentine dance... when well done, is
fierce and wonderful,' while praising 'the calm, quiet, aristocratic,
gentle glide of the true Parisian tango, beautiful, undulating and very
smooth.'[18]  Mrs Crozier carefully explains how the tango should be
danced — there are eight basic figures in her version, with sixteen
optional extra figures.[19] She testifies to the universal popularity of
the dance: 'only a night or two ago a very small and muddy urchin...
greeted me with the shrill demand', "Give me a penny, lidy, and I'll
dance the Tango to yer".[20] The book also has a chapter on the proper
way of conducting a tango tea 'in any ordinary-sized drawing room'.[21]
In Mrs Crozier's view, the tango is ideally suited to fancy dress; she
recommends an 'Argentine peasant' style.[22] She is emphatic, too, that
the dance has considerable educational qualities for children: 'The
sight of a roomful of tiny tots dancing the Tango... is the prettiest
sight imaginable.'[23] The tango was, in fact, danced at the Children's
Fête at the Savoy on Christmas Eve 1913.[24]

Although the tango swept all before it in 1913-14, it did not do so
entirely unopposed. Here indeed is a classic case of history repeating
itself as farce. As with the waltz in the 1810s and the polka in the
1840s, the guardians of the traditional values expressed shock and
horror at the new dance. In France, the Catholic Church had taken
the lead in denouncing it. In England, although the well-known
Jesuit, Fr.Bernard Vaughan, inveighed against the tango ('recently
imported... from the Zoological Gardens,' as he put it), the principal

opposition came from the conservative-minded in general.[25] The most
serious storm of all broke in the columns of *The Times*, in those days
the most respected of the country's newspapers. The attack was
launched on Tuesday 20 May 1913 in the form of a short letter, signed
simply 'A PEERESS', which comprehensively damned the tango, the
Boston and the turkey trot as 'scandalous travesties of dancing'. The
anonymous peeress' démarche roused squeals of protest all round.
George Grossmith sprang to the defence of the tango — 'a most
graceful and beautiful dance' — in the *Daily Graphic* a day later. A
dancing teacher told another newspaper that it was 'one of the most
beautiful dances that have ever been danced'.[26] But it was in *The
Times* itself that battle was most fiercely joined. The correspondence
went on for a fortnight, *The Times*, as was its custom at that period,
striving to hold a balance as between the contending schools of
thought.

*The Times* correspondence aptly illustrates Macaulay's famous
epithet about the British public in its fits of morality. A PEERESS
had several stout sympathisers, some of whom evidently felt that the
degenerate new dances were symptomatic of a general decline in good
manners. 'Is not the whole of our modern moral fibre distinctly
weakening?' asked ANOTHER PARENT on 31 May — after all, many
young men now slouched around London in 'costumes better fitted to
the golf links than to the West End'. The tango's defenders gave as
good as they got. The idea that 'foreigners all over the world are
perpetually inventing snares aimed at the morals of England,' wrote
one of them, was palpably absurd.[27] A 'veteran dancing man' signing
himself SENEX asserted that all the new dances gave him 'positive
sense of rajeunissement'.[28] As always in England, there were those
who thought that the best way to head off the new was to revive the
old — in this case, old dances like the polonnaise and the mazurka.
There was even a plea for the restoration of the minuet: 'What
analogy is there between such a splendid dance... and the degenerate
Tango, with its close contact and indelicate squirmings?'[29]

*The Times* itself did not pronounce on the issue until later in the
year. In November it printed what may well have been the most
intelligent article on the topic to have appeared at any time during
the craze. This made a serious effort to analyse the tango's success.
All dances, asserted the anonymous author, were related to their
historical epoch: 'if the waltz expressed romanticism, the polka was
the triumph of the bourgeoisie'. The tango owed its triumph to the
simple fact that dancing as such was once again popular, thanks in
part to the Russian Ballet. There were other factors as well:

The rage for the Tango is, in fact part of our new sense of pageantry... The last two reigns have given us a revival of royal ceremonial. At the present moment feminine apparel has a note of exotic fantasy, while the staid yellow and brown brick of our streets is being daily replaced by Babylonian palaces with majestic columns. The dances of a spectacular age must likewise catch the eye. That is the secret of the Tango.[30]

After this, *The Times'* own editorial on the tango came as an anticlimax. It saw no real harm in the dance: 'So far from being indecent or immodest, the ballroom tango is ungainly, ridiculous and dull'.[31] It may be doubted whether this very mild condemnation changed anybody's opinion.

One important question remained unresolved at the start of 1914. What was the opinion of the royal family? Royal taste in these matters was rather old-fashioned; the quadrille was a standard dance at palace balls right up to the First World War. It was strongly rumoured (even in the press) that Queen Mary disapproved. Such a fear was not wholly unreasonable. On the continent, the emperors of Germany and Austria-Hungary had forbidden their military and naval officers to dance the tango in uniform. (Punch's comment on this was: 'The KAISER'S hatred of the tango is well known... he has now ordered the CROWN PRINCE to cease being a Danzig man'.[32] The crown prince, who had incurred his father's disapproval on account of his interest in the tango, was then with his regiment in Danzig). As it happened, Queen Mary was not yet familiar with the dance. At a ball given by Grand Duke Michael of Russia at Kenwood, Hampstead, in the summer of 1914, Maurice and Florence Walton demonstrated various new dances, but omitted the tango. The queen had a quiet word with her hostess. Then came a great moment — 'For seven minutes Maurice and Florence tango'd in front of the Queen... When it was over, Her Majesty complimented Maurice and said how charming the dance was'.[33] The battle was finally over.

It was a pyrrhic victory. The tango was very soon to be dethroned, partly by the war, partly by the foxtrot. To judge from the press, the great craze was anyway beginning to abate somewhat in the early months of 1914. In January *The Sketch* began publishing a long series of fanciful cartoons depicting the ever more fantastic new dances that were now to replace the tango. *Punch* even carried a full-page cartoon captioned 'Exit Tango': it shows the Spirit of Dance awakening from slumber and saying 'Well thank heaven that's over; one of the dullest nightmares I ever met!'.[34] The outbreak of war in August spelled an instant decline in dancing all round. This, in fact, was something of a false twilight: the demand was such that dance halls eventually reopened, and the post-war years saw a huge upsurge in public interest in dancing. The Hammersmith Palais (opened in 1919) was merely the first of a series of splendid, capacious new dance halls; in the later 1920s even the Royal Opera House, Covent Garden, installed a dance floor.

The tango's later history in England can only be sketched in outline here. No longer in the forefront of fashion, it had to content itself with being one dance among many. The foxtrot, its immediate successor in popularity, arrived with the war and flourished thereafter, (ironically the foxtrot is the only dance other than the tango to have become a letter in the international radio alphabet) as did the new ragtime and jazz-inspired dances like the shimmy of the early 1920s and the notorious Charleston, whose reception in 1926 was very reminiscent of that of the tango in 1913. In the mid-1920s there was a brief resurgence of enthusiasm for the tango (almost, but not quite, a second craze); in general it fared quite well on English dance-floors until the Second World War. But the constant turnover of new dances from now onwards spelled its inevitable decline.

In the early 1920s there was considerable confusion in respect of the steps of the tango and other new dances. The largely self-appointed authorities of the ballroom dancing world decided to take things in hand. The extremely influential Philip Richardson (founder of *Dancing Times* in 1910 and its editor till 1957) arranged and presided over a whole series of conferences held under the auspices of the Imperial Society of Teachers of Dancing. The fourth conference (October 1922) was entirely devoted to the 'problem' of the tango. Only at the sixth and seventh conferences (April and July 1929) were the steps for this and other major dances finally standardised.[35] The tango as danced in England now had only a slender connection with its rough Argentine ancestor — though it has to be added that this was also true in most other countries, including Argentina. The smooth, gentle version now prevailed, though in the mid-1930s a more staccato form was briefly popularised in England by a German dancer, Freddie Camps.[36]

The Second World War and (especially) the years that followed brought further great changes. The prevailing fashions of the 1940s and 1950s included a number of new Latin American dances (the rumba, the samba, the cha cha cha, and so on), while the rock-and-roll explosion of the 1950s and 1960s signified a complete transformation in the patterns of social dance. A sociological survey of young people conducted in the 1960s showed that a large majority expressed no interest whatever in the tango, or, for that matter, the waltz.[37] The tango, for its part, continued (and continues) to be cultivated, but by devotees, not the general dancing public. From the Second World War onwards it has mostly been danced in two principal milieux; first, the old time dance clubs, which enjoyed an extraordinary growth in the war years (and which continue to exist, though maybe in smaller numbers), and second, the flourishing world of competitive ballroom dancing, both amateur and professional. This world is very well known to the public through BBC-TV's marvellous 'Come Dancing' programme, which in 1986 completed its thirty-sixth series. As admirers of the programme will appreciate, there is a final irony in the contemporary status of the Argentine tango. It is not classified as a Latin American dance at all (it belongs firmly in the old time sections). This is, perhaps, the ultimate mark of domestication.

There remains one last aspect to be considered. While the tango as a dance has played its part in modern English life, the impressive musical tradition to which it gave rise (tango bands and singers dominated popular taste in Argentina between 1920 and 1950) can hardly be said to have made any mark whatever. This has not been the case in some other countries. In France, to take an obvious example, the continuous presence of Argentine musicians (from 1920 until now) has encouraged local imitators. In the 1920s and 1930s Paris was visited at intervals by the greatest Argentine bands (those of Francisco Canaro, Osvaldo Fresedo and Julio de Caro, to name but three), while the greatest of all tango singers, Carlos Gardel, made triumphant appearances in cabaret and music hall in 1928-29 and 1930-31. A less predictable case is that of Japan, where enthusiasm for the tango took hold in the 1930s, and where competent indigenous bands have flourished, the singer Ranko Fujisawa winning very respectful applause when she visited Buenos Aires in the 1950s and 1960s. (This story is the more remarkable since the Japanese learned tango music from gramophone records; not until well after the Second World War did Argentine musicians visit the country.) One might also note here the oddly persistent tango influence in the eastern Mediterranean, the familiar rhythm sometimes sounding forth from Greek bouzoukis and in a current of Turkish popular music — as exemplified in a vocalist like Secaattin Tanyerli.

English popular music has not been marked by the Argentine tradition in any of these ways. Tangos executed by English dance bands in the 1920s and 1930s were nothing special, musically speaking, as British visitors to Buenos Aires realised when they heard the real thing: 'the tinkling insignificance by which most of us understand a tango,' observed Philip Guedalla in 1931, 'would not live for five minutes in the city of its birth.'[38] There is, however, an honourable exception to be mentioned here. The bandleader Gerald Bright (1904-74), a Londoner better known as Geraldo, was attracted early in his career to Latin rhythms. After a trip to South America to study them, he formed his celebrated Gaucho Tango Orchestra to play at the Savoy Hotel, starting in August 1930. The musicians wore vaguely 'gaucho' outfits. The band was heard frequently on the BBC National Programme; Geraldo became known as the Tango King. In the autumn of 1933, however, he formed a more conventional (and by the 1940s altogether more famous) dance band, popular through to the 1950s. The tango band took second place, and disappeared by around 1937. It can still be appreciated from its recordings, some of which have now been reissued.[39] According to one writer, Geraldo's tangos 'had about as much authenticity as the uniforms of his musicians'.[40] This is not quite fair. The Gaucho Tango Orchestra has a thicker, more ponderous sound than any Argentine band of the period; its insistence on the strict tango rhythm can be a trifle monotonous at times; but by and large Geraldo's tangos are easy enough on the ear. In general, the long, sophisticated and exciting tradition of Argentine tango music remains almost wholly unknown in England. It is likely that in recent years other forms of Latin American music (the New Chilean Song of the 1960s, for instance, or the salsa music now coming from the U.S.A.) have made a greater impression. English audiences only get rare opportunities to hear genuine tango musicians — though in March 1984 the Cuarteto Cedrón, a distinguished group based in Paris, performed briefly in London, and in June 1985, making his English debut, the great avant-garde musician Astor Piazzolla brought his Quintet to the Almeida Theatre, Islington. Both received very respectful notices. It remains to be seen whether England will eventually share the modest revival of international interest in the tango that occurred during the 1980s. ('Tango Argentino', a dance show by Argentine artists, had an astonishing success in New York in 1985-86). One may be permitted to hope so. Whatever the future may hold, the story of the past is clear enough. The great tango craze of 1913-14 left permanent traces, even if small ones, on twentieth century English culture. Most of us would be ashamed to admit that we could not (in the words of the American hit song of the early 1950s) tell a waltz from a tango; most of us are aware (as another song by the same authors, Al Hoffman and Dick Manning, has it) that it takes two to tango. England said 'Hullo, Tango!' very firmly in 1913 — and will never quite be able to say goodbye.

## Notes

1. Two useful sources in Spanish are *Historia del tango*, 16 vols., Buenos Aires, 1976-80, especially Vols. I and II, and José Gobello, *Crónica general del tango*, Buenos Aires, 1980, pp.10-20. In English, see D.L. Jakubs, 'From Bawdy House to Cabaret. The Evolution of the Tango as an Expression of Argentine Popular Culture', *Journal of Popular Culture*, 18:1. 1983, pp.133-45.
2. E. Guibourg, *La Calle Corrientes*, Buenos Aires, 1978, p.41.
3. Theodore Zeldin, *France 1848-1945*, 2 vols. Oxford 1973-7, II, pp.662-3.
4. Gobello, *Crónica General*, p.108.
5. 'A New Craze' *Illustrated London News*, 17 May 1913, p.685.
6. See the splendid two-page drawing *Illustrated London News*, 8 November 1913, pp.754-5, with the caption 'The Cult of the Argentine Tango. The Fashionable Dance at a Fashionable Hotel'.
7. *Illustrated London News*, 24 January 1914, pp.126-7.
8. *Ibid.*, 5 July 1913, pp.22-3.
9. A.H. Franks, *Social Dance: a Short History*, London 1963, p.180.
10. *The Sketch*, 12 November 1913, p.159.
11. *The Sketch*, 28 May 1913, p.232.
12. *Daily Mail*, 24 December 1913, p.3.
13. *The Sketch*, 6 August 1913, Supplement, p.3 for photographs.
14. *Ibid.*, 12 November 1913, p.71.
15. *Punch*, 15 October 1913, p.336.
16. *Ibid.*, 3 December 1913, p.458.
17. *Punch*, 12 November 1913, p.413.
18. G.B. Crozier, *The Tango and How to Dance it*, London 1914, p.11.
19. *Ibid*, pp.23-75.
20. *Ibid*, p.18.
21. *Ibid*, p.144.
22. *Ibid*, pp.133-6.
23. *Ibid*, p.147.
24. *Illustrated London News*, 3 January 1914.
25. *The Times*, 26 May 1913, p.9.
26. *Daily Mail*, 23 May 1913.

27. *The Times*, 21 May 1913, p.11.
28. *Ibid.*, 26 May 1913, p.9.
29. *Ibid*, 27 May 1913, p.11.
30. *Ibid*, 10 November 1913, p.11.
31. *Ibid*, 15 December 1913, p.9.
32. *Punch*, 24 December 1913, p.519.
33. P.J.S. Richardson, *A History of English Ballroom Dancing, 1910-45*, London 1946, pp.25-26.
34. *Punch*, 4 February 1914, p.83.
35. Richardson, *History of English Ballroom Dancing*, pp.75-7, 85-7.
36. Kit Hallewell, *Blackpool My Blackpool. One Man's Chronicle of the Blackpool Dance Festival over the years 1931-78*, Birmingham, 1979, pp.10-11.
37. Frances Rust, *Dance in Society*, London, 1969, p.211.
38. *Argentine Tango*, London 1932, pp.151-2.
39. Joy label, Joy 'D' 276, 1983.
40. Albert McCarthy, *The Dance Band Era*, London 1971, p.151.

# 14

# The British Press and the Peróns

*Gwyn Howells*

The detailed interest shown by the British press in Argentine affairs came to an abrupt end in 1956. Although Perón's return to Argentina in the early seventies aroused memories in some quarters, the changes which had occurred in the old relationship made Perón — the radical rabble-rouser of press coverage in the 1940s and 50s — less newsworthy than he had once been. It was not the living Perón but the dead Evita who now became the object of attention. She had grown in stature with the passing of the years and her story had a universal appeal which could be used by film-makers, writers and musicians. But for the British reader of the 1940s and 1950s, Argentina was a serious political matter which involved British national prestige, democratic principles, and the supply of cheap meat.

The amalgam of often contradictory phenomena with the Peronist movement allowed British and American commentators to label it according to their interests. British attitudes were conditioned by commercial considerations, the ideological legacy of the war, party political loyalties and national pride encapsulated in myths of Empire, of military glory and democracy. Perón's Argentina, with its power to affect the British meat ration, its managed economy and animosity towards the former ruling classes was used by journalists to score points against domestic political opponents, selecting material, distorting facts, making spurious parallels, playing on prejudices and stereotypes in press campaigns which bore little relation to what was actually happening in Argentina.

## Argentine fascism

Although by 1951 most journalists had come to accept Perón as a new sort of dictator[1] who ruled over a nation of 'delinquent democrats',[2] he was generally regarded as a fascist. How, in what context, and by what means was he so regarded?

On 4 June 1943 a coup led by Perón overthrew President Castillo. The coup was immediately reported in the British Press and continued to dominate the news for five days. Few first-hand accounts were available,[3] but optimism and war propaganda resulted in the claim that a pro-allied revolt had occurred. A variety of interpretations were put on the scanty facts although the common deduction was that the coup heralded 'the re-appearance of Argentina in its true character'[4] — namely, the old relationship.

Argentine neutrality and tolerance of Axis activists had embittered and shocked all those commentators who had long grown used to regarding Argentina as an informal member of the Empire. On 7 June, *The Times* reported that 'it has never been believed in this country that it was the true mind of Argentina to injure a cause with which her history and her future are both identified.' 'True' Argentina — as opposed to all the other possible false Argentinas — was liberal, democratic and pro-British, as symbolised by the railways, the trams, the freezer ships, and the Roca-Runciman Treaty.

General Ramírez's emergence as leader of the military junta cooled press enthusiasm noticeably and a more cautious attitude of expectancy prevailed. In the *Herald* of 14 June Alistair Cooke sounded one of the first cynical notes: the coup seemed to be no more than a 'strategic dash' for a place on the winning line. The day before the *Reynolds News*, probably the most ideologically intolerant of the left-wing papers, had categorically stated that Argentina was firmly under Nazi control. The prime cause for condemning Ramírez was his failure to sever diplomatic relations with the Axis. Nationalistic excesses, the elimination of the term 'provisional' before the Government title, and rumours of the establishment of a corporate state and the appointment of José M Rosa[5] as Minister of Finance seemed to corroborate the fascist thesis. For the *Herald* and *Reynolds News*, the regime's persecution of unions and communists seemed a portent.

In July an article by John White in the *Baltimore Sun* — based on flimsy evidence from diplomatic sources in Chile — seemed to provide further confirmation that Argentina had indeed become fascist. From early August the British press, leaning heavily and in most cases exclusively on US reports, also concluded that Ramírez and all connected with him were Nazi-style fascists. Indeed, when in early August the US revoked its export licenses to Argentina, *The Times* considered that Ramírez had instituted on American soil 'the kind of totalitarian regime that exists in Germany'.[6] Thus, when Perón's name was mentioned for the first time by an English paper,[7] and in the context of his unionising activities, evidence of fascist aspirations for the creation of centrally controlled unions had already been presented by British papers relaying American reports.[8]

Although many occurrences in Argentina seemed to point to the nationalistic authoritarianism of the regime, the primary reason for United States hostility towards Ramírez was his stubborn refusal to accept Washington's concept of Pan-Americanism even though *La Prensa*, *La Nación*, and the Jockey Club members were urging him in that direction. But not all British papers were totally satisfied with American interpretations of events. Although the *Mail* — stalwart defender of Anglo-Argentine trade — was acutely embarassed by feeling obliged to support trade with a fascist country, it never accepted the American view.

By January-February 1944 a series of events seemed at first to destroy the fascist thesis and then again to support it. The Bolivian coup d'etat and the Hellmuth spy ring affair[9] were taken as indicators of an active and dangerous phase of Argentine fascism. The break with the Axis at the end of January appeared to prove the accusations wrong, but the removeal of Ramírez at the end of February led many reporters to re-state them with increased vigour. The majority view was that Perón and Farrell, the real authors of the revolution, had overthrown Ramírez because of his anti-Axis move.[10] The US government reacted by suspending recognition of the Farrell regime, pending Argentina's strict compliance with a stringent set of conditions. This tough American line was supported by both the *Observer* and the *Telegraph*. The *Mail* took a more independent line, attacking the American consumer-goods imperialism which was providing Argentina with manufactured goods like cars and refrigerators which the British could not provide. *The Mail* considered that Argentina, more orientated towards Catholic Europe than towards Protestant America, was experiencing a Revolution which was 'neither pro-Axis nor Fascist but — both nationalist and anti-American'.[11]

From 1944, the British papers tended to divide along lines determined by the extent of their support for American policy in Latin America. Many drifted between support and reserve, but while most popular papers supported the US, the quality press and the *Mail* preferred Argentine beef to American pork. With the exception of *The Times*' BA correspondent, all were hostile to Perón: the Centre and Right because he did not represent the 'true' Argentina; the Left because of his Fascist tendencies.

The Labour party's view was clearly determined by the wish to be unwaveringly and uncompromisingly anti-totalitarian, and their reluctance to appear as appeasers: Munich had cast a long shadow. The party also had to repudiate the accusations of totalitarianism which had been thrown at it by both Hayek's book — *The Road to*

*Serfdom* — and by Churchill's allusion to a possible 'Socialist Gestapo' in Britain.[12] But whereas the left followed uncritically official American descriptions of Perón, the right was more reserved in its condemnation.

## Perón's apotheosis and electoral triumph

*The Times* report of 15 June preceded the British General Election by a month: it looked as if Argentina was being used as part of the British electoral campaign. *The Times* Buenos Aires correspondent was just starting to build a case for classifying Perón as a socialist. Indeed, the reports by this writer stand out from the mass of tendentious, bombastic and sensationalist columns in other papers. The famous events of October 1945 which climaxed on the 17th — San Perón's day — were accurately described and report by *The Times* correspondent. He was the only journalist who did not adhere to the assertion that Perón and a few henchmen and fanatics were trying to retain power despite the overwhelming opposition of democratic Argentines.[13] Even when paralyzing strikes and mammoth demonstrations followed Perón's resignation and arrest, the *Herald* and the *Express* wrote of Perón's supporters as 'unkempt youths' and a 'howling crowd'.[14] *The Times* itself had been moved to write on 11 October that the Colonel's removal perhaps heralded happier days for Argentina. In the meantime, *The Times* correspondent in Buenos Aires cabled these words on 17 October:'Eye-witnesses were astonished at the extraordinary cordial relations which were apparent between factory workers and the police contrasting with the bitter hatred shown on other occasions when the police clashed with well-dressed crowds'.

A popular revolt in favour of Perón had not been expected by the press in Britain or the US and a sudden flurry of scare-mongering articles were presumably designed to keep the fascist theme alive. Peronist anti-semitism was the *Herald* topic on 20 October; Argentine plans for atomic-bombs that of the *Reynolds News* and the *Pictorial* of the following day. A week later the *Star* summed up the consensus feeling with these words: 'The Nazi inspired gangsters of Buenos Aires glibly promise elections next April. A blunt exposure of them all by Britain and the United States would be salutary.' These words, in fact, echo Assistant Secretary of State Braden's notorious Blue Book, which was published on 12 February 1946 in an injudicious and crude attempt to discredit Perón. Braden's plan, however, backfired, and enabled Perón to coin the vote-catching slogan, 'Braden or Perón'.

Until Perón's victory was conceded by his opponent Dr. Tamborini on 13 March 1946, the British media, following the American lead, mounted an unrelenting campaign of vilification against him. According to the *Economist's* report of 6 April. 'In elections which to everyone's surprise seem to have been fair, Argentine has gone Nazi. Two days earlier *The Times* leader had speculated on the significance for Britain of Perón's 'new and personal left-wing party'.

Left-wing commentators, in particular, were to retain an image of Perón the fascist for many years to come; their venom was directed at Eva Perón for the same reason. As late as May 1953 articles warning of Argentine expansionist ambitions would appear in the *Observer*,[15] but, by then, communism had become the western bogey.[16] The Peróns would also be sometimes accused of that.

With hindsight it seems that although many writers were genuine in their denunciation of Perón as a fascist, their opinions were too closely founded on European parallels and were deliberately encouraged by official Washington policy towards Argentina — a policy based on the assumption that the West would be more secure if the oppressed majority of democrats in Argentina could be returned to power. It is not surprising that the *Mail* and other pro-trade papers should have reisisted the fascist interpretation on the grounds that it was invented by the US to weaken British influence in Argentina, but it is notable that they imagined that the pre-war Anglo-Argentine relationship could resume its old course. They were to be quickly disillusioned.

## The meat question

Between 1946 and 1952 six trade missions left Britain to secure the supply of Argentine meat. Each one of the negotiations was protracted and accompanied by acrimonious and partisan press comment. Perón had the power to perpetuate austerity and the popular press' portrayal of Argentina as a land of sizzling steaks and prosperity was symptomatic of the awe with which Argentine food-power was regarded.

Many features of Peronist policies such as the armaments programme[17] made dealings with Perón problematic for the Labour government although trade and food supplies took precedence over other considerations.

Shortly after Perón's election triumph, the British sent the Eady mission to Argentina to secure a new trade pact to replace the Roca-Runciman treaty of 1933 (renewed 1936) which was due to expire in August. This treaty had been the object of virulent Argentine nationalist hatred and many papers were apprehensive about the mission's chances of success in the new political climate in Argentina.

Early British hopes of smooth negotiations appeared misplaced when, on 17 July, *The Times* reported a speech in which Perón made critical reference to the Anglo-Argentine railways, and stated that the Roca-Runciman agreement would not be renewed after August, and that higher prices would be demanded for meat. Sir Walter Eady's alleged complaint about 'the cold hostility of Buenos Aires'[18] and the *Economist's* deprecation of tactics 'obviously not learnt at a public school'[19] brought a chorus of resentful comment from the papers. The general tenor of comment was one of self-pitying resentment at Argentina's treatment of an old ally which had suffered so badly in war.

Although by 11 September talks seemed on the verge of collapse, agreement was suddenly announced on the 15th. Much of the suspense had, undoubtedly, been part of Peronist domestic propoganda. Only the *Express* withheld its applause and stifled its relief. But the Mission's success allowed the *Herald* of 18 September to make political capital. By sticking to a well-thought-out guiding plan and by bold use of the Socialist policy of bulk purchase for imported necessities, the outlook has been transformed. Perón had not proved such an ogre as had been feared. In fact, 1946 showed him to be willing to trade with Britain in a businesslike manner. Supporters of the old relationship were highly satisfied by the way the conclusion of the treaty appeared to confirm the survival of pre-war understanding. In addition, satisfactory progress had been made on the complex question of the Anglo-Argentine railways.[20]

By 1947, however, a complete reversal of these early favourable trends occurred, and the political issue surrounding Argentine meat would again become crucial for the Labour government. Private trade in meat imports had been replaced on the British side by bulk-buying, and Argentina had established the IAPI to regulate its foreign trade — as a means to direct the economy. Thus, the Conservatives had a keen interest in observing the results of such state control. By the end of 1947, the *News Chronicle* could declare that never had Argentina been of such interest to the British people.[21]

The dollar shortage that led to the suspension of sterling convertibility on 20 August 1947 was the crisis which brought Anglo-Argentine trade to the forefront of the political arena. A *Mail* editorial of
12 September prompted by Miguel Miranda's threat to stop meat
shipments until convertibility was restored, warned Britain that only
hard work and exports would bring success. The editorial concluded:

That is the lesson the British people must learn and if the present
Government, through incompetence, feebleness, woolly-minded-
ness, or sheer stupidity cannot teach it, they will have to make way
for leaders who can.

This comment might be taken as a sign that Conservatives felt that
the political tide was now turning and that there was no better time
to make a point than over the threat to the meagre meat ration.
Shipments of meat to Britain were not suspended but this was not of
interest to the *Mail*; socialist *economic* theory was.

Conservative propagandists were in fact able to extract many
advantages from Argentine affairs, particularly as the Falklands
issue and the *La Prensa* affair were added to the meat ration problem.
For since 1948 the Peronist Government had attempted, unsuccess-
fully, to moderate the critical line followed by *La Prensa*, a prestigious
Argentine daily, with a world-wide reputation, by measures which
included a compulsory reduction in the number of pages — and by
extension — commentaries published by the newspaper. As these
measures had no effect, the expropriation of *La Prensa*, was ordered
by the government in 1951, ostensibly due to an insolvable dispute
between management and the Vendor's Union.

In March 1951 all sections of the British mass media were driven
to further denunciations of the Peróns because of the suppression of
the Argentine quality newspaper, *La Prensa*. The saga of the newspaper's demise and resurrection as a loyal mouthpiece was newsworthy in its own right. There was the murder of a printer, political
manipulation of unions, partisan courts, compliant parliamentarians
and a hero, Dr. Paz, *La Prensa's* editor who had to flee the country to
avoid arrest. But it can be argued that the affair became more
embittered than it might have because the US and British press
turned it into an attack upon Peronism. In her *Historia del Peronismo*, Eva Perón would describe *La Prensa* as 'a capitalist cancer',
whereas for the British right-wing press it was a free voice in an
increasingly totalitarian state. Moreover, some of the most Conservative newspapers utilised the affair to attack members of the Labour

government. A *Daily Mail* leader on 7 March, on the pretext of solidarity with *La Prensa*, assailed the Labour Government in these terms:

> Since the war the British Left Wing have sought on every occasion to discredit the Press. Ministers have gone out of their way to attack it. One, Mr Bevan, called it 'the most prostituted Press in the world'!... What these dupes and pseudo-intellectuals do not realise is that the free Press is the basis of their liberties, and that without it we should all live in ignorance and fear.

The *La Prensa* affair was thus turned by the right-wing British Press into an exemplification of the threat posed by socialism to the fundamental rights of a free society.

Meat, however, was the primary weapon, since crises concerning its supply were annual occurrences and each one reinforced Conservative criticisms of labour's economic management. An *Express* comment on 31 August 1951 crudely expressed Conservative prejudice:

'There will not always be bulk-buyers and state-planners to present Britain in the world's markets as a gaping yokel among the hucksters at a fair ... The system is coming to an end'.

Criticism of the bulk-buying system by the Conservative Press was nearly always associated with the image of Perón as a bullying, devious politician. Popular conceptions of Latin corruption, exemplified by the Mafia, were useful seedbeds for anti-Perón propoganda. Labour supporters, thererfore, could be expected to demand firm handling of Perón by their leaders. Conservatives for their part were fully aware of the efforts that Argentina made to fulfil its meat contracts but such facts were not taken into account until 1952. They were also aware that British home production met 65 per cent of the national requirements in 1951, as opposed to 51 per cent before the war. Moreover, by 1951 New Zealand had become Britain's chief foreign supplier. In short, the Labour government had successfully reduced British dependence on imports, favouring the Commonwealth, just as Argentina's exportable surpluses declined.

The Labour press tried hard to project their politicians as non-appeasers, but to no avail. Between March 1950 and April 1951, Labour fell into a trap. The press had urged the government to refuse to pay higher prices for Argentine meat. By refusing to pay the Argentine price and on account of Argentine difficulties in sending supplies, the British fresh meat ration fell, on 4 February 1951, to eight-pence a week — its lowest point ever.

The policy adopted by Maurice Webb in the summer of 1950 had, at first, been generally regarded as courageous, but by 1951 it had become unpopular with the public, had divided the Labour Party, and had led to a Conservative censure motion on 8 February which Labour won by eight votes. Webb, who had accused Argentina of blackmail in the Commons on 23 March 1950, had seriously miscalculated the balance of advantage. The Argentine claim for a 50 per cent rise in meat prices was being urged on Perón by the cattle producers befriended so consistently by the erstwhile allies of the British Conservative and Liberal Press. The war of attrition with Britain could not harm their interests.[22] The suspension of meat shipments to Britain from 21 July 1950 inevitably caused the reduction of the British meat ration and gave the anti-bulkbuying lobby an opportunity which they promptly seized. Webb had lost the propaganda battle.[23]

After their October 1951 election victory the Conservatives had to bargain with Argentina under the terms of the 1949 Covenant just as Labour had done. The meat deal announced on 20 December 1952 however, was the last to provoke Press furore. Although the arrival of the first post-war chilled Argentine beef at Smithfield in March 1953 was taken by some papers as the final thawing-out of austerity, Argentine meat itself had lost its ability to influence the British elector.[24] In July 1954, the import trade reverted to private enterprise.

## Juan Domingo Perón

By comparison with the attention paid to other Latin American figures, Juan Domingo Perón was singularly honoured by British papers, for Perón was a thorn in the western side. His status as troublemaker is nevertheless puzzling. There were no bloody programs and no real threat to western security in Perón's Argentina. But from the plethora of anti-Perón articles it is clear that he was attacked for his anti-British, anti-American and anti-liberal behaviour. Although some papers might have been able to applaud his anti-American politics, Anglo-American unity took precedence. Until the Cold War began in earnest, Perón was treated as a menacing, Mussolini-style figure. Afterwards he was seen as a threat to Western security.

Within each of these major themes lay several minor ones. For Labour papers Perón's chief sin against social democracy was his abolition of free trade-unions, high-lighted by his struggle to defeat Cipriano Reyes[25] and the devices used to achieve this end. They were also outraged by his use of Evita, and of bribery and corruption to gull the simple worker. No Labour paper paused to question why Argentine workers should have consistently voted for him.

Conservative and Liberal papers, on the other hand, objected to Perón's rough handling of the old Argentine establishment. On 5 November 1948 *The Times* discussed the 1948-9 reform of the Argentine Constitution. The article stated that Perón's success was due to 'the generous social reform and improvement of the lot of the masses in a land where reform was long overdue'. This aspect of the Peronist regime was no recommendation for the Right and Centre papers as it was achieved at the expense of economic stability in Argentina. A constant theme of *Express* and *Mail* reports in 1949 was the precariousness of the Argentine economy despite its 'biliously rich exterior'.[26] James Cameron of the *Express* and Richard Greenough of the *Mail* both concluded that Perón's squandermania was ruining the unruinable. Such eye-witness accounts as those of these two journalists were inspired not only by a puritanical sense of the virtue of poverty but also by outraged economic principles. Perón and his Finance Minister Miranda were not seen as modernisers but as inept managers. Common to all sections of the Press were references to the Argentine masses eager to accept shackles in return for a promise of a better life. In the *Express* of 17 March 1949, James Cameron referred to the blind adulation of the Peróns by the masses, echoing an opinion voiced in the *Economist* two years earlier, on 30 August 1947:

> In Argentina the Perónist movement has indicated that the masses of the country are willing to sacrifice liberty and freedom in return for the promise of a better life.

In essence, these views of Perón's power were similar to those expressed about the Fascist leaders' hold over their countrymen. Perón was believed to be bribing the foolish masses so that he could retain power. British commentators could, according to their political affiliation, interpret Peronism as an example of tyranny of the left or the right and thereby cast doubt on the democratic credentials of their domestic political opponents. If the left stressed the anti-free union side of the Peronist regime, the right claimed that it was a dictatorship based on workers' support.[27] What particularly perplexed all commentators was that whereas Argentine conservatives had allowed freedom of expression but rigged elections, the opposite was true of Perón: between 1949 and 1951, he established a congressional committee to investigate anti-Argentine activities, closed over one hundred newspapers, Peronised education, antagonised the church and used the police to suppress dissent. On 31 May 1950 the *Guardian* summarised Argentine trends as evidence of Perón's 'unpleasant notions of Government'; three months earlier the *Observer* had declared that Argentina was comparable to Nazi Germany.

Even though journalists realised that the decline of British influence in Argentina and Perón's attacks on American policies were all part of a pattern, they saw it as little more than a dictator's ploy to distract his people's mind from the failure of his economic policies. At this stage the Press appears to have been totally unaware of what is now known as Third World politics, development economics, or cultural nationalism. Most British observers were unable to free their minds from the belief that only Western-style democracy is proper government because it is thought to be founded on self-evident truths. Thus, Perón's attempts to Argentinise his country were inevitably criticised. As the reaction to Perón's 1947 broadcast had shown,[28] the British could not understand that his eclectic ideology expressed deeply held views.

By the time that Perón began his second term, Argentine autarky was totally defunct. Rather than submit immediately to United States dominance, Argentina made overtures to Stalin through its ambassador in Moscow, Señor Bravo. In early 1953 Perón courted Chile in another attempt to kindle enthusiasm for a South American trading union. Approaches to Russia and the visit to Chile caused sections of the Press to fall back once again upon parallels with European history.[29]

A turning-point in the Peronist regime was 1953. Bomb outrages, internal struggles in the party, rampant inflation, vitriolic denunciation of imperialism and its agents by the President, were evidence of the depth of the crisis. Most papers were evidently hoping for Perón's overthrow although it had become clear by May that there was no effective organised opposition in Argentina. On 6 June the *Telegraph* reporter, Anthony Mann, speculated on whether Egypt would follow the example of Peronism. The significance of Perón's survival lay in that it quashed the myth that the regime was in power through force. More importantly, some reporters, chiefly of the quality Press, were obliged to examine the roots which had kept the Peronist tree upright in severe storms.

For the great majority of papers all that was of interest now was the ultimate dénouement of the Perón saga. A *Times* editorial of 18

May 1954 entitled 'Divergent Policies' expressed the hope that Argentina would now abandon its economic policies and move back in step with a freer and more competitive system. It was this change of political and economic climate in Britain which altered press focus on Perón. He would, henceforth, be viewed as a dictator in decline, beset by an increasing number of enemies. His clash with the church, which popular papers saw as a struggle between a tyrant bent on self-deification and the outraged Christian community, caused an increase in interest in Argentine affairs between December 1954 and April 1955. Journalists made no attempt to analyse the Argentine church or to explain why, having enjoyed its support in 1945-6, Perón was now at odds with it. However, *The Times* correspondent did note that the Argentine catholics who demonstrated against Perón were mainly upper class. Perón's battle with the church — which ended in his excommunication and the abortive and bloody coup of 16 June — was not primarily due to Catholic incursions into the union field but to the massive propaganda campaign which sought to exalt Peronism above the traditional faith. Indeed, Perón actually demoted Christmas and Easter to second class holidays. The Press commented on the President's anti-Catholic manoeuvres, but not with great passion.

The events from 16 June to 30 September 1955 did, however, lead to considerable coverage. But although over 140,000 words were written on the turmoils which followed the 16 June bombings, British papers were caught by surprise when the end came on 17 September. Such was the belief in Perón's powers of survival that journalists lost interest after the mass rally and vitriolic speeches of 31 August in Buenos Aires. Jack Comben's cryptic cable in the *Express* of 17 September — 'Spain' '36, 'Argentina' '55' — brought attention back with a jolt. But despite Comben's implicit assessment of the Argentine situation, no civil war took place. In fact, journalists were again taken by surprise by the rapidity of Perón's departure. The *Telegraph's* statement of 4 October seemed accurate: the dictator had gone 'with a whimper'.

In the aftermath many papers printed summaries of Perón's career. Although the *Herald* commented that his fall was a ' black day for the workers', most others agreed that Argentina faced a difficult future. Nevertheless, the *Mail* and the *Express* stressed the jubilation of anti-Peronist Argentines. Indeed, the *Mail* claimed that Perón's support had been limited to a few thousand fanatics and opportunist sycophants. Either way, no British journalist claimed that Perón had been of more than Argentine significance.

## Eva Perón

Although Perón received a bad press in Britain, Eva, at least until after her death, received a worse one. Cassandra's obituary in the *Mirror* was the most savage to appear and was replete with all the prejudices and none of the perceptiveness shown by commentators on Eva during her life-time:

> A very old-fashioned lady is dead. Not an old-fashioned lady of lace and lavender and gentle faded smiles, but an old-fashioned lady of mink furs and armour-plated motor cars, a quaint out-of-date lady of violent ambitions embedded in vast and vulgar wealth. Eva Duarte Perón ... has died. Señora Perón was remarkable for the fact that she and her husband were able to rivet medieval ideas of tyranny on to the framework of modern society. She was old-fashioned in that she followed the ancient patterns of ambitious and beautiful women seeking power through the ages without one single new idea of her own.

Of sixteen obituaries which appeared, eleven condemned her for her corruption, ruthless ambitions, and exploitation of simple people's hopes. With the exception of *The Times*, Evita had been consistently treated as a virago whose rise from rags to riches merited the type of treatment given to stories about the stars of Hollywood.

Events in early October 1945 brought her name and her activities to prominence — just as it appeared that she was about to lose her influence. On 16 October the *Mail* carried this report:

> She rose to wield despotic power in a lightening career which ended as abruptly as it began ... In the early days ... she gained virtual control of Radio Belgrano and used it increasingly to boost herself and Perón, none of which did her any good with the public, who hated her.

The key points in this comment — despotic powers, self-glorification — were thereafter to be found in all journalists' reports.[30] Many papers liked to be more specific, by adding a phrase such as 'ex-actress' or 'jumped-up showgirl' to their texts. Much Press comment in the United States was so scurrilous that the Argentine Embassy placed an appeal to journalists for fairness and decorum in the *New*

*York Times* — 'nauseous attacks' on Evita were unworthy of the American Press'.

Eva's 1947 European tour made her name familiar throughout Britain because of the possibility that she would visit England. This issue divided the Press: left-wing papers opposed her visit because of the ecstatic reception she had received in Franco's Spain. With the exception of the *Express*, the right-wing press grudgingly accepted it for the sake of trade. On 18 June the Labour MP Raymond Blackburn showed the depth of Labour divisions by writing in the *Herald*,: 'Personally, I regret that the wife of the Fascist President of Argentina, after being fated by Franco, should seek to visit this island which stood alone against Fascism in the darkest days of the war.' It was, however, an *Express* article of 12 June, written by the foreign editor Charles Foley, which caused greatest embarrassment by claiming: 'Señora Perón Breaks a Tradition Will Visit the Palace But not Stay There'. Foley knew quite well that Eva's visit would be unofficial and not as a Head of State. It became commonplace in the popular Press to attribute the eventual cancellation of the visit to Eva's umbrage at this snub from Buckingham Palace.

The events of August 1951 provided the next opportunity for malicious coverage of Evita's career. Her failure to overcome army resistance to her candidacy for the Vice-Presidency was treated as a long overdue public rebuke. Neither left nor right in Britain were impressed by the willingness of the Argentine masses to idolise her and her husband and, consequently, ridicule was used to debunk her. In August 1951 the farce was compounded by Perón's excuse that since his wife was only twenty-nine she did not meet the constitutional requirements. Soon after the crisis of August and September, newspapers became aware of the gravity of Eva's illness and whether out of respect or a sense of human drama they refrained from attacking her.

Of interest, in view of later newspaper assessments of Perón, was the majority opinion that Eva was a more remarkable figure than her husband. Milton Shulman wrote in the *Evening Standard* that

> Historians may even deny General Perón a complete chapter. For in the turbulent firmament of South America dictators blaze and die with the quixotic incandescence of comets ... Eva made the difference ... She set herself up as a Joan of Arc wearing armour by Dior and brandishing a microphone as her weapon. Her Dauphin was Perón.

The reason why journalists preferred Evita was not because of her politics but because in the end she appeared as a magnanimous, courageous and tragic figure, more sinned against than sinning. In the end she won the acclaim she sought earlier in life for a dramatic role.

When Perón fell, many fanciful and romantic interpretations of his defeat became current. Revelations of Perón's sex-life which were given great publicity by the new Argentine regime eclipsed the more sentimental versions of the grief distracted widower. The political vacuum created by Eva's death was stressed as she was seen as the true leader of the *Laborista* wing of the Perónist movement and as a more sincere and courageous person than her husband. On 3 October 1955, the *Telegraph* quoted these words from *Epoca*:

> We do not mind gold and jewels, we do not mind cynicism and lies, we can even forget his gallant episodes and sexual lusts. What we cannot pardon is that filth has stained her who was a guide to the nation, though in a wider sense, her memory is only purified by the fate of false prophets.

## Perón's return and Evita

With the exception of a few articles occasioned by Perón's abortive attempt to return to Argentina in 1964 there was nothing resembling coherent coverage of Perónism until the early seventies.

It was the rediscovery of Eva's body in a Milan cemetery in 1971 which focussed attention on the imminence of Perón's return. During the brief period from April 1972 to July 1974 there was a slight but detectable shift in Press treatment of Perón. Prior to his return to Argentina in 1973 he was the object of stereotyped criticism. Bernard Levin writing in *The Times* of April 4th 1973 equated him with Hitler and called him a 'populist fascist' who had looted his country 'to deck his dreadful wife in jewels.'

After Perón became president in 1973, an event which merited only eight lines in *The Times*, the Press abandoned its reference to fascism. It was evident that the General's term in office was only a brief interregnum. Less than a year later Perón had died and *The Times* published an obituary entitled 'Flamboyant creator of modern Argentina.' The title and final lines of the obituary recognise the extent of Perón's influence in modern Argentina but suggest that it had been largely negative: 'If the mythology and false hopes which surrounded

General Perón are allowed to die with him it could help to create a
more realistic and forward-looking atmosphere.' Although he had
finally become a more respectable figure worthy of a requiem mass
in Westminster Cathedral, he was still perceived as little more than
a talented pedlar of illusions. There was virtually no comment on the
declaration by Franco's Spain and Castro's Cuba of three days mourn-
ing for Perón. [31]

If Argentine affairs generally (apart from football) failed to arouse
much interest the same was not true of Eva. She was to become the
subject of one of the most successful musicals ever staged in Britain
and which is still in the repertoire over ten years after it first opened
at the Prince Edward Theatre in the summer of 1978. The interest of
Tim Rice who wrote the lyrics was first roused by the television film
*The Queen of Hearts* in October 1972, the first opportunity the British
had of seeing a visual account of Eva's controversial career.

Critics praised the artistic merits of the musical but almost universally condemned the characterisation of the heroin.[32] Tim Rice was
obliged to defend his treatment of Eva in the *Sunday Times Magazine*
of June 11 1978. Journalists of both Left and Right continued to
consider Eva as the unacceptable embodiment of womanhood. She
was 'the whore in office'[33] the cynical exploiter of human hopes and
weaknesses. There was little reflection in the press of the extraordinary influence which her myth exerted in the Argentina of the early
1970s.

It might be argued now, with hindsight, that a better informed
popular press might have played some role in preparing public
opinion for the events of 1982. The sensationalism which greeted
Evita did not deepen the understanding of Argentine affairs. Little
had changed in twenty-five years.[34]

## Conclusion

British Press comment on the Peróns and Argentina fell into three
major periods: the war-time crisis, the Labour years, the Conservative post-austerity years.

The first period was characterised by the ideological commitment
of the left to oppose fascism everywhere and to establish a Welfare
State in Britain. On the right, concern for export markets and
food-supplies took precedence over ideology. The left, surprisingly,
was influenced by American opinion, while the right, especially the

commerical right, was more hesitant in accepting the honesty of American motives.

During the Labour years, meat deals, the Falklands dispute of 1948, and the *Prensa* affair of 1951 gave Conservatives the opportunity to criticise socialist economics, defence policies, and totalitarian tendencies. Perón's 'socialism' with its class bias, offered the right many analogies with trends in Britain. 1949 and 1951 were years when Peronist politics were used by the British Press for electoral purposes, although the meat negotiations of 1947 can be said to mark the beginning of the Conservative onslaught and the Labour defence. This defence was based on trying to destroy any analogies between Argentine and British politics by branding Perón a fascist gangster, and his wife an unscrupulous rabble-rouser.

After 1951 the return of the Conservatives to power, the intensity of the Cold War, reversals of trading conditions in the world, and the withering away of the Anglo-Argentine relationship allowed partisan comment on the Peróns to give way to more objective reporting. Only Eva's death and Perón's last dramatic months in office were to receive extended coverage.

The clash between British political groups, revealed obliquely and directly in their reporting of Argentine affairs, arose essentially from differing views of the functioning and purpose of the state. Fundamentally, the Conservative Press opposed Perón's milking and souring of the Argentine economy to keep the loyalty of his supporters. The economic disasters which beset Argentina after 1948 were seen by the Conservatives as vindication of their viewpoint. For both left and right in Britain the Peronist regime was a focus of concern, for its real moral was how to preserve democracy, based on alternating parties, when electoral success and economic realities do not often prove compatible. Perhaps it was because of the gravity of this thought that so few papers treated Perón's fall as a triumph for the *real* Argentina.

## Notes

1. Words of *Mail* 29.5.51.
2. Opinion of *Guardian* 31.5.50.
3. Out of only 17 articles, 7 came from the US, 3 from Uruguay, 3 from London and only 4 from Argentina.
4. *Observer*, 6.6.43.
5. Rosa was the owner of the printing works where the extreme nationalist *El Pampero* was published.

6. *The Times*, 5.8.43.
7. *Guardian*, 25.10.43.
8. In December the *Herald* published Sumner Welles' criticism of Perón as a 'young, forceful, fanatical Fascist bent upon becoming an Argentine dictator.'
9. In January 1944 Paz Estenssoro came to power in Bolivia and the British uncovered a spy-ring in Trinidad. Oscar Hellmuth, one of the spies caught, was an auxiliary consul of the Argentine in Barcelona.
10. The opposite was probably true. Ramírez did not wish to comply with US demands.
11. *Mail*, 14.3.44, 'Power Politics'.
12. Hayek's book came out in 1944 and Churchill's 'gestapo' speech was made in June 1945.
13. c.f. *Mail* of 5.6.45.
14. *Express* and *Herald*, both of 18.10.45.
15. *Observer*, 15.53, 'Perón's Ambitions', written on the occasion of Perón's visit to Chile.
16. When Braden resigned in June 1947, he had stated thet fascism was now less dangerous than communism.
17. For left-wing fears see *Tribune*, 5.4.46. Fascist rather than Communist aggression was feared and wild stories of Argentina's atomic bomb potential were circulating. Stanley Ross of the *Tribune* had been told by Perón that Argentina needed to militarise against possible threats from Brazil and Chile which were reciving US military aid.
18. Sir William Eady denied using this phrase.
19. *Economist*, 27.7.46.
20. After initial proposals for a mixed company, the railways were sold to Argentina for 150 million pounds (above market value). They passed officially to Argentine control on 9.2.48. Despite Perón's boast, Argentina did not make a good deal; the railways needed massive investment to modernise them.
21. *News Chronicle*, 22 December.
22. On 21 August 1950, Argentina announced higher minimum prices for light steers for packing plants than for heavy steers suitable for the British fresh meat market.
23. In early 1951 Perón was boasting that he had acquired the Anglo-Argentine railways for nothing. In March *La Prensa* was closed.
24. The chief year for coverage of meat deals was 1949 and the second was 195 . Taken together these years provided the

*Herald* with 54 per cent of its meat stories in the Peronist years. Other papers show a similar pattern; *The Times* 42 per cent; *Mail* 70 per cent; *Express* 54 per cent; *Telegraph* 49 per cent. The *Mail* figure is of particular political significance.

25. Cipriano Reyes, an ally of Perón in 1945-1947, represented the Labourite view of the Peronist movement. He tried to prevent the creation of a monolithic trade-union structure by rallying dissidents. In 1948 he was arrested and remained in prison until 5th September 1955.

26. A phrase from the *Express* of 6.9.46.

27. *The Times* headline, 14.11.50.

28. *Economist*, 2.7.47 described it as 'rarely departing from the plane of principle and platitude'.

29. The *Observer* article, 1.5.53 stated that South America allied to Perón would be 'like Europe united under the Nazis'. It was the *Express*, 16.2.57 which quoting *La Nación* recalled the precise wording of the GOU proclamation of 1943.

30. A great deal of the virulent comment against Eva, as well as anti-red hysteria came into the press via the *Sunday Express*, 3.8.52 and the *Mail*, 5.8.52. The original inspirer of this material was Fleur Cowles. Her book *Bloody Precedent* was first published in 1952.

31. Brief agency reports were published.

32. For a more balanced view by Richard Gott see *Guardian* 21.6.78.

33. A phrase used in the *New Statesman*, 30.6.78.

34. During the seventies the press paid little attention to the Falklands. Problems related to the islands were being dealt with at a diplomatic level and were thus unexciting. One article is worth mentioning. This appeared in the *Times*, 23.6.78. In the light of subsequent events it is worth quoting from this article:
'Those who live in the Falkland islands are in a peculiar time vacuum of the Victorian and Edwardian era ... They are an embarrassment to the British Government, to the Argentine Government and almost to themselves ... At present the Falkland islands game is a draw and unless the strong Falkland Islands lobby in London stops urging the home side to adopt 'foul play tactics' it is likely to remain so.'

# 15

# The Unnoticed Era

## Eduardo Crawley

'Link', my dictionary tells me, is 'a connecting part; a thing that connects others; a means of connection.' For the most part, the quest for rescuable links between Britain and Argentina looks like the search for things that will connect little more than dinner-time speeches at Canning House; exercises in nostalgia or strained compilations of 'telling' anecdotes (such as Cesar Milstein coming up with his monoclonal antibodies at Cambridge, or the 'irony' of an *Old Georgian* running the South American Department in the post-Falklands Foreign Office)[1]. All too often, this quest seems rather pathetic and pointless.

The hard evidence accumulated in the decade between 1976 and 1986 points overwhelmingly to the rusting away, the occasional snapping, of old links, amid a general mood too indifferent to be fatalistic. After thirty years of steadily declining presence in Argentina, not many were surprised when Britain failed to open its doors, let alone its arms, to the thousands of Argentines fleeing the terror of the 'dirty war', concentrating instead, first under Labour and then under the Tories, on trying to forge a new link through arms sales to the military in power in Buenos Aires.

Indifference was so pervasive that the war of 1982 did come as a surprise, and it was so briefly and superficially touched by the war that the tale of neglect revealed in the Franks Report caused little concern or regret. It is true enough that never as in 1982 was so much written in Britain, in a single year, about Argentina; but never, either, was so little understanding, or unwillingness to understand, expressed in so many printed words.

There have been, in the post-Falkland years, calls for reconciliation, for the restoration of lost links. Some of these calls, perhaps the ones which will carry most weight in the circles of power, are unashamedly mercantile; their authors would find little amiss in restoring the kind of links that existed immediately before 1982. Theirs is a call to salvage what little remains of an old, nearly exhausted investment.

There are, of course, other calls, of which this book is implicitly one, rooted in the sense that somehow, over the years, links — means of connection — have been created whose value cannot be reduced to economics. Yet there appears to be little on which to ground this feeling save the appeal to a glorious past; glories which belong to a pattern of Argentine-British relations which the evidence of economics shows as dying, if not dead, and which the evidence of politics shows as most unlikely to be resuscitated. Such is the mass of this evidence that the quest for rescuable links seems pathetic and futile.

But the evidence is misleading. Among those few who have been watching, too many have been morbidly fascinated by the spectacle of an old relationship falling apart, or engrossed in the attempt to salvage something from the debris. So much so that little if any attention has been directed towards the fruits of that old relationship, already well on their way to becoming the seeds of new growth.

Never as in the past decade, never perhaps as in the years since the Falklands war, has the Argentine presence in Britain been so significant. And through that presence, never, at least in this century, has British influence been projected so potently back to Argentina — and beyond.

## The new Argentine presence

This Argentine presence to which I refer has its origins in the diaspora created by the 'dirty war' of the mid-1970s. In contrast with the welcome offered the Chileans fleeing the Pinochet regime, Britain did not open its doors to the wave of Argentines forced into exile. Access was limited to those fortunate enough to have a British passport or those able to invoke some other 'normal' entitlement to entry.

The few who came did not arrive with the formal status of refugees or asylees. Though they did not see themselves as permanent expatriates, the very circumstances of their arrival prevented their isolation in the typical ghettos of the exiled, and demanded fuller integration in the host community. The ease with which this integration was accomplished speaks volumes about the nature of the links forged between Britain and Argentina since the early 1800s. Integration, however, did not lead to absorption — in a sense, the Falklands war helped prevent that, by reinforcing their links with the home country over and above the political circumstances which had forced their departure.

Lest this begins to sound too much like vague generalisation, I hasten to mention the concrete dimensions of the Argentine presence in present-day Britain. We have Argentines playing an innovative role and occupying leading positions in important London-based journalistic enterprises; writing an impressive number of books for both the British and Argentine public (including one of the most significant political works of the last couple of decades); even playing, from Britain, an important role in shaping the foreign policy attitudes of Argentina's recently-restored democracy. To their activities in Britain they brought expertise developed in Argentina; to their writings for Argentina (and elsewhere abroad), an outlook with the clear imprint of the British experience — including the most sobering impact of the Falklands war.

## Two leading figures

Two names stand out as examples of these developments. Indeed the two have been personally responsible for most of them: Andrew Graham-Yooll and Rodolfo H. Terragno.

Andrew Graham-Yooll is the Argentine son of a Scot who rose to the position of political editor of the *Buenos Aires Herald*, the idiosyncratic but plucky English-language newspaper which acquired renown as one of the only two dailies to continue reporting on 'disappearances' and other acts of political violence long after their bigger peers had been cowed into silence. Apart from writing in English for the *Herald*, Graham-Yooll was also an indefatigable writer of works, literary and historical, in Spanish, and even of poetry in that peculiar Anglo-Argentine dialect, 'Spanglish'. Researchers into Argentine history since 1955 will always be grateful to him for his painstaking chronologies, the fruits of a daily discipline he somehow fitted in between his reportorial duties, his other writing, and his passion for bringing together intellectuals, artists and politicians.

Death threats forced Graham-Yooll into exile in 1976. He came to London where, after an all-too-brief spate of media interest, he found himself thrust into the obscurity of a sub-editor's desk at the *Daily Telegraph*. A year later, he exchanged for a similar position at the *Guardian*, which he held for seven years.

For Graham-Yooll, it was a good enough base; as in Buenos Aires, all he seemed to need was access to a typewriter and an opportunity to practice hospitality. Soon he was churning out books in English for the British public. *The Press in Argentina* (1978) was an addition to

his series of detailed chronologies, this time recounting how the press
became one of the main targets of political violence in his home
country. *The Forgotten Colony* (1981) told the story of the English-
speaking (and Welsh) communities in Argentina. *Portrait of an Exile*
(1981) provided a most personal, a first-hand insight into the atmosphere and the actors of Argentina's 'dirty war' (in 1986 this book was
re-issued as *A State of Fear*, after being expanded with the account
of his return to Argentina as a witness in the trial of Montonero leader
Mario Firmenich, plus interviews with retired torturers and abduc-
tors). *Small Wars You May Have Missed* (1983) was the oblique
means chosen by Graham-Yooll — a most non-political man in spite
of his background in political reporting — to comment on the
Falklands War.

And while the writing and publishing proceeded, he found the time
and energy to turn his home into the meeting-place for the Argentine
intellectual diaspora. A typical one of these frequent encounters,
modern-day versions of the nineteenth-century *tertulias*, would find
around his table a well-known novelist, an exiled politician, a budding
guitarist, an economist on his way to an executive position with the
Inter-American Development Bank, and fellow-journalists.

In 1984 Graham-Yooll joined *South* magazine as deputy editor and
in 1985 he was promoted editor. *South* is a unique journalistic
venture: an attempt to produce a first-class news and analysis magazine with an editorial team of Third World journalists and reflecting
a Third World outlook on international affairs. It has become a
favourite among officials of international organisations and, in its
still brief lifespan (it was launched in 1980) has begun to figure
frequently as a source in footnotes to academic works on Third World
matters.

Eight years after leaving his home country, Graham-Yooll had
begun to typify a new breed of Argentine exile: not only at home in a
British environment but using a London base to influence international opinion with the professional tools acquired in Argentina.

In many ways, the story of Rodolfo Terragno is similar. In Buenos
Aires he edited *Questionario*, one of the most celebrated magazines
of political analysis of the early 1970s. Following the military coup of
1976, Terragno too went into exile. His first stop was Caracas, where
after a spell as an adviser to the Venezuelan government he led the
launch of the first new daily newspaper the city had seen in years: *El
Diario de Caracas*. In 1980 he left the editorship of the paper to move
to London, initially intending to concentrate on historical research.

His efforts in this field yielded interesting fruit. Delving into the little-known story of one of Argentina's greatest exiles, General José de San Martín, he came up with evidence suggesting that the *Libertador's* campaign to eject the Spanish from Chile and Peru closely followed a blueprint prepared by a British general, Thomas Maitland.

But Terragno was soon drawn back into the field of journalism. In 1981 it looked as if one of the world's leading sources of information on Latin American affairs, *Latin American Newsletters* (founded in 1967) would either have to close down or sell out. Terragno organised a rescue operation, attracting Latin American capital to purchase the newsletters. In 1982 he became the publisher of what was jokingly described as 'the only British company to have gone Argentine after the Falklands war' (though in fact its new shareholders were by no means all Argentine). Within a year the company's financial situation had been turned around, and by 1985, it was expanding with the addition of new titles.

Here too, then, we had an Argentine bringing expertise to a London-based publishing concern; one which, moreover, is most influential in informing international opinion regarding Latin American affairs.

But Terragno's role went beyond that. From London he began to write for the Argentine public as Argentina returned to civilian rule. *Memorias del Presente* (1984) showed the sharp political analysis many remembered from his days in *Questionario*, enriched by the experience of his most active years in exile. His refreshing no-nonsense approach to Argentina's international position in the wake of the Falklands war was one of the factors that made the book a remarkable success when it was launched in Buenos Aires. Indeed, it awakened public expectations of Terragno's return, not so much as an analyst, but as an active politician.

Still in London, Terragno responded to these expectations with *La Argentina del Siglo 21* (1985). In this brief book (published in English in the US in 1988), Terragno issues a challenge to Argentina's political milieu: it is time, he says, to 'assimilate' science and technology into Argentina's culture as a necessary step for development past the year 2000. Advances in cybernetics and biotechnology already incorporated by the industrialised nations, he argues, have already permeated political and economic thinking in the world's leading nations — while Argentina remains culturally in the nineteenth century.

However unlikely the subject-matter seems, the book made a notable impact upon its launch in Argentina. For weeks on end, the book and its author were featured in virtually all press media; throughout the country public discussions were held on its theses and impromptu associations were formed to respond to the challenge. Most unusually for Argentina, the book ran into five printings, with a circulation of more than 70,000 copies.

After years of weariness with the old Peronism — anti-Peronism issue, *La Argentina del Siglo 21* introduced a fresh new approach to the country's political debate. Terragno himself used it as a launching-pad for his return to Buenos Aires to set up his own think-tank, the *Fundación Argentina Siglo 21*; itself seen by many as the base for him to embark upon a political career. He has recently been appointed as Secretary of State in charge of the Cabinet.

Even before returning, Terragno had begun to acquire a reputation as a leading independent adviser on foreign affairs to the Alfonsín government — and to the new generation of Peronist leaders. He has not severed his links with London, where he resides for part of the year and where he retains his role as Publisher of *Latin American Newsletters*.

## An appropriate environment

Graham-Yooll and Terragno exemplify the new breed of Argentine expatriates based in London. They are not alone. Also from a London base, Miguel Angel Diez (founder and first Editor of *Numero*, Venezuela's first business magazine) piloted the rescue of ALA (Agencia Latino-Americana), a syndication service established in the US forty years ago by Joaquin Maurín, and which distributes throughout the region the writings of such prominent figures as German Arciniegas, Victor Alba, Julian Marías, Carlos Andres Pérez, Henri Raymond, Luis Alberto Sánchez, Jose Font Castro and Rafael Caldera. Also from London, in 1987, Diez launched *Al Dia*, a newsletter aimed at Latin American leaders and devoted to interpreting for them the changing fashions of economic and political thinking in the northern hemisphere.

Beyond the news media, it was also from a London base that Oscar Grillo built up his reputation as one of the world's best film animators.

These ventures, moreover, are not freak phenomena. Contrary to common wisdom, they have prospered in an appropriate environment, cultivated by others whose activities have had a much lower profile: the *Club Argentino* first headed by Eduardo Romero and more recently by Augustin Bianco Bazan, which regularly brings together the many Argentines acting in the City and in business; and the tireless, unpublished efforts of Juan Eduardo Fleming (between 1982 and 1989 the head of the Argentine Interests Section at the Brazilian Embassy) to bring together the Argentines in Britain and leading personalities of British political and business life.

That same environment has bred, apart from the instances mentioned and from the deluge of print on the Falklands/Malvinas war, an unprecedented number of major books on Argentina. Among these are Guido Di Tella's *Argentine under Perón 1973-76* (1983), John Simpson and Jana Bennett's *The Disappeared* (1985), David Rock's *Argentina 1516-1982: from Spanish Colonisation to the Falklands War* (1986), and Jimmy Burns' *The Land that Lost its Heroes* (1987).

Awareness of all this has been minimal; mainly because it has gone unnoticed by the press. However, it is in these ventures and the environment that nurtured them that the foundations have been laid for a new chapter in the history of British-Argentine links.

## Notes

1. An old boy of St. George's the premier English school in Buenos Aires.

# FUTURE ISSUES

# 16
# Argentina and Britain: the Antarctic Dimension

*Peter J. Beck*

Most contemporary perceptions of Anglo-Argentine relations tend to be dominated by memories of the 1982 Falklands War and by an appreciation of the absence of diplomatic relations until 1990. With the exception of perhaps the debt question, relatively little attention has been devoted to other international issues of interest to both governments. This chapter will concentrate upon Antarctica, an often-ignored topic which both divides and unites the two governments. Historically, the ownership of Antarctica caused controversy and tension between London and Buenos Aires, but for the past three decades the Antarctic Treaty System (ATS) has served to moderate the impact of the sovereignty problem as well as to provide a focus for Anglo-Argentine interest and cooperation, which has survived, and even developed, in spite of the serious complications arising between them over the nearby Falklands/Malvinas issue.

## The Role of the Historical Dimension

The central feature of the international politics, law and science of Antarctic today is the Antarctic Treaty — Argentina and Britain were among the twelve original signatories in 1959 — which is often interpreted as bringing peace, stability and inter-governmental co-operation to a region which had proved a long-standing source of rivalry and tension, especially between Argentina and Britain (and Chile).[1] For example, the Anglo-Argentine clash at Hope Bay in February 1952, when Argentine troops used machine guns against British scientists, was merely the most serious of a continuing series of problems. In addition, the emerging American and Soviet involvement in the continent during the late 1940s and 1950s prompted fears that the Cold War might extend to Antarctica, even if such developments could not disguise the fact that Antarctica remained still a relatively marginal area and one of the lesser international issues,

albeit one possessing considerable significance to certain governments like Argentina.

Against this background it becomes difficult to understand the
ATS' nature and achievements without a knowledge of the historical
dimension, since memories of the friction prevalent during the 1940s
and 1950s have influenced recent government attitudes during the
1980s, that is, at a time of challenge to the ATS. In this respect several
governments have referred to the danger of a return to the chaos and
controversy of the pre-1959 period as a prime reason for the maintenance of the Antarctic Treaty. In addition, the current Antarctic
position of individual governments can be understood fully only by
reference to the historical perspective, according to which such countries as Argentina and Britain have acquired a polar tradition and
developed strong vested interests in Antarctica through their long-
standing involvement therein. These traditions provide an emotional
chapter in their respective national histories and an influential
framework for the formulation of current and future policies, and in
this connection it is of interest to note the use made of tradition during
the course of the annual United Nations (UN) debates held on
Antarctica since 1983. For example, in November 1983 the British
delegate reminded the UN of his country's Antarctic credentials
dating back as far as Captain Cook, for 'the United Kingdom has been
active in Antarctica since 1775'.[2] 'Similarly, Argentine governments
refer frequently to 'Argentina's long Antarctic history' — like its
Malvinas past this dates back to the activities of Spain in the
fifteenth-sixteenth — as well as to 'the fact that the Argentine
Republic has for more than 80 years continuously and effectively
occupied its Antarctic territory'; thus, their country is 'closely linked
to the Antarctic continent by reasons of sovereignty, history and
geography'.[3]

The Anglo-Argentine relationship proved a central feature of the
international politics of Antarctica during the 1940s and 1950s, and
the tensions arising from this rivalry constituted one of the key
background influences to the conclusion of the Antarctic Treaty,
which was designed in part to contain such sovereignty problems as
well as to clear the way for international scientific cooperation on the
lines of that enjoyed during the International Geophysical Year (IGY)
of 1957-58. Obviously, the positive desire for such cooperation was
influential, but John Heap, currently head of the Polar Regions
Section of the British Foreign Office, has stressed the priority of
negative factors, including 'the fear of chaos' over claims and what
the signatories 'stood to lose without it'.[4] Similarly, Roberto Guyer,

an Argentine diplomat involved in the treaty negotiations of 1958-59, has pointed to the fact that during the late 1950s the governments involved in the continent were 'on the threshold of a conflict which could have had serious political consequences', thereby inclining them to appreciate the advantages of some form of political and legal accommodation.[5]

## The Antarctic Treaty of 1959

The Antarctic Treaty was signed at Washington DC on 1 December 1959 by the twelve nations active in Antarctica during the IGY, and the arrangements came into effect on 23 June 1961. Briefly, the treaty area, defined as the area south of 60° South, was dedicated 'exclusively for peaceful purposes', and in this connection military activities and nuclear explosions were prohibited, while Article IV recognised and protected the differing positions held on sovereignty by the signatories. The continent would be managed 'in the interests of all mankind' through a series of biennial consultative meetings, and in effect the treaty zone was placed under a special type of inter-governmental regime acting through consensus to produce recommendations for the 'government' of Antarctica.[6] The treaty, possessing no time limit, may last indefinitely, although there exist provisions for a review conference during and after 1991. The term Antarctic Treaty System has come to be employed to describe the complex of arrangements constructed around the 1959 treaty, including the 1972 Sealing Conservation Convention and the 1980 Convention for the Conservation of Antarctic Marine Resources. In 1989 Argentina and Britain signed the recently- negotiated Convention on the Regulation of Antarctic Mineral Resource Activities (CRAMA), but this proposal faces an uncertain future because of the opposition of some Consulting Parties, notably Australia and France.[7] The ATS has experienced an extended level of participation, so that the original twelve Consultative Parties have been joined by a further thirteen governments, while another fourteen nations have accepted the treaty's principles as non-Consultative Parties.

## The Nature of Antártida Argentina and of British Antarctic Territory

The territorial claims of Argentina and Britain were an established feature of the Antarctic scene at the time of the conclusion of the Antarctic Treaty, and it seems appropriate at this point to review the nature of their respective claims. Antártida Argentina, comprising about 550,000 square miles between 25°W-74 south of 60°S, was defined during the 1940s, although the actual claim precedes this date. In February 1953 Molina, the foreign minister, stated that:

> Argentine sovereignty over the territory is based on deep-rooted historic rights ... which are spiritually identified with the feelings of the entire people of the nation; on the superior geographical position of the Republic; on the geological contiguity of its land with the Antarctic territories; on the climatological influence which the neighbouring polar zones exercise on its territories; on the rights of first occupation; on the necessary diplomatic action and finally on its uninterrupted activities in the Antarctic territory itself [note dated 20 Feb.1953].[8]

The section of Antártida Argentina between 53°W and 74°W is claimed also by Chile, but the main complication arises from the fact that the whole territory falls within the area defined by Britain formerly as the Falkland Islands Dependencies (FID) but described since 1962 as British Antarctic Territory (BAT).

BAT covers some 700,000 sq.miles and the area was defined in 1908, 1917 and 1962.

> The root of the United Kingdom's title ... lies in British acts of discovery between 1819 and 1843, accompanied by formal claims in the name of the British Crown ... defined by the Crown in Letters Patent in 1908 and 1917. Since then there has been a continuous display of British sovereignty and activity appropriate to the circumstance. [9]

The existence and long-standing nature of their respective claims (see Map 3) explain one of the key policy interests of the Argentine and Britain governments, that is, the desire to maintain, support and protect their respective legal titles. This aspect is reinforced by geopolitical and strategic considerations arising from the concern of both governments about Antarctica's proximity to their territory, and the consequent anxiety to deny the continent's use for military or nuclear purposes; thus, Antarctica as Argentina's 'Near South' or back door is of particular concern to Buenos Aires, as evidenced by the manner in which during the late 1950s Argentina articulated fears about the introduction of nuclear weapons into Antarctica in the wake of American and Soviet involvement. Guyer has identified the value of a nuclear-free zone in Antarctica to Argentina, for 'we are less than a thousand kilometres from Antarctica, and if, for instance, an atomic explosion occurred, it could have very concrete effects for us'.[10] Britain's geopolitical interests derive in part from its control over the nearby Falklands and South Georgia. Economically, both Argentina and Britain are interested in securing an appropriate share in respect to the management and benefits of Antarctic marine and mineral resources, while other interests include those in the sphere of science, communications and environmental protection.[11] Although Argentine and British interests can be classified in this rather unified manner, there are of course differences of degree and emphasis, as evidenced by Argentina's support (with Chile) for the concept of a South American Antarctic through the Donoso-La Rosa Declaration of 1948 and the Act of Puerto Montt of 1978.

At the present time, and indeed over the past twenty-five years or so, both Argentina and Britain have come to believe that, while they maintain conflicting territorial claims and legal arguments, 'their interests were best protected by the maintenance and observance of the Antarctic Treaty System'.[12] This British quote has been echoed by numerous Argentine spokesmen and statements:

Once the Antarctic Treaty was signed, Argentina effectively endorsed the new regime of international cooperation ... the Antarctic Treaty and system have clearly demonstrated that they are efficient, practical, dynamic and open ... all efforts should be made to preserve and maintain them.[13]

The 1984 UN Study on Antarctica recognised the wider significance of the ATS, particularly as the peaceful use provisions meant that: 'The Antarctic Treaty represented the only post-war international agreement for the complete demilitarisation of a sizeable geographical region ... and became a forerunner of nuclear weapon-free-zones.[14] In addition, the Study, guided by submissions from fifty-four member governments (these included Argentina and Britain), observed that: 'No-one challenged the fact that two and a half decades of peace in Antarctica were attributable to the achievements of the Parties to the Treaty in implementing effectively the far-reaching disarmament measures of the Treaty'.[15]

In general, these 'achievements' have been under-rated, especially because the Treaty's success in neutralising Antarctica has served to reduce not only the possibility of conflict but also the region's perceived policy priority by transforming it into a strategic irrelevance.

However, for southern hemisphere governments, like Argentina, Australia and Chile, as well as for governments, including Britain, with territorial and other interests in the southern oceans, Antarctica remains a key strategic concern, while even the superpowers have acknowledged the global significance of the Antarctic Treaty, as evidenced by their strong recent support for the ATS. In turn, the Antarctic Treaty has come to be interpreted as a model to be followed and complemented by other arms control agreements, such as the Treaty of Tlatelolco (1967) and the South Pacific Nuclear-Free-Zone (1985-86) agreements; thus, both arrangements take account of 60 South as the northern boundary of the ATS.

The legal framework of Article IV of the 1959 Treaty has helped to contain the conflict potential of the sovereignty problem, although the apparent simplicity of the legal 'freeze' conceals a rather messy and confused situation, since Article IV merely pushed aside, rather than resolved, the claims question. In practice, sovereignty-related difficulties have never quite disappeared. For instance, the Argentine government, like its Chilean counterpart, has continued to treat Antarctica as a matter of 'fundamental importance' and to act in a relatively hawkish manner. Argentina's assertive, overt and occasionally flamboyant stance on sovereignty has been directed at both domestic and international audiences, as indicated by the significance attached to publicity and symbolic acts, which include the erection of name plates in Antártida Argentina, the issue of postage stamps depicting the nature and extent of the claim, and periodic presidential visits. President Frondizi's visit in 1961 was followed up in 1973, when President Lastiri was accompanied by the Argentine cabinet and Marambio base was declared the temporary capital of Argentina. Press and journal articles refer frequently to the country's research, aviation, naval, tourist and other activities in Antarctica, including the establishment of 'schools' and family groups at bases, the conduct of weddings, and the birth of babies there who were 'all citizens of Argentina and the Antarctic'.[16] The first of these 'Antarctic citizens', Emilio de Palma, was born at Esperanza base (see Map 3) in January 1978, and such events have been presented as further proof of Argentina's 'effective occupation' of its Antarctic territory; thus:

> All this contributes to Argentina's legitimate aspirations to sovereignty. Although all Antarctic claims have been temporarily suspended by virtue of the treaty, they are still pending and are a part

of the genuine prestige of Argentina among the Antarctic countries.[17]

In theory, Argentine activities since the Antarctic Treaty came into
effect in 1961 cannot affect the relative strength of Argentina's title
— according to Article IV this can be neither improved nor weakened
— to Antarctic territory, and the British government, when confronted by parliamentary concern about the impact of Argentine
moves, has stressed always 'the protection given by the Treaty to the
United Kingdom's position in the British Antarctic Territory.'[18] However, some commentators have suggested that, if the Antarctic Treaty
was terminated, Argentina would demand some return for its 'investments' in Antarctic since 1961, thereby prompting problems for
Anglo-Argentine relations. For instance, in 1982 the Shackleton
Report on the Falklands argued:

> The need for awareness of possible threats to the Antarctic Treaty
> ... an example of this is Argentina's action in maintaining armed
> military on their bases, having pregnant Argentinian women flown
> there to have their Argentinian babies and thus to claim rights
> based on 'settlement', and even at one stage declaring Marambio,
> one of their Antarctic bases, temporary capital of Argentina'.[19]

In British and other scientific circles the above-mentioned actions
have prompted criticism to the effect that Argentina has been more
concerned to record its presence for sovereignty and publicity reasons
than to perform Antarctic research. For example, during 1981-2 there
were 132 military personnel stationed at Argentine Antarctic bases
as compared to only 55 civilians, and Dr. Richard Laws, the Director
of the British Antarctic Survey (BAS), informed the House of Commons Foreign Affairs Committee of his visit to San Martín base in
March 1982. 'There were twenty-three personnel who were all military. Two of them were doing meteorological observations and no
other science was being conducted'.[20] The allegedly political and non-
scientific basis of Argentina's presence has been supported by statistics on research work, and Dr. Laws, utilising figures collected by the
Scientific Committee of Antarctic Research (SCAR), stated that 'the
average numbers of papers produced over the last four years is 18 for
Argentina, 14 for Chile and 151 for Britain.'[21] Obviously, this 'British'
interpretation of the evidence needs to be balanced against other
viewpoints. For example, Professor William Budd of the University
of Melbourne has advanced similar conclusions to those of Laws,

whereas Argentina has claimed that it has performed always a significant scientific role in Antarctica, which is reflected inadequately in statistical comparisons.[22] The Argentine note sent to the UN in June 1984 surveyed the country's important Antarctic research contribution in the biological, earth and atmospheric sciences, while the large military presence is excused by the way in which Argentina's logistical activities are performed by the military services — this is true of several other countries also — as compared to the civilian nature of Britain's Antarctic activities conducted through BAS.[23]

## The Falklands War of 1982 and After

Perhaps, the most significant perceived threat to Pax Antarctica, at least recently, arose in 1982 as a by-product of the Anglo-Argentine war over the Falkland Islands, since this conflict served not only to focus attention upon the nearby Antarctic territories but also to foster fears that the war might spread from the Falklands and the FID to Antarctica, another area of Anglo-Argentine rivalry and interpreted by Argentina as part of one territorial claim embracing the Falklands, the FID and Antarctica.[24] Memories of past problems prompted speculation about the Antarctic implications of the Falklands War, and within Britain there arose repeated parliamentary and press suggestions that the issues at stake included Antarctic sovereignty, even if it proved difficult to define the precise nature of the Argentine threat to BAT. Early in April 1982 Lord Shackleton reminded the British government that: 'There is much more at stake than the Falkland Islands ... What is at stake and what understandably is in the minds of the Argentinians is not just the Falkland Islands but their claim to Antarctic territory.'[25] There is evidence also that other ATS powers, such as Australia and New Zealand, were 'very concerned' about the war's consequences for Antarctica.

In the event, fears about the extension of the war to Antarctica proved groundless, partly because of a possible mis-reading of Argentine intentions, partly because of Argentine setbacks in the Falklands and South Georgia, and partly because of a general tendency to underestimate, even to be ignorant of, the protective qualities of the Antarctic Treaty. During the 1982 war Antarctica retained its post-treaty peaceful status, and consequently its relative insulation from disputes between its parties in other parts of the world, even if these clashes occurred in a geographically- proximate area like the Falklands or South Georgia. Obviously, there were occasional difficulties, and Robert Fox quotes the case of Foreign Office advice to BAS scientists at Signy in the South Orkneys to avoid wireless contact with their Argentine neighbours at Orcadas base.[26] But in general, there occurred no serious problems, and the cooperative qualities of the ATS were highlighted by the fact that during the war itself Argentine and British representatives sat down together at the same table, albeit with some adjustments to the normal seating pattern, in Hobart (May 1982) on marine resources and in Canberra (May) and Wellington (June) on a proposed minerals regime. Similarly, the fact that Argentine representatives could attend a meeting in Wellington during the war offered further proof of the ATS's value in the light of the New Zealand government's strong support for Britain, as evidenced by the closure of the Argentine mission there. It was not surprising perhaps that some commentators began to see the Antarctic Treaty as a possible way out of the Anglo-Argentine impasse on the Falklands; thus, it was proposed that the treaty area might be extended to embrace the Falklands and South Georgia in order to 'freeze' the sovereignty question and to clear the way for improved relations on other matters. However, the surface attractions of such a proposal conceal a range of difficulties, including the risk of introducing a destabilising element into the ATS, which has enough other problems at the present time.[27]

In addition, British moves after the Falklands War offer a good example of the continuing inter-connection of politics and science in Antarctica, and especially of the fact that the level of any country's political commitment to Antarctica is often measured in terms of the amount of scientific activity and funding; thus, changes in research expenditure can serve to indicate transformations in government policy towards Antarctica. During 1982-83 funding for BAS increased by over 60 per cent as part of the post-war enhancement of Britain's role in the south west Atlantic, and it is reported that the extra money followed from the personal initiative of the prime minister herself. After some fifteen years of level funding and of a gradual contraction in BAS activities — this included the plans during 1981-82 to close the BAS base at Grytviken on South Georgia (one of the 'signals' alleged to have encouraged the Argentine invasion of 1982) — the British government decided not only to allocate extra funding to BAS but also to reprieve HMS *Endurance*. Although the additional sums of funding involved were relatively small (ie. £4-6 million), particularly in contrast to the amounts devoted to the Falkland Islands, they represented a large proportionate increase for BAS, thereby providing the basis for the rapid escalation of British research activity in Antarctica in the resource-related spheres of the marine and earth

sciences as well as in the atmospheric sciences. These changes offered
a clear and visible symbol of the manner in which political decisions
on Antarctica tend to be reflected through science; indeed, for the
British government BAS provided the only real instrument through
which a re-orientation of British policy towards Antarctica could be
expressed as part of the post-Falklands reappraisal of British interests and role in the South Atlantic.

## War reappraisal of British interests and role in the South Atlantic.

The 1982 Shackleton Report highlighted the value of the regional
perspective, such as when evaluating the future of the Falklands, and
it sought to 'draw attention to wider and longer term issues in the
South Atlantic and the Antarctic'.[28] As a result, the infamous 'Falklands factor' prompted a change of course regarding Britain's role
in Antarctica, since the enhancement of BAS research was interpreted as serving to promote British visibility in the wider South
Atlantic region as well as to indicate an appreciation of the basic
Argentine challenge not only to the Falklands and South Georgia but
also to BAT. These examples suggest that, while the Antarctic Treaty
has helped to contain their territorial rivalry and to remove the
possibility of conflict south of 60°S, sovereignty considerations have
never disappeared from the perceptions of Argentina and Britain. In
this context, John Heap has observed that: 'Where sovereignty has
been claimed, it is unlikely that any State, having claimed it, will give
it up. And, indeed, the more it is attacked, the less likely it is to be
given up.[29] Certainly, Argentina has displayed no evidence of surren-
dering title, while the British government, having appeared to moderate its stance on sovereignty during the 1960s and 1970s, has
assumed, it is reported, a more hawkish attitude in recent years. To
a large extent, this change was caused by the 'Falklands factor', but
one should not forget the impact of developments in the ATS, most
notably the marine and mineral resource regime negotiations conducted during the past decade or so, since these topics concentrated
attention upon the management and ownership of Antarctic resources and thus upon the matter of sovereignty. Similarly, the 1982
war merely accelerated, rather than caused, the emergence of Antarctica as an international issue, as reflected in its status as a regular
UN agenda topic since 1983.[30]

   Since the 1970s the basic politico-legal question of Antarctic sovereignty has been sharpened by the rise of new legal principles, and

particularly by the common heritage concept, which tends not only to deny the validity of the existing claims to a continent depicted as *terra communis* but also to challenge the international acceptability of the ATS. The Malaysian government, acting through the Non-Aligned Movement and other organisations, has led the pressure for some UN-based organization, modelled possibly on the Law of the Sea precedent, to replace the ATS, and since 1982- 83 this campaign has resulted in annual debates on Antarctica at the UN. This episode has raised yet again the problem characteristic of the 1940s and 1950s, that is, whether the question of 'who owns the Antarctic?' can be resolved without making the continent the subject of international discord. In 1985 there were signs of a growing split within the international community on the subject, since the Antarctic Treaty powers came out strongly against outside interference in the affairs of Antarctica.[31] The annual UN debates conducted subsequently on Antarctica have merely reaffirmed this divide, including the difficulty of restoring a consensus between the treaty parties and their critics.[32]

In the face of the UN-centred challenge to the ATS, the Antarctic Treaty powers have displayed a considerable degree of unity towards the critics, and therefore Argentina and British spokesmen have found a common cause in advocating the merits of the ATS and in refuting the criticisms. For example, in November 1983 Victor Beauge, speaking for Argentina, informed the UN that the ATS 'must be maintained and strengthened', and he reinforced this view a year later on the grounds that 'we do not believe it would be possible to create a better system'.[33] Subsequently, in November 1985 Cullen of Argentina referred to the 'balance' achieved by the Antarctic Treaty, such as in respect to Article IV which 'constitutes the best possible balance that could be achieved between the rights and interests of the parties'.[34] The application of the common heritage principle to Antarctica has been strongly opposed by Argentina, for — to quote Cullen again — 'we could never accept the application of other formulas that run counter to our sovereignty rights', thereby reaffirming Beauge's previous statements to the effect that 'we cannot participate in or support any kind of parallel mechanism'.[35] British statements have regularly echoed such sentiments, and in November 1985 John Heap told the UN of 'the delicate balance' achieved by the Antarctic Treaty and of the fact that 'my Government is not prepared in any way to countenance the dismantling of the Antarctic Treaty System'.[36] Significantly, in September 1985 Sir Geoffrey Howe, the British Foreign Secretary, informed the UN General Assembly that:

We firmly believe that an attempt to apply a common heritage regime would upset this proven system, risk destabilising the region and jeopardise the present close international scientific collaboration. We shall maintain our support for the Antarctic Treaty System.[37]

The fact that Sir Geoffrey chose to mention Antarctica at all during the course of his wide-ranging survey of international affairs proved as significant as the message itself. As a result, both Argentina and Britain remain, and will continue to remain, strong supporters of the ATS on account of their belief that it offers the best framework within which to pursue their respective national interests in Antarctica, and especially their joint desire for peace and stability in the region. This point has been suggested by John Heap: 'The world can have peace in Antarctica under the Antarctic Treaty; it can have no such assurance that it can secure the same ends if a group of States attempt to undermine the Treaty'.[38]

## Conclusion

Historically, Antarctica's international political role has proved mainly a function of the sovereignty problem, and especially of the Anglo-Argentine (and Chilean) claim for the same piece of Antarctic real estate, a rivalry which threatened on occasions to spill over into international conflict and which also offered a major challenge to the negotiators of the Antarctic Treaty. As a result, the events of the pre-1959 period are of relevance to an understanding of both the present position and future developments, such as by showing why Argentina and Britain are in Antarctica, why they continue to attach significance to the region, and why recent events have brought them together in support of the ATS in spite of both their rival territorial claims and the perceived threat posed by the 1982 Falklands War to Pax Antarctica. In many respects, the Antarctic future of Argentina and Britain would appear to be a function of the success and durability of the ATS, and significantly both governments have come to regard its indefinite maintenance as a key policy interest alongside the pursuit of their territorial claims. In 1990 the ATS celebrated thirty years of operation, and from this perspective it can be interpreted as a well- established fact of international life — the support of Argentina and Britain is paralleled by that of China, the Soviet Union and the USA — which the Malaysian government and its supporters will find difficult, if not impossible, to dislodge. At present neither Argentine nor British policy-makers see any reason for distinguishing between their support of the ATS and of territorial claims, but perhaps they should give some consideration in the future as to whether priority should be given to the preservation of the ATS in preference to the indefinite maintenance of divisive and unrealistic claims. In the meantime, the Antarctic dimension offers an interesting insight into Anglo-Argentine relations, which tend not only to highlight several points of consensus and cooperation but also to constitute a useful corrective to the divisions consequent upon the 1982 Falklands War.

## Notes

1. Peter J. Beck, *The International Politics of Antarctica*, Croom Helm, London, 1986, pp.21-36.
2. United General Assembly Records (UNGA) A38/C1/PV44 pp.16-18, 29 Nov. 1983.
3. UNGA A39/583 Part II, vol. 1, pp.10-11, June 1984: UNGA A39/C1/PV44 PV53 p.7, 29 Nov. 1984.
4. J.A. Heap, 'Co-operation in the Antarctica: a quarter of a century's experience' in Francisco Orrego Vicuña (ed.) *Antarctic Resources Policy*: scientific, legal and political issues, Cambridge University Press, 1983. pp.104-05.
5. Roberto E. Guyer 'Antarctica's Role in International Relations' in *Ibid*, p.270.
6. Beck, *op.cit.* pp.148-79.
7. Peter J. Beck,'Antarctica enters the 1990s,' Applied Geography, vol. 10 (4) 1990, pp. 247-63
8. W.E. Bush (ed.) *Antarctica and International Law*, Oceana New York, 1982, Vol.1 699. See also, J.A. Fraga, *Introducción a la Geopolítica Antártica*. Dirección Nacional del Antártica, Buenos Aires, 1983, pp.16-19.
9. Memorandum by the Foreign Office 13 Oct. 1982 in House of Commons Foreign Affairs Committee, HCFAC Falkland Islands, Minutes of Evidence, 10 Nov. 1982, p.3.
10. Roberto E. Guyer, quoted in Rudiger Wolfrum (ed.) *Antarctic Challenge*, Duncker and Humbolt, Berlin 1984, p.59.
11. Fraga, *Introducción a la Geopolítica Antártica*, pp.38-9.
12. Foreign Policy Document no. 98: *Antarctic: an overview*, FCO, London, 1983, p.6.
13. UNGA A39/583 Part II, Vol. 1, pp.22-4, June 1984.
14. UNGA A39/583 Part I, pp.44-5, 31 Oct. 1984.

15. *Ibid.*
16. 'Tres generaciones argentinas en la Antártida', *Argentina*, no. 13 1981, p.12.
17. *Ibid*, p.12.
18. Beck, *The International Politics of Antarctica*, p.133.
19. Lord Shackleton, *Falkland Islands, Economic Study*, 1982, Cmnd. 8653, HMSO, London 1982, p.3.
20. HCFAC, Falkland Islands, Minutes of Evidence, 13 Dec. 1982, p.96.
21. *Ibid*, p.94.
22. W.A. Budd 'Scientific Research in Antarctica and Australia's effort' in S. Harris (ed.) *Australia's Antartic Policy Options*, CRES. Canberra, 1984, p.241.
23. UNGA A/39/583 Part II, Vol. 1 pp.12-17.
24. Peter J. Beck, 'Britain's Antarctic Dimension', *International Affairs*, Vol. 59 (3), (1983), pp.435-36.
25. Hansard (House of Lords) Vol. 428 col 1585, 3 April 1982.
26. Robert Fox, *Antarctica and the South Atlantic Discovery Development and Dispute*, BBC, London, 1985, p.60.
27. Beck, *Britain's Antarctic Dimension*, p.440.
28. Shackleton, *Falkland Islands*, p.3.
29. Heap, quoted in Wolfrum, *Antarctic Challenge*, p.58.
30. Peter J. Beck, 'A new polar factor in international relations', *The World Today*, vol. 45 (4), pp.65-8
31. Peter J. Beck, 'The UN goes green on Antarctica: the 1989 session', *Polar Record*, Vol. 26 (159) 1990, pp. 323-5
32. Peter J. Beck, *The Antarctic Treaty System after 25 Years*.
33. UNGA A/C 1/38 PV46 p.2. 30 Nov. 1983; UNGA A?C 1/39, PV53, P.11, Nov. 1984.
34. UNGA A/C 1/40 PV50 pp.22-23, 26 Nov. 1985.
35. UNGA A/C 1/40 PV50 p.23, 26 Nov. 1985: UNGA A/C 1/39 PV53, p.16, 29 Nov. 1984.
36. UNGA A/C 1/40 PV53 pp.11-12, 29 Nov. 1985.
37. UNGA A/40 PV9 p.62, 25 Sept. 1985.
38. UNGA A/C 1/40 PV53 p.12, 29 Nov. 1985.

# 17
# Falklands Futures

*Walter Little*

## Introduction

A considerable number of solutions to the *impasse* over the Falklands/Malvinas have been advanced over the years. Some of them reflect the interest in abstract problem-solving of outsiders — academics, peace researchers, island enthusiasts, amateur strategists, and environmentalists — who have become interested in the future of the islands[1] because they are themselves directly concerned — that is, the islanders and their allies in the UK.[2] And, though it might run counter to their natural instincts, even the politicians and civil servants who are charged with direct responsibility for some sort of a vision of the future.

The tendency to look for solutions is partly inspired by the widespread view that the dispute is something of an opera buffa one. A handful of people, a geographically isolated and economically marginal territory, and a history of close relations between Britain and Argentina, all seem to suggest that it can and should be resolved. But it is worth remembering that the dispute has run for over 150 years, that relations have not always been amicable and have become much weaker over the last forty years,[3] that it does have an 'identity' element (that of the islanders), and that even apparently trivial disputes over territory can be remarkably difficult to resolve.[4]

Seeking long-term solutions is also in itself a source of problems. On the one hand, it is difficult for the parties concerned to agree to explore what small steps might be taken towards reconciliation without having some sense of where these small steps might lead them. On the other, consideration of long-term options to the extent to which they might foreclose upon the very different outcomes preferred by the parties involved, is destructive of agreement about less important issues. The problem has been clearly manifested in the difficulties that have arisen between Britain and Argentina over the question of whether and in what form sovereignty might be included in any agenda for discussions.

Traditionally, there has been much less debate about the matter in Argentina since the preferred outcome — complete and sovereign integration with the mainland — has not only been agreed upon by almost all shades of political opinion but has generally been regarded as non-negotiable. Within this spectrum there are, of course, differences of emphasis. Conservatives, whilst not opposed in principle to integration have tended to downplay it. Both the Radical Party and the Peronist movement have taken a strong line (the dispute was revived in the UN under a Radical government in 1955) though the former have generally laid greater stress upon the pursuit of integration by peaceful means alone than have some of the more extreme nationalist factions within Peronism.[5] But the degree of national consensus over the islands is such that even the internationalist and anti-militarist elements of the Argentine left have been unable to distance themselves from it.

As a consequence of this unity of purpose the onus for finding answers to the problem has tended to lie with the UK. In the last few years, however, as a result of military defeat in 1982 and the subsequent return to civilian rule signs of greater flexibility and a willingness to think creatively about possible solutions have begun to emerge in Argentina. The ultimate goal remains unchanged but the forms which a recovered sovereignty might take are now much more open to debate.

## Unilateral options

Some of the 'solutions' that have been advanced seem utopian — even bizarre — but the fact that they been advanced at all is of some interest. Not only do they reflect the range of perceptions and emotions involved but they also represent an attempt to influence the political agenda. Short of some unlikely act of altruism (essentially the abandonment of their position by one of the three parties to the dispute) it seems certain that a negotiated settlement will require that unilateral approaches be ignored. They do, however, serve to illustrate the intractable nature of the dispute.

Probably the favourite with the islanders themselves would involve the complete integration of the islands into the United Kingdom possibly with an analogous status to that of the Channel Islands or the Isle of Man. They would thus cease to be a colony and would be distinguished from the mainland only by their distance from it. Though few, if any, islanders seem to believe that this dream is ever likely to be consummated its attractions to them are obvious. Quite apart from the additional social and economic services and political rights to which they would be entitled, integration would effectively meet the repeated Argentine argument that the right to self-determination cannot be used to prolong colonial situations; for the islands would no longer have colonial status. Most importantly, given the principle of the indivisibility of the sovereignty of nation states, it would mean that the UK, regardless of the types of government it might have, would be obliged in perpetuity to ensure the defence of the islands against any future aggression from Argentina or, indeed from any other state.

It is of course precisely the binding character of integration which has deterred successive British governments from ever entertaining it. Once established it could hardly be reversed and the vital distinction between peoples and territories would be lost. It would render the currently intractable, but for the moment peaceful, dispute between Britain and Argentina more dangerous, would be regarded even by some of Britain's allies as a mere device to ensure the perpetuation of a *de facto* colonial situation, and would make a strategic imperative out of the South Atlantic. Such a prospect would not appeal even to those who regret Britain's loss of world status far less those in the British government whose job it is to maintain Atlantic and European commitments with ever more stretched resources.[6]

The main problem with the idea of integration — the need for Britain to permanently defend the islands in the face of a potentially hostile and certainly irredentist Argentina — would also arise in those approaches (such as associated statehood, free association, and agency agreement) which have been advanced to decolonise other micro territories in the past. Intended to give a measure of (or lead to) self-government without the need for full state viability, such arrangements can hardly be expected to function when the territory concerned is claimed by another state with a significant offensive capability, which refuses to accept its legitimacy. Not only would Britain continue to be responsible for the defence of foreign relations of the islands but the granting of a greater degree of autonomy could also increase the veto power of the islanders over British policy which at present is purely moral in character. Given their apparent intransigence it is essential for any British government that the colonial and dependent constitutional status of the islands is maintained because this means that sovereignty remains vested entirely in Parliament which can dispose of it as it sees fit.

Similar problems would apply to the option of independence, with or without an agency agreement. Though the idea that tiny peoples and territories should have the right to determine their own futures is an attractive one it is unrealisable in this context. The issue is not primarily one of minimum size for state viability (significant though this is as a practical problem) but whether or not the state concerned is capable of defending itself against its neighbours. Though it could be argued that independence would resolve the colonial issue through the exercise of self-determination, Argentina (and probably many other countries) would refuse to recognise the new state on the grounds that self-determination can only be enjoyed by peoples and that the islanders are an alien and temporary population and not a people in the proper sense.[7]

Whether or not this is so is not strictly relevant. As the case of Grenada dramatically demonstrated, in the absence of an effective international legal regime for micro states (efforts through the 1960s to create one were not fruitful) independence for such states is only possible if they are of no resource, strategic, or ideological interest to their more powerful neighbours. Though the idea of independence has surfaced occasionally, islanders themselves acknowledge that it is not a serious possibility.

A common problem with these somewhat utopian solutions is that they are unilateral in character and go no way at all to satisfying Argentine desires for sovereignty of some sort. The abandonment by Britain of its sovereign claims would no doubt be welcomed by Argentina but if it meant that Argentine sovereign claims also had to be abandoned then it would be much less likely to find favour. This may not always be the case but for the present no solution imposed from London or Stanley would be able to stand unprotected by British arms. In this sense they are not solutions at all but merely constitutional recastings of the current situation.

## Multi-lateral approaches

Partly because of this idea, taking a multilateral approach to the problem has found favour in some quarters. These have the great advantage of introducing a new element into what has been up to now a bilateral stalemate. They also have the undoubted advantage of diminishing at least some of the responsibility for the present state of affairs from those who brought it about in the first place. But their drawbacks are also clear: either they are hypothetical in the extreme or else merely interim solutions and usually very complex ones at that.

One which has arisen on a number of occasions is in some way to couple the future defence and security of the islands to that of the region as a whole.[8] This would involve some kind of multilateral defence agreement analogous to, though not as institutionalised, as NATO. Presumably its members would include at least three states with a traditional interest in maintaining the freedom of the seas in time of war as well as those regional actors with a direct strategic concern in the area: that is, Britain and the USA along with Brazil, Argentina, but not, if the bioceanic principle were applied, Chile. Such an arrangement, it is claimed, would have a number of advantages.

So far as the UK is concerned it could be expected to diminish the financial and political costs of the defence of the islands in the sense that any such arrangement would necessarily require agreement with Argentina about their respective regional roles. In global strategic terms it would provide for the defence of the sea route around Cape Horn (with possible implications for the Cape of Good Hope) in the event of the closure or restriction of use of either the Suez or Panama canals. It would also serve to fill a defence vacuum and counterbalance the trend in recent decades for an increase in alien naval capacity in the southern oceans. For the local powers each of whom sees itself as having a regional security role, it would not only diminish tensions and rivalries but give their militaries a professional role which has up to now been lacking. Lastly, it would defend the interests of Western powers and their local allies alike in securing access to the undersea resources of the region, as well as those of Antarctica, which are currently being sought by external powers.

However, these geopolitical advantages would seem to be outweighed by a number of objections, hypothetical as well as practical. In particular, a 'SATO' arrangement would be likely to provoke an increased Eastern bloc naval presence as has occurred in recent decades in the Indian Ocean. With the exception of marginal Anglo-German conflicts in both world wars, the region has — at least until 1982 — been relatively free of tension and effectively demilitarised. An increased Western military presence could alter this and bring about the very tension it would be intended to prevent.

Moreover, the SATO idea has been promoted on a number of occasions the in the past but has come to nought. Partly this has been because of suspicion about the ideological provenance of its supporters (Brazil, for example, has always vetoed the idea-popular in some Argentine naval circles in the past — of possible South African involvement) but more importantly because for none of the stages concerned are its costs outweighed by its advantages.[9] Bluntly, the security threat to the region is hypothetical rather than real. Not only does the former Soviet Union seem to be having second thoughts about its out of area commitments but recent years have seen a significant rapprochement between Argentina and Chile over the Beagle Channel and between Argentina and Brazil over their military postures in general.

This is not to say that if the sovereignty issue could be amicably resolved that some modest defence cooperation might not be possible. Indeed, an Argentine military presence (presumably notional) would be likely to be part of any such settlement. But as things stand the idea of a multilateral security arrangement without an Argentine presence is as difficult to imagine as their military cooperation with the UK while sovereignty remains denied them.

The idea of extending the principles governing Antarctica northwards to the Falklands/Malvinas is also one that has been occasionally mooted. Since 1959, it is said, the continent has been demilitarized and its exploitation governed by the principle of peaceful negotiation. In particular, the suspension of sovereign claims (under Article 4 of the Treaty) provision for the shared management of resources (Article 9 1F), and demilitarisation (Article 1) might somehow be applied to the islands without geographically extending the ambit of the treaty itself.

This is a superficially appealing notion for though the Antarctic Treaty has not settled the issue of sovereign claims it has effectively suspended it by providing that no acts committed in the interim may form the basis for any claim to or denial of sovereignty. It also establishes that no claim might be advanced while the Treaty is in force and that nothing in the Treaty may be interpreted as a renunciation of any prior claim.

But the circumstances of Antarctica are unique. Its hostile environment puts a premium on cooperation between states. The number of states involved means that unilateral action would effectively result in isolation and exclusion for the state concerned. The fact that it is a club open to new members prepared to invest the necessary resources also renders it a fluid situation. Above all, the fact that it has no permanent resident population to administer means that the practical exercise of sovereignty (that is in legislative and fiscal terms) does not arise.[10]

This is not to say that the idea of Argentina and Britain jointly and simultaneously suspending though not abandoning their respective claims should be dismissed out of hand. As part of some negotiating process it may have its uses. But the idea that sovereignty might be suspended indefinitely while British administration continued in practice is clearly unworkable. Nor is it easy to see how the idea of demilitarising the islands could be pursued outside some agreement over sovereignty. Lastly the idea of cooperation over the exploitation of natural resources, while attractive in principle, has proved up to now to be unworkable.[11] In this sense, some of the elements of the Antarctic system might well be deployed either as part of a final settlement or as a means of reaching one but they are not sufficient in themselves.

One of the most frequently encountered suggestions is that the status of the islands be somehow internationalised. In particular, it has been suggested that the trusteeship system of the United Nations Charter might be an appropriate vehicle. Though there is no direct precedent for a dependent territory being placed under UN trusteeship, Articles 87 and 88 of the Charter do provide for it. Such an arrangement would leave open the nature of the local administration of the islands. This could, in principle at any rate, continue to be British in practice acting on behalf of the UN. Alternatively, it could be managed jointly by Britain or Argentina or entrusted to the UN itself, though this latter has never been tried before.

Such a solution would obviously relieve both Britain and Argentina of some of the financial, political, and diplomatic pressures currently being borne. More importantly, it would also resolve the question of the ultimate location of sovereignty in that the veto powers of Article 79 of the UN Charter could ensure that the territory remained permanently in trust. As an incidental benefit, it might restore credibility to the UN and provide a possible model for the internationalisation of micro territories elsewhere.

However, UN involvement would be unlikely to be greeted with any enthusiasm by the islanders. They are suspicious of the fact that Argentina has always laid great stress upon the importance of the UN as a forum for pressing their claims and are quick to point out that the UN is no more than a congerie of disparate states and (*pace* West Irian) has a poor record in protecting the interests of the small peoples of the world. It is possible, however, that this suspicion is overdone. It is true that Article 79 of the Charter would require Argentine agreement to the establishment of a trusteeship and likely that it would not accept exclusive British administration even in the name of the UN. But UN trusteeship exercised by the UN itself with internal self-government would remove the possibility of any Argentine involvement. This would not be unlike associated statehood with the UN acting as the protecting state and Argentina's very reliance upon the UN also makes it likely, if it agreed in the first instance to trusteeship, that it could not then seek to alter the situation.

A further twist upon the idea of some sort of UN involvement would be the idea of establishing permanent UN sovereignty over the islands with appropriate treaty guarantees for their secure internationalisation for the future. This would probably be acceptable to the UK, might or might not be acceptable to Argentina, but would certainly be a new departure for the UN itself. If for that reason alone it is unlikely ever to be seriously explored.

Quite how an internationalisation option could be achieved is of course a major problem but as a first step a formal invitation from the UK to the Secretary General (the UN Committee of 24 on Decolonization would be likely to receive a hostile response from the islanders) to initiate a study of the islands with a view to reporting to the General Assembly might be worth trying. It could certainly be justified solely in terms of better informing the UN about island realities but also as a useful step in bridge-building.

These realities are less simple than they may seem. For all its 'sturdy crofter' image, island society is characterised by significant territorial and social (if not political) divisions but the overwhelming felt need for solidarity tends to obscure these. At the political level, there is no doubt as to the strength and sincerity of the islanders' desire to remain under British rule. But since the British government is underwriting this attitude by not merely making it painless but actually rewarding this is hardly surprising. How islanders might respond politically to less than ideal options (which, secretly, many fear will one day be put before them) cannot be known until they are posed. If such a day does arise it should be accompanied by offers of adequate compensation, jointly funded and for all inhabitants, in recognition of past Argentine aggression and British neglect. Indeed, had attractive compensation been offered in the past the islanders might have solved the problem by voting with their feet.

## Bilateral options

In essence the dispute is a bilateral one. Though the islanders themselves constitute a third party their status in the affair remains subordinate. The present British position is that their wishes as well as their interests remain paramount but this blanket interpretation is unlikely to be shared by some future British government. Both opposition parties (and elements within the Conservative party) have made it clear that while the islanders' interests must be respected their wishes are a quite different matter. For so long as the dispute is cast solely in trilateral or multilateral terms little progress is likely and while some bilateral resolution will require major compromise in the long run it represents the most promising way forward.

The notion of sharing sovereignty in some way seems to be an obvious one. But just how sovereignty might be divided — territorially, functionally, temporarily — is a much more complex issue. It also depends critically upon whether the sovereignty to be shared is notional or real in character.[12]

Among the options which do not seem promising is the idea of a condominium of the sort exercised in the New Hebrides between Britain and France where separate administrations existed side by side. Quite apart from the fact that such an arrangement requires the goodwill of the contracting parties the practical administrative difficulties of attempting to administer quite different fiscal and legal systems would seem to be insurmountable. It would also encounter fierce resistance on the part of the islanders. If, however, the sovereignty to be shared were to be purely notional or titular in character then these problems need not arise.

It is curious that the idea of submitting the dispute to some sort of arbitration or mediation has rarely been raised. Although the UK did offer to submit the dispute over the Falklands Islands Dependencies of South Georgia and South Shetland to the International Court in 1948 (and made a unilateral application to it in 1955) it did so because it was convinced of the soundness of its title. Neither party has expressed any willingness to submit the main issue to external legal judgment, a recognition possibly of the fact that neither has an unequivocal title in international law.

So far as the issue of sovereignty itself is concerned, neither side has a watertight case. British claims rest fundamentally upon the doctrines of prescription (that is, effective, peaceful, and longstanding rule) and, more recently, self-determination. Argentina's claims are rooted in the principles of inheritance of title from Spain, territorial proximity and decolonization. None of these principles is unambiguous and subsidiary arguments about whether the islands were or were not *terra nullius* prior to 1833, what constitutes effective protest in international law, or what bearing the doctrine of intertemporal law might have in this case only serve to muddy the waters further. The dispute, then, is a political one and the legal arguments are deployed by both sides for purely political ends.[13]

It is possible that even if such a submission were made (it would require both parties to agree) the International Court would not find the matter justiciable. But in that case nothing would be lost to either party other than money and time would have been gained. If the Court found for Argentina then Britain would be obliged to compensate the islanders in some way but would have demonstrated to the world its commitment to the peaceful resolution of international disputes. If Britain were to be favoured then Argentina would be unlikely to accept such a ruling but its international position would be gravely weakened. As things stand neither side has the necessary will to put the matter to the test but it is a possibility which may find a more opportune moment in the future.

One approach to the sovereignty question which has been seriously entertained in the past is the so called Andorran approach whereby sovereignty is divided between the contesting parties but is vested in proxies and not actually exercised on the ground. At one time this was an option favoured by some islanders but never one actively entertained by the British and one opposed by Argentina. It is an open question as to whether what was unacceptable to Argentina ten years ago will continue to be so in the future, but it is worth noting that it has been indifference on the part of France and Spain that has allowed Andorra to work successfully under a proxy system.[14]

One proposal — not surprisingly it is popular in Argentina — is the transfer of sovereignty in return for guarantees that the islanders could continue to live their lives in their own way. This would amount to some sort of home rule for the islands with Argentina remaining responsible for defence, foreign affairs, and possibly some other functions. Such a proposal would require a reform of the Argentine constitution but, some argue, this has precedents of sorts in the Federal system which, in principle at any rate, allows for high levels of provincial autonomy.[15]

The attraction of such a scheme lies in the distinction it draws between sovereignty over territory and sovereignty over peoples, as obtains in the case of the Aland Islands. Under such a scheme the islanders could retain their British nationality, the use of English, and possibly the common law, though how far and in what areas home rule might be extended (would islanders be able to control immigration from the mainland for example?) is necessarily unclear. It rests crucially on the assumption that Argentina is interested more in the principle of sovereignty and in world recognition of the rightness of its claim than in the islands as a piece of territory or the islanders as potential citizens. It is not clear to what extent this is the Argentine position in general though there is evidence of support for such a scheme in liberal political circles.[16]

The main difficulty with such a transfer of sovereignty lies in making the guarantee of effective island home rule credible. Some in Argentina suggest that a constitutional amendment would be sufficient though islanders rightly point to the frequency with which the Argentine constitution has been flouted by *de facto* governments in the past. Such an agreement, they argue, would rest entirely upon Argentine goodwill and while this may exist at present there is no guarantee of it being respected by some possibly non-democratic government in the future. Others have suggested that a treaty with the UK (which would in any case be required) would be sufficient guarantee. Less popular in Argentina but more acceptable to the islanders would be some guarantee endorsed by one or more third parties such as the USA. To the extent that Argentina remains a democracy in future these fears are likely to diminish but this will be a matter of decades and not merely years.

Indeed one of the main problems in scenarios of this sort are the differing perceptions of the actors concerned. Argentine politicians understandably bridle at suggestions that their democracy is fragile and that their constitution has signally failed in the past to protect the rights of their own citizens. They are also at pains to distance themselves from the previous military regime. From the point of view of the islanders, who regard Argentine as an inherently unstable and aggressive neighbour, such distinctions are not convincing.

Possibly the best known option for dealing with the sovereignty issue has been that of leaseback, whereby sovereignty is transferred to Argentina but the islands leased back to the UK for a period to be determined. First mooted in 1977 the leaseback idea attracted the support of ministers and Foreign Office officials and was presented along with condominium and a freeze of the status quo to the islanders as options to consider. Not surprisingly the islanders — ever suspicious that the Foreign Office wished to be rid of them — rejected it. It is unfortunate that an apparently elegant solution failed abjectly and for this the government which failed to prepare either the islanders or the House of Commons must bear much of the blame.[17]

The official position now is that in the aftermath of war leaseback is no longer a possibility. However, the idea has found increasing support within Argentina. A critical issue would be the length of the lease. While previously Argentina was only prepared to consider a short lease of up to ten years, there are signs that it might now be prepared to think in terms of generations. Leaseback of course would involve the withdrawal of British forces and it could be argued that Argentina could then simply seize the islands. However, having achieved their long-term goal in titular sovereignty with effective control in prospect such an act would seem to offer little advantage compared with the damage it would do to Argentina's international standing.

One possibility which has not received much attention is that of combining one or more of these options. Though this would complicate matters there is no reason in principle, for example, why leaseback could not be combined with the idea of home rule. If Argentina's desire is for the principle and not the practice of sovereignty then such an approach would satisfy them, the current generation of islanders over continued British administration, and that of future generations over the maintenance of their own distinct way of life.

## Conclusion

As things stand there is little or no likelihood of any of the above options being seriously pursued. Simply, the reason is that, tangentially or otherwise, they all address the question of who shall have what kind of sovereignty and on this issue the gulf between Britain and Argentina remains very wide. Argentina argues that it is the central issue and must at some stage be addressed even if not immediately. It does not claim to prejudice the outcome of any such discussion but insists that it must take place and that once agreement is reached on this then other points of dispute (such as air links, trade, fishing etc.) will be readily resolved. Britain, for its part argues that Argentina is interested in the sovereignty only if discussions result in its transfer and that for as long as the islanders are opposed to this then Britain is honour bound to respect their wishes; so long as sovereignty is excluded from the agenda anything and everything can be amicably resolved. The positions thus remain irreconcilable.

This difficulty (which led to the breakdown of preliminary talks in Berne in 1984) has led some to suggest that the problem is essentially one of communication and that third parties, through the use of their good offices, might be able to improve matters. It is true that there are a number of agents who might be prepared to lend their good offices but how productive they might be is another matter. Multilateral institutions such as the EEC, OAS, or Non-Aligned bloc, are too cumbersome to be effective and would not in any case command the respect of both protagonists. Other states, such as Canada, might enjoy general respect and actually welcome a mediating role but it is unlikely that they would carry the necessary weight. As so often the onus is left to fall upon the USA.

It is true that the USA occupies a unique position both as a close ally of the UK and a major power within the inter-American system and it has already offered its services as a broker in respect of the vexed question of fishing rights in the region. But the very duality of its role (in evidence throughout April 1982 when Secretary of State Haig tried and failed to prevent hostilities) suggests that there are limits to its usefulness in this dispute. In particular the regional obligations which the USA bears to Europe and Latin America are not complementary and clearly arise in its attitude towards the colonial fact of the Falklands in the Americas. The issue is an irritant for the USA but a bearable one and no initiative over sovereignty is likely from that quarter.

Quite apart from these practical difficulties the idea that com- munication is inadequate is debatable. It is true that there is a cultural and intellectual divide (evident in the understandable Ar- gentine preference for juridical arguments in multilateral fora and the equally comprehensible British distaste for them) but if anything, communication is all too rapid and effective. Indeed the speed with which marginal issues (such as the islands' constitution) have been seized upon by carpetbaggers in both countries is disturbing. Profes- sional diplomats were not responsible for the failures in the past (though their political masters were) and it is perhaps unfortunate that the problem cannot be left to them in the future. They might not be able to resolve it but at least could avoid the disinformation and partial pleading to which politicians and amateurs are prone.

It is also worth recalling that the gains to be made from resolving the dispute might be outweighed by the risks of trying and failing to do so. From the British perspective the continued need to defend the islands is a significant defence burden and though its costs are likely to fall with the commissioning of the new airport, even a rigid deployment capability is an expensive option. It was also one which few defence planners seemed to think was comparable to the defence of the North Atlantic or West Germany in terms of national strategic interests.[18] Lastly it is a diplomatic embarrassment which many would prefer did not exist.[19]

But against this is the fact that the government might well not survive an agreement which could be portrayed as a betrayal. Though the policy was very much that of a Prime Minister acting alone, deep public commitments have been made which would be difficult to reverse. It is not inconceivable that a *volte face* might take place but the pressure for it or calculation of losses and gains to be made from it would have to be very different from what they are today,[20] not only that many are ready to argue that the expenditures have been incurred and paid for and that given the uncertainty about the future of Antarctica (not to mention the possibility of oil exploration) it would be foolish to throw away an advantage so expensively gained, albeit with a quite different purpose in mind.

So far as Argentina is concerned there are also gains and losses to be made. A successful negotiation would further increase the popularity of the government, would further distance it from its military predecessor and so strengthen democracy, and would contribute to the effort of being made to cut defence expenditure. But anything short of some kind of sovereignty (how much is the great unknown) could be disastrous. It could easily lead to the downfall of the government if not at the hands of the military then perhaps those of the electorate. As things stand Argentina has reason to feel that the pressure for a settlement is felt more acutely in the UK and that it would be foolish at this stage to risk any weakening of its claim to full sovereignty. As Foreign Minister Caputo put it, 'If Argentina sits down to negotiate ... after accepting that the sovereignty issue is not up for discussion ... it will constitute a precedent which ... will have serious consequences for future negotiations ... All Argentina asks is that the sovereignty issue should not be excluded.'[21] Too much should not be made of the idea that the dispute is a useful diversion for a government confronted by deep economic problems. If public commitments are anything to go by Argentina does seem sincere in its willingness to make major concessions in respect of the maintenance of the islanders' traditional way of life but on sovereignty its position is unchanged.

Given those political constraints, agreement requires that one of the parties must one day yield and the likelihood is that it will be Britain. Crudely, Britain does not want the islands as much as Argentina does and this will, sooner or later, lead to a shift in policy. Repeated polls in the UK since 1982 indicate that the general public, unlike that of Argentina, is divided over the desirability of retaining the islands and deeply concerned about its cost. Similar uncertainty is evidence in the political class. The opposition parties (and many

Conservatives), though they deny that they favour a sovereignty transfer, are clear that it must be discussed and by implication compromised if the settlement to which they are pledged is to be reached. In contrast, Argentine politicians offer flexibility as to the means of settlement but not as regards the end.

The Argentine government is well aware of these facts. For it, waiting is not only relatively costless but the most likely means of achieving their long-desired objective. In the meantime there is some comfort to be derived from the fact that both sides are determined to avoid a renewal of hostilities.

## Notes

1. They are of course deeply divided amongst themselves, propagandise constantly, and generally did play the fervour typical of single issue politics.
2. They have proved to be remarkably effective lobbyists with Parliament and the press since 1968, partly because of their own deep sincerity and clearness of view and partly because of the sentimental nature of their cause. Their effectiveness has not been based on heavy spending.
3. Those who advocated blockades or attacks on the Argentine mainland in 1982 were not generally aware of the unhappy record of such efforts by Britain against Argentina in the last century.
4. In this case the ethnic dimension is significant. Islanders are well aware of how the inhabitants of Diego García, for example, have been treated by Britain. As one put it to the author, 'It's a good job we're not black.'
5. The 1966 assault on the islands by the New Argentine Movement was unimportant in itself but nevertheless widely applauded within Peronism.
6. Islanders are well aware of this and have a profound mistrust of, and even contempt, for the Foreign Office. See the evidence given by islanders to the *Foreign Affairs Committee, Session 1982-83*, HMSO 1983.
7. This is in fact highly debatable proposition. Many islanders would argue that they are as much natives of the region as any Argentine.
8. See A. Hurrell, *The Politics of South Atlantic Security*: A *Survey of Proposals for a South Atlantic Treaty Organization, ms* St Antony's College, Oxford.

9. Its advocates in the UK, not surprisingly, also tend to be well to the right on the political spectrum.

10. This has not stopped various powers — especially Argentina — from engaging in acts of a 'sovereign' sort. The fact that the two superpowers would lose out if the continent were ever partitioned in the lines of existing claims is a major factor behind the success of the Antarctic regime.

11. Partly because so many nations are involved, attempts to come to a multilateral agreement on fishing have not yet come to anything.

12. It is true that the strength of the rival claims differs as between East and West Falkland but no one has seriously suggested a territorial division of sovereignty.

13. For a brief review of the legal background see *Foreign Affairs Committee, Minutes of Proceedings, Sessions 1982-83*, HMSO, 1983.

14. See UK Falklands Islands Association Memorandum to the Foreign Affairs Committee, Session 1982-83. Published in *Appendices to the Minutes of Evidence*, HMSO 1983.

15. It has even been suggested that the islands might become a separate province of Argentina.

16. The Argentine military, of course, would very much like a base in the islands the better to buttress their claim to a strategic role in the South Atlantic.

17. In large part this was because of low priority given to it. No one anticipated an Argentine invasion until the last moment and careers were not likely to be advanced by becoming an expert on the dispute. See *Franks Committee, Falklands Islands Review*, HMSO, 1983.

18. The pressure to reduce out-of-area commitments is likely to grow with projects cuts in real terms in the defence budget. For a review of the defence issues see *Defence Committee, The Future Defence of the Falkland Islands*, HMSO, 1983.

19. This can be exaggerated. Condemnation in the UN is embarrassing but not fatal. So far as Britain's relations with Latin America are concerned the damage done has been slight.

20. Though the then Prime Minister had repeatedly asserted that the islanders wishes are 'paramount' she had at the same time acknowledged that paramountcy actually lies with Parliament.

21. Cited in House of Commons Library, *The State of Negotiations between the UK and Argentina since 1984, 1986*.

# 18
## Epilogue

*Alistair Hennessy*

These essays have concentrated on aspects of the British-Argentine connection which have so far been little studied. They chart the rise and fall of British influence, finishing in an *impasse* from which there seems to be no clear escape, but in doing so, they may have suggested more questions than answers.

They show Argentina providing a challenge to the nineteenth century entrepreneur looking for adventure and eventual profit. Spinning off from this early period was a body of travel and descriptive literature which was to be an important influence on the way in which Argentines themselves viewed their country. The 'discovery' of Argentina was partly a creation of British travel writers but the momentum of this cultural influence could not be maintained in the era of mass immigration and at a time when immigrants from other nationalities were entering the professions and universities, becoming the ideologists and mentors of a new nationalist generation with a negative and hostile view of British influences. Nor could the pioneering efforts of early British settlers be sustained. Bishop Every, for all his racial assumptions in the 1930s about the moral superiority of the British in the 'debased moral atmosphere' of Argentina, nevertheless recognised the shortcomings of his fellow countrymen as pioneers. Except for a handful living rough (who if they 'went native' risked ostracism), pioneering was not the destiny of most of those arriving in Argentina from the 1890s on. The fittest who survived on the wind-swept sheep ranches of the 'uttermost part of the earth' were far outnumbered by those who, in more comfortable surroundings, could react to the ticker tape of the stock market. This is not to deny the efforts of the early settlers who put down roots, were Argentinised and made an invaluable contribution to their adopted country but once the imperial frontier opened up in Canada, South Africa and Australia, opportunities changed and with these changes came new and different challenges. There is something symbolic in the contrast between the young Cunninghame Graham in the early 1870s, carefree and roaming the pampas, and his brief sojourn forty years later during the First World War, selecting his beloved horses for almost certain slaughter on the Western Front. In retrospect, the decline of British influence in Argentina appears inevitable given the drain of the First and Second World Wars, the cramping constraints of imperial and post-imperial responsibilities elsewhere, the inflexibility of British industry and of ingrained attitudes.

The focus here on social and cultural matters reflects the growth of professionalised Latin American studies in Britain since the 1960s. But it is ironic that academic scholarship, resulting in greater understanding of Argentine society, should coincide with the final breakdown of our 150-year connection and implies a difference between official and popular perceptions on one side and academic perceptions on the other, as well as the failure of most academics to influence anyone but their own kind.

One question posed by the history of the relationship is whether greater official attention to cultural concerns might have prevented the misunderstandings which contributed to the Falklands crisis which has now become one of the most intractable issues in British foreign policy. There has been belated recognition that cultural diplomacy needs to be taken more seriously than in the past but culture is a slippery term and may be used in a variety of ways stretching from the anthropological interpretation of a society's total way of life, reflected in social myths and behaviour patterns at one end of a spectrum of definitions, to the narrow view of culture as the thought of an intellectual minority, with this 'high' culture differentiated from 'popular' culture. Similarly, cultural diplomacy is open to a variety of interpretations — 'it is a Humpty Dumpty term. It can mean more or less what one wants it to mean; it has never been satisfactorily defined.'[1] However, the purpose of such diplomacy should not be only to project the cultural values of one's own country in the widest meaning of the term, as well as its cultural achievements in the narrow sense, but also to interpret and explain the distinctive features of the culture of the country concerned. It is this latter reciprocal element which has often been absent in our official relationship with Argentina.[2]

In cost-benefit terms it is difficult to quantify the spin-off from investment in cultural activities and so justify increased expenditure on them. There is no simple line of cause and effect. Cultural influences can operate independently of commercial considerations which are considered by criteria such as availability of credit, exchange rates, and market factors, but even a knowledge of the market should involve an understanding of cultural traits, in the anthropological sense. Similarly in politics, without some appreciation of political culture — those unspoken pre-suppositions on which politics is based — the possibilities of misunderstanding are endless.

Commercial and financial relationships in the past had consequences affecting narrow social groups in both countries, neither of whom were well attuned to changes occurring in the other, particularly from 1930 onwards. The anglicised Argentine elite, in common with the Anglo-Argentine community, were suspicious of post-war British socialism at a time when Peronism was threatening their own dominance. It is questionable though, how deeply the elite identified with British culture even at the height of our relationship. Although their children might go to exclusive British schools with their continuing social cachet today, or be brought up by British governesses, France tended to remain the first choice for vacations and for forced and self-imposed exile. If Savile Row clothed the men, *haute couture* still lured the women to France. France had, and still has, the largest Argentine colony in Europe, where the climate, physical, moral and intellectual, is more amenable than in Britain. Paris remains the magnet for intellectuals and the Riviera for playboys. How far this is related to the success of French cultural diplomacy or to an affinity with the ambience is an open question (although some hundred branches of the Alliance Française must have some influence). A Frenchman, Paul Broussac, was librarian of the National Library in Buenos Aires and even before the First World War Argentine history was being taught at the Sorbonne. France appealed to a wider spectrum of Argentine political opinion, with its republican tradition, the Catholic Right, Liberal Catholicism and the Marxist left, all of which had some relevance to Argentine conditions. France, with its *marxisant* political culture, has always had more to offer the left than the British left, encapsulated in its non-Marxist traditions, and although anglicised members of the elite might admire British institutions and the ingrained conservatism of its political system, these can have little relevance in the context of republican politics.

Of all Latin American countries Argentina has been the most exposed to European influences. This is partly to be explained by its large and varied immigrant population with each national group perpetuating links to its homeland through keeping the language alive in schools, press and societies. But there was also the repudiation of Spanish influences throughout the nineteenth century when Spain was convulsed by internal discord and could provide no acceptable example to follow — at least not until the Generation of 1898 and the growth of *Hispanismo*.[3] Argentines therefore looked elsewhere, and eclectic in their choice, were attracted to Britain for its commercial and financial expertise and political stability, to France for its literary, legal and republican traditions, to Italy for its opera and architecture, to Germany for its music and science and to the United States, when it was not distrusted, for its dynamism, educational and frontier experience.

So long as British commercial and financial hegemony was assured, cultural influences could be taken for granted, but once the hegemony was challenged the narrow base of such influence was exposed. The burden of sustaining a cultural presence was then borne by British schools, by an under-funded British Council, and by Anglo-Argentine institutions and societies. But their undue concentration on language teaching no longer necessarily benefits Britain unless accompanied by a generous scholarship programme as now English, the world's universal language, is beginning to be divorced from a specific British culture.

There has to be a re-definition of what is meant by cultural influence, how it is exerted and what is the purpose of cultural diplomacy. When does influence shade off into propaganda? Which groups are selected to be targeted and why? What is distinctive about British culture now and how is it changing from pre-conceived notions and stereo-types? These questions are made more urgent by the last unhappy chapter in the relationship where the values portrayed may seem to be at variance with the actuality.

For Argentines the Malvinas question has now become the touchstone of judgement. Whatever the British view, the majority of Argentines believe the British to be usurpers.[4] The major consequence of the war has been to replace the bilateral relations of the pre-war period with complex multilateral manoeuvring with diplomats lobbying international agencies, the United Nations and the European Community, to sustain the British case. Ever since UN Resolution 2065 of the General Assembly in December 1965, inviting Argentina and the United Kingdom to start discussions leading to a resolution of the Falklands question, the British have been on the defensive, cultivating friends to sustain a position which even those friends are coming to regard as increasingly untenable. Sympathy aroused by the Argentine invasion is evaporating on the rock of British obduracy over the principle of sovereignty.

The reasons for this obduracy are many and have little to do with contentious historical claims. The most important is the British insistence on the principle of self-determination. To Argentines as well as to many others this has the appearance of *post hoc ergo propter hoc*, as it was not until after the war ended that British citizenship was granted to all the inhabitants of the islands. 'It's a good job we're not black' was the reputed comment of one of the islanders, recalling the compulsory evacuation of the inhabitants of Diego García in the Indian Ocean to make way for an American base.[5]

Previous to the war, the history of the Falkland Islands had been one of neglect by Britain and of domination of the economy by a handful of commercial interests which allowed little scope to the islanders to have a firm stake in the country. However, once the principle of self-determination was invoked and reforms were introduced, initiative passed to the Falklanders: so long as they wish to remain British there is nothing substantial to discuss. Sovereignty, the one matter of central concern to Argentina, is not negotiable. This is an *impasse* as no Falklander can be expected to accede to Argentine demands after the trauma of invasion (although it must be said that there can be few examples of the invaded themselves having suffered less at the hands of an invader). The war killed any chance of a 'winning hearts and minds' campaign, akin to that which the Foreign Office (the Government's and Falklanders' whipping boy, aware since before the First World War of the need for a settlement and conscious now at a time of cheeseparing economies, of time and energy expended on the Falklands issue) was proposing and which was embodied in the Communications Agreement of 1972.

It would furthermore be unreasonable to expect any Falklander after General Galtieri's disastrous miscalculation of the British response to his invasion to have faith in a society which had succumbed in a dozen or so years to a degree of militarisation and control which has scarcely any parallel in the Western World, nor could they be expected to risk the fate of becoming *desaparecidos*.

The letter written by the *Asociación de Agricultores Británicos* to the Buenos Aires daily *La Nación* in April 1982 would have fallen on deaf ears:

We, Britons and descendants of British husbandmen in Argentina wish to inform Her Majesty's Government that for years and in some cases for generations we have lived and worked happily under Argentine governments of different political orientations. We have lived in keeping with our traditional British way of life, without obstacles of any kind, and our experience has brought us to believe that the inhabitants of the Malvinas have nothing to lose and much to gain by placing themselves under Argentine sovereignty.[6]

Although Articles 104-6 of the Argentine Constitution allow for a large measure of provincial autonomy, the Falklanders are divided by too wide a cultural and social gap from the commercially-orientated Anglo-Argentine community to share their optimism.

The time may indeed by past, given the changing nature of the islands' population, to build bridges such as existed in earlier days when many families on the islands and mainland were linked.[7] Faced with the unknown and the unfamiliar, clinging to the principle of self-determination is seen as a means to preserve a distinctive way of life. Anything else is perceived as a creeping form of capitulation.

Numerous arguments have been deployed in further justification of the sovereignty issue and the retention of the islands, ranging from not creating a precedent for the Spanish to claim Gibraltar (if atavistic emotions could be roused over the Falklands, how much greater would be the reaction over the Rock, the evocative symbol of permanence and British Imperial might for past centuries), to the perhaps now outdated argument that because of the global naval power of the former Soviet Union and possible threats to the Cape Horn and Cape of Good Hope shipping routes, or to a possible blockade of the Panama Canal, the Falklands would recover its earlier strategic importance as a 'Gibraltar of the South Atlantic', as in the battle of the Falkland Islands in 1914 when battle cruisers were hastily despatched from Britain, an extraordinary portent of 1982.[8] Finally, there is the view that as the 'gateway to Antarctica' the Falklands are necessary to bolster British claims there.

The most serious of these arguments involves the Spanish claim to Gibraltar. Interest in the Malvinas and support for Argentina is understandably intense in Spain, anxious to refurbish traditional ties and to act as a bridge between Europe and Latin America much as Britain does between Europe and the Commonwealth. There is also a much greater sensitivity than in Britain (as there is generally in Europe) to the problems of emerging democracy in Argentina, and on how to encourage its growth. There has been a continuity in Spanish foreign policy spanning the close relationship between Franco and Perón and the close ties between Raul Alfonsín and Felipe González, with Spain now providing a model for the transition from authoritarianism to democracy (as in the problem of the military) whereas previously it had been a model for authoritarianism. There is too the recognition that the survival of a democratic regime is dependent on democrats having room to manoeuvre and not be seen to be yielding to British pressure. The accord initiated by Italy and seconded by Spain, making investment conditional on the preservation of democ-

racy is one example of conditional European support, but such initiatives made by other nations in the European Community could be
soured by British intransigence over the islands' future.

Useful though the second argument about Soviet naval power was
to the naval and merchant naval lobby it has little relevance unless
Britain aspires to play an independent world-role, but the Falklands
War underlined dependence on the United States for both intel-
ligence and logistical support. Without this it is difficult to envisage
the British retaining the islands in any future conflict but the cost of
that support might be considered too high if it meant a worsening of
United States relations with the rest of Latin America.

Finally, with the pending re-negotiation of the Antarctic Treaties
any British weakening might be interpreted as a waning of British
interest in Antarctica as was the accounting of the withdrawal of
HMS *Endurance* in 1981. But whatever the future of that continent
the economic potential of the South Atlantic has added a new dimension to the argument. Off-shore oil may still be a dream, and untenable without Argentina's cooperation, but the fish bonanza is a
present reality with the issue of licenses bringing an annual income
in excess of £10 million, thus undermining the argument that the
islands cannot be self-supporting (excepting military expenditure),
although, as Peruvians already know to their cost, fish booms can
burst.[9]

A high price is being paid in elevating principle over pragmatism
and wider British interests. The cost of a 'Fortress Falklands' policy
may be declining after the initial capital expenditure but there is the
potential threat of a low intensity 'war' of attrition by constant
intrusions into the exclusion zone (cf. the Cod War with Iceland), thus
raising the cost of vigilance to unacceptable heights. There is also the
British exclusion from a potentially lucrative market and field for
investment in Argentina although the British share of this had
already dropped to a mere 4 per cent and 0.8 per cent respectively
even before the war. It remains to be seen to what extent the new
accord between Argentina and Britain since Carlos Menem's accession will enable Britain to recover even its feeble pre-war presence.
In addition, there are the hypothetical wider consequences of Britain's standing in the rest of Latin America. Although the long-term
effects of Latin American solidarity with Argentina are difficult to
assess, a further escalation of the crisis could mobilise Latin American opinion, impatient with British intransigence.[11]

The primacy given to Falklands affairs in Britain over the wider
issue of relations with the rest of Latin America is a reflection of the

strength of the Falklands lobby in comparison with the debility of the
Latin American lobby. This can be partly explained by the incompati-
bility of the two major interests concerned with Latin American
affairs — those firms traditionally associated with the region and
those critics, mostly professional Latin- Americanists, who criticise
British policy from the perspective of human rights, arms sales to
military dictatorships, the meagre scale of our aid programme, and
who were opposed to Reaganite-style policies and attitudes towards
Latin America.

In overall strategic and economic terms the Falklands are marginal to British interests and constitute a drain on resources which
could be more profitably deployed elsewhere. But too much emotional
and political capital has been invested in the 'Falklands factor' to
envisage any change of the British position so long as the present
government remains in power, magnanimity is not a word in its
political vocabulary, and it is unprofitable to speculate on an alternative domestic political scenario as a softening of attitudes by a
government of any persuasion would mobilise the popular press —
for whom the war had been a godsend — by legitimately recalling the
sacrifices of the dead and mutilated.[12]

Whatever the weight given to the above factors there is an element
of unpredictability on the Argentine side. If negotiations have been
fruitless under Alfonsín with his democratic credentials, what chance
will there be now that Carlos Menem is in power? The portents, much
to everyone's surprise, are more favourable than expected. Diplomatic relations were resumed in March 1990. And there is the added
irony that Thatcherism is becoming respectable in some Argentine
financial circles. Nevertheless, Peronism has cast a long dark shadow
over British-Argentine relations and it can only be hoped that anti-
British feeling which it fuelled in the 1940s and the 1950s has been
mitigated by the rise of a moderate wing within the party.

Innumerable solutions to the dispute have been proposed and
canvassed, from preserving the status-quo, to international and
multi-lateral initiatives but none of them satisfies both parties. The
British are refusing to yield on sovereignty: the Argentines are
convinced of the justice of their case even if many disapprove of the
means used to enforce it. On one side are the memories of invasion
and the disturbance of a way of life which has vanished forever, and
the risks of living under an unpredictable regime. On the other, there
is an unassuaged sense of historical grievance at territorial loss.[13] To
the latter must be added a deteriorating economy, spiralling inflation,
an unresolved debt problem, a growing disillusion with the ineffi-

ciency of democratic solutions and the ever-present military –
divided, bruised, pilloried but now re-armed and anxious to be re-vin-
dicated after absorbing the lessons of a war they could have won and
indeed could have done so had bombs been properly primed.

Given these factors the prospects do not seem promising for the
peaceful solution of what Ossie Ardiles — an Argentine who has been
a hero on the football terraces of Tottenham Hotspur both before and
after the war — had described as a family quarrel:

> The Falklands war, he writes, was particularly stupid in being
> between two countries with similar lifestyles who had everything
> to gain from friendship but had stumbled into hostilities because
> their governments had adopted positions from which there was no
> retreat.[14]

Or to quote from one of the British dead:

> ... I cannot think of a single war in Britain's history which has been
> so pointless. They have been either for trade, survival, maintaining
> a balance of power, world [economic] growth etc. This one is
> re-capturing a place which we were going to leave undefended from
> April and to deprive its residence of British citizenship in Oc-
> tober.[15]

David Tinker's posthumously published letters are one among
many poignant accounts of the war — more numerous on the Argentine side, impelled by the bitterness of defeat, humiliation, criticism
of mismanagement and clouded by memories of the 'dirty war'.
Personal testimonies, films, poetry and plays have given the war a
greater resonance than any foreign event in this country since Suez.[16]
The war also not only enabled the press to stir the latent flame of
jingoism but provided a laboratory for strategic planners in which
equipment and weapons, from the design of boots to missile systems,
and perhaps laser rays could be tested. The war also engendered an
important literature with implications beyond the Falklands itself
concerning crisis-management, the conduct of cabinet government,
and the problems of crises in mini-states. [17]

In contrast to glorification and analysis has been a growing critical
literature, questioning the basic principles of national policy. For the
hard left, the war was an inevitable consequence rising from contra-
dictions within two capitalist societies in crisis, brought into conflict
by an outdated colonialism. [18] Criticism by the soft left has focused

on the conspiratorial nature of decision making on issues such as the sinking of the *Belgrano*, undermining peace initiatives, control of the media, the deception of parliament and lack of government accountability.[19]

The war solved nothing, except to leave the British for the time being, in Dr. Johnson's words, the 'undisputed lords of tempest-beaten barrenness', and the only lessons learnt seem to have been how to secure the islands more effectively against the next Argentine invasion, and for the Argentines, how to rectify the military shortcomings which robbed them of what they felt should have been a certain victory. The solution is as far away as ever and will, in fact, only be found when both sides consider it equally expedient, but for that to occur many years will have to elapse.

Faced with a surreal situation where neither side shows any inclination to yield, and where international law and outside agencies seem powerless to help, other solutions need to be explored. As the mere descriptive use of 'Falklands' or 'Malvinas' implies commitment, as a first step the islands might be renamed the Hudson Islands (W.H. to the British but Guillermo Enrique to the Argentines) in honour of the only person apart from George Canning to have monuments to him in both Buenos Aires and London and whom both countries can proudly acknowledge as their own without conflict and whom H.J. Massingham once described as:

> a primitive in habit of mind, yet so modern that he diverted the evolution of human thought and revolutionised the relations between man and nature ... virtually the parent and inspiration of a new driving force in the world. [20]

For the islands to be denationalised, and to become a bird sanctuary and a wilderness area, a haven for reflection by lovers of solitude and nature, both Argentine and British, would be an assertion of the sovereignty of nature over the sovereignty of nationalism and might be no bad solution at a time of encroaching environmental doom.

## Notes

1. House of Commons, the Foreign Affairs Committee Report 1986-87 on *Cultural Diplomacy*, HMSO, London, 1987, p.54. The most sophisticated discussion of the relationship between diplomacy and culture, together with definitions, and useful for

comparative purposes in Frank A. Ninkovich, *The Diplomacy of Ideas: US Foreign Policy and Cultural Relations, 1938-50*, Cambridge University Press, 1981. See also Sir Anthony Parsons British Council's fiftieth anniversary lecture 'Vultures and Philistines: British Attitudes to Culture and Cultural Diplomacy'. By far the best discussion of British cultural policy in Latin America is Gerald Martin's pessimistic and hard-hitting chapter 'Britain's cultural relations with Latin America in Victor Bulmer Thomas (ed.) *Britain and Latin America: a changing relationship*, Cambridge University Press and the Royal Institute of International Affairs, 1989. See also J.M. Mitchell, *International Cultural Relations*, Allen and Unwin and the British Council, London, 1984.

2. It is odd that the principle of seconding experts from the large (much of it unemployed) pool of available academic talent to act as press or information officers in embassies has not been pursued more vigorously. The French have realised the importance of intellectuals, expert in the countries to which they are attached, in influencing opinion. Given the importance accorded to intellectuals in Latin American societies (although not in Britain) it would seem an obvious strategy to utilise the Latinamericanists who have been overproduced by the Latin American Centres since they were established in the 1960s.

3. The swing to Spain was partly a reflection of the *criollismo* of the traditional elite, of solidarity with Spain during the Cuban-Spanish-American War of 1898, the influence of Ortega y Gasset and the *Revista de Occidente*, and of Unamuno, one of the first European critics to appreciate the genre of gaucho poetry, seeing it as an extension of the Spanish romance. Spanish neutrality during the First World War was also seen as a virtue when immigrant groups in Argentina were divided along national lines.

4. The Malvinas/Falkland issue and the war have generated an enormous literature. Perhaps the best single book is Michael Charlton's radio interviews published as *The Little Platoon: Diplomacy and the Falklands Dispute*, Blackwell, Oxford, 1989 (the title is a quote from Edmund Burke), and the penetrating chapter by Malcolm Deas 'Further Thoughts on the Falklands' in Bulmer Thomas,*supra*. The war itself has generated a large literature. Good studies looking at the war from both British and Argentine viewpoints are Martin Middlebrook, *Task Force: the Falklands War*, Penguin, Harmondsworth, revised edn.

1987, and *The Argentinians in the Falklands*, The Viking Press, London, 1989. A useful bibliography is in Jimmy Burns, *The Land that lost its heroes, Argentina, the Falklands and Alfonsin*, Bloomsbury, London, 1987. The author was the only full-time British journalist to be in Argentina during the war and it is required reading for an understanding of the Argentine viewpoint. The most comprehensive study is by L. Freedman and V. Gamba-Stonehouse, *Signals of War: the Anglo- Argentine Conflict of 1982*, Faber, London 1990.

5. For Diego García see the Minority Rights Group Report No. 54, London. *Diego García: a contrast with the Falklands*.

6. Quoted in Fritz L. Hoffman and Olga Mingo Hoffman, *Sovereignty in Dispute: the Falklands/Malvinas 1493- 1982*, Westview, Boulder and London, 1984, p. 176

7. See Alexander Betts, *La verdad sobre las Malvinas: mi tierra natal*, Emecé, Buenos Aires, 1987 and Michael Mainwaring, *From the Falklands to Patagonia: the story of a London pioneer family*, Alison and Busby, 1983, which relates the story of William Halliday who emigrated from Dumfries as a shepherd to the Falklands in 1862 and then moved to Patagonia in 185. Members of the family were interviewed by the author. The problem of the islands could be solved if unmarried Argentine girls, possibly of Irish, Scots, Welsh or English antecedents, married Falklands bachelors. The 'kith and kin'argument is clearly operative in the case of the Falklands as it was in Rhodesia although it did not prove insuperable then. British attitudes to Hong Kong make the point. One wonders if the Chinese would have been trusted in negotiations had the inhabitants not been Chinese- but British-born.

8. See Geoffrey Bennett, *Coronel and the Falklands*, Batsford and Pan Books, London 1962.

9. It is odd given the depressed state of the British fishing industry that British trawlers are not jostling with Taiwanese, Polish, Esthonian trawlers and others for a share of the catch, or are fishing licences another example of the rentier mentality?

10. One estimate puts the total expenditure over the period 1982-92 on the war, 'Fortress Falklands' and economic aid in the region of £5 billion. See Appendix to G.M. Dillon, *The Falklands, Politics and War*, Macmillan, London, 1989, pp. 237- 42.

11. There are conflicting views about Latin American reactions to the war. Some people undoubtedly were not averse to seeing Argentina discomfited but I suspect solidarity with a fellow

power against a European incursion outweigh this. Although pragmatic considerations seem in the long run to have outweighed other feelings. Chile was the one state to benefit from the conflict because of the British need for support in case of a renewal of hostilities.

12. It is worth recalling the way in which Michael Stewart was howled down in the House of Commons when in 1968 he suggested that sovreignty might be negotiable.

13. For a pungent analysis of how, since the break from Spain, Argentines have been obsessed by a perceived sense of national loss see C. Escude 'Argentine territorial nationalism', *Journal of Latin American Studies*, 20 May 1988.

14. Ardiles with M. Langley, *Ossie: my life in football*, Sidgwick and Jackson, London, 1983, p. 163.

15. Tinker, H. (ed.) *A message from the Falklands: the life and gallant death of David Tinker Lieut. R.N. from his letters and poems*, Harmondsworth, Penguin Books 1983, P. 198.

16. Such as the films *Los chicos de la guerra* and *Veronico Cruz* in Argentina, and *Tumbledown* and *Resurrection* in Britain.

17. For a good example of crisis management see Virginia Gamba, *The Falklands / Malvinas War: a Model for North-South Prevention*, Allen and Unwin, Boston and London, 1987. For cabinet government see G.M. Dillon, *The Falklands, Politics and War*, Macmillan, London, 1989. There is a new field of study concerning small islands with their inherent development problems and susceptibility to destabilisation, especially through the use of drug money, although this does not seem to be a Falklands problem — yet.

18. For the 'hard left' see Anthony Barnett, *Iron Britannia: Why Britain waged the Falklands War*, Alison and Busby, London, 1987 and Vol. 134 of *The New Left Review*. It is parallelled on the Argentine side by A. Dabat and L. Lorenzano, *Argentina: the Malvinas and the end of military rule*. Verso, London, 1983.

19. For one famous example see C. Ponting, *The right to know: the inside story of the Belgrano affair*, Secker and Warburg, London, 1984. A dispassionate analysis of the media question is V. Adams, *The media and the Falklands War*, Macmillan, London, 1986. See also the pertinacious Tam Dalyell, *One Man's Falklands*, Cecil Wolf, London, 1982 and *Thatcher's Torpedo: the Sinking of the Belgrano*, Cecil Wolf, London. 1984.

20. Quoted in R. Tomalin, *W.H. Hudson: a biography* Faber and Faber, London, 1982, p. 25.

# Contributors

*Peter J. Beck* is Reader in International History at Kingston Polytechnic. He graduated from the London School of Economics and is a leading authority on Antarctica and the Falklands on which he has published *The International Politics of Antarctica, The Falkland Islands as an International Problem* as well as many articles in British and foreign journals.

*Simon Collier* is Reader in History and Director of the Centre of Latin American Studies at the University of Essex. He graduated from Cambridge and among his many publications in Latin American History are *From Cortes to Castro: an Introduction to the History of Latin America (1492- 1973), Ideas and Politics of Chilean Independence*, and *The Life, Music and Times of Carlos Gardel*. He was co-editor of the *Cambridge Encyclopaedia of Latin America* and is editor of the *Cambridge Latin American Monograph series*.

*Eduardo Crawley* is Editor of the London- based *Latin American Newsletter* and a distinguished journalist and writer on Latin America. He is the author of *A House Divided: Argentina, 1880- 1980*.

*Harry S. Ferns* was Emeritus Professor of Political Science, University of Birmingham and author of a wide range of books and articles on Argentina including *Britain and Argentina in the Nineteenth Century, Argentina* (The Nations of the Modern World Series), *The Argentine Republic, 1519- 1971: an Economic History*, as well as many other books on a wide variety of topics.

*Evelyn Fishburn* is Senior Lecturer in Latin American Literature at the North London Polytechnic. A graduate of the University of London, she was brought up and lived in Argentina until the age of twenty. She is the author of *The Portrayal of Immigration in Nineteenth Century Argentina Fiction 1845-1902*. She has published articles on Borges and has recently published a *Dictionary of Borges*.

*Roger Gravil* is Professor of Economic History at the University of Natal. A graduate of the University of London, his monograph, *The Anglo-Argentine Connection, 1900-1939* is being published in translation in Buenos Aires. A sequel entitled *Britain and Perón's Argentina, 1943-1955* is in preparation.

*Alistair Hennessy* is Professor of History and has been Chairman of the School of Comparative American Studies at the University of Warwick where he is also Director of the Centre for Caribbean Studies. A graduate of Oxford he is the author of *The Federal Republic in Spain: Pi y Margall and the Federal Republican Movement 1868-1874* and *The Frontier in Latin American History*, an expanded edition of which is in preparation. He is editor of the Macmillan Warwick University Caribbean series and is at present directing a research project on West-European Cuban relations.

*Gwyn Howells* is Principal Lecturer in Spanish at Coventry Polytechnic. A graduate of Liverpool University, his M.Phil. at Warwick was on the treatment of the Peróns in the British popular press. He has published articles on contemporary Spain, on automatic translation and on Peronism.

*Charles A. Jones* is Lecturer in International Studies at the University of Warwick and a graduate of Cambridge. He has specialised in the history of British business interests in the River Plate and has published numerous articles on Argentine history in British and foreign journals in addition to *North-South Relations: a brief history* and *International Business in the Nineteenth Century*. He is at present working on the Argentine intellectual and politician Vicente López.

*Dermot Keogh* is Professor of European Integration, University College, Cork. He is a graduate of University College, Dublin and the European University Institute, Florence. In addition to his many publications on Irish labour history, Irish religious history, and foreign policy, he has edited *Central America: Human Rights and US Foreign Policy* and *Church and Politics in Latin America*.

*John King* is Senior Lecturer in Latin American Cultural History at the University of Warwick and is a graduate of Edinburgh and Oxford. He is a leading authority on Argentine cultural history on which he has published *Sur: a Study of the Argentine Literary Journal and its role in the Development of a Culture, 1931-70, El Di Tella y el Desarrollo Cultural Argentino en la Decada del Sesenta* and has edited *The Garden of Forking Paths: Argentine Cinema*. His book on the Latin American Cinema is to appear shortly in the new Verso Books series on Latin American culture of which he is also an editor.

*Walter Little* is Lecturer in Latin American Politics at the University of Liverpool. He graduated from Cambridge where his PhD was on Peronism. He has published numerous articles both in Britain and abroad on Peronism, Argentine labour relations and the military. He was specialist adviser to the House of Commons Foreign Affairs Select Committee on the Falklands.

*Callum MacDonald* is Senior Lecturer in Comparative American Studies at the University of Warwick. He is a graduate of Edinburgh and Oxford. In addition to articles on Argentine foreign policy he has published *The United States, Britain and Appeasement, 1936-1939*, and *Korea: the War before Vietnam*. A second book on the Korean war is about to be published. In addition to many articles he has also published a book on Heydrich's assassination.

*Oliver Marshall* is a Research Assistant at the Institute of Latin American Studies, University of London. He graduated from the University of East Anglia and Manchester. He is currently researching on Colonia Victoria in Argentina.

*John Walker* is Professor of Spanish at Queen's University, Kingston, Ontario, Canada. He graduated from Glasgow and London. He has published extensively on nineteenth and twentieth century writers of the Southern Cone including Manuel Gálvez, Eduardo Mallea and Eduardo Barrios. He has also written numerous works on British writers in Argentina including *The South American Sketches of R.B. Cunninghame Graham*.

*Glyn Williams* is Reader in Sociology at the University College of North Wales at Bangor. A graduate of the University of Wales and Berkeley he is the leading authority on the Welsh in Chubut on which he has published extensively in British and foreign journals. His book *The Desert and the Dream: a History of the Welsh Settlement of Patagonia, 1865- 1915,* is one of the most detailed accounts of any foreign agricultural colony in Argentina. A sequel *The State and the Ethnic Community: the Welsh in Patagonia* is the press. He is also a leading authority on Welsh society and sociolinguistics.

*Jason Wilson* is Lecturer in Spanish and Spanish American Poetry at University College, London. A graduate of London University he lived and researched in Argentina and Mexico between 1970-81. His publications include *Octavio Paz: a Study of his Poetics, Octavio Paz* and *An A to Z of Latin American Literature in English*. In addition he has published widely on contemporary Argentine and Spanish writers and on W.H. Hudson and Charles Darwin on whom he is completing a book.

# Short Chronology

1527   Sebastian Cabot establishes short-lived settlement on Lower Paranà

1593   John Hawkins' alleged discovery of Falklands

1690   Straits between East and West Islands named Falkland Sound in honour of Anthony Cary, 3rd Viscount Falkland, later 1st Lord of the Admiralty.

1730   T. Falkner S J begins life among Patagonian Indians

1717-50   British South Sea Company holds *asiento* to import slaves into Buenos Aires

1765   Commodore John Byron names Port Egmont and takes possession of Falklands in the name of George III.

1770   British driven out by Spanish force from Buenos Aires

1771   Spain hands over Port Egmont to British

1774   British withdraw from Port Egmont

1806   British expedition under Sir Home Popham, on return from Cape of Good Hope, occupies Buenos Aires. Colonial militia under Santiago Liniers force British surrender

1807   British under General Whitelocke occupy Montevideo and attack Buenos Aires. British again forced to surrender

1811   Spanish garrison withdraws from Falklands

1815   Rivadavia's diplomatic mission to London. Correspondence with Bentham

1824   The Baring Loan

1825   Treaty of Recognition between Britain and the Provinces of the River Plate

1828   Argentine – Brazil war in which British sailors fight on both sides – one of whom, William Brown from Ireland, is made an Argentine admiral. The Banda Oriental becomes Uruguay as a buffer state between Argentina and Brazil under British auspices

1828   Louis Vernet appointed Military and Political Governor of Malvinas

1828   Robertson brothers establish a Scottish colony at Monte Grande

1833   British re-occupy Falklands/Malvinas. Capture of Antonio Rivero

1828-52   Juan Manuel de Rosas' domination of Argentina

1838-40   French blockade of Buenos Aires

1841   W.H. Hudson born in Quilmes, outside Buenos Aires

1845-8   Anglo-French blockade of Buenos Aires

| | |
|---|---|
| 1842 | *Facundo: or Civilization and Barbarism* published by Sarmiento |
| 1852 | Rosas defeated at battle of Caseros, flees to England where he dies in 1877. Buried at Southampton. |
| 1853 | Constitution incorporates clause encouraging immigration |
| 1856 | Buenos Aires municipal gas company founded |
| 1862 | Bank of London and River Plate founded |
| 1865-70 | War of Triple Alliance between Paraguay, Argentina, Brazil and Uruguay |
| 1865 | The *Mimosa* sails from Liverpool with first Welsh settlers for Chubut |
| 1866 | The Great Southern Railway opens first line |
| | Buenos Aires Water works financed by British capital |
| 1869 | Buenos Aires Water works financed by British capaital |
| 1870 | City of Buenos Aires Tramway Company founded |
| 1870 | Rosario-Córdoba railway 'The Central' completed |
| 1871 | Tandil massacre |
| 1872 | Consul General Macdonnell's report on immigration |
| 1874 | W.H. Hudson travels to England. |
| 1876 | *Le Frigorifique* makes first voyage |
| 1879-85 | The Conquest of the Desert – followed by opening of the frontier and land speculation |
| 1885 | *The Purple Land that England Lost* published |
| 1889 | High point of British investment in Argentina |
| 1890 | The Baring Crisis |
| 1893 | W.H. Hudson, *Idle Days in Patagonia* published. |
| 1912 | Saenz Peña Law widens franchise |
| 1916 | Irigoyen comes to power |
| 1918 | W.H. Hudson, *Far Away and Long Ago* published |
| 1922 | W.H. Hudson dies aged 81 |
| 1925 | Visit of Prince of Wales |
| 1928 | d'Abernon mission |
| 1930 | Revolution overthrows Irigoyen and after short period of military rule the oligarchy return in the *Concordancia* |
| 1933 | Roca-Runciman treaty |
| 1936 | Roca-Runciman renewed |
| 1936 | Cunninghame Graham dies in Buenos Aires aged 84. |
| 1943 | Military coup ends *Concordancia* |
| 1946 | Perón elected President |
| 1947 | Nationalisation of British-owned railways |
| 1952 | Eva Perón dies, aged 33 |
| 1955 | Perón removed from power and goes into exile in Spain |

| 1965 | UN Resolution 2065 invites UK and Argentina to enter discussions over the Falklands/Malvinas issue |
| 1966 | Operation Condor: symbolic seizure of Malvinas by twenty members of Perón Youth Group |
| 1971 | Borges awarded honorary degree at Oxford |
| 1973 | Perón returns |
| 1974 | Perón dies, aged 79 |
| 1978 | *Evita* opens at 'Prince Edward's Theatre', London |
| 1978 | Argentina wins the World football cup |
| 1982 | Falklands/Malvinas war |
| 1983 | Raul Alfonsín elected president |
| 1984 | Borges receives honorary doctorate from Cambridge. |
| 1986 | Borges dies in Switzerland, aged 87 |
| 1989 | Carlos Menem elected President Juan Manuel de Rosas re-buried in Buenos Aires |
| 1990 | (March)  Argentine-British diplomatic relations resumed. |

# Select Bibliography

For further detailed reading see Notes to each chapter. Good accessible bibliographies are in David Rock, *Argentina, 1516-1982*, Tauris, London, 1986, James Scobie, *Argentina: a city and nation*, Oxford University Press, 2nd edition 1981. Eduardo Crawley, *A House Divided, Argentina 1880-1980*, Hurst, London, 1984 and especially A. Graham Yooll, *The Forgotten Colony: a history of the English-speaking communities in Argentina*, Hutchinson, London, 1981. José Evaristo, Uriburu, *La República Argentina a través de las obras de los escritoíres ingleses: Compilación*, Claridad, Buenos Aires, 1948 and S. Samuel Trifilo, *La Argentina vista por los viajeros ingleses: 1810-60*, Gure, Buenos Aires, 1959.

Adams, Valerie, *The Media and the Falklands War*, Macmillan, London 1986.

Adamson, Gladys and Pichon Rivière Marcos, *Indios e inmigrantes: una historia de vida*, Galerna, Buenos Aires 1978.

Ardiles, Osvaldo with Mike Langley, *Ossie: my life in football* Sidgwick and Jackson, London, 1983.

Andreru, J. Bennassar, B. Gaignard R. et. al. *Les Aveyronnais dans la Pampa: fondation, développement et vie de la colonie aveyronnaise de Pigüé, Argentine 1884-1974*, L'Université Toulouse, Le Mirail Privat Toulouse, 1977.

Bailey, J.P. *Immigration and ethnic relations: the British in Argentina.* La Trobe Sociology Papers no. 44. Bundoora, 1978.

Barnett, Anthony, *Iron Britannia: Why Britain waged the Falklands War*, Alison and Busby, London, 1987.

Barager, Joseph R., *Why Perón came to Power: the 1968 background to Peronism in Argentina*, Knopf. New York, 1968.

Bayer, Osvaldo, *Los vengadores de la Patagonia Trágica* 3 vols. Galerna, Buenos Aires, 1974.

Beaumont, J.A. *Travels in Buenos Aires and the Adjacent Provinces*, London, 1828.

Beck, Peter, *The International Politics of Antarctica*, Croom Helm, London. 1986.

— *The Falklands Islands as an International Problem*, Routledge, London, 1988.

Betts, Alexander, *La verdad sobre las Malvinas: mi tierra natal*, Emecé, Buenos Aires, 1987.

Blinn, Reher, Vera, *British Mercantile Houses in Buenos Aires 1810-1880*, Harvard Studies in Business History no. 29, Harvard University Press, Cambridge, Mass., 1979.

Braden, Spruille, *Diplomats and Demagogues*, Arlington House, New York, 1971.

Bridges, E. Lucas, *Uttermost Part of the Earth*, Century Travellers, London, 1987.

Bryce, James, *South America: observations and impressions*, London, 1912

Bullock, Donald & Mitchell, Christopher. *The Aland Islands Solution*, South Atlantic Council, Occasional papers no.2, London, 1987.

Bulmer Thomas, Victor, *Britain and Latin America: a changing relationship,* Cambridge University Press in association with the R.I.I.A., 1987.

Burgin, Miron, *The Economic Aspects of Argentine Federalism*, Harvard University Press, Cambridge Mass. 1946.

Burns, Jimmy, *The Land That Lost its Heroes: Argentina, the Falklands and Alfonsin*, Bloomsbury, London, 1987.

Cady, John F. *Foreign Intervention in the Rio de la Plata 1830-50: a study of French, British and American policy in relation to the dictator Juan Manuel Rosas*, Philadelphia (University of Pennsylvania, 1929).

Cardosa Paul, Kirschbaum Ricardo, Van de Kooy, Eduardo, *Falklands: the secret plot*, trans. Bernard Ethell, East Moseley, Preston Editions, 1987.

Cara-Walker, Ana, 'Cocoliche: the art of assimilation and dissimulation among Italians and Argentinians'. *Latin American Research Review* 22.3.1986.

Charlton, Michael. *The Little Platoon: Diplomacy and the Falklands Dispute*, Basil Blackwell, Oxford, 1989.

Clemenceau, *South America Today*, London, 1911. (incomplete)

Cochran, Thomas C. and Reina Ruben E., *Entrepreneurship in Argentine Culture: Torcuato di Tella and SIAM*, University of Pennsylvania Press, 1962.

Collier, Simon, *The Life, Music and Times of Carlos Gardel*, University of Pittsburgh, Pittsburgh, 1986.

Cordell, Hull, *The Memoirs Vol. II*, Hodder and Stoughton, London, 1948.

Cornblitt, Oscar, 'European immigrants in Argentine industry and politics' in Claudio Veliz (ed.) *The Politics of Conformity in Latin America*, Oxford University Press, London 1967.

Crawley, Eduardo, *A House Divided: Argentina: 1880-1980*, Hurst London, 1984.

Crassweller, Robert D., *Perón and the Enigmas of Argentina*, Norton, New York, 1987.

Dabat, Alessandro and Lorenzano Luis, *Argentina: the Malvinas and the end of military rule*, Verso, London 1983.

Darwin, Charles, *Journal of Researches into the Natural History and Geology of the countries visited during the voyage of H.M.S. Beagle around the world*, London, Dent, 1906.

Denis, Pierre, *The Argentine Republic: its development and progress*, Fisher & Unwin, London 1922.

Dent, Martin, *Shared Sovereignty: A solution for the Falklands/Malvinas Dispute*. South Atlantic Council, Occasional papers no. 5, London, 1989.

Diaz, Alejandro, Carlos F. *Essays on the Economic History of Argentina*, Yale University Press, New Haven, 1970.

Di Giovanni, Thomas, *In Memory of Borges*, Constable, London

Di Tella, Guido, *Perón 1973-6*, Macmillan, London, 1983.

Di Tella, Guido, and Watt, D. Cameron, *Argentina between the Powers 1939-46*, Macmillan, London 1989

Donaldson, Frances, *The British Council: the first fifty years*, London, 1984.

Duncan, T. and Fogarty, J., *Australia and Argentina: on parallel paths*, Melbourne University Press, 1984.

Editit, Robert C., *Pioneer Settlement in North-East Argentina*, University of Wisconsin Press, Madison, 1971.

Echeverría, Juan *The Slaughterhouse* translated and edited by Angel Flores, New York, Las America Publishing Co. 1959.

Elliott, L.E. *The Argentina of Today*, London, 1925.

Escudé, Carlos, 'Argentine territorial nationalism', *Journal of Latin American Studies*, 20.1.May 1988.

— *Patología del nacionalismo: el caso argentino*. Instituto di Tella, Buenos Aires, 1987.

— *Gran Bretaña, Estados Unidos y la declinación Argentina 1942-1949*, Belgrano, Buenos Aires, 1983.

Falcoff, Mark, 'Raul Scalabrini Ortiz: the making of an Argentine nationalist', *Hispanic American Historical Review* 52.1.1972.

Falcoff, Mark and Dolkart, Ronald H. *Prologue to Perón: Argentine in Depression and War 1930- 43*, University of California Press 1975.

312                                          THE LAND THAT ENGLAND LOST

Falkner, Thomas S.J. *A Description of Patagonia and the Adjoining Part of South America*; with an introduction and notes by Arthur E.S. Neumann, Armann and Armann, Chicago, 1935.

Faundez, Julio and Borón, Atilio (eds), *Malvinas hoy: herencia de un conflicto*, Editorial Puntosur, Buenos Aires, 1990.

Ferns, Harry S., 'Britain's informal empire in Argentina', *Past and Present*, 4. 1954.

— *The Argentine Republic 1516-1971: an economic history*, David and Charles, Newton Abbot, 1973.

— *Argentina*, Benn, London 1969.

— *Britain and Argentina in the 19th Century*, Clarendon Press, Oxford, 1960.

Fishburn, Evelyn, *The Portrayal of Immigration in Nineteenth Century Argentine Fiction* (1845-1902), Berlin, 1981.

Fogarty, J., Gallo, E. and Dieguez, H. *Argentina y Australia*, Instituto Torcuato di Tella, Buenos Aires, 1979.

Ford, Alec G. *The Gold Standard, 1880-1914: Britain and Argentina*, Oxford University Press, London, 1962.

Fraser, John F. *The Amazing Argentine: a new land of enterprise*, London, 1914.

Fraser, Nicholas, and Navarro, Marysa, *Eva Perón*, André Deutsch, London, 1980.

Freedman, Lawrence, and Gamba-Stonehouse, Virginia, *Signals of War: the Anglo-Argentine conflict of 1982*, Faber, London, 1990

Freedman, Laurence, *Britain and the Falklands War*, Blackwells, Oxford, 1988.

Galasso, Norberto, *Scalabrini ortiz y la lucha contra la dominación inglesa*. Ediciones rel Passarmiento Nacival, Buenos Aires, 1985.

Gallo, Ezequiel, *La Pampa gringa: la colonización agrícola en Santa Fé (1870-95)*, Editorial Sudamericana, Buenos Aires, 1983.

— *Farmers in Revolt: the Revolution of 1893 in the province of Sante Fé, Argentina*, Athlone Press, London 1976.

Gálvez, Manuel, *Vida de Don Manuel de Rosas*, Buenos Aires 1940.

Gamba, Virginia, *The Falklands/Malvinas War: a model for North-South crisis prevention*, Allen & Unwin, London 1987.

García Heras, Paul, *Automotores norteamericanos, caminos y modernización urbana en la Argentina 1918-39*, Buenos Aires, 1984.

George, Bruce and Little, Walter, *Options in the Falkland/Malvinas Dispute* South Atlantic Council Occasional Papers No. 1 April, London, 1985.

Gibson, H., *The History and Present State of the Sheep Herding Industry in the Argentine Republic* Buenos Aires 1893.

Goebel, Julius Jr. *The Struggle for the Falkland Islands*, Yale University Press, New Haven (reprint) 1971.

Goodwin, Paul B., *Los Ferrocarriles Británicos y la UCR*, 1916-31, La Bastille, Buenos Aires, 1974.

Graham, W. *English Influence in the Argentine Republic*, Buenos Aires, 1890.

Graham-Yooll, Andrew, *The Forgotten Colony: a history of the English-speaking communities in Argentina*, Hutchinson, London, 1981.

— *The Press in Argentina 1973-1981*, 2nd Edit., Index on Censorship, London, 1984.

— *Así vieron a Rosas los ingleses*, Rodolfo, Alfonso, Buenos Aires, 1980.

Gravil, Roger, *The Anglo-Argentine Connection 1900-1939*, Westview, Boulder 1985.

— 'Anglo-U.S. trade rivalry in Argentina and the D'Abernon mission of 1929' in D. Rock (ed.) *Argentina in the 20th Century*, Duckworth, London. 1975.

— 'British retail trade in Argentina, 1900- 1940' *Inter American Economic Affairs* 24.2.1970.

Greenup, Ruth and Leonard, *Revolution before Breakfast: Argentina 1941-6*, Greenwood Press, Westport 1942.

Guedalla, Philip, *Argentine Tango*, Hodder and Stoughton, London, 1932.

Gustafson, Lowell, S., *The Sovreignty Dispute over the Falklands (Malvinas) Islands*. Oxford University Press, London.

Guy, Donna J., 'White slavery, public health, and the Socialist position on legalized prostitution in Argentina 1913-36', *Latin American Research Review* XXIII 3 1988.

Hammerton, J.A. *The Argentine Through English Eyes*, London n.d.

Hanson, Simon G., *Argentine Meat and the British Market: chapters in the history of the Argentine meat industry*. Stanford University Press, 1938.

Hennessy, Alistair, *The Frontier in Latin American History*, Arnold, London 1978.

Head, Sir Francis Bond, *Rough Notes taken during some rapid journeys across the Pampas and among the Andes* ed. with an introduction by C. Harvey Gardner, Carbondale 1967 (orig. published 1826).

Henty, G.A., *Out on the Pampas: or, The Young Settlers*, London 1871.

Hobson, J.A., *Imperialism: A Study*, Allen & Unwin, London 1962.

Hoffman Fritz L. and Olga Mingo Hoffman, *Sovereignty in Dispute: The Falklands/Malvinas 1493-1982*, Westview, Boulder and London, 1984.

House of Commons, *Cultural Diplomacy*, The Foreign Affairs Committee Report 1986-7. H.M.S.O. London 1987.

Howells, Gwyn, *The British press view and treatment of Argentine affairs 1943-1955 with particular reference to the popular press.* Unpub. M. Phil. Thesis, University of Warwick 1972.

Hudson, W.H., *The Purple Land that England Lost: being the narrative of one Richard Lamb's adventures in the Banda Oriental in South America as tried by himself.* London, 1922.

— *Idle Days in Patagonia*, Dent, London 1984.

— *Far Away and Long Ago: A History of my early life*, Dent, London 1951.

Humphreys, R.A., *Latin America and the 2nd World War*, Athlone Press, London, 2 vols. 1981-2.

— *Liberation in South America 1806-1827: The career of James Paroissien*, Athlone Press, London 1915.

Ibarguren, Carlos, *Juan Manuel de Roasas, su vida, su tiempo, su drama*, Buenos Aires, 1930.

Imaz, Jose Luis de, *Los que mandan*, Eudeba, Buenos Aires, 1968.

Irazusta, Julio and Rodolfo, *La Argentina y el imperialismo británico*, Buenos Aires, 1934.

Jefferson, March C., *Peopling the Argentine Pampas*, American Geographical Society, New York, 1926.

Johnson, Samuel, 'Thoughts on the late transactions respecting the Falklands Islands', in Vol. X of *The Works of Samuel Johnson*.

Jones, Charles, A. 'British financial institutions in Argentina, 1860-1914',unpublished Ph.D. Thesis, University of Cambridge 1973.

— 'Business Imperialism and Argentina 1875- 1900: a theoretical note: *Journal of Latin American Studies*, 12,2,1980.

Joslin, David, *A century of banking in Latin America*, London 1963.

Jurado, Alicia, *Vida y obra de G.E. Hudson*, Buenos Aires, 1971.

Kelly, Sir David, *The Ruling Few or the Human Background to Diplomacy* Hollis & Carter, London, 1955.

King, John, *Sur: a study of the Argentine literary journal and its role in the development of a culture 1931-70*, Cambridge University Press 1986.

King, John and Torrents Nisa (ed.) *The Garden of Forking Paths: Argentine cinema*. London, British Film Institute 1988.

King, John, *Argentine Cinema*, Plymouth Arts Lecture 1986.

— *El Di Tella y el desarrollo cultural argentino en la década del sesenta*, Ediciones de Arte Gaglianone, Buenos Aires, 1985.

Koebel, W.H., *Argentina: past & present*, Kegan Paul, London 1910.

Korn, Francis, *Buenos Aires: los huéspedes del '20*, Sudamericana, Buenos Aires, 1974.

Kovol, Juan Carlos and Sábato, Hilda, *Como fué la inmigración irlandesa en la Argentina*, Buenos Aires, 1981.

Kroeber, Clifton, B., 'Rosas and the revision of Argentine History 1880-1955', *Revista Interamericana de Bibliografía*, 11.1.1960.

Kruger, DW, 'Afrikaners in Argentina', *Standard Encyclopedia of Southern Africa*, Vol. 5, Editorial Nasau, South Africa.

Latham, Wilfred, *The States of the River Plate*, 2nd edit., London 1868.

Latin America Bureau, *Falklands/Malvinas: Whose crisis?* London 1982.

Lewis, Colin, *British Railways in Argentina 1857-1914: a case study in foreign investment*, Athlone Press, London 1983.

Little, Walter, 'The popular origins of Peronism' in D. Rock (ed.) *Argentina in the Twentieth Century*, Duckworth. London 1975.

— 'Party and State in Peronist Argentina', *Hispanic American Historical Review*, November 1973.

— 'Electoral aspects of Peronism' *Journal of Latin American Studies*.

— 'La organización obrera y el estado peronista', *Desarollo Economico*, October, 1979.

Livermore, Seward, W., *'Battleship diplomacy in South America'*, *Journal of Modern History*, XVI, March 1944.

Lloyd, Reginald (ed.), *Twentieth-century Impressions of Argentina: its history, people, commerce, industry and resources*, London 1911.

Londres, A., *The Road to Buenos Aires*, London, 1930.

Lucas, Bridges., *The Uttermost Part of the Earth*, Century, London, 1987.

Lynch, John, *Argentine Dictator: Juan Manuel Rosas, 1829-1852*, Oxford University Press, London, 1981.

MacCann, William, *Two Thousand Miles' Ride through the Argentine Provinces*, 2 vols. London, 1853.

McGann, Thomas, *Argentina, the United States and the Inter-American System*, Harvard University Press, Cambridge, 1957

316 THE LAND THAT ENGLAND LOST

McGee, Deutsch, *Conservatism in Argentina 1900-32: the Argentine Patriotic League*, University of Nebraska Press, Lincoln, 1986.

Macdonald, C. 'The politics of intervention: the United States and Argentina 1941-6', *Journal of Latin American Studies*, 12, (2), 1980.

— 'The United States, the Cold War and Perón' in Abel, C. and Lewis, C. (eds.), *Latin American Economic Imperialism and the States*, Athlone Press, London, 1985.

Main, Mary, *Evita: the woman with the whip*, Corgi Books, London 3rd Edit. 1978.

Mainwaring, Michael, *From the Falklands to Patagonia: the story of a pioneer family*, Alison and Busy, London, 1983.

Manchester, A., *British Pre-eminence in Brazil: its rise and decline*. Octagon Books, New York 1964.

Marsal, Juan, *Hacer la América*, Instituto Di Tella, Buenos Aires, 1969.

Martínez Estrada, E., *El mundo maravilloso de Guillermo Enrique Hudson*, Buenos Aires, 1951.

*X-Ray of the Pampa*, trs. Alan Swietlicke, University of Texas Press, Austin, 1971.

Masefield, John, *Collected Poems*, London, Publisher, 1923.

Mörner, Magnus, *Adventurers and Proletarians: the story of migrants in Latin America*, University of Pittsburgh, Pittsburgh, 1985.

Mulhall, M.G. and E.T., *Handbook of the River Plate Republics*, London, 1885.

— *The English in South America*, Buenos Aires, 1878.

Naipaul, V.S. *The Return of Eva Perón*, Harmondsworth, Penguin Books, 1981.

Nairn, Tom, *The Break-up of Britain,* Verso, London, 1981.

Newton, R.C. *Germans of Buenos Aires 1900-1933: social change and cultural crisis*, University of Texas Press, Austin, 1977.

Ninkovich, Frank A., *The Diplomacy of Ideas: U.S. foreign policy and cultural relations, 1938-1950.* Cambridge University Press, 1981.

Ocampo, Victoria, *Autobiografía*, 6 vols. Ediciones *Sur.* Buenos Aires, 1979-1984.

Ortega Peña R. and Donhalde E.L. *Baring Brothers y la historia política argentina*, Buenos Aires, 1923.

Owen, G.D. *Crisis in Chubut: a chapter in the history of the Welsh colony in Patagonia*, Christopher Davies, Swansea, 1977.

Parsons, Sir Anthony. *The Future of the Falklands: a view from Britain*.

Payne, John R. *W.H. Hudson: a bibliography*, Anchor Books, Hamden Conn. 1977.

Petersen, Harold F. *Argentina and the United States 1810-1960*, State University of New York, Albany, 1964.

Platt, D.C.M. and Guido di Tella (eds.), *Argentina, Australia and Canada: studies in comparative development 1870-1965*, Macmillan, London, 1985.

— *The Political Economy of Argentina 1880-1946*, Macmillan, London 1986.

Platt, D.C.M. (ed) *Business Imperialism 1840-1930: an inquiry based on British experience in Latin America*, Clarendon Press, Oxford, 1977.

— *Latin America and British Trade 1806- 1914*, A & C Black, London 1971.

— 'British agricultural colonies in Latin America' *Inter-American Economic Affairs*.

Ponting, Clive, *The Right to Know: the inside story of the Belgrano Affair*, Secker & Warburg, London, 1984.

Rapoport, Mario, *Gran Bretaña, Estadosbridos y las clases diaigeatos argentinos 1940-1945*, Edit. Belgrano, Buenos Aires, 1981.

Reid, George, *The Afro-Argentines of Buenos Aires, 1800-1900*, University of Wisconsin Press, Madison, 1980.

Rennie, Ysabel, *The Argentine Republic*, Macmillan, New York 1945.

Robertson, J.P. and W.P., *Letters on South America*, London, 1843.

Rock, David, *Argentina, 1516-1982*, Tauris, London, 1986.

Rock, David, ed., *Argentina in the 20th Century*, Duckworth, London, 1975.

— *Politics in Argentina 1890-1930: the rise and fall of radicalism*, Cambridge University Press, 1975.

Rodríguez Monegal, Emir, *Jorge Luis Borges: A literary biography*, Dutton, New York, 1978.

Rumbold, Sir Horace. *The Great Silver River: notes of a residence in Buenos Aires in 1880 and 1881*, London, 1890.

Sáenz Quesada, María. *Los estancieros*. Buenos Aires, 1980.

Sarlo, Beatriz, *Una modernidad periférica: Buenos Aires, 1920 y 30*, Nueva Visión, Buenos Aires, 1988.

Scalabrini Ortiz, Rául, *Historia de los ferrocarriles argentinos*, 4th edition, Buenos Aires, 1964.

— *Política británica en el Río de la Plata*, F. Blanco, Buenos Aires, 1957.

Scarzanella, Eugenia. *Italiani d'Argentina: storie de contadini, industriali e misionari italiani in Argentina 1850- 1912*, Venice 1983.

Scobie, James R., *Revolution on the Pampas: a social history of Argentina wheat 1860-1910*, University of Texas, Austin, 1964.

— *Argentina: a city and a nation*, Oxford University Press, New York 2nd edit. 1971.

— *Buenos Aires: plaza to suburb 1870- 1910*. Oxford University Press, New York, 1974.

— 'Buenos Aires of 1910: the Paris of South America that did not take off', *Inter-American Economic Affairs* 22.2.1968, pages.

Sarmiento, Domingo Faustino, *Life in the Argentine Republic: or civilization and barbarism*, Collier Books, New York, 1966.

— *Travels in the United States in 1847*. trans. and edited by M.A. Rochland. Princeton University Press 1970.

Seymour, R.A. *Pioneering on the Pampas*. Publisher, London 1869.

Shuttleworth, Nina K., *A Life of Sir Woodbine Parish*, Publisher, London 1910.

Slatta, Richard W., *Gauchos and the Vanishing Frontier*, University of Nebraska, Lincoln, 1983.

Solberg, Carl E., *Oil and nationalism in Argentina*, Stanford University Press, Stanford, 1979.

— *The Prairies and the Pampas: agrarian policy in Canada & Argentina, 1880-1930*, Stanford University Press, Stanford, 1987.

— *Immigration and Nationalism: Argentina and Chile 1890-1914*, University of Texas Press, Austin, 1970.

Szuchman, Mark, *Mobility and Integration in Urban Argentina: Córdoba in the Liberal era*, University of Texas Press, Austin, 1980.

Tabbush, Alan, *Argentina-British Trade and the South Atlantic Conflict*. South Atlantic Council, Occasional Papers No. 7, London, 1989.

Tamagno, Roberto, *Sarmiento, los liberales y el imperialismo británico*. Peña Lillo, Buenos Aires, 1963.

Taylor, Carl C., *Rural Life in Argentina*, State University of Louisiana Press, Baton Rouge, 1948.

Taylor, J.M., *Eva Perón: The myths of a woman*, Basil Blackwell, Oxford.

Terragno, R. *The challenge of rural development: Argentina in the twenty-first century*, Rienner, Boulder, 1989.

Tinker, Hugh (compiler). *A message from the Falklands: the life and gallant death of David Tinker, Lieut. R.N. from his letters and poems*, Penguin Books, Harmondsworth, 1983.

Tomalin, Ruth, *W.H. Hudson: a biography*. Faber & Faber, London, 1982.

Trifilo, W.S., 'Catholicism in Argentina as viewed by early 19th century English travellers', *Americas* XIX, 1962-3.

Tulchin, Joseph S., 'The Malvinas War of 1982: an inevitable conflict that should never have occurred', *Latin American Research Review* XXII 3 1987.

Vidal, Emeric Essex, *Picturesque Illustrations of Buenos Aires and Montevideo*. Ackerman, London, 1820.

Walker, John, *The South American Sketches of R.B. Cunninghame Graham*, University of Oklahoma Press, Lincoln, 1978.

Watts, Cedric & Davis, Lawrence, *Cunninghame Graham: a critical Biography*, Cambridge University Press 1979.

Willetts, Peter, *Fishing in the South West Atlantic*. South Atlantic Council Occasional Paper no. 4. London, 4 March 1988.

Williams, Glynn, *The Desert and the Dream: a study of Welsh colonization in Chubut 1865-1915*, University of Wales Press 1965.

Williford, Miriam, *Jeremy Bentham in Spanish America: an account of his letters and proposals to the New World*. Louisiana State University Press, Baton Rouge, 1980.

Wilson, Jason, *The Colonial's Revenge*. University of London. Institute of Latin American Studies Occasional Paper, London, 1979.

Winsburg, M.D., *Colonia Baron Hirsch: a Jewish agricultural colony in Argentina*, University of Florida monograph 1 9 1963.

Woodbine Parish Sir, *Buenos Aires and the Province of the Rio de la Plata*, 2nd edit, London, 1852.

Wright, Winthrop R. *British-owned Railways in Argentina: their effect on economic nationalism 1854-1948*. University of Texas, Austin, 1972.

Wolf, Cecil and Moorcroft Wilson, Jean (eds) *Authors Take Sides: the Falklands War*, Cecil Wolf London 1982.

# Index

Patagonia, 17
*Patagonia Rebelde*, 18, 23
Peel, Sir Robert, 52
Pellegrini, Carlos, 30
Pendle, George, 98
Pendle and Rivett, 98
Perez, Carlos Andres, 252
Perón, Eva, 88, 89, 93,
  168, 227, 233
  unpopularity in Britain,
  239-40
  death, 241
  Evità, 241-3
Perón, Juan, 5, 24, 37, 47,
  59, 80, 85-6, 93, 120,
  121, 164, 166, 197
  denigration of, 93-102
  Blue Book, 98-101
  debate as to the nature
  of regime, 168-9
  return of, 170, 197, 227
  and the meat question,
  227, 231-5
  overthrows President
  Castillo, 227-8
  election victory 11
  March 1946, 231
  fall, 238
  and Eva Perón, 239-43
  return to power, 241-2
  death, 241-2
  and Franco, 294
Piazzola, Astor, 223
Plummer, Miss Gladys,
  222
Popham, Sir Horace, 12,
  198
Ponsonby, Lord, 13
Potash, Robert, 99-100
Prince of Wales, 58, 79,
  82, 166
Puerto Rico, 145
Puerto Victoria, 17-19
*Purple Land that England
  Lost, The*, 3, 21, 176,
  178-9, 180-1

Quesnay, 68

railways, 11, 12, 33, 38, 80
Ramírez, General, 228
Raymond, Henri, 252

Regulation of Antarctic
  Mineral Resource
  Activities (CRAMA), 259
Rennie, Governor, 129
Rhodes, Cecil, 98
Rice, Tim, 242
Richardon, Philip, 221
Richepin, Jean, 214, 218
Riestra, Alvaro de la, 69
Riestra, Norberto de la,
  70, 71, 74
Rivadavia, 16, 28, 53
Robertson brothers, 14
Roca, President, 116
  genocide against
  indigenous
  population, 113
Roca-Runciman Treaty,
  1933, 37, 59, 83, 85, 87,
  89, 228, 232
Rock, Professor David,
  125, 253
Rojas, Ricardo, 33
Romero, Eduardo, 252
Rosa, José M., 228
Rosas, Juan Manuel de,
  15, 16, 30, 32, 34, 49,
  51, 52, 53, 66, 130, 159,
  166, 168, 187
  re-interment, 60
  character and
  achievements, 60-2
  campaign of terror, 69
  fall of, 70-1
Roscoe, William, 69
Rothschild, Lord, 55
Rumbold, Sir Horace, 22
Rural Society, 81, 83

St. Andrew's School, 161
Salisbury, Marquis of, 55
Sanchez, Luis Alberto, 252
Sarmiento, Domingo
  Faustino, 15, 17, 24,
  28-9, 32, 70, 159-61,
  162, 165, 185-6, 187
'SATO', 275-6
Schelm, Adolf J., 144-7,
  148, 151, 152
Schmidtmeyer, Peter, 184
Sclater, Dr., 174, 175
Scott, Sir Walter, 28

Sealing Conservation
  Convention, 259
Seymour, R.A., 18-19
Shackleton, Lord, 264
  Report, 266
Shand, William, 29, 183,
  195-9
Shennan, David, 165
Shuckburgh, Sir Evelyn,
  88
Shulman, Milton, 240
Smith, Adam, 53, 58
Smith, W.H., 55
Solar, Maria Hameres, 8
South American
  Antarctic, 261
South Pacific
  Nuclear-Free-Zone, 262
South Sea Company, 65
Spain
  influence of, 194-5,
  289-90
  sport, 11-2, 161, 164-5
Stalin, Joseph, 96
Stunz, Hugo, 100
'Sunshine Girl', 215

Tamborini, Dr. José, 100,
  231
Tango, 213-24
  origins, 213, 214
  international diffusion,
  214-7
  teachers, 216-7
  at London theatres, 217
  books on tango, 218
  attacks, 218-9
  defenders, 219-20
  later history, 220-3
Tanyerli, Secaattin, 222
Taylor, Philip Meadows,
  205
Terragno, Rodolfo, 249,
  250-2
Terry, Simone, 99
Thomas, Hugh, 99
Tinker, David, 295
Tower, Sir Reginald, 81
Treaty of Friendship,
  Commerce and
  Navigation, 51, 56
Treaty of Recognition, 14